Sakamoto Ryoma
and the
Meiji Restoration

Sakamoto Ryōma
and the
Meiji Restoration

BY MARIUS B. JANSEN

COLUMBIA UNIVERSITY PRESS
NEW YORK

Columbia University Press Morningside Edition
Columbia University Press
New York   Chichester, West Sussex

Morningside Edition with new preface
Copyright © 1994 Columbia University Press
Copyright © 1961 Marius B. Jansen

Library of Congress Cataloging-in-Publication Data

Jansen, Marius B.
Sakamoto Ryōma and the Meiji restoration / by Marius B. Jansen.
p.   cm.
Originally published Princeton, N.J. : Princeton University
Press, 1961.
Includes bibliographical references and index.
ISBN 978-0-231-10173-8 (pbk.)
1. Sakamoto, Ryōma—1836–1867. 2. Japan—History—Restoration,
1853–1870. I. Title.
DS881.3.J28 1995
952'.025'092—dc20   94–39075
CIP

Printed in the United States of America
c 10 9 8 7 6 5 4 3 2 1
p 10 9 8 7 6 5 4

for Jean

CONTENTS

CONTENTS

Map follows page 3

PREFACE TO
THE MORNINGSIDE EDITION

*I*T IS gratifying to know that there is enough interest in Sakamoto Ryōma to justify this printing, now thirty-three years after the book first appeared. For the historian of Japan's modern history, this provides some evidence of changes in Japan and of the way Japanese view their past.

When I began work on Sakamoto in the 1950s he was not very high in the consciousness of most Japanese. They were keenly aware of the changes that war and occupation had brought to their country, but frequently inclined to see the Meiji Restoration as prelude to the ruinous rounds of militarism and war that had dominated their lives and destroyed their cities. The participants and leaders in the upheaval that led to the Meiji Restoration were at best shadowy figures; prewar education had measured their merit by their contribution to imperial modernization, and among them representatives of minor domains like Tosa took second place to the stalwarts of the Satsuma and Chōshū who had dominated the modern governments and armed services.

Shiba Ryōtarō, whose best-selling historical novel about Sakamoto did much to change these attitudes toward Sakamoto, recently wrote that from the standpoint of the Meiji imperial state Sakamoto was more likely to seem a troublemaker, or even rebel, than hero. He violated filial piety by deserting his ancestral home and family, and he violated canons of loyalty by walking out on his feudal lord and his domain. His proposals could be linked to the movement for freedom and democratic rights. And he was not from Satsuma or Chōshū, the domains that provided the leaders of the Meiji state. Official textbooks moved smoothly from Sakamoto's contemporaries Saigō, Kido, and Ōkubo to the Meiji emperor's senior statesmen, Itō and Yamagata. To be sure, Sakamoto and Nakaoka were given imperial rank posthumously in 1891, but that hardly compared with the praises heaped on their counterparts from Satsuma and Chōshū. Nobody needed a rōnin from Tosa.

Moreover, even when Sakamoto did make the textbooks by appearing to the Meiji Express on the eve of the Battle of

Tsushima Straits in the Russo-Japanese War, the story had some curious elements. As it is described in this book, the empress must have been worrying about the outcome of the battle, for she dreamed that someone appeared and told her that he was "a person who had played some part in late Tokugawa times, Sakamoto Ryōma from Tosa," and that she need not be concerned about the battle at hand.

Now the interesting thing about this is that the empress had clearly never heard of Sakamoto. When she asked who the figure in her dream might have been, the court official Tanaka Kōken, who was from Tosa, had to assure her that there had indeed been someone by that name. Mr. Shiba concludes that since conversations like that seldom got outside the palace, it is reasonable to think that the Tosa people in the palace saw to it that it did become known. At any rate, although the story quickly qualified Ryōma for the pantheon in the Japanese empire of armies and navies it remained a rather trite fable, and it gave little indication of what Sakamoto's real contribution might have been.

The fact is that outside of Tosa, where he was part of local lore, Sakamoto was relatively little spoken of; his image was that of a swashbuckler and a stormy petrel whose early death prevented him from excercising much influence on the modern state. In the 1950s it often seemed to me that my research topic, when disclosed, tended to draw the kind of compassionate and bemused response that bright graduate students at Harvard or Columbia might have given an earnest young Japanese who said that he was working on the political thought of Davy Crockett.

Today things are very different, for Sakamoto is one of the most popular heroes of the Restoration times. What produced this change? First of all, the end of imperial Japan and its replacement by a democratic and peaceful order has made for new interest in people who were nonconformists in the old society. The generals and admirals of the old textbooks have had to make way for other forerunners of the new Japan.

Second, the scholarly base for reassessment has grown prodigiously thanks to the labor of a devoted group of local historians in Tosa. Hirao Michio, whose name appears frequently

in this volume and a scholar to whom I remain deeply indebted, continued to write until his death in 1979, sharpening and refining his knowledge of Tosa history in a bibliography of notes, articles, and books that numbers close to 2,500
items. His earlier biography of Sakamoto was reissued several times, and in 1966 his *Ryōma no subete* (All about Ryōma) added to that coverage. Mr. Hirao and Hamada Kameki-
chi also collaborated in a translation of this book that has
gone through many printings from Jiji Press. Hirao's collaborator Miyaji Saichirō continued his work by completing a
massive *Sakamoto Ryōma zenshū* (Complete Writings of Sakamoto Ryōma) that appeared in 1988; it now becomes the standard documentary source. Mr. Miyaji went on to do the same
for Nakaoka Shintarō in *Nakaoka Shintarō zenshū,* which
appeared in 1991. The widest swath, however, was surely
that cut by Shiba Ryōtarō's *Ryōma ga yuku* (1966), a brilliant
historical novel that brought Sakamoto fully into the public
domain. Since then a flood of illustrated books, magazines,
and articles for all age levels has continued to be published.

The diffusion of this image was further speeded by the
technology of our information society. The Sakamoto boom
began during the great age of Japanese cinema. The director
Itō Daisuke's *Bakumatsu* (End Tokugawa, 1970) portrayed Sakamoto as a revolutionary, full of admiration for Western
technology and imbued with democracy. Had he made the
film before the war, Itō said, he would not have been able to
show how critical of his society Sakamoto really was. Gosho
Heinosuke, director of *Firefly Light* (Hotarubi, 1958) focused on the events of the incident at the Teradaya, in which
Sakamoto, by taking up with Oryō, implied equality between
classes and between the sexes. In Shinoda Masahiro's *Assassination* (Ansatsu, 1964), Sakamoto enters as the friend of
the assassin of the Tairō, Ii Naosuke, in 1860. Perhaps most
famously, Kuroki Kazuo's *Assassination of Ryōma* (Ryōma
no ansatsu, 1974), focused on the futility of individual effort
in a time of revolutionary betrayal.[1] These film writers uti-

---

[1] See Joan Mellen, *The Waves at Genji's Door: Japan Through Its
Cinema* (N.Y., Pantheon Books, 1976), pp. 61-77.

lized Sakamoto to make of him a proponent of their own progressive and often revolutionary ideology, but they were able to do this because he had become an attractive and progressive historical figure.

Television did the rest. As Japan recovered confidence and wealth its media returned to the events of Meiji to seek a starting point, and a series of highly successful historical runs made household figures of Sakamoto Ryōma and other heroes of the Meiji Restoration.

The "new" Sakamoto stood out for his youth and courage; he was optimistic and quick to accept new ideas. A pistol was better than a sword, and commerce better than war. Councils would be better than rule by a hereditary elite, and democracy more viable than daimyo.

As a result Sakamoto emerged as an attractive and believable personality for postwar Japanese, especially young Japanese. For some years the curator of the Kyoto Ryōzen Historical Museum, which is rich in materials relating to the Meiji Restoration, was receiving, and answering, letters from young people who wrote to "Sakamoto Ryōma" to ask advice for personal problems. Sometimes people even telephoned the museum and asked to speak to "Mr. Sakamoto". As a *Yomiuri* reporter explained it, "a generation that has grown up knowing Sakamoto in the era of film, television, and novels, seems to be able to think of him as a direct contemporary." What Ryōma might have thought of some of the advice, as when a lonely youngster would be told to "try joining some clubs" is another matter.

More substantial is the surge of private and public effort to memorialize the man and his significance. In Kōchi a splendid new public museum chronicles the events of the Movement for Freedom and People's Rights of the 1880s; near the Kōchi airport a small private museum records the stages of Sakamoto's life with tableaux whose English explanations are taken from this book. Most recently, on the Katsurahama beach, close to the great statue of Sakamoto that was erected by private subscription of young men's organizations in the 1920s, Kōchi Prefecture dedicated a Sakamoto Ryōma Memorial Hall in 1991. A striking glass structure pointing to the ocean beyond, it stands as witness to the image of a Japan open to the world, its trade and ideas. That image has come to be the legacy of Sakamoto Ryōma for contemporary Japan.

Marius B. Jansen

Princeton, August 1994

INTRODUCTION

$\mathcal{I}$N ASIA, as in the Western world, the middle decades of the nineteenth century were filled with unrest and violence. Movements were in progress whose end result was fully as momentous as were the ending of slavery in America and serfdom in Russia. But the differences were equally important, for the Asian developments were speeded and affected in varying degree by the intervention of the West. Even where, as in Japan, the West impinged on traditional society with no thought of conquest, its evidence of the vitality of progress, constitutionalism, and industrialization provided new formulations which attracted or repulsed men who wanted change. In India the Sepoy Rebellion of 1857-1859 brought on the full measure of English control. In China the great Taiping Rebellion of 1850-1864 utilized a bizarre version of Christian doctrine to try to drive out the Manchu rulers and erect a new theocratic and communist state. The Taipings failed to win the support of the Chinese elite, but their military successes produced a setting in which foreign technology first became acceptable, because it was essential, to Chinese leaders.

At mid-century Japan too faced the Western threat. Japan's crisis came after those of India and China, and foreign conquest was never as real a danger as Japanese leaders thought. The decade between the negotiation of a commercial treaty with Townsend Harris in 1858 and the fall of the military government of the Tokugawa shogun in 1867 saw animosities and tensions that had long been present burst into flame, however, and the intellectual and political ferment of those years produced the Meiji Restoration.

The Restoration led to a unified national state which struggled to achieve international equality and leadership in Asia. The successes of the Japanese leaders had an effect on neighboring Asian societies as stimulating as was that of revolutionary France on Europe. Sun Yat-sen, K'ang Yu-wei, Kim Ok-kiun, Emilio Aguinaldo, Subhas Chandra Bose, and many others dreamed of creating in their own countries something of the drive and unity that had first established in Japan the equality of Asian with European strength and ability. Many of these men credited the Japanese achievements to the colorful and dedicated nationalists who had led the Restoration movement, and as a result the Restoration activists became heroes for Asians who aspired to approximate their deeds. Within Japan the Meiji Restoration leaders also served as examples of a new and ideal type in politics: that of the idealistic, individualistic, and courageous patriot who gave his all for the Imperial cause—the *shishi*. In the days before World War II in Japan the young officers of the armed services laid claim to this tradition as they flouted conventional standards of morality and discipline in their efforts to carry out a twentieth century "Shōwa Restoration."

In view of the importance and the interest of the Japanese revolution, it is astonishing that Western scholarship has given it so little attention. In recent years Western writers, following the lead of social scientists in Japan, have concerned themselves more with the "motive forces" and with the significance of the Restoration than with the changes themselves and the men who helped bring them about. These are certainly vital concerns, but they ought properly to come after, and not before, descriptions of the events themselves.

In this book I have chosen to tell the Restoration story by examining the career and thought of Sakamoto Ryōma and, to a lesser extent, Nakaoka Shintarō. Both men were from Tosa, one of the fiefs that played an important role in Restoration politics. Both were of relatively low rank, and neither was at all at home in the circles of Japan's "Western experts." Tosa, their home, contributed to, but did not lead the Restoration process, so that regional power politics and ambition were at first less involved in their education in world affairs than was the case with their counterparts in more powerful fiefs. Sakamoto and Nakaoka were murdered shortly after the shogun's resignation in 1867, and our view of their Restoration activities is not colored by their subsequent eminence or failure. Nevertheless they had important and exciting roles in the Restoration drama. Sakamoto's colorful career, in fact, has drawn to it the talents of so many Japanese authors and playwrights that romance has to some degree come to overshadow fact. The foreign scholar, however, is less affected by this; published sources, which retain enough flavor of personality to explain the man's attraction for biographers and authors, provide abundant opportunity to sift fiction from fact.

I first became interested in the *shishi*, these "men of high purpose," in research on the Chinese revolution. In later Meiji days the "China *rōnin*," as the Japanese adventurers called themselves, and their Chinese friends like Sun Yat-sen compared themselves to the Restoration heroes. Further investigation in the democratic movement of nineteenth century Japan, a movement dominated by men from Tosa, led me to the Tosa scene in Restoration days. It is an area of tremendous interest and opportunity, and one which has hardly been touched. So few historians have concerned themselves with this, one of the great themes of recent world history, that my subject, Sakamoto Ryōma, has hitherto been scarcely mentioned in the Western literature on Japan. In telling his story I have necessarily had to concern myself with the way in which the Restoration came about, instead of discussing, in the terms common in Japan today, why it had to come. No doubt some light on those reasons has nonetheless emerged; the idealism, dedication, and courage of the *shishi* was usually combined with a practicality and desire for self-attainment that made for something of a pattern of response to the challenge that was brought by the West. The influences and opportunities of the day had first to work on individuals, however, and it has seemed to me that the late Tokugawa scene had in it enough variety and contrast in motivation and belief to make it unlikely that it could be summed up in any single theory of causation.

Much of the material on which this study is based was gathered in Japan during 1955 and 1956 during a stay made possible by a Ford Foundation fellowship. While in Tosa I was fortunate to make the acquaintance of Mr. Michio Hirao, an authority on local history to whom all Japanese and many foreign historians are indebted. Through the assistance of the Asia Foundation it became possible for Mr. Hirao to spend the summer of 1958 at the University of Washington, where he quickly became the center for a seminar which dealt with the history of Tosa in Tokugawa days. Out of this has developed a documentary record of social and economic developments in Tosa, still in preparation, on which I have been engaged with the assistance of my colleague Noburu Hiraga under the auspices of the research program of the Far Eastern and Russian Institute of the University of Washington. My debt to Mr. Hirao is suggested by the frequency with which citations in this study note his numerous publications. For help with the map I am indebted to Hiroe Kiyoshi, who is preparing a historical atlas for Tosa under the auspices of the Kōchi City Public Library, and I am grateful to Yoshimura Shokuho of Kōchi and (Judge) Inoue Kazuo, presently of Tamashima City, Okayama Prefecture, for their help in photographing and lending copies of the pictures which appear in the book. A grant from the Princeton University Research Fund has helped make publication possible.

I have thought it best to use the contemporary Tosa reading of numerous names, trusting that cross-references in the index will prevent confusion for readers accustomed to Yamanouchi instead of Yamauchi. All dates have been converted to the Western calendar, since specialists who read further will have no difficulty in reconverting to the Japanese original. Names, however, are given in the Japanese order with surname first. Macrons have been retained to indicate long vowels in all but the most common geographical names.

I must acknowledge also the help and encouragement of my colleagues in the Japan Seminar at the University of Washington, where an earlier draft of this work was taken up during the year 1958-1959. My obligations to them, as to specialists and librarians in this country and in Japan, are too numerous to itemize. More specific is my gratitude to Miss Grace Brewer and Mrs. Ann Yaney for their assistance in preparing the manuscript. I remain, of course, solely responsible for all errors of fact and interpretation and for all translations not otherwise acknowledged.

Marius B. Jansen
Princeton, N.J.
May 1960

SAKAMOTO RYŌMA
AND THE
MEIJI RESTORATION

I. SAKAMOTO'S JAPAN

*T*HE outstanding intellectual and political experience in the formative years of Japan's Restoration activists was the discovery that their society was incapable of successful resistance to the Western threat. In the wake of this realization came proposals for political and social change that were designed to make good the weakness and inadequacy of their country. Reforms that had previously seemed desirable to some were now put forward with the urgency of desperation. Programs for change were conditioned by the tensions that had existed long before the appearance of the West, but they were increasingly fashioned in the image of the West in hope of approximating its power. The programs toward which Sakamoto Ryōma and his contemporaries found themselves drawn were also moderated by the values of the world they knew. It is therefore useful to begin with a survey of the society of the 1830's into which the Restoration leaders were born.

1. The Tokugawa Setting

"The government of a country has a great deal of influence on the values and the customs of a people," begins the account of the Chief Factor of the Netherlands trading station at Nagasaki in 1830, "and I will begin with a brief account of the government of Japan in general and Nagasaki in particular as an introduction to the sketches which I plan to give."[1] Meijlan's little book, based as it was on limited observation, contains many errors, but like the accounts of other resident Hollanders it is instructive for the evidence of the way in which even observers with limited freedom were able to recognize many of the principal features and problems of Japan.

Japan in the early nineteenth century was still organized along the lines of feudal autonomy that had been worked out after the great battles of the early seventeenth century. After his victories and appointment as military overlord by the prestige-holding but powerless emperor, the Tokugawa shogun had arranged and ranked his vassals and defeated rivals with a view to perpetuating the rule of his family. The first Tokugawa shoguns reapportioned

---

[1] G. F. Meijlan, *Japan: Voorgesteld in schetsen over de zeden en gebruiken van dat ryk, byzonder over den Ingezetenen der stad Nagasaky.* Amsterdam, 1830.

PRINCIPAL SUBDIVISIONS OF TOSA
Dots indicate points of origin of the Restoration activists

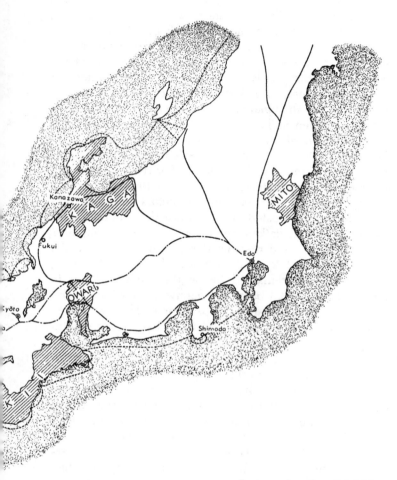

Japan in the 1860's
PRINCIPAL AREAS AND ROUTES
OF RESTORATION DAYS
————— principal land routes
.... principal shipping lanes
. — . — . Tosa *sankin-kōtai* routes to Edo

fiefs almost at will, and they gradually reduced the number and territories of their erstwhile rivals and enemies, *tozama daimyō*, or "outside lords," in favor of the *fudai daimyō*, "hereditary retainers," and *shimpan*, "related houses." The related houses, together with the most honored of the fudai daimyō, staffed the central councils and the boards that conducted national affairs for the military government, or bakufu, whose capital was at Edo (modern Tokyo). The shogunate kept under its close control lands producing nearly seven million *koku* of rice, approximately one-fourth the national total; of these, lands producing some three million koku were allotted to direct vassals of less than daimyō rank, the so-called bannermen (*hatamoto*). For these and its own lands the shogunate maintained responsibility through commissioners (*bugyō*), bailiffs (*daikan*), and inspectors (*metsuke*) appointed from among its trusted vassals. Since the shogun's lands were so vast, individual daikan might, on occasions, administer lands greater in extent and revenue than those of many feudal lords. They were subject to rotation and replacement, however, and consequently they remained below the daimyō group in tenure and prestige. Feudal barons of daimyō rank administered fiefs of at least 10,000 koku annual rice income. They were free from close control except for periodic visits by bakufu representatives and supervisory functions connected with controls on Christianity. Most importantly, however, the lords contributed no regular part of their tax revenue to the shogunate; they limited their tribute to ceremonial gifts, guard service, and attendance at the shogun's capital. At times the shogunate requested extraordinary loans from all vassals of daimyō rank, but never for very long; in emergencies it had also provided loans for the daimyō.[2]

Although the daimyō were not regularly taxed, they were nevertheless controlled by such ingenious measures that Japanese historians sometimes utilize the term "centralized feudalism" to indicate the anomalous political order that resulted. The barons' marriages and movements required shogunal approval; they were expected to contribute lavishly to bakufu projects; they were forbidden to erect or repair castles or fortifications without permission; and they could not establish toll stations. Most important of all were the requirements established in connection with the

---

[2] Thus Tosa received a *bakufu* loan in 1732. Kōchi chihōshi kenkyūkai, *Kōchi Ken rekishi nempyō*, Kōchi, 1958, p. 52.

system of alternate attendance (*sankin-kōtai*) under which lords were resident in the shogun's capital at Edo in alternate years; during their absence from Edo they left their heirs and wives as hostages. The processions to Edo, carried out according to the most exacting specifications and rules, involved the lords in great expenditures, while residence in Edo tended to substitute ceremonial and courtly concerns for the military preparedness of the previous era. Since the barons were accompanied by their principal retainers and maintained extensive installations while in attendance in Edo, the effects of the system penetrated far beyond the ranks of the great vassals primarily concerned. It involved expenditure, adventure, and opportunity for the most lowly who followed in their lord's train.

Among the devices for control stressed by the early shoguns were measures designed to prevent the growth of political and social contacts between their leading vassals, particularly those most recently subjected, and the imperial court in Kyoto. The emperor was supported by modest grants of income that made his economic status little better than that of the lesser feudal lords, and the aristocratic families at court (*kuge*) were supported less liberally. Shogunal officials stationed in Kyoto dominated appointment of nobles to the offices of chancellor and other posts created to transmit messages to the military government in the east.[3] The shogunate took particular care to prevent daimyō visits to Kyoto, and matrimonial alliances between the feudal and court aristocracy were also scrutinized carefully. With the passing of the years of Tokugawa peace, however, the rigor of supervision lessened. The third shogun, Iemitsu, had visited Kyoto with a mighty military array in 1634 to overawe the court, and an emperor who overstepped the limited bounds permitted by shogunal preference was later forced into abdication. In later years the growth of Confucian scholarship with its respect for legitimacy, combined with the absence of indications of danger from Kyoto, made for an easing of the early restrictions. The principal tozama daimyō gradually developed matrimonial alliances with noble families. The Shimazu of Satsuma had long-standing ties with the Konoe, whose estate stewards they had once been, while the Yamauchi of Tosa developed similar ties with the Sanjō family;

[3] For the controls on the Kyoto court, Ishin shiryō hensan jimukyoku, ed., *Ishin shi* (Tokyo, 1941), Vol. I.

Mōri, of Chōshū, had enjoyed a special sort of Imperial favor since the warfare of an earlier day. As a result, the representatives of these fiefs were likely to look to the further development of such ties whenever shogunal weakness, indecision, and incapacity might provide the opportunity and incentive in the nineteenth century.

The exclusion of all westerners except Netherlands traders had come about through the same fear of subversion and change that distinguished the political controls on daimyō and court. Although the early shogunate was fully aware of the benefits to be won through trade and eager for its extension, the gradual conviction that Christianity would follow trade led to the bans against Christianity and those who had brought it. After the last stand of Christian adherents in 1637-1638 had been crushed, a modest amount of trade was permitted to the non-Catholic Netherlanders, who were forced into the restrictive and humiliating conditions that had originally been devised in Nagasaki for the Portuguese. The conditions of life for the Hollanders improved somewhat during the years that followed. Even so, the restrictions on movement and contact experienced by Meijlan in 1830 gave point to his rueful estimate of the "friendly relations" he had known: "if this is the way friends are treated, then Heaven spare any who fall into the hands of the Japanese as enemies!"[4]

Although most of the institutional measures worked out by the early shoguns seemed to retain their vigor and effectiveness in the 1830's, there had been important changes behind the surface. Tokugawa society was based upon a rigid stratification of classes whereby the warrior class of samurai governed the agriculturists whose labors supported their betters. Merchants and artisans were, in the Confucian ranking of occupations, less esteemed and less productive; consequently they were not taxed in any regular manner. But although the arts of peace and commerce developed greatly during the Tokugawa years of peace, the military who governed society had had little occasion or stimulus to revise or improve their organization or techniques. Their bureaucratic organizations had become highly developed, but their martial capabilities had declined markedly. The bearers of their ancestors' swords and armor had done little to develop further formations and weapons last used in the seventeenth century,[5] and when new

---

[4] Meijlan, p. 30.
[5] Thus one writer described the Tokugawa troops that marched against Chōshū

8

military techniques and concepts were introduced from the West in the nineteenth century they seemed to threaten both the prerogatives and traditions of feudal society. The warrior class had by that time become concentrated in the castle towns, where they lived in relative indolence in attendance upon their lords. Under the spell of urban influence they had lost their martial vigor to the pleasures of peace. Until the challenge which was posed by the return of the Western ships with their superior armament in the nineteenth century there were relatively few who maintained a lively interest in the military arts. Those who did were divided into schools of fencing and tactics which carried on intact the teachings of their founders generations earlier. The initial reaction to the Western threat was to emphasize anew the importance of the traditional military skills, and the anti-foreign movement of the 1860's was led and dominated by specialists in the outmoded arts of swordsmanship.

If the military tradition had not made great strides, however, the activities of the townsmen had increased in scope and importance. This was possible in part because the political institutions which had been devised to guarantee the primacy of the warrior class and the Tokugawa family had important economic consequences. The absence of the feudal lords from their fiefs while in attendance in Edo meant that they had to sell a major portion of their tax rice to defray the costs of travel to and residence at the shogun's capital; in so doing they found themselves forced to negotiate with the dealers of the Osaka rice market. In Edo and in the provincial castle towns retainers were increasingly absent from their fiefs and estates and forced to sell their rice income for the necessities of urban life. Everywhere the warrior class found itself dependent upon merchant assistance and services. Since merchants lacked full security in law for their property, they were intent on the opportunity of the moment. In periods of irregularity or laxity merchants attained considerable influence through the cooperation of officials willing to compromise their Confucian standards for monetary advantage. Even where corruption was not involved, however, the problems of urban life found

---

in 1866 in these terms: "Lord Ii's soldiers wore the armour of their grandfathers and marched along, carrying long banners, blowing on trumpet shells, and beating drums, just as a daimyo with his retainers paraded along the Tokaido road to and from Edo." Quoted in Yosaburo Takekoshi, *The Economic Aspects of the History of the Civilization of Japan* (London, 1930), III, p. 371.

samurai involved in ritual ostentation and display, accumulating debts, and increasingly forced to concern themselves with problems for which their education and outlook, concerned as it was with honor rather than practicality, equipped them poorly. In all sectors of life there was an increase of relationships expressed in money rather than in payments of kind; the shogunate's decision to pay some retainer salaries in coin was indicative of the growth of the money economy. It was nowhere stronger than in the shogunal domain, and merchant influence there was also considerably greater than in the peripheral areas controlled by the great tozama daimyō. Merchant collusion and governmental inefficiency combined with the undeveloped state of transport to create a food market sensitive to natural disasters and susceptible to human manipulation. The uncertain fluctuation of the price of rice produced sporadic and electric tension in the life of the towns, where protests were usually directed against the wealthy rice dealers, and it created problems which occupied many of the best minds in the government.

Relationships in the countryside had also changed a great deal. The peasants, praised, cajoled, and oppressed by the feudal administrators, had proved sensitive to the changes produced by production for urban markets and the possibilities of transfer of land to new entrepreneurs. In some backward and remote areas class gradations and conditions of serfdom continued almost unchanged from the original subjection to farmer-soldiers who had remained on the land to become village leaders.[6] Closer to the paths of trade and the metropolitan centers, however, the use of money, indebtedness, and contractual relationships for the production of handicraft goods had resulted in new forms of tenantry. Diligence and sloth produced the inevitable minimum of fluidity between rural groups, but in the competition for land and influence the established rural leaders were not necessarily bested by urban forces or groups.[7] The countryside nowhere presented the scene of a uniformly oppressed and undifferentiated "peasantry"; there were heads, elders, landlords, landholders, tenants, and

[6] See, on this point, Thomas C. Smith, "The Japanese Village in the 17th Century," *Journal of Economic History* (New York, 1952) XII, 1, pp. 1-20.

[7] Thomas C. Smith, "Landlords and Rural Capitalists in the Modernization of Japan," *Journal of Economic History*, XVI, 2 (June 1956), pp. 165-181, draws on a wide range of secondary literature discussing this problem.

servants.[8] With the separation of most samurai from the land, the prestige of village leaders, and the authority that passed into their hands, made for new types of self-assertion and self-confidence. Tokugawa commentators noted both the wealth and the poverty of farmers with disapproval, but they were never able to devise measures to tap the former or relieve the latter.

During Tokugawa days the agricultural production increased steadily. Land reclamation, better seeds and fertilizers, and more intensive cultivation consequent upon the growth of population resulted in an increase in the agricultural yield that was frequently estimated to be double the formal estimate of koku with which the Tokugawa vassals were credited. Despite this, the official tax rates failed to rise proportionately.[9] Undoubtedly irregular and special taxes siphoned some of this added wealth out of the countryside, but much of it remained in the village. And since the breakdown of the tax requirement, which was levied on the village, was usually in the hands of the village headmen and elders, it is clear that the increase in yield tended to go to the landowning farmers in the villages, sharpening the distinction between them and their tenants.[10]

After the warrior class moved to the castle towns, local administration was the work of village elders and headmen who worked under the general supervision of the district commissioners. Their wisdom in judging the middle path between evasion and exploitation kept their fellows in a strategic position for the accumulation of land, wealth, and literacy. When new taxes and monopolies threatened the pattern they had developed and maintained, it was usually the village leaders who organized the protest and, if it failed, the resistance to the feudal overlords. That their judgment was in the main wise and that they protected their area of interest is evidenced by the many contrasts drawn by foreign travellers in the 1850's and 1860's between the smiling, prosperous countryside and the poverty-stricken, run-down towns. Thus Rutherford Alcock commented on the evidence of "Peace,

[8] *Shōya, toshiyori, jinushi, hombyakusho, nago, mōtō,* were the most prevalent terms used for these distinctions.

[9] Thomas C. Smith, "The Land Tax in the Tokugawa Period," *Journal of Asian Studies,* xviii, 1 (November 1958).

[10] Economic, social, and technological changes in the countryside during Tokugawa days are ably described in Thomas C. Smith, *The Agrarian Origins of Modern Japan* (Palo Alto, Calif., 1959), 250 pp.

plenty, apparent content, and a country more perfectly and carefully cultivated and kept, with more ornamental timber everywhere than can be matched even in England," while Hugh Mitford, writing of a different area, noted that "We could not help being struck by the great prosperity of the country . . . a happier people it would be difficult to find."[11] Meijlan's astonishment at the extensive development of institutions for credit and trade, and his sweeping assertion that all groups, even in the countryside, possessed at least minimal literacy, is further evidence that the areas of which he had knowledge prospered under feudal rule.[12] The Tosa Restoration protagonists were, as will be seen, drawn chiefly from these rural leaders; in their case, at least, political ambition accompanied economic well-being and social esteem.

The problems of the ruling class in early nineteenth century Japan were dominated by the fact that its income had failed to keep pace with the rising productivity of the society of which it formed the apex. Individual samurai competed for a share of their lords' tax yield, a yield which was still comparable to that of the seventeenth century. Rewards of position and office could improve the position of some members of the class, but usually at the expense of the less successful. The growth of numbers of the samurai class further complicated the problem, and although some younger sons dropped out of the privileged ranks, others remained attached as dependents. Family heads often found their stipends inadequate to meet needs. To make matters worse the daimyō frequently tried to meet their economic problems through the euphemism of declaring a loan of part of stipends, thereby reducing their expenditures. As a result the majority of the samurai lived in honorable but austere circumstances, and the literature of Tokugawa days has numerous examples of samurai who pawn their swords, run up debts, are unable to pay for desperately wanted books, and, in some areas, resort to infanticide to reduce

[11] Alcock's full statement about the Kantō plain, was, "Here in outward form we have feudalism, without its chivalry, reproduced. . . . Yet what do we see? Peace, plenty, apparent content, and a country more perfectly and carefully cultivated and kept, with more ornamental timber everywhere than can be matched even in England." Yet, of Kyushu, he noted, "the extreme richness and fertility of the soil were in striking contrast with the apparent poverty of those who lived on it." *The Capital of the Tycoon: A Narrative of a Three Years' Residence in Japan* (New York, 1863), I, 383, 75 respectively. Mitford's comment, applied to the domain of Kaga, may be found in *Memories by Lord Redesdale* (New York, n.d.) II, 405.

[12] Meijlan, p. 134.

encumbrances on a limited family budget. Great regional varia-
tions existed between the fiefs, which knew a wide disparity of
samurai incomes and numbers as well as of agricultural productivity; Nakaoka Shintarō commented that samurai stipends considered low in Tosa would seem generous in Satsuma.[13] It is clear,
however, that everywhere the number of "upper" and comfortable
samurai was small, and that the well-being of rural leaders was
frequently greater than that of the mass of ordinary samurai.

To cover the discrepancy between costs and income, the shogunate and its vassal states licensed and utilized monopoly guilds,
and they also borrowed from merchants.[14] Regional specialties
for central markets were made the preserve for authorized guilds
which acted as official agents and which were given monopoly
rights over them; the feudal authorities attempted, through their
merchant allies, to buy cheaply and sell at a profit. Such measures
could, however, succeed only to the degree that they failed to
antagonize rural leaders. The shogunate also attempted to solve
its problems by devaluating its currency through reminting. On
the fief level the vassals, forbidden to mint coins, could approximate such measures by the issue of paper currency. But their
notes had currency only within the realm, and the device was
practicable for only a small number of large and integrated fiefs.
Since even their economies were increasingly drawn into the central orbit through compulsory services of attendance for the Tokugawa shogun and through marketing of fief produce at the great
shogunal cities of Osaka and Edo, such note issues were seldom
successful; knowledgeable merchants, conscious of the conversion
problems that would arise from their extension into other markets, resisted their use.

Related to such efforts for greater revenue were periodic drives
designed to curb excessive popular consumption. Periods of official reform usually followed hard on long periods of laxity and
favoritism, typically those that had developed during the long and
relatively untroubled reign of a successful shogun or daimyō. Not
infrequently the new ruler under whom such reforms were ordered was an adopted son, one who had avoided the debilitating

[13] Nakaoka's *Heidan* is reprinted in *Jinketsu Sakamoto Ryōma den* (Osaka,
1926), p. 362.
[14] For a brief account of relations with merchants, John W. Hall, "Bakufu and
Chonin," in *Occasional Papers* (Michigan Center for Japanese Studies, Ann Arbor,
1951), 1, pp. 26f.

13

physical and mental effects of growing up in the luxurious round of favoritism and triviality which resulted from the compulsory residence of vassal heirs in Edo. In periods of reform restrictive legislation affected all forms of display and ostentation and sought to limit consumption by commoners. Such efforts, however, struck more at the signs than at the cause of the financial problems of the ruling class, and as the Tokugawa period entered its last fifty years the traditional reforms were patently inadequate to meet the problems at hand. Instead of revising the system which had produced the urbanization, specialization, and commerce, instead of lightening the tax burden on areas close to the cities which had resulted in the flight of farmers to the cities, such measures succeeded chiefly in dramatizing the dilemmas of the day.

Sometimes spectacular signs of discontent showed how little the shogunate had solved its economic and social problems. One such occurred in 1837 when a model Confucian bureaucrat of the samurai class led a demonstration of desperate townsmen against wealthy profiteers and the officials who supported them. The insurrection of Ōshio Heihachirō took place in Osaka, the shogunate's commercial crossroads, and its warnings were read in all parts of Japan.[15] In the countryside the tempo of peasant protests and demonstrations also rose noticeably in the 1830's. While the meaning and evaluation of the rural riots is still subject to much scholarly debate, there can be little question of the alarm they inspired in feudal administrators.[16]

The last, and least successful, of the bakufu's attempts to deal with these problems came during the 1840's, with the elevation of Mizuno Tadakuni to leadership of its central council in 1841.[17] Mizuno tried to strengthen the position of the shogunate in all respects. He attempted to lower food prices by edict. Seeing danger in the powers and profits of the merchants, he ordered the great shipping guilds to dissolve, in the mistaken belief that a free market without the price fixing of the monopolists would

[15] There are a number of biographies of Ōshio. Kōda Shigetomo, *Ōshio Heihachirō* (Tokyo, 1910), pp. 175ff., provides a good description of the rising.
[16] Peasant revolts increased sharply in number in the mid-1830's, after which a period of relative calm lasted until the final years of Tokugawa rule. The rice price also rose sharply in the last years of Tokugawa power. There are convenient charts provided by Tōyama Shigeki in *Meiji Ishin* (Tokyo, 1951).
[17] The Council of Elders, *Rōjū*, consisted of 4 or 5 fudai daimyō whose fiefs were rated at 25,000 koku or more a year; it was the bakufu's highest council and dealt with control of the daimyō, the court, and other top-level matters.

14

bring about lower prices for consumers. Instead the producers were able to raise their prices. He regarded the swollen population of Edo as proof of peasant disobedience of laws against flight and as a cause of the insufficient production of food, and therefore he ordered villagers to return to their fields. Sumptuary legislation restricted city amusements and curtailed costs and ornamentation of dolls, dress, hair styles, and houses. At the same time Mizuno tried to increase the area directly held as shogunal territory around the cities of Osaka and Edo by removing the lords who had been allotted fiefs there. This cost him his support in bureaucratic circles, and in the end even his backers turned against Mizuno. His dismissal in 1843 ended his desperate efforts to return Japan to the pre-commercial order of things, and soon after an Edo mob attacked his house.[18] The reforms of this period, known as Tempō for the year name in which they fell, thus failed. The shogunate had, to a degree, fallen victim to the centralization which it had carried out for political reasons. There was no real hope of reverting to a decentralized, feudal natural economy, for neither samurai nor commoners would accept without protest enforced frugality and smaller incomes. With hopes of financial solvency and strength dashed, the Tokugawa shogunate was quite unable to respond vigorously and imaginatively to suggestions that it should open the country to foreign trade lest that opening should be forced upon it at disadvantageous terms. A suggestion to this effect from the Netherlands king in 1844 went unanswered. With an empty treasury and a backward defence system, the regime was anxious to avoid foreign contacts.

Intellectual and institutional unpreparedness paralleled the economic incapacity of the shogunate. The Tokugawa councillors conceived their function, as one writer has put it, as that of stewards who had received a system intact and had the obligation of passing it on undamaged and unchanged.[19] Although a few advisers might venture to suggest changes in the system of alternate attendance, to permit the lords to spend more of their income on defence measures, and of seclusion to permit importation of more Western equipment and advice for defence measures, the prin-

[18] This analysis follows Sakata Yoshio, "Meiji Ishin to Tempō kaikaku," *Jimbun Gakuhō* (Kyoto, 1952), 2, pp. 1-27; a description of Mizuno's policies and failure can be found in Mikami Sanji, *Edo jidai shi* (Tokyo, 1944), II, 544-628.

[19] W. G. Beasley, *Select Documents on Japanese Foreign Policy, 1853-1868* (London, 1955), p. 3.

cipal bakufu councils, staffed by fudai councillors whose ancestors had led the Tokugawa hosts in the sixteenth century, were committed to the preservation of the work of their forebears.

Much of the intellectual life of Tokugawa days tended to reinforce the conviction that the established order was just and proper. Confucian moralist thought stressed the nobility of agriculture as the basis of the state, and this emphasis on a natural economy, known as *nōhon shugi*, made it inevitable that commentators should be more concerned with recreating the virtuous order of the past than with utilizing and adopting the commercial possibilities of the present. Nor was there, in any case, a very wide variety of political speculation. It is true that there were many Confucian schools, and that the official school of Chu Hsi Confucianism was declared official for government purposes only in 1790. But most of the proposals for change that were put forth stressed the hope of returning warriors and farmers to the soil and ending the corruption of urban life. By 1800 some of the students of the learning that filtered in through the Dutch station at Nagasaki were prepared to question the tenets of their society. They were nevertheless few in number and little known or read. A sweeping plan for abolition of feudalism in favor of a centralized, authoritarian state which was put forward by Satō Shinen in the early nineteenth century was little known and not at all taken seriously until shogunal officials were attracted to it in the crisis years of the 1860's.[20]

But although clearly drawn formulations of political alternatives were few and little known, a number of potential bases for heterodox positions had been prepared by the 1830's. The small but growing body of intellectuals who were finding interest in Western learning was turning from the narrowly technical and medical to writings of broader interest. The shogunate itself reflected and stimulated this trend with the establishment of a bureau for translating Western books within the Bureau of Astronomy.[21] Private scholars were prepared to go even farther, and their readings in the stories of Western advances in technology and weapons, their realization of the British advance on south China and the Russian advance from the north, provided food for discontent with Toku-

[20] Ishii Takashi, "Satō Shinen gakusetsu jissen no kito," *Rekishi gaku kenkyū*, No. 222 (August 1958), pp. 1-10.
[21] Shimmura Izuru, "Ransho yakukyoku no sōsetsu," *Shirin* (Kyoto, 1916), I, 3.

gawa policies and weakness. Potentially, they constituted a body of intellectuals discontent with at least the manner, if not yet with the fact, of Tokugawa rule. It is worth noting that the Tempō reforms of Mizuno Tadakuni had included measures against scholars of foreign learning whose loyalty had been impugned.[22]

Other bases for theoretical opposition to Tokugawa rule had been prepared by scholars who investigated the Shintō tradition to find in it the theories of Imperial divinity and of priest-rule in antiquity. Studies of Confucianism indirectly tended to support the legitimacy of the primacy of the court at Kyoto over the military government at Edo.[23] Still, before such theoretical positions could become in any sense directed toward a change in the balance of authority between Edo and Kyoto, specific instances of conflict between court and camp and proof that the imperial will was being disregarded would be required. Ideological misgivings were held, in the early nineteenth century, by numbers of intellectuals; but they were not voiced on a significant scale until there were new and dramatic episodes of disrespect to substantiate theoretical misgivings. It would require times of crisis, times when accepted solutions and accustomed procedures were patently inadequate to deal with unprecedented difficulties.

It must be emphasized that the actors in the Restoration drama worked within a social and political framework which, until the very end, they felt was sound. At the mid-point of the nineteenth century, the shogunate had two and a half centuries of prestige behind it. It was in every sense the longest, most stable, and most successful system of social and political organization which Japan had yet known. Its economic crises and social dislocations may well have been becoming more troubled, but these were variants of problems with which Japan's rulers had been dealing since the seventeenth century. Confucian and Shintō studies had seemed so far from being subversive that they had enjoyed centuries of shogunal patronage and favor. *Kokugaku*, or national learning, had been conducted almost entirely within the patronage of the Toku-

---

[22] Grant K. Goodman, "The Dutch Impact on Japan (1640-1853)" (Univ. of Michigan Ph.D. Dissertation, 1955), pp. 270f.

[23] This was particularly important in the case of the Mito school of historians, whose writings and scholars came to exert national prestige and influence. Fujita Tōko, for instance, lectured before the Tosa daimyō. And the famous *Nihon gaishi* of Rai Sanyō, which popularized some of these views, influenced men as different as Itō Hirobumi and Yoshida Tōyō, the Tosa minister.

gawa family in the centers of Tokugawa authority. It was the same with Western studies. Interest in the West and sponsorship for study of the West dated from such Tokugawa leaders as Arai Hakuseki and the shogun Yoshimune, and while toward the end of the eighteenth century centers of "Dutch studies" had been developed by fiefs which, like Satsuma and Saga, later came to figure importantly in national politics, it would be an oversimplification to credit their later political activity to subversive trends brought in by scholars of Western learning. For nowhere were Western studies as vigorously pursued and as generously sponsored as within the shogunate itself at Edo. Western books, techniques, and experts, far from being hoarded or concealed by jealous lords with guilty consciences, were exchanged, borrowed, and shared between the great centers of activity. No sponsor stood to gain more from such exchange, and none had greater power of attraction and reward for scholars from other areas than the shogunate itself.

It may be that some modification of these statements is required for the private schools of Dutch learning which came to flourish by the middle of the nineteenth century. Yet, since schools like that of Ogata Kōan in Osaka (where Fukuzawa Yukichi studied) lacked powerful backers, they had to be more circumspect and cautious, and they guarded their libraries and resources more jealously. Even so, the benefits of the shogunal centers were not to be closed to them. Fukuzawa, although his memories in old age are full of scorn for the Tokugawa regime under which he grew up, could use the library of the shogunal institute, and he also attained shogunal employment.[24]

Fukuzawa's memories of bitterly anti-Confucian feelings and prejudices should not be allowed to obscure another important fact. Individual scholars of things Western were, for the most part, soundly rooted in traditional Confucian and feudal values; far from going into Western studies out of the desire to release pent-up feelings of revolt and frustration, they sought livelihood in fields which promised them interesting work as technicians of a new day. The nature of that day was not apparent to them, but

---

[24] Fukuzawa found the shogunate's library in the new Institute for Investigation of Barbarian Books (*Bansho Shirabesho*) open to him, but left in annoyance when they would not allow him to borrow a valuable dictionary overnight. *The Autobiography of Fukuzawa Yukichi* (Tokyo, 1948), p. 108.

it was evident that knowledge of Western applied science in medicine and armament was going to give them a good competitive position in the national search for talent. For many students this initial practicality led on to real intellectual curiosity. Yet it did not have to become in any sense subversive. These scholars were obeying the instructions of their fiefs and of the shogunate, and ideologically then were proceeding within what seemed to them a quite normal application of the Confucian "investigation of things." In late Tokugawa and early Meiji times the term "investigation of principles," *kyūri*, changed in content from the study of the Neo-Confucian universals of Chu Hsi to the "science" of the West. For those fully conscious of the significance of this, and remorselessly logical, this might well have resulted in a questioning of the entire Confucian synthesis. This seems to have been the case for Fukuzawa. Yet many others managed a kind of compartmentalization of mental experience that was made the easier by the absence of works discussing the theory and methodology which lay behind the Western science. And even in the case of Fukuzawa, it is well to remember that his famous autobiography gives the memories of old age in which he could easily exaggerate the rebellion of his youth; in addition, he had personal reasons for resentment with the system of class and rank under which he had grown up.[25]

It required, in other words, some new, extraordinary, and external problem to bring to the surface all the latent dissatisfactions which had awaited articulation. This challenge was supplied by the advent of the West. It was a problem that had been foreseen by those worried about the defence of the northern islands against the Russians. It was an appearance that was preceded by the stories of the British activities in China. It was an appearance that had been announced by the Dutch from their Nagasaki trading station, who presented solemn warnings of what was to come. And it was a danger whose details and results were soon available to all who could read, for besides the "Dutch scholars"

[25] Fukuzawa, while at Nagasaki studying Western lore, had been ordered home because his progress was in advance of that of the son of his lord's chancellor. *Autobiography*, p. 25. Still, in his *Kyūhanjo*, he notes that the lower samurai tended to accept their station without rancor. (Translated by Carmen Blacker in *Monumenta Nipponica* [Tokyo, 1953], pp. 304-329.) And Fukuzawa himself, however critical of Tokugawa feudalism in his writings after the Restoration, restricted himself to publishing factual accounts of the West and kept his political views to himself prior to 1868. Numata, *Bakumatsu yōgaku shi* (Tokyo, 1950), p. 262.

19

who speculated, however guardedly, on its significance, there were writings from China that needed no translation for any well-educated Japanese. All this information, suitably simplified and refracted by Japanese writers and analysts, quickly spread to the broad mass of literate Japanese.

These generalizations may now be substantiated by turning from the national scene to the province of Tosa and the social and economic setting which Sakamoto Ryōma and Nakaoka Shintarō knew. In Tosa, as in other fiefs, severe economic problems led the administration to attempt ambitious reforms to increase its revenues. The reforms ran afoul of traditional interests and groupings and helped to produce the setting of distrust and fear in which the Restoration leaders were first to win prominence. Knowledge of the West was not widespread, and the revelation of Japan's weakness acted as a powerful stimulant for young warriors. Many of these men sprang from the groups of rural leaders who, in the absence of their warrior superiors, controlled the countryside. A loyalist party formed, its leaders schooled in a blend of Shintō studies and Confucian loyalty; their first reaction to the foreign danger was a xenophobic one. In these respects Sakamoto and Nakaoka were representative of their contemporaries. They were not so much innovators as followers of the opinion of their peers; they were literate but by no measure were they intellectuals. They were traditional but not obscurantist in their outlook, and they were loyal to but not zealots for the institutions and overlords they knew. Though they accepted most of the loyalist and Shintō thought of their school days, they were not students or intellectuals, and hence not closely associated with Shintō, with Confucian, and still less with Western studies and values. They were at first slightly, and only later fully, aware of the economic dilemmas of the ruling class to which they owed a nominal adherence. The manner of their education was importantly conditioned by the problems peculiar to their region, but their response was in large measure one typical of their generation.

2. Tosa

Kōchi Prefecture retains almost unchanged the boundaries of the Tosa fief of Tokugawa times. A fan-shaped, mountainous province in the southern part of the island of Shikoku, it is one of the least accessible and least visited parts of Japan. A rail connection from Takamatsu in the northeast came only in 1936, and travel in the direction of the other neighboring castle towns of Tokugawa days, Matsuyama and Uwajima, is still by slow bus along primitive roads which thread through the steep defiles of the surrounding mountains.

Kōchi, or Tosa, to use the ancient provincial name preferred by its inhabitants, was an integrated realm with natural mountainous frontiers. In Tokugawa times communications were slow and roads were kept in a state of disrepair in all parts of Japan in order to discourage contacts between fiefs. The Kōchi authorities were particularly intent upon maintaining such restrictions. In the seventeenth century the Tosa rulers had been troubled by the flight of frightened farmers to neighboring realms, and in later years villagers in border areas several times expressed their resistance to new levies or policies by seeking sanctuary across the mountains until the issues at stake had been worked out. Therefore the principal passes were carefully guarded, and since the mountainous terrain made it easy to bar entrance to neighboring fiefs for all but the most determined refugees, only Satsuma (modern Kagoshima) in southern Kyushu was as effectively secluded during Tokugawa days. Much official travel and authorized merchant transport moved to Osaka and other Inland Sea ports by ship, but land routes were few and difficult.

The Tosa climate is mild, with a growing season of 241 frost-free days which makes double-cropping of rice possible; the more than abundant rainfall of more than one hundred inches also simplifies problems of irrigation. The soil is less friendly than the weather, however, and the small amount of flat valley land suitable for paddy cultivation was long ago supplemented by vigorous terracing measures that give the countryside much of its interest. The population, which is estimated to have numbered approximately 300,000 at the beginning of Tokugawa rule, grew to an estimated 500,000 by 1842.

Popular writers sometimes distinguish between two types of personality which developed under the warm skies, sudden storms, and difficult terrain; the mountaineer, harsh, intolerant, rigid, and unyielding, and the coastal dweller, who is credited with a more supple approach in negotiation and with an open-minded curiosity about the new and strange. One can have little confidence in such stock types and less in their geographic roots, but it is worth noting that these distinctions were worked out to describe the principal subjects of this study—Sakamoto Ryōma, supposedly the "coastal," manipulating type, and Nakaoka Shintarō, the more single-minded backwoodsman.[26]

Tosa was ruled by the head of the Yamauchi family, a daimyō who, despite membership in the group of tozama ("outside") daimyō, had experienced many favors at the hands of the Tokugawa. After the great battle of Sekigahara in 1600 Tokugawa Ieyasu, the founder of the shogunate, relieved the daimyō of Tosa, Chōsogabe Morichika, of his fief, which was then turned over to Yamauchi Kazutoyo. This man, lord of a small (50,000 koku yield) domain in Tōtōmi, had joined the Tokugawa side before the battle, but he had taken no part in the fighting. His rewards therefore seemed to go far beyond his services, and such fortunate treatment placed his successors under a great obligation to the Tokugawa house. Their gratitude was often cited as justification for their reluctance to work actively against the Tokugawa cause during the last years of the shogunate. Whether put forward from conviction or from caution, it furnished an irrefutable argument in Tokugawa times. "We are after all in a very different position from you," Kazutoyo's 14th descendent Toyoshige (Yōdō) could point out to the Satsuma representative Saigō Takamori, "since we bear the Tokugawa a moral obligation."[27]

The lord of Tosa ranked nineteenth in revenue among the vassals of the Tokugawa shogun. As Lord of a Province and hereditary holder of a Fourth (Imperial) Court Rank, he was one of the great tozama, and he sat with his peers in the Great Hall when in ceremonial attendance upon the shogun in the Edo Chiyoda Castle.[28] Ceremonial obligations and honors were proportional to rated rice income. Tosa was ranked at 202,600 koku of rice annually. In fact, however, it was known to be more productive from the first, and the willingness of Tokugawa officials to overlook the probability of an additional 50,000 koku yield was

[26] Introduction by Iwasaki Akigawa, *Sakamoto Ryōma kankei monjo* (Tokyo, 1926), p. 2; cf. also Tokutomi Iichirō, *Tosa no kinnō* (Tokyo, 1929), p. 4, who adds other examples.

[27] Quoted in Osatake Takeshi, *Meiji Ishin* (Tokyo, 1947), III, 773.

[28] A description of the ceremonial functions in Edo, where the lords were obliged to reside in alternate years, may be found in John W. Hall, *Tanuma Okitsugu (1719-1788): Forerunner of Modern Japan* (Cambridge, Mass., 1955), pp. 24-25.

usually cited as an example of Tokugawa good will; the lower rating made possible important economies.[29]

The Tosa daimyō was able to tap other sources of wealth besides the rice income of his realm. Dense forests covered the mountains, and under Yamauchi rule exports of lumber to the main island increased markedly. Some went as tribute offerings for shogunal needs for castles, temples, and ships, but large amounts also went on concession to Osaka merchants to add to the fief income. From the forests also came firewood and, more important, Tosa paper. The waters of the bay also made possible a flourishing fishing industry, and dried bonito (*katsuobushi*) from Tosa found its way from the fishing villages, via the proper guild channels, to the markets of Osaka and Edo. In addition land reclamation, more intensive cultivation, and better agricultural methods increased the rice and other agricultural yield as well.[30] The Tosa potential placed the Yamauchi among the very great and very powerful lords.

Yamauchi rule was exerted through bureaucratic institutions that were on the whole similar to those of the shogunate and the majority of its major vassals. Problems relating to entrance into and continuity within the administrative structure were at the heart of much of the political maneuvering of late Tokugawa times, and it will be useful to indicate the main divisions of the fief, or *han*, government. They were as follows:

A Court Office (*Naichōkan*) was responsible for the administration of the affairs of the lord's household.

A Division of Internal Administration (*Naikan*) was charged with supervision of the samurai, with operation of the Yamauchi

[29] The koku (4.96 bushels) was the unit of capacity in which rice was measured; in Tosa, it was often used interchangeably with the unit of area (*tan* = .25 acres) which, in theory, produced one koku of rice annually. For the Tosa *kokudaka* problem, see Hirao Michio, *Kochi han zaisei shi* (Kōchi, 1953), pp. 1, 2, and Numata Raisuke, "Tosa koku taka kō," *Rekishi Chiri* (Tokyo, 1924), Vol. 28, 1, pp. 45f.

[30] Recent publications by Hirao Michio document each of these Tosa industries. In *Tosa han ringyō keizaishi* (Kōchi, 1956) Hirao gives charts of tribute shipments of lumber from 1634 to 1838 as well as evidence of commercial use. Conservation and reforestation plans began as early as 1617, and by 1691 Tosa was divided into 25 zones, with a rotation plan for logging. Careful figures recorded the number of trees cut and planted each year thereafter. Fisheries are covered in Hirao, *Tosa han gyogyō keizai shi* (Kōchi, 1955), and handicrafts in *Tosa han kōgyō keizai shi* (Kōchi, 1957). The over-all fiscal picture is treated in *Tosa han zaiseishi* (Kōchi, 1953).

residences in Edo and elsewhere, with instruction in the samurai college, and with records and archives.

An Outer Office (*Gaichōkan*) carried on the administration of the realm.

It will be seen that in practical, as opposed to honorific, terms, it was the third division that counted for most; this was the division whose policies and personnel would be seen by commoners and samurai as constituting the han government. Its most important offices were often termed the "Three Offices":

Commissioners General (*Bugyō-shoku*), three high ranking retainers with ultimate authority and responsibility.

Assistant Ministry (*Shioki-yaku*), a board of three assistants to the Commissioners General. It also headed the Bureau of Shrines and Temples, thereby assuming responsibility for religious surveys and the census.

The Great Inspectors (*Ōmetsuke*), a board of three men who headed the elaborate police and surveillance services of the realm.

Of these offices it was usually the second, Shioki-yaku or Assistant Ministry, that played the most important role. Under this bureau served the magistrates of towns, districts, taxes, finance, public works, construction, shipping, coastal districts, forests and mountains. Of these magistrates, in turn, it was the District Magistrates (*kōri bugyō*) who formed the link between central administration and local affairs. The District Magistrates, whose offices were to be found in each of Tosa's seven districts, dealt, sometimes through subordinating bailiffs (*daikan*), with the village heads.[31]

For the bureaucratic posts of the han, of which only the most important have been listed, eligibility was limited to samurai of specified rank. Rank, in turn, bore appropriate income from subfief, which bore name appropriate to the holder's status, or from stipend. In addition, rank and title also signified command in the military organization that had last seen service in the sixteenth century. Although they had served little more than ceremonial and

---

[31] This summary is based on standard sources for Tokugawa Tosa: *Kōchi Ken shiyō* (Osaka, 1924), pp. 201ff., and the recent *Kōchi Shi shi* (Kōchi Shi shi hensan iinkai, Kōchi 1958), pp. 316ff.

review purposes for many years, the formations had been retained. The principal ranks of late-Tokugawa days were as follows:

"Upper" samurai (*jōshi; osamurai;* also termed *shikaku*):

Karō (House elders) Eleven in number. Lands with tax base of 1,500-10,000 koku. Headed the Court and Internal Administration departments and served as Commissioners General (Bugyō-shoku). Headed the major military formations. Granted permission to use the Yamauchi family name, and served the daimyō in the way the most trusted fudai and shimpan lords served the shogun.

Chūrō. Eleven in number. Lands with tax base of 450-1,500 koku. Staffed some of the more important offices, usually at a level closer to that of implementation than did the more honored *karō*.

Of whom were "Regular" samurai (*hira-zamurai*):

Umamawari (Mounted guard). Approximately 800 in number. Lands with tax base of 100-700 koku. Their name derived from their position around the daimyō's headquarters in the field. Field-grade officers in battle formations. Furnished the bulk of the leadership at the administrative level, particularly in the Assistant-Ministry (shioki-yaku), which they and chūrō staffed.

Koshōgumi, number not definitely fixed. Lands producing 70-250 koku. Staffed with *umamawari,* most magistracies.

Rusuigumi, number not fixed. Lands producing 50-200 koku. Staffed with koshōgumi, some magistracies, and lesser offices.

These five ranks provided the official classes for the bureaucratic institutions that distinguished Tokugawa feudalism. Office normally brought with it an additional reward in salary. The Assistant Ministers, for instance, received 450 koku annually in addition to their regular income, while district magistrates received 250 koku. Regulations specified appropriate scales of consumption for each grade.[32]

[32] These provisions are as specified in Yoshida Tōyō's codification of administrative procedure in late Tokugawa times, the *Kainan Seiten.* There were fourteen classes of land, scaling from the lord's domain, *O-kurairi,* to *Sashiagechi,* a Supplementary grant made to officials or samurai whose incomes seemed inadequate. See Matsuyoshi Sadao, *Tosa han keizaishi kenkyū,* p. 7. When an estate com-

There was some mobility within the lower ranks of the upper samurai, but very little between these favored ranks and the five below them, collectively known as "Lower" samurai (*kashi; keikaku*):

Gōshi, 900-1000 in number. Lands producing 30-250 koku.
Yōnin, number not fixed.
Kachi, number not fixed, income 12-17 koku.
Kumigai, number not fixed, 10 koku.
Ashigaru, "foot soldier," further subdivided into many groups, and maintained on the subsistence level at 3-7 koku.

Men in the last four ranks received their income in the form of a stipend from the lord's warehouse. While they might receive official employment of a modest sort, it would be at the lowest levels and paid, if at all, poorly, usually with rations for dependents. The lowest-ranked ashigaru, in fact, performed a labor service that was utilized in logging operations.[33] There was thus a substantial gulf between the first five ranks and those below them, and this gulf proved important in the development of the loyalist movement, many of whose early members were from families of the sixth rank.

Just as the Tokugawa collected their retainers in their cities, the Tosa administration gradually assembled most of its retainers in Kōchi City. The city grew beneath the castle which, together with the elevation upon which it was constructed, was erected by forced levy of all the populace of the Kōchi shortly after the consolidation of Yamauchi rule.[34] During the years of peace the warriors tended to have less and less contact with the lands which had been allotted them, with the result that rural administration gradually passed into the hands of the district magistrates. The granting of sub-fiefs came to a virtual stop, as payments in stipends of rice, collectable in Kōchi, became the rule. The one completely

---

prised an entire village or group of villages the grantee would supervise its administration. If, however, his holdings represented only part of a village, as was more often the case, the entire village would be under the rule of the han-appointed headman except for tax collection, which the grantee would arrange with a group leader selected from among the heads of five-man units.

[33] Hirao Michio, *Tosa han ringyō keizai shi*, p. 165.

[34] Hirao Michio, "Kōchi Shi no konjaku," *Kōchi Ken kenchiku shikai hakkō* (n.d.) pp. 2, 3. *Kōchi Shi shi*, pp. 289ff., gives the daily labor force at 1,200 to 1,300, including women and even children who helped to carry soil and stones.

autonomous sub-fief in Tosa, which had been granted to Yamauchi Kazutoyo's younger brother, reverted to Kōchi control at the end of the seventeenth century after the bakufu had dismissed its holder.[35]

Among these ranks the *gōshi*, who topped the classification of "lower" samurai, will figure importantly in this narrative. From their ranks came many of Tosa's Restoration leaders and heroes, among them Sakamoto Ryōma and Takechi Zuizan. The *gōshi* as a grade owed their origin to problems of administration which the Yamauchi encountered after their entry into Tosa. At the time the Yamauchi entered Tosa in the seventeenth century their warrior following was small, as befitted their realm, and it was inadequate to staff all of the ranks that have been described. Tosa itself was still under the control of retainers of the Chōsogabe family, men whose roots in the land were very strong. For a time there was sporadic resistance by the Chōsogabe men against the new lord; several rebellions and widespread flight kept the new authorities hard-pressed to restore order. The Yamauchi tried therefore to utilize and placate some of the Chōsogabe retainers by granting them the rank of *gōshi*.

The rank of *gōshi*, "country samurai," was instituted in 1613, when it was granted to a small number of Chōsogabe retainers in the area near Kōchi city. The *gōshi* were expected to reside in the countryside, administering areas later defined as producing between 30 and 250 koku. They were given military assignments roughly comparable to those of non-commissioned officers, and their rank was considered sufficiently honorable to permit their presence in the review held for the daimyō at the new year's ceremonies. They sometimes accompanied the Yamauchi on duty in Edo.

These initial grants represented measures designed to establish and maintain order in the countryside. In 1644, however, the Tosa administrator Nonaka Kenzan changed the pattern by utilizing

[35] This was Nakamura, in present-day Hata district. Its holder declined appointment to the Tokugawa Junior Council (*Wakadoshiyori*) in 1689, hoping to avoid the ceremonial costs which this honor would have involved. The abolition of his fief meant loss of his mansions in Edo, destruction of his castle, and of the incomes and, ultimately, the residences of his 400 retainers, who were scattered, most of them entering lower class livelihoods of artisans and merchants. The effect on Nakamura was "as though a fire had ravaged it." The bakufu appropriated the sub-han's income for several years before returning it to the Yamauchi main family. Nakamura chō yakuba, *Nakamura Chō shi* (Kōchi, 1950), p. 32.

the rank as an incentive for land reclamation.[36] Any qualified applicant who had reclaimed an area of new fields (*shinden*) producing a minimum of 30 koku of rice annually could apply for one of one hundred *gōshi* patents which Nonaka made available. At the time, it was still necessary to establish descent from Chōsogabe retainers, but subsequent regulations, designed as they were to encourage reclamation in outlying districts, placed their chief emphasis on character rather than on family. Major grants of rank in 1763 and 1822 brought the total number of *gōshi* to over 800 families.[37]

At the very time that political and economic measures were drawing the upper samurai into the castle town, then, reclamation incentives provided by the administration were encouraging the growth of a new group of landed samurai. Many of them must have accumulated estates of very considerable size, since the codes of 1690 provided for possible transfer to the "upper" grade of *rusuigumi* for *gōshi* of samurai descent whose lands produced a minimum of 100 koku annually. It is difficult to determine the frequency of such transfers, but since new qualifications for rusuigumi issued in 1735 raised the minimum acreage to lands producing 200 koku it may indicate that too many had made the shift.[38]

It is not possible, however, to characterize the *gōshi* simply as a group of samurai-farmers maintaining the agrarian and feudal

---

[36] Nonaka Kenzan (1615-63) was a scholar and administrator who devised intellectual, economic, and political policies which established Tosa as one of the great fiefs. Extensive reclamation and riparian works extended cultivation, while han monopolies tapped other products to augment official income. Neo-Confucian scholarship was introduced, and scholars like Yamazaki Anzai and the Tani line of Confucianists were encouraged. Shortly before his death Nonaka was the victim of bureaucratic rivalry and demoted and banished on charges of oppressing the people. There are many biographies. For an account of Nonaka's career and fall, Ozeki Toyokichi, "Kambun no kaitai ni tsuite," *Tosa Shidan*, No. 24 (Kōchi, 1928), pp. 24-40.

[37] The *gōshi* system is described by Irimajiri Yoshinaga, *Tokugawa bakuhansei kaitai katei no kenkyū* (Tokyo, 1957). Other accounts can be found in Ozeki Toyokichi, "Kōchi han no gōshi ni tsuite," *Tosa shidan*, No. 48 (Kōchi, 1934), pp. 117-154; Matsuyoshi Sadao, *Shinden no kenkyū* (Tokyo, 1936), pp. 233-311. Basic documents for the development of the class are contained in the recent volume of the Kinsei sonraku kenkyū kai, *Kinsei sonraku jichi shiryōshū*, Vol. II, *Tosa no kuni jikata shiryō* (Tokyo, 1956), pp. 383-431. In English there is a short appendix in E. H. Norman, *Soldier and Peasant in Japan: The Origins of Conscription* (New York, 1943), pp. 58-65, based largely on Matsuyoshi; and R. B. Grinnan, "Feudal Land Tenure in Tosa," TASJ, xx, 2 (Tokyo, 1893), pp. 228-247, based on conversations with a Tosa karō (Shibata Kamichirō) and gōshi (Hosokawa Gishō.)

[38] Irimajiri, p. 296.

ideal in a society that had become commercialized. By mid-Tokugawa times it was unlikely that prospective applicants would find lands of requisite size in one parcel capable of development by their servants. *Gōshi* estates now tended to be made up of scattered lands, and their development required capital to pay workers and tenants to do the work. Effective management of such estates required managerial ability. The han regulations, probably out of eagerness to maintain the fullest possible use of land, therefore became less insistent upon samurai background for would-be *gōshi*. The notices of 1763, when Hata district was to be developed, made it known that applicants would be considered regardless of family occupation; "even a person who is engaged in merchant activity can be chosen if he proves suitable." Only those with criminals in their lineage were now excluded. The notices of 1822 furthermore provided for free sale of *gōshi* titles, provided that the buyers met standing qualifications of character and record.[39]

As a result of such changes, the *gōshi* were infiltrated by representatives of merchant or rural wealth who bought titles of rank. More noteworthy still is that significant numbers of new, and some old, *gōshi*, preferred to live in or near the castle town of Kōchi instead of on their lands. A survey made in the early decades of the nineteenth century showed that of the approximately 800 *gōshi* eighty-two families were resident in or very close to the town of Kōchi. It is not surprising that surviving members of the original *gōshi* groups as well as many of the upper samurai looked down on these urbanized "country samurai," and that a number of petitions deplored such developments.[40] It was into such a family that Sakamoto Ryōma was born in 1835. His grandfather, a wealthy sake brewer, had purchased *gōshi* rank in 1771, but the family had continued to reside in Kōchi.

The great majority of the Tosa *gōshi* lived in the countryside, however, and in the absence of the upper samurai, all of whom had moved to the castle town, they were in touch with popular sentiment and helped to mold it. The *gōshi* also provided a literate and educated group of rural leaders throughout Tosa with a good

---

[39] Irimajiri, p. 281, and "Tosa han 'chōnin gōshi' no kaisei ni kansuru ichi shiryō," *Shakai kagaku tōkyū*, ɪ (Tokyo, 1956), p. 102.

[40] *Kōchi Shi shi*, pp. 330-337, gives the names, incomes, and estates of these families. For a memorial of 1787 condemning such urbanized *gōshi* as of no use to the lord, p. 329.

deal of pride and solidarity. A number of incidents found them pitted against their betters. In 1797, for instance, a *gōshi* named Takamura insulted an upper samurai named Inoue, who promptly drew his sword and wounded Takamura fatally. The han's first response was to justify the act on grounds of lower class discourtesy. Soon murmurings among the *gōshi* resulted in meetings and petitions protesting this, and as tension mounted the han reconsidered its attitude and penalized the upper samurai by lowering his rank and income. But the *gōshi* were still dissatisfied, and group and individual petitions gave evidence of organization and determination. In 1801 the daimyo became alarmed and banished Inoue. A general wave of resignations and sudden illness among the han officials who had allowed the incident to become so explosive followed this settlement.[41] From this and similar incidents one can sense the degree to which *gōshi* resented the arrogance of their superiors.

Important as the *gōshi* were, they had no direct authority for administration in the countryside. This rested with village headmen, or *shōya*, who provided, together with the *gōshi*, most of the Tosa Loyalist Party members. In order to understand the manner in which *shōya* like Nakaoka Shintarō and Yoshimura Toratarō could come to assume a political role in late Tokugawa days, it is useful to summarize the powers of their office and the content of their education.

The *shōya* functioned as the lowest unit of han control, but since they were in fact commoners and not samurai they were simultaneously the highest point of village organization and most effective spokesmen for local and rural interests. *Shōya* were appointed by the district magistrate (*kōri bugyō*) from among the leading families in the village. Actually most of them were members of families whose heads had served in the office for many generations, and many traced their eminence to pre-Tokugawa days when the distinction between farmer and samurai was still a hazy one. In such cases they descended, therefore, from Chōsogabe farmer-soldiers, and as a result many claimed the same sort of background the oldest *gōshi* families did. Numerically such families may have been in the minority, as they probably were

---

[41] Details and documents are provided in Hirao Michio, *Nagaoka son shi* (Kōchi, 1955), pp. 88-92.

among *gōshi* by the nineteenth century, but so useful and prestige-filled a social and psychological myth required no statistical backing to serve its role. There were many links between the two groups, for it was from the *shōya*, more specifically younger sons, that most *gōshi* were recruited.

The *shōya* ran the village, and in the case of great *shōya* (*ōjōya*) like Nakaoka, as many as thirteen or more villages. They had powers of justice and police for all but the most serious infractions of order, and they were held responsible for seeing that the land tax was paid. *Shōya* also felt it their task to protect their villagers against unfair demands from the absentee samurai, who were in any case their natural rivals for influence and authority. Surviving documents make it clear that they considered themselves the "head of the people," and since their tax-collecting and reporting functions usually included residence taxes on retainers' houses and religious affiliation reports for all within their area, including *gōshi* and other samurai, they had grounds for being impressed with their own importance. Their responsibility usually led them to protest to the central authority at times when literal execution of duties or collections would imperil rural well-being and order. Thus one finds Nakaoka Shintarō making several trips to distant Kōchi to plead the case for his district.[42] The han regime recognized the *shōya* as the fulcrum upon which feudal authority rested. The official *shōya* registers include praise for headmen who prevented or reported incipient protests and revolts; cases in which the revolt was not successfully headed off found the *shōya* held accountable.[43]

Despite the importance of their social role, the *shōya* were below the *gōshi* in rank and, indeed, not formally members of the ruling class at all. *Gōshi* who lived within their areas enjoyed immunity from many of the powers exercised by the headmen, an immunity they won in the seventeenth century after protests at being subservient to their social inferiors. *Shōya* occasionally

---

[42] See the biography of Nakaoka by Hirao Michio, *Rikuentai shimatsu ki* (Tokyo, 1942), p. 9.

[43] A convenient summary of monographic studies of *shōya* powers in other parts of Japan can be found in Kodama Kōda, *Kinsei nōmin seikatsu shi* (Tokyo, 1957), pp. 94-130. It is clear that *shōya* powers were considerable in most areas, but few groups could claim as honorable a past as the Tosa village heads. Not only did they claim the memory of Chōsogabe days, but in addition they operated under a feudal hierarchy that was relatively, in national terms, understaffed and hence, in all probability, less intensive in its control.

asked for a return of their jurisdiction over *gōshi*, and there were undoubtedly many grounds for friction between the two groups in the routine of daily life and administration. In other respects, however, the *shōya* and *gōshi* seem to have had more reason to ally than to compete. They were both discriminated against in favor of the urban, higher ranking samurai. On the whole they both represented rural, village interests, particularly the interests of the village wealthy, in potential opposition to the Kōchi administration with its desires to secure greater revenue from the countryside. Their sons were similarly educated, usually in the same schools; they shared the same general outlook, and the *shōya* provided the largest number of recruits to the *gōshi* class. As a result it is natural that the emergent movements of political protest of late Tokugawa days, in particular the loyalist movement, were led by groups of *gōshi* and *shōya* who had been schooled together in fencing and in letters.

An examination of the economic and social antagonisms that could develop in Tosa between the policy of the Kōchi administration and the rural leaders shows a good deal about the problems feudal administrators faced everywhere in Japan by the nineteenth century. In essence the antagonisms grew out of a struggle for the surplus of the countryside, the only real wealth that was available to the ruling classes.

At first impression, the Tosa countryside must have seemed under much more efficient and effective control than was the case in most parts of Japan. This is because the Yamauchi rulers had restored, in 1622, a system of periodic redivision of lands classified as *honden*, the principal, or lord's domain. Under this system, which derived from Nara-Heian times and, ultimately, from T'ang China, lots were drawn for strips of land of varying desirability every five, or seven, or sometimes ten years. The "lot lands" (*kuji chi*) so drawn were tilled until the next redivision, or *jiwari*. In outlying areas the intervals between allotments were very erratic, and it was undoubtedly most efficiently carried on in the Kōchi plain around the castle. It is perhaps an indication of the system's unpopularity, or at least of the helplessness of the peasant before the tax collector, that migration from honden villages to Kōchi and other towns was common. In some areas, lands so lost to cultivation were later reclaimed as shinden, often by would-be *gōshi.* Honden lands were taxed at the ratio of 6:4, the larger being the lord's share of the yield, while on shinden lands, since they were likely to be marginal and because incentives were required to secure their reclamation, the tax ratio was reversed. In late Tokugawa times other fiefs experimented with attempts to restore the redivision system in order to increase their revenue, but none seems to have been successful. The tenacity of the institution in Tosa must be considered evidence of successful work by the officials and *shōya* who administered it.[44]

Since the agricultural revenue alone was inadequate, the han administration developed a number of auxiliary sources of income. Chief among these were the measures taken to market lumber, paper, and other products in Osaka. An office of provincial products under the finance magistrate encouraged production and regulated marketing of salable commodities. Private enterprise in profitable merchandise was limited in scope, as important business was delegated to specially authorized guilds which were given monopoly purchase rights in Tosa. In return for such privileges the merchants involved paid the han a license fee. Inevitably, close contacts developed between officials of the finance magistracy and the privileged merchants.

Monopoly enterprise of this order hurt both the rural suppliers, who sold at a disadvantage to the monopoly guilds, and local entrepreneurs who operated the same type of enterprises, albeit on a smaller scale, during periods of free competition. Typically, the periods of stringent enforcement were denounced as periods of corruption, since merchants became important to han policy, and of bad government, because the commoners suffered. Thus while there was no positive enunciation of the right or value of private enterprise, there was a lively opposition to the evils of official enterprise.

The manner in which monopolies and collusion could affront rural and local susceptibilities is well shown by the famous Ikegawa "paper rebellion" of 1787. In that year villages which produced paper were stirred to protest by the way in which the privileged guilds were keeping prices depressed at the collection points in order to realize a maximum profit on the transactions. Some six hundred inhabitants of Ikegawa presented petitions of protest and then fled across the mountain barriers to the neighboring fief of

[44] *Kōchi Ken nōchi kaikaku shi* (Kōchi, 1952).

Matsuyama. It required prolonged negotiation with the Matsuyama officials, assurances to the refugees, and the proper number of official resignations and dismissals to bring about a settlement.[45]

It was thus always the case that "reformers" who sought to bolster han finances by increasing revenue and by limiting non-official consumption were sharply attacked as responsible for oppressive measures and reproached with opening the way for corruption by encouraging the administration to enter the unseemly path of trade. This was the fate of even the great Nonaka Kenzan, whose policies had done so much to enlarge and bolster the Tosa economy by riparian measures, reclamation, and monopoly trading. Nonaka was driven out of office and into exile in 1663 by complaints that his policies had caused hardship for all classes. As will be noted in later chapters, the same fate was prepared for the reformer of the 1860's, Yoshida Tōyō. After Nonaka's fall, monopolies were periodically revived and dissolved in response to han distress and commoners' protests. But commoners' protests had little chance of being heard unless they were expressed by the gōshi and shōya in the countryside. Nor, it may be added, did the reforms stand much chance of success unless they received the cooperation of the same groups who, since their wealth made of them economic as well as social and political leaders, were personally affected by the reforms. It may be observed that since many students of Tokugawa economics, among them Satō Shinen, praised Tosa as one of the few areas where ancient feudal virtues and institutions could still be found in all their integrity, such sentiments tell us more about the rest of Japan than they do about Tosa.[46] Presumably, it was the Tosa gōshi that brought such praise from Satō, since they seemed one of the few survivors of the self-sufficient farmer-soldier ideal of an earlier day. Actually, as has been noted, many of the gōshi were neither self-sufficient, farmers, nor soldiers.

It would nevertheless be highly misleading to conclude that gōshi and shōya represented simply rural enterprise versus urban monopoly, and that their activities in the 1850's and 1860's derived from anti-feudal or commercial-capitalist ideas. The articulation of opposition in those decades was conditioned by the climate of

---

[45] Hirao Michio, *Tosa nōmin ikki shikō* (Kōchi, 1953), pp. 31-61, for details and documentation.
[46] Quoted by Matsuyoshi, *Keizaishi*, p. 182.

opinion within which young men were brought up and educated, and the ideological setting was more conducive to thoughts of restoring agrarianism than to promotion of mercantile enterprise.

Most *gōshi* and *shōya* sons received their education in private academies (*shijuku*) of which there were nearly twenty in or near Kōchi itself. Retainers' sons were eligible for instruction in the official han schools, and commoners received the rudiments of literacy in the temple schools (*terakoya*) which were everywhere. The han encouraged sons of lower ranks and sons of leading village families to devote themselves to learning and military arts, and most of them did this in the private academies. The shijuku were of several kinds and their teachers of different persuasions, but on the whole the prevalent teaching was that of Chu Hsi Neo-Confucianism as it had been transmitted through the line of Confucianists which stemmed from Tani Shinzan (1663-1718). Tani, a student of Yamazaki Anzai, had absorbed much of his teacher's emphasis on Shintō, and he called for a blend of patriotic learning with the wisdom of the Chinese sages. It is perhaps significant that Tani began his teaching while banished from the castle town, a punishment he had received for his refusal to obey han orders by accepting the direction of a disciple of Itō Jinsai who had received han favor in the 1670's. The private academies were thus capable of heterodox teaching from the first. Tani was pardoned in 1711, however, and thereafter his teaching, known as *Nangaku*, gradually dominated official training institutes as well as most private academies. By the nineteenth century there were also private schools which specialized in purely Shintō studies.[47]

Whatever the political leanings of Nangaku teaching, there is little support for attempts to find in it thought disruptive of the values of agrarianism upon which Tosa and Tokugawa society were based. Historically the teaching derived from Yamazaki Anzai, whose patron had been Nonaka Kenzan. Tani Shinzan's original difficulty was probably caused in part by the association of his teaching with the discredited cause of Nonaka and Yamazaki. In later years most of Nonaka's methods were reintroduced, and it was fitting to refurbish his philosophical protégés as well. In no sense was the teaching of the private schools any more anti-feudal than that of the han schools for higher ranking students. One meets with little success in crediting the *gōshi* or *shōya* gradu-

[47] *Kōchi Shi shi*, pp. 495-497.

ates with progressive thought. Indeed, they were probably less forward-looking than the administrators of higher rank who, faced with responsibility for the problems of the realm, were inclined to experiment pragmatically while looking for solutions. In contrast, the early loyalist leaders, without the sobering responsibilities of leadership, could remain ideologically consistent and "feudal" long after their superiors had shifted their ground. Takechi Zuizan, an urbanized *gōshi* and the leader of the Loyalist Party, usually thought in terms of confiscation of merchant capital in order to finance needed military reforms, and his followers were scarcely more partial to merchants.[48] Far from representing antifeudal thought, the *gōshi* and *shōya* spokesmen of the second quarter of the nineteenth century were usually insistent upon the necessity for returning to a purer form of agrarianism. In so doing, however, they sometimes called into question the values and contributions of the urbanized upper samurai.

3. Tosa at Mid-Century

The second quarter of the nineteenth century, the one into which Sakamoto, Nakaoka, and the other Restoration leaders were born, was remarkable for indications of a rising tide of discontent and for official policies designed to restore the position of the ruling groups. Everywhere in Japan protests and rebellions were put down without, as it seemed, lasting damage to the ruling class. The attempts to bolster feudal rule that followed were, in some fiefs, successful. But when the arrival of the envoys from the West at mid-century precipitated a national crisis, there were to be seen in new dress types of discontent which had earlier asserted themselves, just as in the official response of reform and reconsolidation there were evidences of potentialities and limitations that could be traced to earlier policies. With this in mind, it will be useful to turn to the trends of the Tempō Period (1830-1843) in Tosa.

During these years there were striking instances of *shōya* dissatisfaction in Tosa. It would seem that the *shōya* felt their position threatened by the increasing tide of commercialization that worked to the advantage of the town merchants. Ordinary village

---

[48] The Loyalists will be considered at length in future chapters, but it may suffice to note that one follower suggested to Takechi that Osaka merchants, if they resisted pressure for forced loans, could be intimidated by having *shishi* commit hara-kiri on the spot, and predicted that no merchant could resist more than three suicides. *Ishin Tosa kinnō shi* (Tokyo, 1912), pp. 294-296.

leaders like elders (*toshiyori*) were, in places, being treated like appointed officials and were becoming competitors for honors once reserved for the *shōya* themselves. Many *shōya* had utilized their advantages of position and wealth to enter local and small-scale entrepreneurial ventures whose profits might go toward the acquisition of land or of rank for their sons, with the result that they also tended to resent han policies which favored the monopoly guilds of merchants. It may be possible, as one writer suggests with reference to a different fief, that the feudal rulers in their search for income had now shifted from a policy of mercantilist, regional self-sufficiency, from which they could reap no further benefits, to one of competition with the moneyed class in their own area for the agricultural and handicraft surplus of which they were getting only a part.[49] If so, such policies would inevitably bring them into direct competition with the *shōya* who dominated the countryside.

Shōya dissatisfaction, however, was expressed in terms of a traditional set of values associated with an earlier noncommercial order. The intellectual training absorbed in the private academies was focused on the wisdom of the past, and Confucian values and Japanese tradition tended to instill hopes of a return to a purer society in which their own role would know no competition or humiliation. In the 1830's that competition was being provided by town interests, both merchant and samurai. Complaints tell of inspection tours by petty and insignificant retainers who brought with them all the hauteur once associated with their betters.

The currents of "return to antiquity," which provided such useful slogans in Restoration days, were also much in evidence in Tosa. Teachers of private academies like Kamochi Masazumi (1791-1857) trained a generation of *shōya* and *gōshi* students in the teachings that Motoori Norinaga had worked out earlier. It is not surprising that such students furnished the members for the subsequent Loyalist Party of Takechi Zuizan in the 1860's, and it is worth noting that Takechi himself was a nephew as well as a student of Kamochi's.[50]

The dissatisfactions of which records have survived were *shōya*-

---

[49] Seki Junya, *Hansei kaikaku to Meiji Ishin* (Tokyo, 1956), p. 56.

[50] Matsuzawa Takurō, *Man'yō to Kamochi Masazumi no shōgai* (Tokyo, 1943), p. 254, and Ogata Hiroyasu, *Kamochi Masazumi* (Tokyo, 1944), reprint a good deal of Kamochi's writings as well as describing his life and influence.

centered, and it is interesting to find in these documents desires for improvement of *shōya* status vis-à-vis the *gōshi*. It is likely that the *gōshi* resented were those who had entered the ranks through purchase and who remained resident in or near Kōchi, for the *shōya* complaints of which we have record were centered in villages near Kōchi. These complaints need not, therefore, seriously invalidate the assumption of a common *shōya-gōshi* interest; the later Tosa Loyalist Party, its membership drawn from the two groups, is proof of this.

In the 1830's and 1840's several incidents served to dramatize the dissatisfaction that the *shōya* felt. In 1837, during a shrine festival in Maehama Village, town officials tried to take seats more honorable than those occupied by *shōya*. A group of *shōya* seized upon this incident to make it symbolic of the distorted values that were putting merchant and town above farmer and village, and they petitioned the authorities to prevent recurrences of such an outrage. "There is," they argued, "a distinction of superior and inferior within income. That gained from rice fields is superior while income gained in silver or copper is inferior." Town officials worked with selfish merchants, and they could not possibly compare with *shōya* whose associations were with virtuous farmers. *Shōya*, the argument went on, performed the most important tasks of their society: "We encourage farming and fishing, we see to the payment of the yearly tax and the performance of public works, and, if it become necessary, even the conscription of workers for military preparations. . . . In the final analysis, ours is the office which is entrusted with carrying out all the really important affairs of the realm"; to try to compare this with the life of town officials was "like comparing sky and ground."[51]

The most remarkable indication of *shōya* dissatisfaction came with the formation of a *Shōya* League (*Shōya Dōmei*) in 1841. The *shōya* involved petitioned for a return to earlier administrative practices which had granted them honors they saw slipping away. They wanted exclusive authority over all who resided in their administrative areas, they wanted the privilege of family names and swords for their sons, the right of using force in interrogations, and the dignity of being addressed as "*dono*" (esquire) by *gōshi* in correspondence. In the papers meant for league members, however, the *shōya* went much farther than this. Loyalist

---

[51] Quoted in Hirao Michio, *Tosa nōmin ikki shikō*, p. 126.

teachings and wounded pride went hand in hand to argue that *shōya* had been entrusted with their stewardship in antiquity by the Throne, and that they were properly Imperial servants. The ancient honors of the *shōya* were contrasted to those of the samurai, who, it was implied, were an unprofitable luxury of recent date. "Within the four seas under heaven," the argument ran, "there is only one who is supreme. . . . That supreme being, in all reverence, is the Emperor. The shogun is his deputy, the daimyō are his commanders who head the administration, and the *shōya* are the officers to whom is entrusted responsibility for the land and the people." The samurai, it will be noted, did not enter this table of command. Elsewhere they were referred to as "the feet of the nobility," and contrasted to the *shōya*, "the head of the people."[52] There is no record of any official response to these protests, but they go far to account for the enthusiasm with which so many *shōya* entered national politics in the decade that followed. And, to the degree that the teaching reflected was absorbed in equal measure by *gōshi* and *shōya* sons, the private academy students were not likely to be inhibited by their social and military superiors when a clash of will or interest developed.

The *shōya* protests are noteworthy for the indication of strong influence of loyalist thought among the group. Presumably this is to be credited to the nationalistic leanings of the Tani school of Nangaku which flourished in Tosa education and to the influence of individual Shintō specialists like Kamochi Masazumi. It does not seem possible, as yet, to speak with any confidence about the growth of such thought in Tosa and to speculate as to the enthusiasm with which different groups espoused it. Members of the higher ranks as well were students of Kamochi.[53] It may be that Kamochi was more likely to influence students of *gōshi* and *shōya* rank because they provided the greatest numbers of students who frequented the private academies. At any rate, there is no doubt of the importance of the Shintō thought in the *shōya* documents that have been mentioned. Argumentation begins from the *Kojiki*, and a reference to Imperial service and precedent obviously outweighs recourse to feudal practice as a justification for action or

[52] The full document can be found in Hirao, *Tosa nōmin ikki shikō*, pp. 128-140.

[53] Among them, Sasaki Takayuki, whose career demonstrated the difficulty of remaining true to his peer group while simultaneously maintaining loyalist ideas. See his memoirs, *Kinnō hishi: Sasaki Rō Kō sekijitsu dan* (Tokyo, 1915).

for change. It was to be so again with the enthusiasts of the Loyalist Party in the 1850's and 1860's. It is evident that for men of the lower ranks, resentful of the automatic superiority that their superiors enjoyed, and conscious of their own social role and importance, the thought of a higher loyalty and antecedent order of Imperial rule would have particular appeal. It is therefore no surprise to find Sakamoto Ryōma and his confederates citing such legitimacy confidently in their explanations to parents and friends of their disobedience of the orders of their feudal superiors.[54]

Immediately following the protests that have been described, the Tosa administration launched reforms designed to strengthen the fief's economic position. The reforms may have had little or no reference to the specific protests of the *shōya*, but they were certainly designed to strengthen the institutions of authority and monopoly which had produced the evils of which the *shōya* complained. The Tosa reforms had a broader significance, however, in that they took place amid a general and virtually national attempt to restore the imbalance that had developed between commercial and feudal rights.

The Tempō Reforms followed the long and easy-going rule of the shogun Ienari, who ruled from 1787 to 1837. As was typical during such long reigns, favoritism, ostentation, and corruption had become common. Nor was this restricted to the shogunate. The Satsuma daimyō Shimazu Shigehide (1745-1833) had formally retired in 1787, but continued to affect han policy thereafter until his death in 1833. Through his lavish patronage of cultural and scientific projects, and by the scale of his life in Edo, he left as legacy a mountainous debt. The Tosa daimyō Yamauchi Toyosuke (1794-1872) had ruled for 34 years when he retired in 1843. The Chōshū lord, Mōri Narihiro (1783-1836) had ruled for 27 years at the time of his death in 1836, at which time his fief was also in debt to an amount equivalent to 37 years' regular

---

[54] Thus Sakamoto wrote the parents of a friend who had fled, "The daimyō . . . do not understand the idea of returning the Emperor to a position of power, and yet it is the thing that needs most to be done. What, then, are men of low rank to do to ease his Majesty's mind? You know that one should hold the Imperial Court more dear than one's country, and more dear than one's parents. The idea that in times like these it is a violation of your proper duty to put your relatives second, your han second, to leave your mother, wife, and children—this is certainly a notion that comes from our stupid officials . . . ," from an unpublished letter in the Seizan (Tanaka) Bunko, Sakawa, Kōchi Prefecture.

revenue. When these lengthy reigns ended, everywhere financial problems and new personnel suggested the desirability of reforms.

The earliest Tempō reforms began in the Tokugawa branch of Mito, where Tokugawa Nariaki, who succeeded to rule in 1830, attempted to reverse the tide of agricultural distress that had resulted in depopulating much of the Mito plain, whose peasants left for nearby Edo. Nariaki attempted to cut costs and luxuries and to force some of his samurai out of the castle town and back into the countryside where they would be less expensive and more useful. He was, however, not successful in this.

Meanwhile the startling rising which Ōshio Heihachirō, a minor official and Confucian scholar, led in Osaka in 1837 brought home to all the urgent need of reforms on the national level. Through his influence in bakufu councils Nariaki brought influence to bear on behalf of the minister Mizuno Tadakuni, who took over leadership of the Tokugawa Council of Elders in 1841 and launched the bakufu on a series of sweeping reforms. Mizuno tried to break the monopoly guilds, and he attempted to limit and lower popular levels of consumption. His vigorous measures alienated daimyō whose support he required, however, and he was dismissed in 1843, his desperate efforts to return Japan to the lower standard of living which it had known before the spread of commercialization a failure. As has been mentioned, an Edo mob attacked his house after his dismissal in 1843.[55]

The shogunate's reforms had failed. Its expenses continued to outrun its income. The attempt to do without the guilds had shown their importance, for food had temporarily ceased to be shipped to Edo. In addition prices, which had to some degree been depressed by the monopoly guilds at the point of origin, had risen under free competition instead of falling as Mizuno had expected.

Elsewhere in the same years, however, individual fiefs with less complex economic relations and a more attainable mercantilist goal, were more successful in their reforms. The Satsuma feudatory adopted a variety of measures to deal with indebtedness and inadequate revenue. Merchant debts to Osaka brokers were in part refinanced, in part evaded. Costs were cut by temporary retrenchment of the extensive measures that had been begun to

---

[55] Mikami Sanji, *Edo jidai shi* (Tokyo, 1944), II, 544-628. Mizuno drew the wrath of fudai daimyō because of his plans to incorporate territories near the major shogunal centers into the bakufu holdings in order to centralize administration and defense.

experiment with and develop European studies at Kagoshima. Samurai stipends were pared to the absolute minimum and han revenues were raised by measures which concentrated on the production of cash crops for the national market. From the Ryukyus a profitable trade in luxury goods could be maintained. From the Satsuma domain itself came wax, cotton, and sugar cane which peasants were forced to grow, which they were carefully prevented from utilizing or enjoying themselves, and which helped to balance the han's accounts. As a result Satsuma went into the last decades of Tokugawa rule in a comparatively strong financial position. Satsuma had succeeded where the shogunate had failed because it was possible to isolate the area to some degree from outside contact, because its large population of samurai could be utilized to supervise and enforce the measures which were taken to restrict the commoners' standard of living, and because it could exploit its geographic advantages and its control of the Ryukyus for profitable trade. Satsuma leaders succeeded, some writers have it, not because they were more "modern," but because their society was less modern than that with which the shogunate had to deal.[56]

In the domain of Chōshū at the western extremity of the main island of Honshu different measures achieved a comparable result. Here too the han administration, which had been threatened by a large rebellion in 1831, faced a large and mounting debt. In a series of steps begun in 1838, a reform administration acted to consolidate administrative posts and improve samurai livelihood by the reduction of ceremonial and by placing a moratorium on samurai debts. This in turn made possible a slight alleviation of peasant distress. Most important were the measures taken to deal with the reduction of the han debt. Land reclamation projects were begun, salt works developed, and the increased revenue was made available for loans to coastal shipping interests. By reversing the traditional pattern of indebtedness to merchant entrepreneurs, the Chōshū authorities were able to take advantage of their strategic geographical position to accumulate a sizable reserve which stood their han well in the turbulent days that followed. Although the measures taken to control the economy were less draconian than those in Satsuma and considerably more enlightened than

[56] For a brief account of Satsuma reforms with bibliography, Tōyama Shigeki, *Meiji Ishin* (Tokyo, 1951), pp. 34-41.

those of the bakufu under Mizuno, the Chōshū policies were on the whole a logical continuation of the reform pattern of Tokugawa days. They were chiefly remarkable for the way in which the han administration moved into fields of private enterprise like usury, which had previously been left to merchants. Chōshū money lenders were forced to accept cancellation of or moratoriums on their loans to samurai, and measures were taken to prevent samurai from contracting further loans.[57]

The Satsuma and Chōshū reforms differed less in intent than in execution from those attempted by Mizuno in Edo. Their greater success can probably be ascribed to the location of the areas in which they were carried out, which were at once strategic for trade and isolated for control. In one point, however, they showed a significant contrast. Mizuno was thoroughly reactionary and exclusionist in his views on study of the West, and during his ascendancy a number of "Dutch scholars" in Edo were persecuted.[58] In Chōshū the Tempō reforms resulted in changes in the official han academy which included emphasis on Dutch learning; the han also sponsored translation of major works. In Satsuma the Tempō period saw no great increase in interest in Western studies, because none was needed; the previous daimyō, Shigehide, had incurred a goodly portion of the han debt by expensive experimentation with applied Western science. Satsuma expenditures were reduced in Tempō times, but there was no sharp revulsion from things Western.[59]

In the Tempō era the Tosa han administration also sponsored reforms which provide an interesting variant to the more celebrated processes in Satsuma and Chōshū. The thirteenth Yamauchi daimyō, Toyoteru, succeeded to the rule in 1843. He found the fief in debt and operating at an annual deficit. Of the net han income of 141,689 koku of tax revenue, over two-thirds, or 98,372 koku were earmarked for expenses in Edo, Osaka, and Kyoto-Fushimi, leaving 43,317 koku for running the domain. Added taxation and monopolies would not provide easy answers, for the previous year a peasant rebellion in Nanokawa, where several hundred peasants fled across the border into the neighboring do-

[57] The most recent summary of the Chōshū reforms is that of Seki Junya (n. 48).
[58] Grant K. Goodman, "The Dutch Impact on Japan" (n. 22).
[59] Numata, Bakumatsu yōgaku shi, pp. 163-172 for Dutch studies in Satsuma and Chōshū.

main, showed that the countryside was not prepared to accept further exactions without protest.[60] In addition it was evident that indebtedness and commercialization were affecting the entire ruling class. A good index of this can be seen in the increasing rate of transfer of *gōshi* patents of rank. There were 742 *gōshi* registered in 1845; between 1830 and 1867, over one-third of the total, or 212, changed hands through sale.[61]

The Tosa administration began with traditional measures. In 1842 an edict undoubtedly modelled on the Mizuno notices of the previous year had abolished the thirteen principal guilds in Tosa. Further edicts decreed lower prices and forbade raising them again. The administration also set about curbing expenditures and, as was customary, announced that samurai stipends would be lowered. It sought for some means of cutting off connections, and therefore obligations, with the Osaka merchants to whom it was indebted. Inevitably, objections rose from merchants, from some members of the samurai class, and most particularly from the top levels of the privileged group who disliked having their ability to float new loans limited, and who feared that their incomes might be the object of han retrenchment.[62]

But the Tosa Tempō Reforms were to founder not so much on economic difficulties as on personal and ideological issues. Toyoteru, in his search for new men to staff his reform administration, selected a member of the rusuigumi, the lowest of the upper samurai ranks, named Mabuchi Kahei. Mabuchi had served as an official of the finance magistracy in Edo during the 1820's, and in the course of his dealings with Edo merchants he had come in contact with a new syncretic thought which had spread among the merchant class. *Shingaku* (literally, "heart study") had been developed by Ishida Baigan (1685-1744), a Kyoto merchant apprentice who had given up his commercial career and instead developed, out of an amalgam of Confucian, Shintō, and Buddhist thought, a teaching which he called the "way of the merchant" (*shōnindō*). While he justified commerce and profit as proper for the merchant, Ishida also made capital virtues out of honesty,

---

[60] Hirao, *Nōmin ikki*, pp. 76-88, provides details and documents.

[61] The figure is given by Ikeda Yoshimasa, "Tempō kaikakuron no saikentō: Tosa han o chūshin ni shite," *Nihon shi kenkyū*, No. 31, p. 5.

[62] Ikeda Yoshimasa, and also in "Hansei kaikaku to Meiji Ishin: Kōchi han," *Shakai keizai shigaku*, Vol. 212, Nos. 5, 6, pp. 561-582, and "Tosa han ni okeru Ansei kaikaku to sono hantai ha," *Rekishi gaku kenkyū* (Tokyo, 1957), No. 205, pp. 18-29.

fairness, reverence, and loyalty. Shingaku teachers avoided criticism of the ruling class, and indeed held up the samurai as the ideal ethical type for all classes.[63] As Shingaku spread along the trade routes of the Tokugawa domain, it began to interest many members of the ruling class, among them the Tosa samurai Mabuchi Kahei. The shogunate saw much virtue in Shingaku—the Tempō reforms banned all public performances except Shingaku and Shinto lectures, lectures on military works, and story-tellers— but it was nevertheless undesirable to have samurai espouse an ideology that properly belonged to merchants. In 1827 Mabuchi had been recalled from Edo to Tosa in partial disgrace. In Tosa he had continued his studies and teachings of jūjutsu, a secondary interest, and he retained a good deal of prestige.

Toyoteru inaugurated his program by appointing Mabuchi as an official of the fiscal office serving directly under the Finance Magistrate. From this post, Mabuchi took charge of the han's economic reforms. Around him he gathered his disciples in jūjutsu, students who had learned of shingaku from him as well. Among these were high-ranking retainers, including even a *karō* (house elder) named Shibata. Mabuchi's following grew in numbers and in influence, and it included some devotees of Western-style medicine as well as Shingaku students.

Naturally, members of the Tosa samurai group who felt their positions and incomes threatened by the Tempō reforms resented the influence and eminence of Mabuchi's group; they dubbed them the "*okoze*" band, after a good luck shell. Soon they were maligning Mabuchi. A vigorous whispering campaign about his beliefs defamed him as a secret Christian, and the old memories of his Shingaku deviation were revived and given new currency. Lord Toyoteru was finally persuaded to have his minister put under surveillance, and when it proved that Mabuchi was still in fact a believer in Shingaku he was jailed and his followers dismissed. With him went his reform policies; the Tosa Tempō Reforms came to an end late in 1843.[64]

The Tempō Reforms have been the subject of much scholarly attention. The coincidence of failure on the part of the bakufu

---

[63] On *shingaku* see Robert N. Bellah, *Tokugawa Religion: The values of preindustrial Japan* (Glencoe, Ill., 1957), Chap. VI.

[64] *Kōchi Shi shi*, pp. 395-399, and Hirao Michio, "Tempō 'Okoze gumi' shimatsu," *Tosa shidan*, No. 36 (Kōchi, 1931), pp. 23-39.

and success on the part of Satsuma and Chōshū has given rise to a school of interpretation that credits the success of the great southwestern han to the fact that they were less "modern" and more draconian in their measures than were the Tokugawa, whose realms included the most commercially advanced parts of Japan. It is also suggested that the young samurai administrators of Satsuma and Chōshū gained experience during these reforms which equipped them to become the bureaucrats of the national scene in the latter part of the nineteenth century. And because the early years of the Meiji Period, characterized as they were by feudal and capitalist elements which were given unity and direction by the cult of loyalty to the throne are often described as "absolutist," many writers have traced the origins of this new political and state structure to the Tempō Reforms. It is difficult, however, to find lasting or significant economic or political results in the short-lived burst of reform in Tosa. Some military reforms were begun, and some steps in the direction of fiscal solvency were taken, but their design and purpose were hardly very different from those of earlier days. Furthermore, in Tosa, as in Chōshū and Satsuma, the Tempō Reforms found most of the Restoration leaders schoolboys hard at their lessons and not yet students of the bureaucratic arts. It may be suggested, however, that it was during the Tempō years that junior officials in Tosa as in other areas gained some of the experience that made them effective reformers in the Ansei era of the 1850's, and that Restoration leaders of the 1860's first reacted against the Ansei reformers and then profited from the strength with which those reforms had given their realm. Still, it is likely that what gave the Ansei reforms their urgency and effectiveness was not so much a new motivation or orientation within a segment of the ruling class as it was the appearance of new and compelling dangers from the West.[65]

In Tosa the years after Mabuchi Kahei's fall were not, so far as can be seen at this distance, years of imaginative attempts to deal with the problems of late feudal society and economy. One of Mabuchi's appointees, Yoshida Tōyō, a man who had served as

[65] Tōyama Shigeki, *Meiji Ishin*, has provided one of the most influential statements of Tempō as the beginning of the new absolutism. For Chōshū, Naramoto Tatsuya, *Kinsei hōken shakai shiron* (Tokyo, 1948), provided an early statement considerably refined by Seki. Ikeda (nn. 60, 61) applies the same considerations to Tosa.

shipping magistrate and district magistrate, utilized the years of enforced idleness which followed the fall of his patron to indulge his interest in reading history and gathering information about the West. In the 1850's his sweeping plans for changes within Tosa were to owe much to his years of study. Among his texts were imports from China like the *Hai-kuo-t'u-chih* of Wei Yuan.[66] But Yoshida was the exception. One of his contemporaries, Sasaki Takayuki, later recalled that learning suffered in Tosa in the years that followed Mabuchi's disgrace and fall. Any samurai displaying undue interest in intellectual activities was likely to be reproached by his fellows and charged with secret leanings toward the now proscribed Shingaku band and its thought, and even Yoshida Tōyō, when he came to power in the 1850's, was to be maligned as the organizer of a "new okoze" band of spiritual conspirators.[67]

A final and highly important element in the Tosa picture at mid-century was the accession of a vigorous and able daimyō in the person of Yamauchi Toyoshige (Yōdō) in 1848. Yōdō had been adopted from a branch family of the tenth daimyō, Toyokazu. He was one of a handful of able daimyō who influenced national politics during the last decade of Tokugawa rule. He was a shrewd judge of character and ability in his subordinates, and his reading of history, along with his confidence in able ministers like Yoshida Tōyō, gave him a sense of the significance of the times in which he lived. He was a celebrated drinker, a quality in which Tosa men attained a national reputation, and a person of great personal charm and magnetism. Yōdō was also a vigorous extrovert; his scorn for formalities and contempt for empty ceremonial led him to broaden his contacts with persons far below him in rank at the same time that it led him to shock those with whom he dealt as equals. An example can be found in his first meeting with the Tokugawa Councillor (*rōjū*) Abe Masahiro after his accession to the rule of Tosa. Yōdō muttered some perfunctory sentences about the heavy responsibilities Abe bore by serving in such a high sho-

[66] Fukushima Nariyuki, *Yoshida Tōyō* (1927, Tokyo), p. 11. Wei Yuan's famous work was first published in 1844, and was made up of abstracts of translated passages on Western geography which were prepared by order of Commissioner Lin Tse-hsü at the time of the Opium War. For brief note and some excerpts, see John K. Fairbank and Ssu-yü Teng, *China's Response to the West* (Cambridge, Mass., 1954), pp. 29-35.

[67] Sasaki Takayuki, *Kinnō hisshi: Sasaki Rō Kō sekijitsu dan* (Tokyo, 1915).

gunal position, and then abruptly spoke his mind: "What I really think is that you must have a very easy time and enjoy yourself in dealing with these stupid daimyō. But be careful with me."[68] Yōdō dealt with vigor, humor, coarseness, and gentleness as the situation demanded, and he balanced factions and personalities in such a way as to retain firm control of han policy and developments whenever possible. He had the full respect of all his retainers, including those who disagreed with him; this was not always the case in late Tokugawa times.

Below Yōdō, in the top positions, were the representatives of families of high ranking retainers. If we are to believe the judgments of their contemporaries these were for the most part men grown soft and overconfident in their security, slothful and limited in ability, totally devoid of imagination and resourcefulness. In Tosa, as in other han, the *mombatsu*, or family cliques, were deeply conservative and fully satisfied with the status quo, which guaranteed their continued eminence. Moreover, they had the support of the former daimyō Toyosuke. They feared change of any kind, whether in han administrative policies or in shogunal policies. Most of all they feared policies which might bring the han into conflict with the will of the shogunal councils. Therefore thoroughgoing measures which might, under a reform administration, have strengthened the han fiscal and military picture received only grudging support lest they should lead to shogunal suspicion and disapproval. Yōdō later moved adroitly to eliminate their influence, but he could not or would not eliminate their persons from the official scene. When the reformers led by Yoshida Tōyō undertook their reforms in the 1850's and 1860's, the mombatsu proved willing to sacrifice their pride to cooperate with the lowest ranking malcontents in order to remove Yoshida's influence and person from the scene.

The main reservoir of officialdom in the Tosa samurai class lay in those ranks of samurai below the most favored, but within the five ranks collectively known as "upper" samurai. It was particularly within the ranks of mounted guard (umamawari) and headquarters guard (koshōgumi) that Yōdō sought and found his ablest officials. Yoshida Tōyō himself, a relatively low-ranking umamawari with an income of 200 koku, was the descendant of a Chōsogabe retainer who had entered Yamauchi service. From

---

[68] Told in Ōmachi Keigetsu, *Hakushaku Gotō Shōjirō* (Tokyo, 1914), p. 20.

among his following and students, middle-upper samurai like Gotō Shōjirō, Itagaki Taisuke, Fukuoka Kōtei, and others, came the men who led Tosa policy in late Tokugawa days and who went on to figure large in the political history of the Meiji period.

Below the regular samurai (hirazamurai) were the lower samurai classes, and of these it was chiefly the gōshi, with their rural allies and neighbors the shōya, who had a social and economic base that provided security for protest as well as the impetus for resentment against the centralizing policies of overenthusiastic reform administrations. These were also groups among whom Confucian and loyalist thought had made great headway. Arbitrarily kept from eligibility for high han posts, they were nevertheless in control of the areas that counted most to them. As foreign and domestic dangers multiplied in late Tokugawa times, they would become increasingly aware of the need for military training, especially in swordsmanship. Their fencing academies became the seedbeds for future political leagues. Out of this environment came many of the ideologists and fanatics of the Restoration struggles to come. The gōshi Yoshimura Toratarō, who lost his life in 1862, first wrote his father an explanation of his actions that contained echoes of the resolutions of the Shōya League of 1841.[69] No group fought better and more bravely in the Restoration wars than the Tosa companies of shōya and gōshi sons. For many of these men, those wars provided the opportunity for entry into the samurai class that had long been denied to them. Nakaoka Shintarō, the son of an ōjōja (Great Headman) of eastern Tosa, embodies this development perfectly. Beginning as a member of a Loyalist Party, he was to leave for Edo with a group of volunteers, mostly gōshi and shōya. There he would be utilized for a time by Yōdō and later, leaving Tosa, he was to form his own command under the aegis of the Chōshū military organization. Out of these same groups came another whose initial training and outlook led him to subscribe to platforms of the gōshi loyalists and who later helped work out a scheme which, with some modifications, emerged as the first program of the new Meiji government. In Sakamoto Ryōma, the grandson of a sake brewer who had received gōshi rank in 1771, it will be possible to see the develop-

[69] Hirao Michio, *Yoshimura Toratarō* (Tokyo, 1941); *Tosa nōmin ikki shikō,* pp. 149-150.

ment of currents of thought and action which typified the political education of his generation.

Tosa at mid-century thus faced economic and social problems none of which had been met by the attempted reforms of the 1840's. An unusually able daimyō had just succeeded to his post. Hereditary obligations to the Tokugawa house would condition his consciousness of the need for political change and limit his participation in the anti-shogunal movements of the 1860's. Obligations and privileges combined to make of his chief councillors spokesmen for the established order, but below them, at the level of practical administration, were to be found individuals of considerable official experience and mental flexibility. Among the social and political leaders of the countryside, however, many associated themselves with the tradition of a deposed daimyō of the sixteenth century, and their separation from the bureaucratic opportunities of the upper ranks was paralleled by their separation from the castle town in which the upper samurai had come to reside. Numerous instances and examples of social tension had come to light by 1850. By themselves, however, these had not sufficed to make for change or for program. When the need for both change and program was demonstrated by the lack of preparedness to face new problems in the 1850's, the form and much of the content of the suggestions from below were likely to be couched in the language of the Shintō teachers, whose concern for their sacred soil and ruler had penetrated into the private academies.

II. THE RESPONSE TO THE WEST

*T*HE arrival of Commodore Perry's flotilla in the summer of 1853 opened a period of new problems and possibilities for the shogunate, for its vassals, and for their retainers. The shogunate was faced with decisions in the field of foreign relations and of national defence. To meet these it made efforts to rally daimyō support. The foreign danger also offered the bakufu possibilities for consolidation of its position, however, for, as was to be seen, rivalry between the Western powers might make support possible from one or more countries hopeful of winning special favors in a newly opened Japan. Under such circumstances it would inevitably occur to some shogunal officials that it might be possible to enlist the assistance of a Western power to gain absolute control over the daimyō. Those vassals, however, were some years in asserting themselves sufficiently to make such measures seem necessary. Their initial problems concerned the formulation of opinions in response to shogunal requests and the preparation of measures for regional defence. In so doing, as will be seen of Tosa, substantial changes in long-established patterns of privilege and power were forthcoming. For the daimyō's retainers, meanwhile, the new currents of thought and activity opened the way to organization and intrigue previously unthinkable, which could now be justified by slogans about preserving the national and cultural heritage. It will be useful to detail these developments by observing the response that the Western threat evoked within the shogunate itself, the changes that accompanied that response in the realm of Tosa, and the manner in which all of this impinged on the formative years of the young *gōshi* Sakamoto Ryōma.

1. The Tokugawa Response

The institutional patterns of the Tokugawa hegemony which have been described could be grouped around three major concerns. The first had to do with control of the great landed barons. The daimyō were graded in the order of their ancestors' affiliation, and their time and resources were exhausted in the requirements of residence at the shogun's capital. The second problem had been to guard against the development of an indigenous counterweight to shogunal authority. This was done by isolating and denigrating the Imperial court at Kyoto. The emperor's doings had been watched and controlled by shogunal representatives, contacts between the great shogunal vassals and the Kyoto nobility were kept to an authorized minimum, and the separation of the court from governmental functions had been maintained so successfully that large numbers of Japanese were undoubtedly little if at all aware of the political and religious claims of the imperial family. Netherlands traders referred to the court as an ecclesiastical entity only, and the shogun was frequently and reasonably considered Japan's legitimate ruler. Kyoto had seemed to represent so little danger that the shogunate itself provided principal sponsorship for the scholars of Japan's national learning who exhumed again the ancient myths and claims of imperial divinity and authority. By the nineteenth century many of the earlier interdictions on contacts between vassals and court had been relaxed also, but the bakufu was always ready to reassert its authority. When Hirata Atsutane went too far in reviving Shintō claims it seemed natural to quiet him; it was the same during the bakufu's Tempō Reforms, and when, as will be seen, elements at court first asserted themselves in 1858 they were struck down without hesitation by Tokugawa traditionalists. The third concern reinforced all of this by guarding against possible contacts between the great vassals and the outside world. The exclusion system had limited foreign trade to safe and useful contacts between the Netherlands traders and properly designated shogunal channels at Nagasaki, so that foreign relations were restricted to the minimum of goods and information useful for the shogunate itself.

The challenge that Perry posed to the third traditional Tokugawa control led to questioning of the other two. This was inevitable because of the substantial changes that had taken place during the years of peace. The shogunate approached the crises of the nineteenth century with its coffers empty; the unsuccessful reforms of the 1840's had succeeded only in dramatizing its inability to order economic affairs according to its will. Its great vassals were for the most part equally lacking in resources. This was particularly true of the fudai and cadet houses whose support was most vital to the bakufu; their realms, situated in the great plains around the urban centers that had developed, were areas in which the development of a commercial market had gone farthest to weaken the ruling class. It was clear that little could be hoped for in terms of effective rearmament and support from the feudal lords unless they were relieved of the expenses that had been designed to keep them weak. Furthermore, since the crisis Perry brought was foreign in origin, it was inevitable that appeals for daimyō cooperation would be accompanied by considerations of national defence and national good. These, in turn, invited consideration of what was national and not foreign, what was traditional and not imported. All such roads led inevitably to Kyoto. The writings of the Shintō scholars had made much headway among the literate and the articulate, so that, as has been shown, their influence was felt in places as remote as Tosa. The shogunate had been able to legislate against extremes of interpretation in the 1840's when its principal defences still seemed impregnable, but the breach of one now revealed important defects in the others as well.

Commodore Perry's request for treaty relations presented the shogunate with hard alternatives. A refusal would, it was thought, lead to war—a war which the Japanese could not expect to win. It was, nevertheless, a course certain to be advocated by many responsible persons. Since the beginning of talk about a Russian danger in the late eighteenth century, a considerable body of speculation about ways of warding off foreign aggressors had accumulated, and the British opening of China in the nineteenth century had added new urgency to the problem. "Opening" (*kaikoku*) and "exclusion" (*jōi*) were the two poles of the controversy that dominated policy in the 1850's and 1860's, but between the two extremes there remained a wide spectrum of possible positions. Those who held for refusal of the American demands were by no means restricted to obscurantists ignorant of the power of the West. In many quarters it was rather a lively appreciation of the technological and military superiority of the enemy that persuaded spokesmen to advocate rejection of Perry's note. Acquiescence, such men reasoned, would lead to Japan's subjection by the West; rejection, on the other hand, would lead to danger and probable defeat, but such a catharsis was required to rejuvenate Japan's spirit and remilitarize Japanese society. Such a position, with its emphasis on Japan's spiritual essence, was logically related to the intellectual developments that had attempted to make clear that spirit. For most literate Japanese it was associated with the line of scholars subsidized by the great Tokugawa branch house on the Mito plain headed by Tokugawa Nariaki. The Mito scholars, heirs to some of the most influential Confucian and loyalist traditions of the Tokugawa period, were fully aware of the power of the West. Important representatives of the Mito tradition like Aizawa Seishisai and Fujita Tōko insisted, however, on the need for shoring up the national spirit before entering into relationships with the foreigners. Their lord, Tokugawa Nariaki, who combined an urgent desire to utilize Western military techniques with a determination to deny Westerners the right of entry to Japan, was an effective proponent of such a position in the 1850's.

The alternative course, that of granting the American requests, held out the hope of satisfying the foreigners' demands before they became excessive, warding off an unsuccessful war of resistance, and opening the way for full-scale importation of the armament that would make possible an eventual rejection from strength. This view was associated, in the popular mind, with the scholars of Western learning—the "Dutch scholars," or *rangakusha*, as they were called. These authorities on the outside world grew in importance and in self-esteem in mid-nineteenth century Japan. Sakuma Shōzan, who served the lord of a small domain northwest of Edo, taught and wrote vigorously, and his lord's prominence in Tokugawa councils made him known there as well as in other fiefs which sought his services. Among his many students was the young Chōshū scholar Yoshida Shōin, who later trained a generation of future leaders while under restriction in the village of Shoge.

It is important to note that these positions, although described as poles within the controversy that developed, had a good deal in common. The exclusionists realized the advantages and superiority of Western techniques, while the advocates of opening the country did so with hope of strengthening it for a future defence against the barbarians. Thus Sakuma Shōzan, who bitterly opposed the agreement ultimately reached with Perry as unequal and insulting to Japan, was murdered by a true obscurantist who thought him a traitor, while his disciple Yoshida Shōin, long known in the West chiefly through Robert L. Stevenson's sympathetic description of his attempt to board one of Perry's ships in order to learn firsthand of the foreign danger, went on to become the idol of the Chōshū loyalist and exclusionist party through his fervent teaching and reckless scheming against the "traitorous" shogunal officials who had negotiated with the West. Furthermore, the content of the kaikoku and jōi slogans changed considerably with the passing of time and the development of new political possibilities. Neither position was firmly fixed, and neither was entirely exclusive of the other.

The formulation of bakufu policy in these matters was primarily the function of the Senior Council (rōjū), a group staffed by four or five fudai daimyō who served by turn for periods of one month. The fudai chosen for this most important of posts were selected from among the houses whose founders had followed the Tokugawa cause from the latter quarter of the sixteenth century. With a vital stake in the existing order of things, they were keenly conscious of the importance of maintaining their institutionalized advantage. Thus unrestricted foreign access that would have made for foreign contacts for tozama daimyō, was to be avoided at all costs, but on the other hand a partial opening managed by and restricted to Tokugawa areas was preferable to a war with the foreigners in which the same tozama lords might increase their importance or independence. The Tokugawa branch families, and particularly that of Mito, also had some measure of responsibility in major bakufu decisions. In the event a shogun failed to produce an heir, succession was normally from the branch houses of Owari or Kii, while the Mito house, traditionally excluded from the succession, maintained a special position of responsibility and guardianship. In view of the strong views held by Tokugawa Nariaki of Mito in regard to the foreign threat and the prophetic role assumed by the scholars of his domain, the distinction between Mito and the fudai daimyō with their bias in favor of the status quo gave promise of important conflicts and internal divisions within the bakufu itself.[1]

Division and discord were more than likely to come out of this setting. They were guaranteed when the bakufu solicited opinions on what to do. In an effort at unanimity and in hope of diffusing

[1] See particularly the authoritative discussion of Japanese alternatives and positions in the introduction by W. G. Beasley, *Select Documents on Japanese Foreign Policy 1853-1868* (London, 1955), pp. 3-93.

the responsibility for decisions that could not be avoided, Abe Masahiro, the head of the Senior Council, circulated a translation of the letter Perry had brought from President Fillmore a month after Perry's arrival. With it went a request addressed to all the feudal lords, to selected officials and scholars, and even to some merchants. "The country faces a difficult time," it read; "please give serious consideration to the meaning of the letter and express your opinions freely."[2] This novel and ingenious approach bore within it dangerous implications that the opinions would be heeded. It was the first indication that the bakufu itself realized that the new and extraordinary crisis required a readjustment of machinery which, while it had worked well enough in times of peace, had no provisions for securing daimyō support as opposed to obedience. The youthful Abe Masahiro, who initiated the step, demonstrated that the Tokugawa ranks had room for men of considerable flexibility and enterprise. Events were to prove, however, that he lacked the firmness to persevere in his policies, and that less of this reasonableness would be shown after rancor and dissatisfaction built up.

The fifty-nine daimyō replies that are extant show that, although Abe had not solved his problem by his attempt to consult others, he did ease it. The lords, whose views naturally reflected those of their highest ranking retainers, were agreed on the theoretical desirability of continuing in seclusion; they were aware of the impossibility of effective armed resistance and therefore urged avoiding immediate war, and they were very much in favor of rushing defence preparations. It is possible to construe the majority of replies that have survived (about one-fifth of the total) as favoring at least temporary acquiescence in Perry's demands. The strongest statements, however, came from within the Tokugawa circle, and since these were the opinions of men who had a share in policy decisions, Abe was still faced with the necessity of alienating some whose opinions he had solicited. An important statement for the negative came from Mito, where Tokugawa Nariaki's son, the titular daimyō, advocated unwavering refusal of the American demands. An equally significant statement urging acceptance of the American request came from the head of the great fudai house of Hikone, Ii Naosuke, who advocated a period of trade

[2] *Ishin shi*, II, 69.

which would allow Japan to perfect its defences. The existence of two such different counsels within the bakufu itself made bitter disputes in the future certain. Ii's position received important support from a number of junior officials charged with direct responsibility for defence and trade, men who were furthermore under the bureaucratic patronage of Abe Masahiro himself. The sentiments of the tozama daimyō, on the other hand, contained little of the concerted opposition to presumed shogunal intentions that would appear in the years to come. Thus the Satsuma daimyō suggested a delaying action to allow the shogunate and vassals to work on plans for defence, Mōri of Chōshū advised rejecting the suggestions for trade and concentrating on defence, Nabeshima of Saga urged immediate and total rejection, while Yamauchi Yōdō of Tosa advised turning the Americans down and turning to the Hollanders for help in a rush program of self-defence. Still other tozama daimyō like Kuroda of Fukuoka, on the other hand, recommended opening the ports to trade. The shogunate's request for counsel had thus solved no problems. It had forced a number, perhaps the majority, of the lords to consider the alternatives and to advise against measures that would lead to war with the foreigners. It had revealed what was known from the first, a general lack of enthusiasm for the idea of renewing intercourse with the Western world. And it had made clear a decided split of opinion within the ranks of those to whom the bakufu normally turned for advice and leadership.[3]

When Perry returned for the Tokugawa reply in 1854 the bakufu, which had assured its vassals that it would strive to preserve peace while trying to avoid a definite reply to Perry, found itself constrained to grant approval to a treaty which, although it made no clear provision for trade,[4] met Perry's goals. The bakufu had also promised its daimyō that defence preparations would be speeded, and these were now in order. Prerequisite to the success of the military steps were political moves to allay discontent. In

[3] A useful analysis of replies will be found in W. G. Beasley, *Great Britain and the Opening of Japan* (London, 1951), pp. 106-110. See also E. Honjo, "The Views of Various Hans on the Opening of the Country," *Kyoto University Economic Review* (Kyoto, 1936), xi, 2, pp. 16-31. Some daimyō replies will be found in W. G. Beasley, *Select Documents*, pp. 101-119.

[4] Beasley, *Select Documents*, p. 126, quotes the report of the responsible officials: "We refused this, however, pointing out that in Japan we had little experience of trade and could not lightly permit it; that the main theme of his present request was kind treatment for the citizens of his country. . . ."

order to win support for the American treaty, Abe Masahiro appointed Tokugawa Nariaki of Mito to a post of responsibility for national defence. In this manner the foremost exponent of the jōi position was persuaded to cooperate with policies with which he was in disagreement, by being put in charge of measures that would make possible a stronger policy in days to come.

But Nariaki's vigorous espousal of administrative and military changes had awakened the resentment and concern of bakufu traditionalists who saw themselves threatened by sweeping changes. It was indeed true that a search for talent which disregarded fief lines (such as Nariaki talked about) might by-pass men who would otherwise receive sinecures. A new institute for Western learning, for instance, recruited a staff of two professors, ten assistants, and three readers, of whom only the last named and lowest ranking were Tokugawa retainers.[5] The struggle against Nariaki was, however, a short one. His chief supporter, Abe Masahiro, proved to have no stomach for prolonged bureaucratic fighting. In the fall of 1855 Abe appointed Hotta Masayoshi a member of the Senior Council and handed over leadership to him. Two years later Abe died, but well before then he had been eclipsed by Hotta, who had from the first espoused a vigorous kaikoku position. Deprived of Abe's support, Nariaki's position within the Tokugawa bureaucracy had become untenable; thereafter the jōi position no longer received sympathetic or even full hearing at Edo.[6]

In 1856 Townsend Harris arrived at Shimoda to begin the careful negotiations that bore fruit in the commercial treaty he negotiated with shogunal officials in 1857. By this time the power of the West had become a good deal more obvious to everyone. The second Western triumph over China had stirred many to advocate resistance to the Harris treaty, although others, like the Tokugawa officials who negotiated the treaty, were instead convinced of the futility of warfare with the West. Nariaki had weakened somewhat his stand for jōi by this time, but he was firm in his opposition to the shogunal negotiations. Instead he proposed colorful measures to hold the Westerners at arm's length, measures that suggested that he objected more to the manner than the fact of

---

[5] Marius B. Jansen, "New Materials for the Intellectual History of 19th Century Japan," *Harvard Journal of Asiatic Studies* (Cambridge, December 1957), p. 580, treats the *Bansho Shirabesho*, the "Institute for the Study of Barbarian Books."

[6] Beasley, *Select Documents*, p. 26.

Japan's policies. If, he argued, the Americans could not be put off without some trade, he himself should be sent to America with three or four hundred rōnin and younger sons of farmers. This would not "inflict serious hurt on the farmers, townspeople, and others, for you would be granting me only the younger sons, always unwanted, and hence the existence of the families would not be endangered whatever happened."[7]

Since he was unheeded at Edo, it is not surprising that Nariaki sought for friends at the imperial court in Kyoto. In view of the traditional loyalist emphasis of Mito scholarship, the Kyoto nobles were his natural allies. More remarkable was the fact that the shogunate, sensing the opposition to the new commercial treaties among its vassals, also turned to Kyoto for support. Tradition required that the shogun secure imperial approval for major decisions, but Hotta Masayoshi saw this as an opportunity for getting an imperial decree endorsing the decision to trade with the West. So the two wings of the bakufu turned to Kyoto for support among non-Tokugawa forces. This momentous development made Kyoto the center of national politics. With this the political education of young nobles who had previously been carefully shielded from contact with national affairs began. Now, also, began talk of the fact that the course of national events was causing "concern to the Emperor." The shogunate had long justified, on the few occasions when it felt called upon to do so, its rule as easing and protecting the Emperor; from this date on it would have to face propaganda that it was on the contrary responsible for dishonoring and grieving the sacred presence. It is true, however, that the erosion of Tokugawa influence had barely begun and that such arguments carried weight chiefly among the sophisticated loyalists and unsophisticated activists, but this second category, among whom Sakamoto will be numbered, grew rapidly in numbers.

Kyoto became a center for internal as well as international policies. The urgency of the times and the inability of the shogun Iesada to provide effective leadership had brought home to many the fact that Japan desperately required an able and vigorous shogun. Since Iesada was childless, the exercise of choice became possible in the selection of his heir. Tradition and blood relationship suggested a successor from the branch house of Kii, and the fudai daimyō favored this. But because this youth (the future sho-

---

[7] *ibid.*, pp. 168-169, for the text of Nariaki's proposal of 30 December 1857.

gun Iemochi) was young and inexperienced, the suggestion had been advanced that a better candidate was at hand in the person of Keiki, an able son of Tokugawa Nariaki of Mito, who had been adopted into the cadet house of Hitotsubashi. Nariaki was now in the fortunate position of being able to back his own son by endorsing the selection of "men of ability." Keiki's candidacy won the enthusiastic support of the small number of able daimyō with whom Abe Masahiro had consulted informally a few years earlier, among them Shimazu Nariakira of Satsuma, Yamauchi Yōdō of Tosa, Date Munenari of Uwajima, and within the Tokugawa collaterals, Matsudaira Shungaku (Keiei), lord of Echizen. These lords' emissaries in Kyoto urged that the court express its preference for a mature and able shogun. It should be noted that there was little or no thought as yet of anti-bakufu animus among this group. What these men sought was the modification of Tokugawa practice through the selection of an able shogun who would be sufficiently imaginative to revise the existing system in ways conducive to national unity and strength against the foreigners who stood at the gate.

In the spring of 1858 Hotta Masayoshi himself came to Kyoto to speed the imperial decree endorsing shogunal policy, and after his arrival the issues of the Harris treaty and the succession became hopelessly confused. Kyoto now became a center of intrigue. The great lords who backed Keiki were for the most part affiliated through marriage with families at court, with the result that it was easy for them to make their influence felt. To act as their spokesmen they sent trusted retainers, usually men of modest rank and fame best suited for the delicate and inconspicuous task at hand. But the ancient city, less closely invested and guarded by bakufu police than Edo, proved a natural center for independent and self-appointed guardians of the national virtue as well. Numbers of rōnin, agitators, and anti-foreign zealots added their influence to the scene.

The court nobles were of many ranks and grades of sophistication. The senior officials were, as Hotta knew, responsive to Tokugawa desires, but the younger and lower-ranking groups outnumbered them and, in the end, they won the dispute. Hotta won what seemed a safe though narrow victory, and an Imperial decree was issued endorsing the shogunate's policy. Word then spread that the decree was in fact contrary to the personal preferences of the Emperor, and junior court officials, among them the later Restoration leader Iwakura Tomomi, organized a protest meeting which resulted in revocation of the decree. A revision reversed the court's position, and became an instruction to the shogun to be faithful to existing Tokugawa institutions. Violations of the "sound laws handed down from the time of Ieyasu would disturb the ideas of our people and make it impossible to preserve lasting tranquillity." The provisional treaty, the decree went on, would make impossible the preservation of national honor. Therefore the bakufu was instructed to consult once more with the feudal lords and to approach the Court thereafter.[8]

Hotta returned to Edo with plans to add his weight to the support for Nariaki's son Keiki as shogunal successor. A Regent, or *Tairō*,[9] was to be appointed to head the Senior Council in view of the national emergency. Matsudaira Shungaku, who had inaugurated the campaign for Keiki, seemed a possible person for this post, and if this appointment could be made others would follow naturally. Kyoto, its confidence won by this evidence of bakufu cooperation, would add its support, and the great lords who had intervened in Kyoto would have won their goals as well. But these plans miscarried because the fudai daimyō, who still held the balance of power within the Edo circles, were alarmed by the evidence that their special prerogatives were being lost. They secured the appointment of Ii Naosuke, lord of Hikone, as Tairō. Soon the succession issue was settled in favor of the branch house of Kii, and shortly thereafter a purge of Keiki supporters began in bakufu councils and gradually extended to the court and to the feudatories. The purge was particularly severe in its effects on the personal agents who had been sent by powerful daimyō to Kyoto to lobby, and a number of them were executed or died in prison.[10] Amid these indications of renewed bakufu vigor, if not wisdom, came tidings of new and still more vigorous Western advances

---

[8] *ibid.*, pp. 180-181.

[9] An office normally filled only in times of crisis, and one which took precedence over the Senior Council. Traditionally restricted to fudai daimyō of first rank, and in practice to four such, of which the house of Ii, lord of Hikone, was one. Matsudaira Shungaku, a collateral and not a fudai, therefore would have represented new and, in a sense, "independent" power in this important post.

[10] Among those who fell were Yoshida Shōin in Chōshū; Hashimoto Sanai, adviser to Matsudaira Shungaku of Echizen and one of the first to speculate about conciliar organization, and Umeda Umpin, an independent and itinerant loyalist scholar who had influenced many of the nobles at court.

in China. The bakufu's negotiators grew panicky on hearing of these from Townsend Harris and urged immediate ratification of the treaties. This was done by Regent Ii in July 1858 without Imperial approval. This swift succession of events alienated many tozama daimyō, as it did the Kyoto kuge and the Mito group within the Tokugawa camp. It was against this background that movements of loyalism would form in Tosa and other areas.

These political and diplomatic changes dominated national affairs in the years after Perry's coming. The bakufu reaction to the Western problem included measures designed to advance its military preparedness, however, and it is useful to summarize them briefly. The 1850's marked the height of Netherlands influence. It was apparent that, trade or no trade, more Western weapons and know-how were required to strengthen the nation's defences, and the Netherlanders were the logical transmitters of this information. The period thus marked the last stage of the transitional avenue to Western technology, for the full opening of the ports in 1860 replaced the Dutch influence with that of Great Britain and France. The 1850's also marked the emergence of several figures who rose to prominence in later shogunal politics as specialists in naval warfare, one of whom, Katsu Rintarō, later befriended Sakamoto Ryōma. Unfortunately for Tokugawa plans, the political disputes that have already been summarized took their toll in interrupted continuity and backing for technological programs, with the result that much less was accomplished than had been expected. This had an important bearing on the bakufu's strength in the crucial decade that lay ahead.

The import of books and weapons from the Netherlands traders increased remarkably in the 1850's. At the end of the decade the trade offensive was heightened by the return to Nagasaki of P. F. von Siebold, whose presence earlier in the century had meant so much to Japanese study of the West.[11] In 1854 the *Soembing*, a steamship captained by Lieutenant G. Fabius, was sent to Nagasaki. With him Fabius carried a letter explaining that a prior Japanese request for the purchase of a warship could not be grati-

[11] Siebold was in Japan from 1823 to 1829 and again in 1859 to 1861. During his second stay he recorded his impressions of the political scene in an interesting little work, *Open Brieven uit Japan* (Deshima, 1861), p. 64.

The standard biography is by Kure Shūzō, *Shīboruto Sensei, sono shōgai oyobi kōgyō* (Tokyo, 1926), pp. 492, 923.

fied because the Crimean War made it impossible to secure warships at the time. In order, however, to show the friendship which the Netherlands monarch bore his Japanese counterpart, Fabius had been ordered to Japan; and while there he would do what he could to acquaint the Japanese with ship construction and navigation. Between August 21 and October 26 Fabius gave instruction to over 200 students in Nagasaki. Shortly before his departure Fabius was presented with two swords as a sign of gratitude.[12]

Fabius' return with his report produced new steps to help the Japanese, the most important being the dispatching in 1855 of a detachment of twenty-one men under Lt. G. C. C. Pels Rijcken with the *Soembing*, which was now presented to the shogunate, to offer instruction in seamanship. The *Soembing*, renamed the *Kankō Maru*, served as the first medium for instruction in modern sailing for the Japanese. In March 1857 the ship sailed for Edo commanded and manned by men who had been instructed by the Dutch detachment.[13] A second Netherlands detachment, which replaced the first in September 1857, continued instruction with other ships which were sold to the shogunate by the Netherlands government. The program was discontinued in March 1859, probably because the Edo administration had grown suspicious of officials connected with it. A school of medicine in Nagasaki, however, continued until 1863.[14]

The reports of the two Netherlands training detachments to their government showed only moderate satisfaction with the progress of the Japanese students; the instructors were impressed by the difficulties which feudal status made for instruction in modern techniques. The Japanese seamen, they reported, were fine healthy fellows, but since they were of low rank they were not, at first, permitted to drill or practice with firearms of any sort. With no sort of commissariat arrangement, the men prepared their own meals on board the *Soembing*, while the nervous commander hoped their fires would not spread. The Japanese of higher

[12] J. A. van der Chijs, *Neerlands Streven tot Openstelling van Japan voor den Wereldhandel* (Amsterdam, 1867), p. 115.

[13] van der Chijs, Appendix II, gives the history of the naval detachment, pp. 414f. The departure of the *Kankō maru* made it difficult to continue instruction for a time. p. 467.

[14] For the memoirs of the instructor in charge of the medical course, J. L. C. Pompe van Meerdervoort, *Vijf Jaren in Japan (1857-1863)* (Leiden, 1868), 2 vols., of which the second contains personal experiences.

rank, on the other hand, were at once too old (in their late twenties and early thirties) and too haughty to concern themselves with the routine drudgery which effective command required. Gradually, under the protestations of the Netherlands commanders, changes were made. The sailors were permitted to train with weapons. Classes in Dutch were held for all officers, and thereafter calculation and navigation could be taught without the use of interpreters. But it remained the opinion of the instructors that their Japanese students were deplorably rank conscious. They showed ready interest in the more colorful or pleasant aspects of their training ("Drummers' instruction was a perfect pandemonium, and the ten to twelve men equipped with drums and trained by Seaman Second Class Heftij banged away all day long every day"), but they were considerably more reluctant to undertake the more prosaic mental discipline that was required. The reports were particularly insistent on the mental and institutional inelasticity of the Tokugawa officers as contrasted to the students and officers from the daimyō domains. In particular, those from Hizen (Saga) were considered far superior to those sent by the Tokugawa.[15]

There were of course exceptions to this discouraging estimate of Tokugawa retainers, men of whom van Kattendyke, commander of the second Netherlands detachment, wrote "there were also some among the Imperial [i.e., Tokugawa] and domainal officers who distinguished themselves by their energy and of whom one can have good expectations." One such was undoubtedly Katsu Rintarō, who assisted in instruction and who commanded the *Kankō Maru* when it sailed for Edo in 1857. The Netherlands training program thus served both to begin modern naval training and to bring to prominence men of future leadership potentiality. In the case of Katsu, Sakamoto Ryōma's future patron, this experience was of particular importance.

[15] Extracts from the reports submitted by Pels-Rijken and his successor Kattendyke can be found in the appendices, van der Chijs, pp. 457-495. Kattendyke's conclusions were as follows: "They are a light-hearted people. They can best be compared to the French. Most polite, cheerful, and witty, they lack the determination without which one cannot perform a difficult task; and as a matter of fact the making of sea officers is not a very easy task. It is true that they are blessed with a quick understanding; it is not difficult for them to get enough knowledge of a science in a relatively short time to suffice for a superficial impression, but then their curiosity is satisfied and they transfer their attention to something else."

During the same years, most of the books imported through Nagasaki were destined for use in a new institution for Western learning that was being set up in Edo. Designed to concentrate and control the accumulation and dissemination of Western knowledge, this establishment had been strongly urged by the same Katsu in a memorial shortly after Perry's arrival. Katsu argued the desirability of a school to tap Western and Chinese knowledge in military matters, gunnery, astronomy, geography, and all related sciences. Only in this way, he argued, could Japan prepare to strengthen herself for the dangers that would accompany the new contacts with the West. His suggestion was well received by men high in the Tokugawa hierarchy, and out of much planning came the *Bansho Shirabesho*, "Institute for the Investigation of Barbarian Books," which opened for activity in Edo early in 1857. To staff this the shogunate drew upon talent from all over the country, and the institute became one of the most important centers of Western learning.[16]

Despite the twists and turns of internal politics, then, and despite the rapid changes in the position which the shogunate occupied vis-à-vis the lesser feudatories and the court, the years which followed Perry's arrival witnessed a steady trend toward greater acceptance of Western techniques, trade, and contacts on the part of the shogunate. This first stage was symbolized and underscored by the dispatching of Japan's first embassy to the Western world in 1860. The party of official ambassadors travelled on an American ship, but a group of sailing men who had received their instruction from the Dutch at Nagasaki sailed their own ship, the *Kanrin Maru*, to San Francisco to demonstrate their ability.

From that embassy came new pieces of Western lore in the form of books and personal experience. The firsthand proof of the greater importance of English than Dutch had already resulted in trends away from study of Dutch toward that of English in Japan; firsthand contact with the United States and acquisition of books in America now guaranteed that the change-over would be a permanent one.

The mission also produced differing views of national policy. It included three individuals whose reactions to Japan's problems were strikingly different. Each, in his way, came to represent

[16] Jansen, "New Materials for the Intellectual History of 19th Century Japan," p. 580.

a recognized approach to those problems, and in a sense the last years of Tokugawa rule would be years of oscillation between their views. The least political of these was Fukuzawa Yukichi, the product of a private school of Dutch learning in Osaka who had laboriously made the switch to English shortly after the foreigners came to Yokohama to trade. Fukuzawa came to the conclusion that the problems that faced his country were chiefly those of education and enlightenment, and he devoted the rest of his life to popularizing and spreading his considerable knowledge of the West. With relatively little direct interest in politics and less in politicians, Fukuzawa concentrated on his backward countrymen.[17] Katsu Rintarō, who had advocated in the *Bansho Shirabesho* an institute which should help to serve to advance Western studies and techniques of many sorts, returned more convinced than ever of the importance of a program of general modernization and liberalization. Katsu was to be among the first to suggest the shogun's renunciation of his powers. In his dealings with men of many ranks and many areas in the years that followed, men as different as Matsudaira Shungaku and Sakamoto Ryōma, Katsu would show the development of unconventional and liberal ideas. A third man, Oguri Tadamasa, who would later succeed Katsu as commissioner of the bakufu's new navy, returned equally convinced of the need for a thorough program of modernization. Unlike Katsu, however, Oguri felt it was possible and desirable to do this under the aegis of the bakufu. He gradually accepted the proposition that the bakufu, with outside help as needed, should crush its opponents, end the feudal system, and establish a modern unified state under its own authoritarian control.[18] However different these responses, it will be recognized that each of them, if carried through to its logical conclusion, would have been equally destructive of the traditional bakufu.

[17] Fukuzawa sums up his reactions this way: "I disliked the bureaucratic, oppressive, conservative, anti-foreign policy of the shogunate, so I could not side with it. Yet the followers of the imperial cause were still more anti-foreign and more violent in their action, so I had even less sympathy with them . . . an ambitious man might cast his lot with one or the other of the parties to win a place for himself . . . but there was no such desire in me." *The Autobiography of Fukuzawa Yukichi*, tr. Eiichi Kiyooka (Tokyo, 1948), p. 198. This attitude perhaps justifies describing Fukugawa as the first modern Japanese intellectual.

[18] There is a biography by Abe Dōzan, *Oguri Kozuke no Suke seiden* (Tokyo, 1941). Oguri, who favored last-ditch shogunal resistance with French help, was executed by the new government.

Thus the first years of Western contact saw profound changes in political outlooks in Japan. A small number of able daimyō had dared to enter realms of policy planning previously forbidden to them, and although their temerity would bring shogunal punishment for several of them, they continued influential and, in several cases, equally powerful from retirement. The bakufu, by its invocation of daimyō opinion and court authority, had unloosed forces which it was to find difficult to control. Finally, programs of Western training and Western contact could not be abandoned once they were begun; they provided new groups of advisers and experts whose opinions, based as they were on special and firsthand knowledge and experience, counted for much in the days ahead. The process had begun whereby self-confidence and assertiveness would be substituted for the respect for authority, rank, and tradition that had characterized Tokugawa Japan. The direct participants in the events so far related numbered very few. As their efforts were felt on the fief level, however, handfuls became hundreds and thousands. Therefore it is necessary now to turn next to the Tosa of Sakamoto's youth.

2. Reforms in Tosa

The bakufu's efforts to cope with the new foreign policy created many problems for its vassals. Opinions had to be delivered on topics normally considered beyond their competence, and emergency measures for regional defence were rushed to completion. At the same time, however, the critical situation the country faced could be used as justification for sweeping changes in bureaucratic procedure that would have been difficult to justify in normal times. In many fiefs weak leadership was responsible for timid responses to the bakufu queries and ineffective gropings for administrative and military reforms. Yamauchi Yōdō (Toyoshige) of Tosa, however, was one of the few daimyō whom Abe Masahiro found worth consulting, and he was not afraid to speak his mind. He was one of the members of the little group of daimyō who did their best to secure the succession of Hitotsubashi Keiki as shogunal heir in 1858. He also had strong views on the necessity for changes within Tosa, and he utilized the crisis to remove or by-pass the pedigreed incompetents who controlled the Tosa bureaucracy. As a result the Tosa response to the West, and to the bakufu's overtures for cooperation, was dominated to an unusual degree by the personal ideas of this able daimyō.

The Tosa reply to the bakufu's initial request for opinions on the Perry letter advised against granting the American requests. Yōdō wrote that the Western nations seemed bent on total domination of Japan, and that their tactics began with intimidation through the use of warships; "first they demonstrate their military might to open up trade, then they subdue and round up our innocent people by giving the impression of brotherhood and good will." Even trade for a trial period, he felt, could not be restricted to America alone and if such privileges were once extended to the European powers and Russia, Japan would be on the road to poverty and subjection. He recommended as an alternative course the preparation of measures for coastal defence, the employment of Dutch engineers and military instructors, and full utilization of the sense of crisis to bolster the morale of the samurai class.[19]

In the years that followed Yōdō adhered to this position, which might be described as between the jōi and kaikoku camps. Japan should not give in to Western demands, but neither should it neglect the task of developing its military defences by importing technical and military specialists and products from the West through the Netherlanders in Nagasaki. It was, of course, unrealistic to reproach the bakufu for the negotiation of treaties it could scarcely avoid and Yōdō seems to have realized this, since he took little part in the recriminations that followed the major concessions to the West. On the other hand, his stand enabled him to influence both sides in the dispute, each of which considered him sympathetic to its view. As a result Yōdō's advice was of unusual importance and interest after the commercial treaty with Townsend Harris had been worked out.

Yōdō wrote to the bakufu to express his disapproval of the new treaty, making particularly clear his objection to the provisions for extraterritoriality. "If we grant America the right to treat its official buildings and area as if they were in its own country, it will have tragic consequences in the future. Furthermore, there are many impolite and insulting requests contained here that make me furious. I would like to urge the bakufu to take firm steps to

---

[19] The actual text was written by Yoshida Tōyō and is given in Fukushima Nariyuki, *Yoshida Tōyō* (Tokyo, 1927), pp. 60-61.

uphold its prestige and to overpower the foreign countries."[20] At the same time, however, he was writing to Kyoto to support the bakufu's position. He wrote his uncle, the court noble Sanjō Sanetsumu, that it was out of the question to speak of driving out the barbarians. In view of the critical situation the country faced, he advised, the Emperor should leave negotiations with the foreign powers to the shogunate and not try to direct them. It was essential that the bakufu's commitments be honored, in order to maintain a united front on the great issues of military preparedness.[21]

At this time, then, one sees Yōdō maintaining a discreet pressure on the bakufu to convince it of the necessity for changes in order to establish principles of national defence. Support for the Kyoto nobles in their unrealistic and obscurantist hopes of expulsion of all foreigners would weaken the nation and divide it rather than strengthen it. In any case, Yōdō was a true feudal baron full of the pride of his class, and he had little respect for the political wisdom and competence of the Kyoto aristocrats. In a conversation with Matsudaira Shungaku of Echizen in 1858 he is said to have warned that "If we succeed in the reorganization of the bakufu the reckless opinion of the court will have to be controlled by some means, or else they will start disturbing the public mind."[22]

By "reorganization of the bakufu" Yōdō meant the selection of Hitotsubashi Keiki as future shogun. This would bring with it political importance for Keiki's sponsor, Matsudaira Shungaku, a close friend of Yōdō's, and it would guarantee the full cooperation of Keiki's father, Tokugawa Nariaki. Therefore when these decisions seemed near, Yōdō, evidently convinced his tactics had been successful, altered his stand on the Harris treaty. If reforms within the bakufu itself were certain, the harm of the treaty would be balanced by preparation of new strength within Japan. Thus when the bakufu, at the instruction of the court, asked the feudal barons once more for their advice, Yōdō's reply urged ratification of the

[20] Tokyo Teikoku Daigaku, *Dai Nihon Komonjo: Bakumatsu gaikoku kankei monjo*, Vol. 18 (Tokyo, 1925), p. 380.

[21] Text in Iwasaki Hideshige, *Sanjō Sanetsumu shuroku*, Nihon Shiseki Kyōkai (Tokyo, 1925), Vol. 1, p. 201, translated in part in Noboru Hiraga, "Tosa in the Meiji Restoration" (unpublished M.A. thesis, University of Washington, Seattle, 1955).

[22] *Dai Nihon Ishin shiryō*, Part 3, Vol. 4, pp. 809-810; also discussed in Hiraga, p. 103.

treaty—provided that a series of reforms was inaugurated simultaneously. These reforms, he wrote, should include administrative changes within the shogunate, abandonment of the traditional policies designed to keep the daimyō weak and impoverished, and attempts to gain broader support among the vassals for bakufu programs.[23] Yōdō's price for agreement involved a revision of traditional methods for the selection of shogunal leadership, relaxation of the *sankin-kōtai* system of daimyō residence in Edo, and a larger voice in national affairs for the principal daimyō. This was the essence of the program Matsudaira Shungaku and his friends were urging under the slogan *kōbu-gattai* ("union of court and camp"), and it was a program totally unacceptable to the Tokugawa fudai daimyō who remained jealous of their special privileges.

It is tempting to see in this set of proposals steps toward a more representative system for making decisions and it will be possible at a later point to trace much of the talk of conciliar organization (which would lead, in the 1870's to the movement for a constitution) to these modest proposals of Matsudaira Shungaku and his advisers.[24] As important as the potentially "modern" touches of this program, however, were its Confucian and feudal roots. "Rule by ability," and consultation among the vassals in the determination of major policies, were shibboleths of much of the political thought upon which the statesmen of the mid-nineteenth century had been reared. Neither they nor their advisers were as yet thinking of anything remotely democratic or truly representative in nature, although the speed with which events moved found the original content of their proposals and slogans seriously altered within a decade. Then, as those who first formulated these plans were removed from the arena by death or assassination, related programs, newly infiltrated with Western ideas, moved far beyond the original formulations. The speed of events and the rapid dissemination of Western thought thus had the effect of telescoping into decades a process that had required far longer in Western Europe. While it is important to note the derivation of subsequent ideas of political organization that Sakamoto Ryōma and other figures later grasped and utilized, it is equally necessary to retain

---

[23] *Ishin shiryō*, Part 3, Vol. 7, pp. 341-342; also discussed in Hiraga, p. 107.
[24] Chief among them were Hashimoto Sanai and Yokoi Shōnan, the latter of whom later influenced Sakamoto Ryōma.

the outlook of the contemporaries who first coined these slogans, lest they seem to mean more than they did to the feudal barons who talked about "national unity" in 1858.

In the event, however, Yōdō's hopes for an easy transition to new policies were doomed to disappointment. The temporary victory of the Kyoto obscurantists led, as has been noted, to an assertion of traditional prerogatives within the bakufu itself. The post of Tairō went, not to Matsudaira Shungaku, but to Ii Naosuke of Hikone, and the shogunal succession went, not to Hitotsubashi Keiki, but to the youth who became the shogun Iemochi. The new bakufu administration then began to weed out supporters of the moderate position from its own ranks, and having purged itself, took steps against the Kyoto nobles who had rashly sought to influence shogunal policy. The principal rōnin and scholars who had thronged to Kyoto to urge their views on the court nobles were arrested, as were the servants and assistants of the nobles through whom they had worked. Numbers of heroes for the future Restoration list of martyrs fell to Ii Naosuke's purge, among them Umeda Umpin, a scholar of Chinese learning who had helped to write some of the chief documents that had emanated from the court. One who escaped death was Sosaku Ki, whose daughter Sakamoto Ryōma later married. The agents the great lords had sent to Kyoto were also the targets of the bakufu police, as were those whose teachings seemed to implicate them in the agitation that was inconveniencing the bakufu. Thus Hashimoto Sanai and Yoshida Shōin—the former, Matsudaira Shungaku's adviser; the latter, the Chōshū scholar-teacher who had gradually come to advocate and plan assassination of bakufu officials loyal to Ii Naosuke—were condemned. Gradually Ii Naosuke prepared to strike at the lords themselves. Tokugawa Nariaki and Matsudaira Shungaku were forced into retirement and placed under house arrest, and Yamauchi Yōdō too was destined to receive similar treatment.

Yōdō helped to speed his own departure from the scene by objecting to bakufu instructions that he fortify and defend Osaka against possible foreign attack. He countered with a reminder that his strength was already inadequate to defend his own coast line, and suggested that he be allowed to defray the added expenses he would incur by receiving a seven-year moratorium on his sankin-kōtai duties in Edo. Furthermore, he suggested the desirability of getting help from the bakufu in the form of munitions and a ship recently ordered from the Netherlands. He went on to suggest the desirability of evacuating Osaka in order to simplify its defence.[25] This did not endear Yōdō to the new officials in Edo; indeed, as a supporter of Keiki he was already slated for disciplinary action. Yōdō was first ordered to resign as daimyō. Little by little his activities and freedom were restricted, until in 1859 he was ordered confined to his villa at Shinagawa, outside Edo, forbidden even to receive letters from the outside. Here he remained until the spring of 1862.[26]

Besides urging changes in the national administration, Yōdō had used the crisis precipitated by Perry to make drastic changes in the Tosa administrative system. According to the recollections of Sasaki Takayuki, Yōdō had long been waiting for an excuse to launch a reform program. If so, he found it soon after the arrival of the bakufu's request for advice. Yōdō was in Kōchi in the summer of 1853 when a special messenger arrived with the Tokugawa message and the translation of President Fillmore's letter. The messenger had sped to Tosa from Edo in nine days instead of the normal thirty. According to a work compiled to commemorate the activities of the lower-ranking loyalists, when Yōdō showed the documents to his top retainers not one of them could make sense out of the language into which the American letter had been translated.[27] This, one suspects, would have sufficed to convince the most tradition-bound daimyō that his administration was in need of a shake-up.

Yōdō now appointed a new group of officials who organized the changes that have become known as the Ansei Reforms for the year period (1854-1859) in which they took place. The new team was headed by Yoshida Tōyō (1816-1862), a samurai of the uma-mawari (mounted guard) rank who had first gained prominence during the short-lived Tempō Reforms of Mabuchi Kahei. Yoshida was appointed to the *shioki yaku*, or Assistant Ministry, and from this post he supervised virtually all personnel appointments and

[25] Zuisan kai, ed., *Ishin Tosa Kinnō Shi* (Tokyo, 1911), pp. 53-54. For text, Hirao Michio, *Yōdō Kō ki* (Tokyo, 1941), pp. 65-70.

[26] Sakazaki Bū, *Geikai Suikō* (Tokyo, 1902), pp. 104f. *Geikai Suikō*, "The drunken lord of the whale seas," was the way Yōdō styled himself.

[27] This, at any rate, is the account given by the partisan loyalist account, *Ishin Tosa kinnō shi*, p. 32. Ikeda, "Tosa han ni okeru Ansei kaikaku to sono hantei ha," *Rekishigaku kenkyū* (Tokyo, 1957), No. 205, p. 19, feels "this must surely be spoken figuratively."

administrative policies during the next years. Yoshida and most of his colleagues in the central administration, although of honorable rank, were nevertheless several grades lower than the men whom they replaced, and their appearance was not calculated to please the old guard. Yoshida was a scholarly man with a strong interest in history and political economy. He had had concrete experience in government as shipping and district magistrate. While in service in Edo he had had contacts with the noted Mito scholar, Fujita Tōko. Through his reading of translations from China, among them the *Hai-kuo-t'u-chih,* he was also well aware of the state of the Western advance elsewhere in the Orient.[28] Besides secondhand accounts from the Chinese press, Yoshida's impressions of the West gained a good deal from conversations with Nakahama Manjirō, the Tosa fisherman who was rescued by an American whaler and educated in the United States.[29]

Until 1858 the policies that Yoshida inaugurated were dominated by preparedness for war. This was because until the final signing of the treaties with the West it seemed unlikely that the issues could be resolved without battle. Military preparations were undertaken immediately after the receipt of the news about Perry. Tosa troops were ordered to defend Sumiyoshi near Osaka, and the hustle of troop movements convinced many that war had already begun. The young men, Sasaki recalled later, were delighted by the prospect of travel outside the borders of the fief for military assignments. Preparedness also took the form of efforts to produce new weapons, including cannon, in Tosa, and it is interesting to note the degree of inter-fief cooperation that accompanied such efforts. In 1854 han officials were sent to Satsuma to study weapons manufactured there. A reverberatory furnace was begun, but not finished in Tosa, and cannon were constructed, although their performance was not particularly impressive. Copper-based armaments, which were easier to make, were more successful, and to make them possible patriotic contributions of copper were offered by many.

The most significant military innovation was the People's Corps,

[28] Fukushima, *Yoshida Tōyō,* p. 11.

[29] There is a recent biography by Emily V. Warriner, *Voyager to Destiny; the amazing adventures of Manjiro, the man who changed worlds twice* (Indianapolis, 1956), based in part on the standard biography by Nakahama Tōichirō, *Nakahama Manjirō den* (Tokyo, 1936).

or *Mimpeitai*, a small Western-style formation of 10,000 men, aged 17 to 50, recruited from peasants, fishermen, and seamen. Battalions, each of 100 men, were commanded by a *gōshi*, and squads and sections selected their own officers. The Mimpeitai were among the first units of this sort formed in late Tokugawa days. The better known Chōshū *Kiheitai*, a private army formed by Takasugi Shinsaku that included more samurai than peasants, was organized almost a decade later in 1863. By 1863, however, the Tosa units had been disbanded, and as a result Takasugi's Kiheitai, formed to fight the Tokugawa, achieved considerably greater fame. The Tosa Mimpeitai, on the other hand, formed by official han policy on the premise that war with the West was likely, seemed less essential after the signing of the Harris treaty in 1858. It declined in importance and numbers until 1869, when it was reactivated.[30] Yoshida Tōyō set these changes in motion, and his appointees supervised them. He himself, however, was forced to take a less active role from the summer of 1854 until early in 1858. The way in which this came about provides an illuminating illustration of the importance which relations with the bakufu had for even a powerful lord like Yamauchi. In the summer of 1854 Yōdō went to Edo on sankin-kōtai duty, and there one evening he invited a distant relative, now in bakufu service, to a party. Yoshida and other high officials were also present. As the evening grew late and sake had its effect, the Edo guest began to tease the Tosa officials and treat them disrespectfully by patting them on the head with his fan. Yoshida bridled at this, warning that he considered it a form of disrespect for his lord; when he could stand it no longer he struck his tormenter. The insulted and aggrieved guest suggested to Yōdō that hara-kiri would be a proper punishment for his disrespectful vassal. Yōdō, however, was anxious to avoid an incident, and so he had Yoshida resign and return home, where he lived quietly in a small village. There he taught, and thought, and planned for his eventual return to power.[31]

Yoshida was reinstated in office early in 1858, at a time when Yōdō was particularly active in connection with the Harris treaty

[30] Egashira Tsuneji, "Kōchi han ni okeru Bakumatsu no shinseisaku," in *Bakumatsu keizai shi kenkyu* (Tokyo, 1925), pp. 125f. A longer and basic account is by Hirao Michio, "Kōchi han no mimpei seido," *Tosa shidan*, No. 35 (Kōchi, 1931), pp. 79-84.

[31] Fukushima, *Yoshida Tōyō*, pp. 80f.

and the Keiki succession issue. The bakufu was, it seemed, about to be liberalized, and Yoshida's was no longer a dangerous appointment. Yōdō was eager to have someone take over most of the burden of han administration, and so he reappointed Yoshida despite the opposition of the old guard in Kōchi. Shortly after his reappointment Yoshida placed his friends and students in high positions; Fukuoka Kōtei, Gotō Shōjirō, and Itagaki Taisuke, to name only three of Tosa's Restoration leaders, gained prominence at this time as protégés of Yoshida.

A few months after Yoshida's return to power Ii Naosuke was appointed Tairō in Edo, and Yōdō's participation in national politics came to an end. Since Yōdō was forced by Ii to remain in Edo and Shinagawa, Yoshida was in effect the regent as well as first minister for the boy Toyonori who became titular daimyō in Kōchi. There was some uncertainty as to how far Ii Naosuke's vengeance would extend, and Kōchi conservatives feared that the aroused bakufu leader might even relieve the Yamauchi of their domain. Yoshida naturally avoided any appearance of interest in national politics lest he jeopardize his lord's position further, and concentrated on the administration of Tosa.

The principal problems he faced were those of rebuilding the financial strength of the han. Tosa had incurred heavy expenses by its program of hasty militarization, trying to train and equip units like the Mimpeitai. In addition a great earthquake in 1857 had caused heavy damage throughout Tosa. Despite heavy borrowings from Ōsaka merchants, more permanent solutions to the problem were required. As a result Yoshida worked to increase the han income by increasing production of cash crops like sugar, lumber, and charcoal, by increasing the production of paper, by developing copper mines, and by levying higher taxes on goods imported from other fiefs.[32] These measures were similar to those that Tosa reformers had followed since Nonaka Kenzan had first experimented with them in the seventeenth century, but in the late 1850's the first beginnings of foreign trade permitted a few additions to the standard list of fund-raising, as they did of fund-spending, methods.

[32] Egashira, "Kōchi han hi okeru Bakumatsu no shinseisaku." There was a widespread view in Bakumatsu times that the new techniques would guarantee wealth. Thus Yōdō could write his neighbor Date in Uwajima suggesting that he develop some mines there too. *ibid.*, p. 119. See also Ikeda, p. 19, for comparison of these policies to earlier and later reforms.

Shortly after the Harris treaty went into effect Yoshida dispatched Iwasaki Yatarō, in later years the founder of the Mitsubishi firm, to Nagasaki to make arrangements for the export of Tosa camphor, dried bonito (katsuo bushi) and paper. Nagasaki became an important outlet for Tosa products as well as a port of entry for Tosa weapons in the next few years. But Yoshida's plans did not stop here, for he thought in terms of shipping development and the occupation of undeveloped islands in the South Pacific.[33] Related to these steps were Yoshida's measures to secure more dependable knowledge about the West. He was able to attach Yamada Umajirō to the first Tokugawa mission to the United States. A group of students was sent to Nagasaki to study under the Dutch, and after they returned Yoshida even made attempts to learn Dutch himself.

Education also came in for Yoshida's attention. A school for samurai, the *Bumbu Kan* ("Arts and War," later renamed the *Chidō Kan*, "Arriving at the Way") replaced the previous han school in 1862. The school offered studies in both native and foreign studies, and for a time, all regular samurai (*hirazamurai*) between 15 and 40 were required to take at least one course each in the divisions of letters and military science.

Yoshida also revised and simplified the system of samurai ratings from the numerous differentiations of rank which had grown up to the relative simplicity of the ten ranks which had prevailed earlier. Administrative and social regulations were defined and spelled out in the famous *Kainan Seiten*, the last of Tosa's great compilations in Tokugawa times.

When Ii Naosuke's punishment of Yamauchi Yōdō removed Yoshida's sponsor, Yoshida inevitably became the object of much dislike. His reforms had struck at many of the special privileges of the well-born upper samurai, and, especially after the abolition of the new military units, it was clear that they had not opened significant new opportunities for the lower ranks. The old-guard conservatives criticized him for having led Yōdō into the paths that led to confinement in Shinagawa, while the lower ranks were impatient with the cautious, hands-off policy Yoshida pursued lest he further damage Yōdō's case. The new monopolies and economic reforms constituted another in the long list of han attempts to get

---

[33] A famous paper of Yoshida' developing this idea may be found in Ōtsuka Takematsu, *Yoshida Tōyō ikō* (Tokyo, 1929), p. 270.

more income from the agricultural, paper, and fishing industries, and they brought the danger of irritation and discontent on the part of rural leaders. The old guard scornfully referred to Yoshida's group of followers as a "new *okoze-gumi*," thereby comparing them to the reform group of the 1840's that had been attacked on ideological grounds.[34] All Yoshida's enemies, high and low, complained of the expense of his measures, and spoke darkly of popular suffering and discontent. Both groups tried to remonstrate with Yoshida, but he proved little inclined to listen to the opinions of those with whom he disagreed. With considerable arrogance and full confidence in his own ability, Yoshida continued along the path he had mapped out for himself, confident that only thus could Tosa strength and power be developed. Yoshida's dogged conviction of being in the right was the element in his character that the Tosa loyalists could least forgive, since it ran squarely athwart their own, equally dogmatic, conviction of superior wisdom. Their antipathy toward Yoshida and his disciples became so intense and personal that it was nearly a decade before men like Sakamoto Ryōma discovered to their surprise that men like Gotō Shōjirō were kindred spirits. The reasons that the gulf between the two groups became so broad will emerge more clearly if we turn next to the formative years of Sakamoto Ryōma himself.

3. The Education of Sakamoto Ryōma

The crisis and strains of the 1850's left their mark on young samurai everywhere in Japan, and it will be appropriate to observe how they affected the formative years of Sakamoto Ryōma. As was the case with most of his contemporaries in Tosa, Sakamoto's reaction to the Western threat was strongly emotional. His natural aptitude and training equipped him better for direct action against the agents of that threat than for analysis of ways in which it might best be countered, and the associations he formed in his years in fencing schools reinforced his instinctive preference for simple solutions to complex problems. Like his fellow fencers, Sakamoto came to judge his feudal superiors by simple moral standards of courage, and when they seemed to hesitate and hold back out of fear of endangering the fief and country, Sakamoto and his friends reproached them with cowardice and incompetence. Gradually the foreign issue became the occasion for the

---

[34] See especially Sasaki, who disapproved of Yoshida's stand in national policy matters, for consistent use of the term *okozegumi*. *Sekijitsudan*, p. 90.

revelation of resentments of long standing, and anti-foreignism became associated in the minds of Tosa youth with antipathy toward the ruling groups. In view of the schooling in loyalism which many of the youths had received, such resentment would certainly find its justification and focus in the Imperial cause, whose higher morality transcended feudal obligations. The Tosa *gōshi* and *shōya* had their complaints against their feudal betters, and they did not lack for inequality and prejudice as spurs to their efforts. But it will become apparent that these earlier resentments lay largely dormant until the overriding question of the foreign danger could be used to justify breaches in traditional patterns of subordination.

Sakamoto was born in 1835, the youngest of five children. His elder brother, Gompei, succeeded to the family headship. Of the three elder sisters, the youngest, Otome, was a woman of force and character who encouraged Sakamoto in many of his activities. A large number of extremely frank and engaging letters addressed to her testify to Sakamoto's affection for his sister. They constitute the best, and, for some periods, the only, guide to his activities.

The Sakamoto genealogy serves as an excellent illustration of social mobility in Tosa in Tokugawa times. Sometime about the middle of the sixteenth century the family founder, Tarōgorō, left his native province of Yamashiro and came to Tosa in hopes of avoiding the wars and destruction that cursed the area around Kyoto at that time. He took up unoccupied land in the hamlet of Saitani, Nagaoka district, and became a farmer. In 1666 his great-grandson moved to the castle town of Kōchi and entered trade under the name of "Saitani Shop" (*Saitaniya*); from this time on, a pawn shop and, in 1677, a sake brewery became the primary sources of family income. By the middle of the eighteenth century minor administrative responsibilities such as "elder" (*toshiyori*) were being given the Sakamoto family head. In 1763 the han regulations announcing new *gōshi* titles for those who reclaimed land in Hata district made provision for the first time for applicants of merchant descent. Eight years later, in 1771, the seventh family head resigned in favor of his younger brother, formed a new "branch" family himself, and petitioned for and received *gōshi* status.[35]

[35] A standard account by Chikami Kiyoomi, *Sakamoto Ryōma* (Tokyo, 1914),

The Sakamoto family thus provides an excellent example of the "merchant *gōshi*." The main family continued in business, and adoptions between the two branches maintained the connection. A number of accounts survive, emphasizing that the family was one of wealth.[36] The *gōshi* registers give the family estates as producing 161 koku, 8 *tō*, 4 *shō*, and 3 *shaku* of rice. This was third highest of the 82 *gōshi* who were resident inside or near Kōchi city. Only six of those families were rated over 100 koku, and the average holding was only 50 koku. Sakamoto fields were scattered throughout eight villages, and they were obviously not farmed by family members.[37] According to one account Sakamoto was sent by his father to Hata district at an early age, so that it is reasonable to suppose that there were holdings there to enable the family to qualify for the Hata issue of *gōshi* titles. The principal holdings were listed for Tosa district, closest to Kōchi; it is not certain whether any of the original holdings in Nagaoka district remained in the main family. For military purposes, the Sakamoto family was attached to the units commanded by the *karō* family named Fukuoka. This brought with it certain ceremonial relationships, as when the Fukuoka, on visiting their ancestral tombs early each January, visited the Sakamoto home and presented a wine cup. It is noteworthy that the Fukuoka also made gifts of fish to the main family, which had continued its business as the Saitaniya. Thus the merchant branch may have had business relations with the Fukuoka as well. At any rate, Sakamoto's was no impoverished, underprivileged warrior family; it was a farming family that had found it possible to move to town and enter trade, in the process becoming a wealthy merchant house able to buy its way into the only rung of the ruling class open to it. It is also interesting to note that at the dawn of the Restoration, when the old order seemed to be breaking up, Sakamoto took as his alias the name Saitani,

---

pp. 25-30, speaks of descent from a relative of Akechi Mitsuhide who was said to have fled to Tosa upon the collapse of his family's fortunes in 1582. I have followed the more impressive documentation in Takezaki Gorō, "Sakamoto Ryōma Sensei keizu: Ōhama Ke yori izuru," *Tosa shidan* No. 76 (Kōchi, 1941), pp. 35-37.

[36] cf. Iwasaki Hideshige, ed., *Sakamoto Ryōma kankei monjo* (Tokyo, 1926), I, 31.

[37] Chikami gives the family income as 197 koku, but I have followed the more recent and authoritative tables in *Kōchi Shi shi*, p. 331, and *Tosa han gōshi chōsa sho* (Tosa shiryō sōsho, Kōchi, 1958), p. 30. For names and incomes of *gōshi* resident in Kōchi castle town, *Kōchi Shi shi*, pp. 330-337.

thereby harking back to his ancestors' agricultural and merchant background.[38]

Sakamoto was a younger son, and therefore less burdened with duties than his brother. The latter, Gompei, is described as a model elder son—strong of physique, well educated, skilled in versifying, and excelling in military arts. In later years he served the han administration in several posts. His brother's fidelity to han and family duty made it possible for Sakamoto Ryōma to be freed from such concerns, while his own rapport with his elder sister Otome provided him with encouragement and counsel for his plans. As a *gōshi* dependent, Sakamoto benefited from the income and status of rank without being hampered by its duties, and it is possible that some of his readiness to consider new ideas as he began to mature should be credited to this relatively carefree and independent status. Some writers have tried to see in Sakamoto a representative of merchant interests, but his letters, though never very communicative about his ideas on the merchant class, make it clear that he considered himself a samurai first and foremost. It would probably be safe to assume that most of his early ideas were absorbed from the companions with whom he learned the military arts. Their ethos, in the 1850's, was certainly overwhelmingly that of a warrior class.

In 1846 Sakamoto's family enrolled him in one of the private schools below the Kōchi castle. If Sakamoto had applied himself to his lessons he would now have been drilled in the Confucian classics, but since he showed little liking or aptitude for the learning to which he was exposed, he was withdrawn after a short time. The family fortunes did not in any case rest on his shoulders, so that there was no need to force him into proper paths of learning. Sakamoto's literary ability remained at a low level. In later years a friend, Hirai Shūjirō, warned his sister against getting involved in Sakamoto's plans: "Although Ryōma is a splendid fellow, he doesn't have any learning, and therefore he sometimes makes serious mistakes."[39] Sakamoto's letters, especially those to his sister, show numerous signs of awkward construction, and his vocabulary was limited. When he dabbled with learning Dutch in later years he restricted himself to the simplest words, and there is no indica-

---

[38] Sakamoto shifted to this name in the fall of 1866.
[39] Iwasaki Hideshige, ed., *Sakamoto kankei monjo*, I, 60. Letter dated 1862.

tion that he made much headway.[40] It is tempting to credit some
of Sakamoto's disregard for his feudal obligations in later years
to this failure to absorb the Confucianism of the schools. "It is a
lot of nonsense to say that, in times like these, it is a violation of
morality to put your relatives second and your country first, to
abandon your mother, your wife, and your children;—this comes
from our stupid officials," he was to write the parents of a friend
who fled the han in 1864.[41] It must be remembered, however, that
the moral training Sakamoto received at home, like that of his
contemporaries, was firmly within the Confucian tradition of Tokugawa days, and that the rejection of normal duties was justified
for him by the overriding importance of the Imperial cause. Since
he received little formal book learning, this cult of loyalism must
have been absorbed by him in the fencing academies to which he
was sent next.

In the late 1840's and 1850's the consciousness of danger from
the West and the need of remilitarizing Japan's ruling class produced a new interest in the traditional military arts. In Tosa, as
in other fiefs, samurai of all ranks were encouraged to perfect
themselves in fencing, or *kenjutsu*. No group threw themselves
into this program of preparedness with more enthusiasm than
those of the lower ranks, who could match only their enthusiasm
and valor against the special command prerogatives of their betters. It is not surprising that the fencing academies, filled to over-
flowing with ambitious and restless samurai, became the centers
of extremist and obscurantist thought and action. Tournaments
and conventions provided ideal opportunities to refresh contacts
and friendships made in Edo fencing centers, and as the time for
action neared, the swordsmen tested their ability by domestic disorder and political assassination. Sakamoto's excellence in fencing
therefore meant that he would be associated with the most extreme and reckless young men of his time and place.

Sakamoto was sent to a school for swordmanship conducted by
one Hineno Benji on the outskirts of Kōchi in 1848. He soon became one of Hineno's best students. In 1853, since his family was

[40] *Sakamoto monjo*, II, 44f., contains scraps of notebooks with Dutch expressions
for military commands, numbers, and alphabet; there are also a few English notes,
evidently designed for personal use: young man, bride, girl, love potion, etc.

[41] From a letter to the parents of Ike Kurata, a colleague who fled Tosa in 1863,
unpublished, in the Seizan Bunko, the private library of Count Tanaka Kōken, in
Sakawa, Kōchi Prefecture.

able to pay his way and his tuition, he was sent to Edo to continue his study of kenjutsu. Travel and study in Edo opened up tremendous vistas of activity for the young samurai from Tosa. He was boarded in the barracks of the principal Tosa residence at Kajibashi, near the center of the city. From there he walked daily to the Kyōbashi fencing academy of Chiba Sadakichi, who was a younger brother of one of Edo's three greatest masters of kenjutsu.[42]

On his travels Sakamoto carried a simple set of injunctions from his father which serve as a useful summary of the values which the young gōshi had been trained to maintain:

1. Never forget, even for a moment, that loyalty and filial piety are the most important elements in your training.

2. Do not become attached to material things and squander gold and silver for them.

3. You must not give yourself up to sensuality, or forget the importance of the nation, or allow your heart to be corrupted.

I want you to keep these three rules in your heart and to give first importance to returning successfully from your training.[43]

Sakamoto had not been in Edo very long before the appearance of Commodore Perry's flotilla changed the state of affairs. When the bakufu declared measures to guard the coastal districts, most of the Edo han barracks were emptied of samurai; special assignments and details rushed even private students to stand guard with their colleagues who were there on official duty. The Tosa levies were stationed along the coast near the Shinagawa han residence, and Sakamoto was among their number. At the same time hurried preparations were made in Tosa to dispatch more men to Edo.[44] Although Perry stayed only long enough to leave his letter with a promise to return the following year, the defence preparations continued frantically after his departure. Later in 1853 Tosa took steps to fortify the Hama River near Shinagawa, and when the American ships reentered Tokyo Bay in February of 1854, Tosa levies, reinforced by new groups called up from the

[42] Chikami, *Sakamoto*, p. 31, as corrected by Hirao, *Kaientai*, p. 12.
[43] *Sakamoto kankei monjo*, I, 37.
[44] The Shinagawa residence was not one of the principal Tosa Edo mansions, which were at Kajibashi, Tsukiji, and Mita. Sasaki, *Sekijitsu dan*, pp. 67, 119.

province, guarded these emplacements. Sakamoto also was involved in these preparations, and until the bakufu signed its Treaty of Amity with Perry in March 1854 and disbanded the emergency forces, Sakamoto was on military duty. Sakamoto shared the general impression that war was imminent. "Since foreign ships have come to several places," he wrote his father in October of 1853, "I think there will be a war soon. If it comes to that you can be sure I will cut off a foreign head before coming home."[45]

After the crisis subsided Sakamoto returned to Tosa in the summer of 1854, and he was back home by the time a tremendous earthquake did enormous damage to Kōchi in the fall of that year.[46] The costs of reconstruction complicated the task of military and economic reconstruction that the reform administration of Yoshida Tōyō had undertaken.

Sakamoto's return to Tosa gave him the opportunity to renew contacts with former acquaintances. Some he enlightened with tales of his experience in the metropolis, and from others he learned of the steps that were being taken by the Tosa han to strengthen its defences. His friendships serve to illustrate further the degree of social fluidity in Kōchi society. One visitor, for instance, was Kondo [later Uesugi] Chōjirō, the son of a man who made his living baking small bean jam buns. Kondo later entered a Confucian academy, and then paid his own way to travel to Edo to a school of "Dutch" learning, where he studied Western armaments under Takashima Shūhan. Still later he would join Sakamoto as a lieutenant in his enterprises. For Kondō, the talk with Sakamoto was a revelation of the power and danger of the West.[47] Kondo was also a friend of Kawade Shoryō, an artist who had been in Satsuma as member of a military mission charged with reporting the progress in Western weapon-making there. No doubt Kawade's skill in painting was utilized to record the techniques that had been observed in Kagoshima. Kawade had also had many contacts with the returned castaway Nakahama Manjirō, and therefore he was in possession of considerably more accurate information about the West than Sakamoto was.

[45] Hirao Michio, *Ishin Kinnō ibun sensho: Sakamoto Ryōma, Nakaoka Shintarō* (Tokyo, 1943), p. 4; *Sakamoto kankei monjo*, I, 20.
[46] Hirao, *Kaientai*, p. 20, corrects the usual version which has it that Sakamoto returned home after the earthquake out of concern for his parents.
[47] Chikami, *Sakamoto*, pp. 34-35.

Years later Kawade recorded his reminiscences of a talk with Sakamoto shortly after the latter returned to Tosa. He recalled that Sakamoto pressed him vigorously with questions about the burning question of seclusion or of opening the country. Kawade spoke of the need to develop trade and economic measures in order to strengthen the country against the Western threat. Japan's weapons and ships, he explained, were still childish things compared to those of her enemies. It would be necessary for all the han to work together to perfect their defences. If the argument over opening or seclusion continued to rage while foreign ships continued to come, as certainly they would, the country would be lost. It was Kawade's personal opinion that it would be best to engage in trade, not so much from a point of view of profit as to strengthen the country; a foreign ship should be purchased, manned with men who believed in what they were doing, and it should carry both official and private cargo to East and West. The sailors would learn navigation, and the way would be prepared for greater things in the future. As Kawade recalled the conversation, Sakamoto was much impressed with his argument. "Sakamoto clapped his hands, and said 'I have been studying fencing since my youth, but it deals with only one enemy. If you cannot accomplish some great purpose, it is very difficult to extend your ambition.'" Further conversations were devoted to problems of recruiting personnel for such enterprises from able members of the lower classes. "Those who have had hereditary incomes," Kawade explained, "have no ambition"; therefore, he thought, ability was more likely to be found among the less favored groups.[48]

This enlightening conversation, although recorded much later in the full memory of Sakamoto's later interests, is one of the few sources for Sakamoto's outlook during his stay in Kōchi. It shows that his contacts were varied and that they included men from whom he could learn a good deal. It is easy to imagine Sakamoto as one of a fairly numerous group of bright, inquisitive young men who visited elder men like Kawade, whom they respected and asked for their opinions on affairs of the day. In the absence of other means of communication and persuasion, individual figures like Kawade who were capable of inspiring such respect undoubtedly achieved considerable influence among those who concerned themselves with national affairs. And it is clear that

[48] *Sakamoto kankei monjo,* I, 38-49.

Nakaoka Shintarō

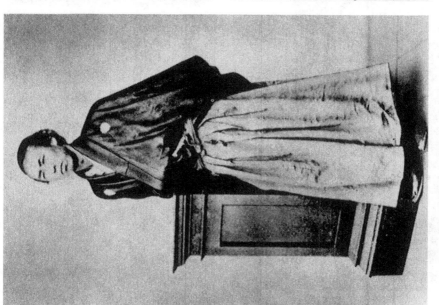

Sakamoto Ryōma

Fukuoka Kōtei at the time of the Restoration

Fukuoka Kōtei in later life

Tanaka Kōken in rōnin years

Tanaka Kōken in maturity

Itagaki Taisuke (center front) and followers
during the Restoration wars

Itagaki Taisuke in early years

Itagaki Taisuke in maturity, as leader
of the Liberal Party

Yoshida Tōyō

Iwasaki Yatarō

Takechi Zuizan

Gotō Shōjirō

Yamauchi Yōdō

Sakamoto was beginning to number among the politically aware.

Sakamoto remained in Kōchi until the autumn of 1856. During this period his father's death was followed by his brother Gompei's succession as head of the family. Sakamoto continued to perfect his skill in fencing, and occasionally he served as instructor in his old master's school. In September 1856, Sakamoto left for Edo again to continue his studies in kenjutsu. His Tosa travel permit was good for slightly more than a year. Two months before Sakamoto left Kōchi, Townsend Harris had come to take up residence in Shimoda under the terms of the Perry treaty, and shortly after Sakamoto had reported to the Tosa Tsukiji residence in Edo, Harris made his first request to come to Edo to present the president's letter.

During these years the Edo fencing academies became the centers of anti-foreign feeling. As the shogunate hesitated in selecting its course, those who were identified with a consistent course gained in stature among the samurai. No position had an appeal comparable to that of the anti-foreign enthusiasts; their position was clear, their solution dramatic, and their patriotism seemed unassailable. The young men in the fencing academies tended to look to Tokugawa Nariaki of Mito as the leader of their cause. Although his actual position was somewhat more ambivalent than they realized, Nariaki's hostility to the bakufu's tactics and the association of Mito scholarship with the Imperial cause made him a natural hero for the samurai who were perfecting their skill in fighting with traditional weapons. Then, as Nariaki lost favor with the bakufu leaders, and as the commercial treaty negotiated with Townsend Harris began to take form, the young fencing students began to take a position increasingly hostile to what they understood to be the shogunal position, and Nariaki became for them a neglected prophet. Ii Naosuke's measures against Nariaki and his ratification of the Harris treaty without Imperial approval clearly identified the Tairō as a despotic and evil figure. This rising trend toward extremism was true of many fencing students in Edo, and it had particularly important consequences for those of lower rank. These were, in any case, more numerous, and they had more incentive to apply themselves to their studies than did their superiors who were assured of command positions. In addition, however, the lower-ranking samurai were more free from official restraints than their betters. Often they were not even quartered in the Edo fief barracks. Since they lived with and trained with their contemporaries from other areas, they could easily go on to conspire with them. As a result fief lines did not mean as much for the low-ranking swordsmen as they did for their superiors. The development of an extremist and loyalist position can be shown with particular clarity for the contingent of Tosa fencing students which numbered Sakamoto among its members, and the process was inseparably connected with the personality of Takechi Zuizan (Hanpeita).

Takechi Zuizan was 27 in 1856. He was the eldest son of a *gōshi* of Niida village in the Nagaoka district of Tosa. The family lands were divided between the villages of Nishinochi, Uenoko, Niida, and Ike, and their production was rated early in the nineteenth century at 50 koku, 1 to, 8 shō, and 7 gō of rice. These resources placed the family in the upper third of the 189 Nagaoka *gōshi*, but *gōshi* income there was astonishingly uneven; Takechi's family income was far above one family listed for 4 koku, but even farther behind another listed at 363 koku.[49] The Takechi family had entered the ranks of *gōshi* in early Yamauchi times with other Chōsogabe retainers. Among Takechi's relatives was the scholar of national learning Kamochi Masazumi (1791-1858), who was an uncle. Takechi imbibed considerably more conventional learning than did Sakamoto. His great enthusiasm, however, was kenjutsu. He began its study at the age of twelve. After receiving training in several of the Kōchi academies he became an accredited teacher of the art. In 1854 he moved his family to Kōchi and opened his own academy there. Here he trained most of the future loyalist leaders of Tosa; in all they numbered over 120.

The han administration recognized Takechi's talents and leadership, and assigned him to several district magistracies to train young men of the vicinity in fencing. Yamauchi Yōdō was anxious to encourage the practice and study of kenjutsu to promote preparedness in Tosa, and to that end he sponsored jousts by visiting specialists and also sent his own experts to train with their peers elsewhere in Japan. As a result, Takechi was ordered to enter Momonoi Academy in Edo in 1856. He was granted 7 ryō as supplementary expense money, and with him went five of his students.

[49] The Nagaoka *gōshi* family incomes are listed in *Tosa han gōshi chōsa sho*, pp. 15-25.

That same fall Sakamoto returned to Edo to continue his studies, and he soon came under Takechi's influence.

Takechi was unusually well fitted to assume a position of leadership among the young students of swordsmanship. As a recognized master of his art in Tosa, he received special privileges of residence near the Edo academy, away from the han barracks; shortly afterward he became the adjutant of the fencing master. Takechi made a profound impression on all his students. They often referred to him as "The India Ink Dragon" (*Bokuryū Sensei*) because his appearance—great height, pale and intense face, and a frame tempered in fencing practice—suggested that of a dragon in a monochrome painting. His was a strong personality, and he easily gained ascendancy over the fencing students from Tosa. His ideas triumphed together with his person. There was in Takechi a drive, only gradually articulated, for loyalism and for administrative reform. The latter must have sprung from his own handicaps of rank and it found expression in his argument that the han should select its leaders according to ability and not according to rank. His respect and reverence for the Emperor, furthermore, were so notable and so marked that he became known as *Tennōzuki*, "Emperor lover."[50] In 1856 Sakamoto came to board at the same lodging as Takechi, and he quickly fell under his influence.

It is not surprising that in such company Sakamoto's emergent espousal of opening the country, which Kawade had noted in the talks the previous year in Kōchi, was relegated in favor of the brand of fervent, emotional, anti-foreign obscurantism that reigned in the fencing schools. Sakamoto took part in a few Edo tournaments and acquitted himself creditably. He helped a relative of Takechi's, who had incurred serious punishment and possible death for a drunken prank, slip out of Edo. And he made friendships with similarly minded young men from many parts of Japan. He and the other Tosa men saw a good deal of young swordsmen from Chōshū and from Mito, both centers of dissatisfaction with shogunal policies.

In October of 1857 Sakamoto and Takechi returned to Tosa, Takechi because of his grandmother's illness, and Sakamoto be-

---

[50] The Takechi career and character are described in *Ishin Tosa kinnō shi*, compiled in 1911 for the (Takechi) Zuizan Society, and Hirao Michio, *Takechi Zuizan to Tosa Kinnō Tō* (Tokyo, 1943). See also Marius B. Jansen, "Takechi Zuizan and the Tosa Loyalist Party," *Journal of Asian Studies*, xviii, 2 (February 1959), pp. 199-212.

cause his permit had expired. Sakamoto made a leisurely trip back, one in which he is said to have indulged in the arts of deliberate carelessness which traditionally marked the true samurai. He gave away his travel money, and lived off the land during a leisurely trip on which he included many of the historic places of loyalism and valor in the Yamato country.[51] His transportation problems from Osaka to Kōchi were solved by han regulations which required merchant vessels to carry any samurai who needed passage to Tosa.[52] Then, back in Kōchi, Sakamoto continued his work in kendō. He also delved into serious reading, but without, one gathers, startling results. An engaging story that dates from this period illustrates the relative amounts of self-confidence and learning which Sakamoto possessed. To one of his friends who visited him, he announced that he had begun to read books, and he showed him a copy of the *Tzu-chih t'ung-chien*. The friend admired the work, but admitted it was beyond him. Thereupon Sakamoto picked it up and began reading at the top of his lungs, making any number of mistakes in reading and paying no attention to the punctuation indicated. "Do you mean to say you can understand it that way?" asked the startled visitor. "Well," Sakamoto replied, "I get the general idea."[53]

Takechi, for his part, resumed his work as fencing master in Tosa, and his fame and influence grew. He now had additional converts. Among them, from Aki district, was Nakaoka Shintarō, who ruled 13 villages as *Ōjōya* (Great *shōya*) and whose holdings were rated, with the precision that characterized Tosa records, as producing 25 koku, 1 to, 3 shō, 7 gō and 6 shaku.[54] Takechi's group of disciples began to take on the character of a league of *gōshi* and *shōya* sons. Sakamoto remained among the number of his assistants and admirers.

Shortly after Takechi's return to Kōchi his followers drew up a formal request to his former fencing instructor, Asada Kanshichi, urging him to nominate Takechi for a special han award. Their petition explained Takechi's skill in the art of swordsmanship, and cited his experiences in Edo and his position in the Momonoi

[51] Chikami, *Sakamoto*, p. 37. Sakamoto is credited with a visit to the grave of Kusunoki Masashige, a pilgrimage most loyalists made.
[52] Hirao Michio, *Tosa han gyogyō keizai shi* (Kōchi, 1955), p. 208.
[53] Chikami, *Sakamoto*, p. 38.
[54] Hirao Michio, *Rikuentai shimatsu ki*, p. 5.

Academy there. It was lavish in its praise of Takechi's personal and moral qualities. As a result of the recommendation from Asada, the han regime (which was again headed by Yoshida Tōyō, who had just been reappointed) awarded Takechi an additional life income of two rations in the spring of 1858.[55]

The contacts that had been made in the Edo fencing academies served to introduce Takechi and Sakamoto to national politics in the fall of 1858, when they were approached by messengers from Mito. Takechi and Sakamoto had returned to Tosa in the fall of 1857. The months that followed saw the failure of attempts in which their lord, Yamauchi Yōdō, participated, to utilize the bakufu's need for imperial ratification of the Harris commercial treaty to secure administrative changes and the succession for Hitotsubashi Keiki. In the late spring and summer of 1858 a new Edo administration under the Tairō Ii Naosuke acted with great vigor in crushing those who had presumed to influence shogunal decisions. Tokugawa Nariaki of Mito, who had served as spearhead of the movement to secure bakufu concessions to the vassals in order to make possible real national unity, was ordered confined to his Edo mansion in late August of 1858. This action infuriated a large group of Mito samurai who had imbibed the loyalist teachings of the fief scholars, and they now tried to utilize the contacts they had made in kenjutsu to organize opposition to the Edo regime. Since Takechi and Sakamoto came to the attention of the Mito men for this purpose, it is evident that the two had made their mark in the society of the swordsmen in Edo the previous year.

Late in 1858 a group of Mito men set out to win support for their cause. Their mission was a difficult one. Mito was deeply and, as it proved, irretrievably divided between factions which favored a greater or lesser degree of opposition to the bakufu policies. Internal strife was to cost Mito leadership of and participation in the events of the final decade of Tokugawa rule. For the time being, however, indignation against the punishment of Nariaki seemed likely to have the upper hand; it was a party of four representatives of the extremist faction, led by Sumiya Toranosuke, which came to Tosa in search of help from their acquaintances.

[55] Hirao, *Takechi*, p. 19.

Their reception in Tosa illustrates both the effective way in which the realm was kept separated from its neighboring areas and the limited degree of knowledge of political affairs that Sakamoto Ryōma had developed. The Mito emissaries were unable to gain admittance to Tosa at the Tachikawa border station. Instead a small party of Tosa men, headed by Sakamoto, came to meet them. Presumably Takechi Zuizan sent them as his representatives. After a talk at the border, Sakamoto and his party returned to Kōchi to see if they could arrange entry into Tosa for their guests, but two days later word was sent back that it could not be done. Failing in this, the guests waited at the border for some days to see what response might come to the letter they had given Sakamoto. None was forthcoming, however, and so they gave up hope of cooperation and moved on.

The diary of the Mito messenger, Sumiya, gives a revealing glimpse of the contrast in political awareness between Mito and Tosa men at that point. "The two outsiders [Tosa men]," he noted, "don't know a thing about their han's affairs; Ryōma [Sakamoto] doesn't even know the names of any of the ministers. We wasted several days; it's a great shame."[56]

If Sakamoto was really this ignorant of national affairs, he could have learned a good deal from the Mito letter which he carried back to Kōchi. It was a detailed indictment of the arbitrary actions of the Regent Ii, written from the point of view of the partisans of Tokugawa Nariaki. The Regent Ii, they charged, had ignored and despised the sound advice of their lord, and he had flouted the Imperial will. He had seized the men of high purpose who had been working in Kyoto for the good of the country, and he had dared to punish Lord Nariaki himself. Naturally, the letter went on, Mito samurai were tremendously agitated, and it was necessary to give some thought to the course that should be followed.[57]

It may be that Takechi and Sakamoto failed to acknowledge this message because the news it contained still seemed to them to affect chiefly the relations between Ii and Nariaki. While their resentment of the foreigners was acute, they were a good deal farther away from the proposed ports and from Tokugawa policy than were the Mito men. As yet their own han had felt neither hurt nor danger from the policies of Ii, for Yōdō's punishment was

---

[56] *Sakamoto kankei monjo*, 1, 56.
[57] *Sakamoto kankei monjo*, 1, 52-54, gives the letter.

yet to come. But if this was the case the next few months showed them wrong. The Regent's purge of his enemies extended to Ya-mauchi Yōdō, who was gradually restricted in his movements un-til he was under house arrest in his Shinagawa residence outside Edo. Fearful of further bakufu retribution, the han administration under Yoshida Tōyō moved cautiously. Yoshida, indeed, ap-proached Edo to voice the hope that the Yamauchi family would not lose its fief altogether. Then, because the signing of the trea-ties with the foreigners removed the likelihood of an early foreign war, the emergency measures of armament that had been begun in 1854 were slowed and stopped while Yoshida tried to repair the damage those measures had done to the han treasury.

Takechi and his followers were not likely to applaud such cau-tion. Instead, they showed a rising and emotional resentment of bakufu internal and external policies. When their wishes were not honored, their anger extended to the political system in which they had so little voice. Meanwhile, throughout the months of 1859 and 1860 their leader's prestige and repute continued to grow. In 1859 Takechi was appointed general inspector for kendō training for all of *gōshi, shirafuda* rank and above, and in the fol-lowing year, when he was thirty-one, he was authorized to leave Tosa with a small party of followers to survey fencing techniques and training in central and southern Japan.[58]

During the period in which Yōdō had counted for a great deal in national politics—the years between the Perry and Harris trea-ties—the lower samurai of Tosa had remained remarkably unin-formed of national issues. Instead they trained themselves in kendō and echoed uncritically the sentiments which they felt all around them. But after Yōdō was confined in his Shinagawa residence the Tosa *gōshi* and *shōya* led by Takechi became increasingly drawn into national politics. They were critical first of bakufu policy, then of their han minister Yoshida Tōyō for submitting to it, and finally they organized to see what they themselves could do on both fronts. In a sense, their behavior was like that of the Toku-gawa vassals who became restive after they felt the lack of a strong hand and consistent policy in bakufu administration. They too had associated external issues with the need for selection of "men of ability."

[58] Hirao, *Takechi*, pp. 22-27.

It will be seen, however, that the Tosa retainers, like the bakufu vassals, were not driven by an integrated or purposeful program for the future. They knew that something was wrong with their country, if only because it was weak and defenceless. But they were still far from thoughts of overthrowing the han administration (or the shogunate) or "restoring" the Emperor. It remained for the course of events to stimulate their tendencies toward radical solutions and for their extremist reactions to speed the process of political change; when this process began, vague ideas of respect for the Emperor would be formulated into a program. The speed with which such developments could come depended on the flow of the times. The old order and the old answers were no longer convincing for Sakamoto and his friends, but no clear alternatives had yet presented themselves.

III. THE LOYALIST YEARS

*T*HE year 1860 brought a period of tremendous change and ferment in the lives of young men like Sakamoto Ryōma. They now began to resist the orders of their feudal superiors and to follow what they considered to be the interests of the Emperor. The opening of the ports to foreign traders brought the foreign problem home to many Japanese and to all the members of the ruling class. The traders in the new town of Yokohama, hard by Edo, furnished an inviting target for young swordsmen anxious to try their blades on the hated foreigner, and a number of incidents were utilized by the powers in demands for further privileges from the shogunate. In 1860 the bakufu's first minister, who was held responsible for the arrival of the traders, fell victim to assassins. His death marked the beginning of several years of lawlessness. Not since the seventeenth century had there been so much of change, of decision, and of opportunity in the air.

For Sakamoto Ryōma and for many of his contemporaries, these years brought a new sense of involvement in the major issues of the day. Like his fellows, Sakamoto saw those issues as simple questions of right and wrong, of moral and immoral policies and leaders. Until a gradual realization of the complexity of the choices came to him, his responses were dominated by an emotional desire for direct action to eliminate the agents of policies he considered disloyal to the throne.

In Tosa these issues were complicated by new expressions of hostility between the lower ranking samurai and rural leaders and their feudal superiors in the castle town. The reforms of Yoshida Tōyō had added to these tensions, and they now made possible a strange alliance between the highest and lowest ranking groups of the warrior class, both of whom had found cause for complaint. However different their interests and objections to his measures, their common hatred of the fief's first minister made possible the assassination of Yoshida Tōyō and his replacement by bureaucratic rivals who did not mount a vigorous search for the swordsmen who had slain him. These tensions and their political consequences must be considered below, for they do much to explain the shifts of Tosa policies as well as the responses of Sakamoto and his friends to the challenge of their times.

The Tosa scene, in turn, was one variant of a national picture in which bakufu policies, internal bureaucratic rivalries, and social and economic tensions made for contrasting and contradictory policies followed by the great fiefs. The han authorities alternately utilized and repressed the activities of their subordinates according to the way in which they read the signs of the times. In many respects the years after 1860 were remarkable for the degree to which samurai from different fiefs worked together, often in continuation of patterns of conspiracy that had begun in the Edo fencing academies. A comparable sense of common interest and danger produced cooperation between a number of great lords who saw in the slogan *kōbu gattai*, reconciliation of court and camp, an opportunity to improve their own positions relative to those of the bakufu and its other vassals. Not that national interests were beginning to predominate for the daimyō; the regional advantage might be interpreted in various ways, but it was never ignored. After 1860 all groups looked for allies and claimed the support of tradition, with the result that the court nobles were drawn into the political picture once again. The loyalist years were remarkable for the boldness with which some of the Kyoto aristocrats turned to national politics.

The new decade was one in which bakufu policies determined the political alternatives available to the great lords and court nobles. After the assassination of the Regent in 1860 a relaxation of controls over the vassals was offered in hopes of allaying resentment and promoting cooperation. Instead, it opened new possibilities of independent action which were utilized and directed by anti-foreign extremists to produce a near-paralysis of Tokugawa planning and action. Out of this came a promise to exclude the traders who had just arrived—a promise which, when taken seriously by one element of the loyalist group, revealed the exclusionist position for what it was, an emotional and irrational fantasy. Until 1863, however, loyalism and exclusionism, combined in the slogan *sonnō-jōi*, were taken seriously by many, and especially by young swordsmen like Sakamoto. The conviction of a higher morality, and the intensity of belief in direct and simple solutions gave to the loyalist years a coloring of fearlessness and fanaticism, courage and cruelty. These were qualities in which Sakamoto Ryōma and his fellow fencers excelled.

1. The SHISHI Type and Ideal

The activists of the 1860's styled themselves *shishi,* "men of high purpose." Although they made much of traditional values and virtues, they represented a new social and ethical type, one which was later glorified by the new government they helped to bring about and one which could be emulated by future enemies of that government, the assassins of the 1930's. Sakamoto's actions during the early 1860's, and the manner in which his image was projected by later histories and romances, cannot be understood without some consideration of the pattern according to which he and his friends lived.

The intellectual armament with which the activists were prepared consisted of conventional Confucian values as modified by the needs of Japanese feudalism. Duty, above all to a higher political calling, was superior to family considerations and responsibilities. Loyalty was the mark of the good warrior, and, since Japanese feudalism was strongly familistic in thought, loyalty and filial piety were one; they reinforced the demands of duty. In the armory of the fighting man, these qualities outweighed others of humanity and trustworthiness in secondary situations and relationships.

The Mito scholars, whose works and attitudes colored the thinking of the nineteenth century loyalists, had focused on parts of the Confucian tradition which rationalized and moralized these ethical demands. In particular it was the phrase of Chu Hsi, *taigi meibun,* "the highest duty of all," which was central to the Mito teaching. It recurs with great frequency in the papers of the Restoration activists. *Taigi meibun* included, in its second element, emphasis on "name and function," or the necessity to make political function correspond to social name or status. In the thinking of the Confucian preceptors of the traditional han colleges, this teaching should have made for deference and obedience on the part of the loyalists, many of whom bore only modest rank. That it had different effects was due to the tendency of much of Tokugawa Confucianism to focus on other matters with this text in mind, in particular on the supreme desirability, or higher duty, of making the political function of the emperor correspond with his name. *Taigi meibun* in this sense had been reinforced by the tradition of national, or Shintō, studies, which had recreated—in a sense, indeed, created—the ideal of the divine Emperor, responsible to and counseled by Imperial ancestors, who ruled the sacred and inviolable land as father-priest.[1] Nothing could have been farther from this ideal than the years after 1860, when impure foreigners forced their way upon the sacred shores because of the vacillation of an intervening bakufu. The shogunate's political position, however anomalous, had been defensible so long as it protected the court, but when its weakness could be shown to cause the emperor grief it would inevitably seem an immoral usurpation. At such a time the "highest duty of all" would dictate steps to correct the situation even though they were taken in defiance of conventional discipline and duty. Such duty would outweigh duty to lord, and it would justify suffering caused family and even parents by defection from fief. For many activists, however, the antithesis between lord and emperor was non-existent; they preferred to believe that their lord was really on their side, although he might temporarily be the victim of bad advice or wicked councillors. Few lords committed themselves unequivocally on the issues of the day, so that this interpretation had as much to substantiate it as did the conviction of the military activists of the 1930's that they spoke the real mind of an emperor whose conservative advisers kept him from taking a strong stand.

This interpretation of duty had particular attractions for samurai of modest rank and slight sophistication in the world of politics. In the case of Sakamoto, for instance, it could justify activity and aspirations on the part of a second son of a citified gōshi, a man whose political future would normally have been restricted to a possible role as teacher explaining taigi meibun to schoolboys who were more interested in their lessons with practice swords. Men born to responsibility and status, on the other hand, were more likely to weigh alternatives before committing their lives to a cause, and with political experience they would see the impracticability of thoroughgoing anti-foreignism, however attractive it might be in theory.

If lack of official or familial responsibility was useful, courage was an essential element for the shishi. Here the training of the fencing schools stood them in good stead. The romantic overtones

---

[1] Brief discussions of loyalist thought can be found in Herschel F. Webb, "The Mito Theory of the State," in Columbia University East Asian Institute Studies No. 4, *Researches in the Social Sciences on Japan*, ed. John E. Lane, 1957, pp. 33-52, and W. Theodore deBary, ed., *Sources of the Japanese Tradition* (New York, 1958), pp. 371ff.

of the cult of the swordsman—the wise and courageous samurai, eye ever fixed on the ultimate objective, with a heart as pure as his shining blade, trained to set aside all personal considerations, cultivating self-perfection in order to be a more perfect instrument of justice—all of this contributed to the romantic view the *shishi* held of themselves.

There was cruelty as well as courage in the conduct of the rōnin swordsmen. Since they took for themselves the highest of morality and duty, their enemies could be dismissed with hatred and contempt. The samurai cult had never, in any case, made much of mercy and compassion, and in the fevered excitement of the 1860's there would be even less room for them. It must be remembered that these were virtues little practiced anywhere in Japanese society; honor to one's name and status far outweighed them in value, even in cases where no moral or political issues were at stake. Sasaki Takayuki relates an incident of these years in which a nephew of his, an eldest son sixteen years of age, came to cross swords with a samurai of much lower rank, a second son twenty years old, in Tosa. Friends and relatives had separated them, and that same night the two parties were gathered—Sasaki and his group outside, and the others inside the house—deliberating how best to combine honor with justice. Sasaki, as senior relative and ranking warrior present, reasoned that temporizing might bring on charges of cowardice, while concerted action against the lower-ranking man involved would produce inter-rank tensions of major proportions. A duel, he decided, was the way to handle it; this would give the "enemy" more honor than he could expect. When he shouted this suggestion to the other party, they answered that they preferred a bloodless solution. Impatient, Sasaki ordered his nephew to go ahead. "Kannosuke, escorted by several of his relatives, dashed toward the inner garden, . . . recognized his assailant, shouted 'Meet my challenge!'—and dispatched the other," who had not, because of a wound just received, been able to rise to resist. Everyone, Sasaki notes, praised his conduct of the business as being fair and straightforward.[2] If this was a reasonable procedure within Tosa, there was little reason to expect the *shishi* to stay their swords in what they conceived to be the Imperial cause.

[2] *Sasaki Rō Kō sekijitsudan*, pp. 243-248.

Courage, devotion to an ideal, however vaguely articulated, and scorn for practical or personal considerations which deterred their fellows—these were the marks of the true idealist. The samurai was trained to be careless and indifferent to material interests, and the *shishi* carried this improvidence to an extreme. If funds, whether public or private, were available, they were shared; if they were not, the *shishi* were sufficiently confident of their superior morality to expect the more lowly social orders to enhance their morality by supporting them. The *shishi* had no care for the morrow. He was brave, casual, carefree, took himself very seriously where "first things" were concerned, and was utterly indifferent where they were not. Irresponsible in many matters, he was also a roisterer, given to wine and to women. Tokugawa police measures made it inevitable that conspiracies would be hatched in restaurants and brothels, the only places where men could gather without arousing suspicion. This coincided with the preferences of the *shishi*, whose actions underscore Bertram Wolfe's remark that "there is something in the hunted man's way of life which makes a moment's respite and physical ease seem intensely precious."[3] There are several instances in the fragmentary diary of Nakaoka Shintarō in which he prepared himself for danger by a last visit to the brothel, only to meet the rest of the group there, with the result that the evening was made up in equal parts of self-indulgence and political discussion. Thanks to this the Restoration received its quota of female heroes, for the entertainers and hotel maids frequently saved the lives of their carefree customers.

The activists first concerned themselves with national politics during the crises in foreign relations that arose in the mid-1850's. For the most part they were in the service of lords who took an active part in the discussion about the ports and the shogunal succession, and the agents of those lords who fell to the vengeance of Ii Naosuke were in many cases the tutors and companions of the heroes of a later day. Then, as the Regent extended his punishment to the lords themselves, the fief governments did their best to restrain their young enthusiasts. Yamauchi Yōdō of Tosa and Matsudaira Shungaku of Echizen were confined, as was Tokugawa Nariaki of Mito; the conservative course their fiefs now took in national politics meant that the retainers who had been full of

[3] Bertram D. Wolfe, *Three Who Made a Revolution* (Boston, 1955), p. 374.

hope for a new dispensation and an anti-foreign war had now been returned to their status and station. In many cases these frustrated hopes contributed to the conviction that a higher duty required action to right the wrongs. In the catalogue of wrongs drawn up by the young samurai their own immobilization was not given prominent place, although the Confucian slogans of "rule by ability" might suggest alternatives. On the other hand, the bakufu's punishment of their lord was another matter, and their fief government's cautious refusal to protest those steps, and its apparent acquiescence in the bakufu's surrender to the West, justified their indignation and action.

Thus the "purpose" for which the *shishi* strove came to have overtones of preservation of the "sacred land" from the impurity of foreign occupation and of reverence for the Kyoto court wherein lay the essence of "national purity." A sense of destiny and a conviction of being in the right colored all future disputes for the loyalists. They easily arrogated to themselves and their partisans terms which indicated their own moral superiority. Thus, in Mito they were the "righteous" (*seigi*), in Chōshū the "enlightened" (*kaimei*), and in Tosa the reverent (*kinnō*) party (*tō*). Their opponents were usually the partisans of a "vulgar" or "pedestrian" (*zokuron*) view, and collectively they could be dismissed with epithets for "corrupt" and "evil" officials. Success depended on the seizure of positions of responsibility for their own group, and this involved the selection of officials not by rank or family but by "ability." From these social and intellectual grounds, in the fevered emotionalism of the literate but unlettered swordsmen of the early 1860's, came the outlook which converted personal preferences into moral necessity and partisan tactics into religious crusades. By their confusion of means with morality and of clique with character, the *shishi* left a political legacy for future generations that was not an unmixed blessing.

However great the indignation the activists felt for the policies of their superiors in the fief, they had little real hope of getting them to reverse their policies. Violence might strike down one minister, as would be the case in Tosa, but it would result in the appointment of new men of comparable status and view. The status restrictions of feudal society were becoming strained but not broken, and those of low rank had little likelihood of affecting policy on their own. The *shishi* were not, in any case, constructive planners or thinkers. It was their special ability to create the disorder in which others might come to the fore, but they themselves were often little more prepared with alternatives than were many of the young officers who assaulted civilian politicians in the 1930's. The young officers trusted in "the army," and the *shishi* swordsmen trusted in "the court." As one of the assassins who took the life of the prime minister in 1932 explained, "We thought about destruction first. We never considered taking on the duty of construction. We foresaw, however, that the destruction once accomplished, somebody would take charge of construction."

The *shishi* turned to the Kyoto nobles as a counterweight to the feudal superiors they no longer respected. The small establishments of the Kyoto nobles had always supported a few rōnin who turned to them for employment. As loyalists from many areas turned to the Kyoto capital, it came to seem far nobler to be a "noble's samurai" (kuge zamurai) than a low-ranking worker in a han. The pay might be no better or worse, but there was an exhilaration about being attached to a national figure in an establishment where the individual was not kept in low estate by the pressure of many ranks above. And since only the adventurous and courageous turned to Kyoto, the atmosphere for the nobles' retainers must have been a far more stimulating and exciting one than it had been in the status society they had left.

So many samurai fled their han to become rōnin in late Tokugawa days that the problem of masterless warriors, which had seemed solved after the 1650's, once again became an urgent political and social matter. In the years since the seventeenth century the severity of the punishments for leaving one's lord and land had become considerably moderated. The stringent laws had remained on the books, but they were honored more in the breach than in the keeping. Runaways tended to be left alone unless they ran afoul of the Tokugawa police through infractions of the criminal laws. Even Tosa, a well-policed and remote fief, illustrated this laxity. Numbers of Tosa samurai had left their duties in the Edo barracks to leave the samurai class altogether, some to become townsmen and others to join previous runaways who had developed new fields at Ue-no-hara, a community in modern Yamanashi Prefecture. If the head of a samurai family defected to other regions or classes, the han usually confiscated or terminated the status and income of the family. Younger sons, however, posed less of a problem, and since they had little enough opportunity within Tosa many of them chose to leave. Of all the Tosa *dappan rōshi* (rōnin who fled the han) who left in late Tokugawa times, only one received the ultimate punishment. Okada Izō, a fencing student of Takechi Zuizan, fled to Kyoto. There he fell on evil days and into evil ways, robbing and murdering above and beyond the *shishi's* "high purpose." He was arrested by the Kyoto officials and handed over to Tosa authorities, who tried and beheaded him.[4] But this case serves chiefly to set off the numbers of refugees who fared better.

When, however, the flight of samurai became tinged with politics and with disapproval of the course of han administration, and particularly when it followed political assassination in Tosa, it came to be considered in a different light from previous defections caused by economic dissatisfaction. Pursuit and punishment now became common. Tanaka Kōken's memoirs make it clear that the *shishi* felt themselves in very great danger. "After all," he wrote, "the power of the bakufu then seemed very great, and even our [Yamauchi] lord's Sakawa retainer was very powerful." To flee from the han was like escaping prison, and even in Osaka or Edo, places where Tosa barracks were maintained and Tosa administration functioned, one could never be sure when he was being followed and might be caught. If caught, stringent measures to learn the whereabouts and plans of other defectors were certain. Numbers of samurai were apprehended even before leaving Tosa, and if they made off successfully their parents could be the sufferers. Tanaka continues, "At the time when I absconded my father was punished on that account; he lost his rank and stipend, and also his house. It was a dreadful thing, but my father had to become a rōnin on my account, barely able to support himself by a little teaching and things of that sort."[5] Obviously it required a higher duty to justify such unfilial conduct. Sakamoto and his fellows found it in the priority of the Imperial claim over those of daimyō and parents, which were championed by "stupid officials" and women. As Sakamoto would write to Tosa after his own flight, the daimyō did not seem to understand the idea of returning the

<hr />

[4] Teraishi Masaji, *Tosa ijin den* (Kochi, 1914), pp. 328-331, gives a brief account of this formidable swordsman assassin.

[5] Kumazawa, *Seizan Yoei*, pp. 110-113. But it must be remembered that Tanaka defected after the assassination of Yoshida Tōyō at a time when police measures might be expected to be particularly severe.

emperor to power: "Well then, what are we men of low rank to do to ease His Majesty's mind? As you know, one ought to hold the Imperial Court more important than his own province, and more important than his parents."[6] This, clearly, was the "highest duty of all." Fortunately for the *shishi*, it coincided with action and excitement.

The Tosa defectors were a year or more behind their fellows from Mito and Satsuma in activity and indignation. The *shishi* ideal was shown first of all in Mito, the center of loyalist teachings and the domain of Tokugawa Nariaki, whose denunciation of bakufu foreign policies had been most vigorous and whose hopes for the adoption of his son as shogunal heir had been dashed. Nariaki was confined to his residence by order of the Tairō Ii, and his retainers were full of indignation. It has already been noted that a party of Mito men which came to the Tachikawa border station in hopes of contacting confederates in Tosa had little success; its members found Sakamoto uninformed, and they failed to reach Takechi Zuizan. They had better success in their attempts to contact Satsuma *shishi*. The death of the able daimyō Shimazu Nariakira in 1858 had resulted in the emergence of a fief administration which discriminated against the favorites of Nariakira, and as a result there was abundant resentment of domestic policies as well as hatred of the bakufu minister who had thwarted their lord's last projects. Furtive messengers between Mito and Satsuma prepared the plans for an armed rising, and they also made their plans known to young nobles in Kyoto. For a time it was thought that the Satsuma administration could be won over to the use of armed force in the vicinity of the Imperial capital. Traditional cases of heroism and "higher duty" in violation of conventional obedience were cited in the documents prepared, and a plan to assassinate Ii Naosuke, attack foreigners in Yokohama, and occupy the Kyoto area under banners decorated with cherry blossoms (the Cherry Blossom Society of Colonel Hashimoto in the early 1930's comes to mind here) illustrated the combination of the cultural traditionalism, political resentment, and anti-foreignism that were to be invoked.

When the Satsuma administration proved unsympathetic to these goals, a group of forty men prepared to flee the confines of

[6] From the unpublished letter referred to in Chap. I, n. 54, preserved in Sakawa, in the Takana Kōken library, *Seizan bunko*.

Satsuma to fight the battle on their own. Police measures deterred them, but not their Mito associates.[7]

The loyalist years began on a snowy day late in March 1860, when a small party of eighteen *shishi*, one of them from Satsuma and the others from Mito, attacked the bodyguard of Regent Ii Naosuke as his procession was about to enter the Sakurada Gate of the shogunal castle. After the guard, encumbered by its protection against the snow, had been feinted out of position, one of the assassins took the Regent's head, made off with it, and disembowelled himself in front of the mansion of a member of the Senior Council. The shogunate's first minister had been struck down at the very gate of the castle in a daring plot that set the stage for years of violence to follow.

The Mito *shishi* had first prepared a lengthy document explaining their action; it serves as a useful guide to what it meant to be a loyalist in 1860.[8] There was not, as yet, any expression of determination to do away with the bakufu. Instead, the Regent was blamed personally for the evils of recent policy; his mistakes had resulted in a crime against the nation, and not only against the Tokugawa—that of admitting the foreigners to Japan. The Regent had disregarded the Imperial will, and this had led to a situation in which all Tokugawa fudai retainers should turn with shame and penitence to the Sun Goddess at her Great Shrine at Ise. In the face of such outrages "the highest duty of all" could be met only by resolute steps to drive out the barbarians. But, instead of taking steps to that end, the Regent had punished and humiliated those who had sought to keep him from his errors. Among those so discriminated against had been a "number of virtuous daimyō like the lord of Tosa." Such immoral policies had required the death of Ii Naosuke.

Throughout the document, Shintō and the Ise shrines of the Sun Goddess were invoked to rebuke the bakufu's first minister. It was apparent that anti-foreign feeling and loyalism would hereafter play a major part in gathering support for opposition to bakufu policies. The rebellion of Ōshio Heihachirō in Ōsaka in 1837 had brought home to all of Japan the severity of economic crises in the shogun's realm. The murder of the Regent Ii in 1860 revealed for the first time the strength and intensity of opposition

---

[7] These plots are described in *Ishin shi*, II, 663-730.

[8] Text in *Ishin shi*, II, 731-738.

to the new political and diplomatic moves. Small wonder, then, that in the principal castle towns young samurai whose training and sympathies gave them everything in common with the Mito *shishi* would consider their success a call to duty on the local and, later, national scene.

The Tosa Loyalist Party

The news of the assassination of the Tairō Ii Naosuke reached Tosa by way of a han merchant vessel returning from Ōsaka. The word spread quickly in Kōchi, but because of its lowly source and the difficulty of believing that the Regent could really be dead it was not immediately believed. Shortly thereafter confirmation came from the han residence in Edo through regular official channels, and then the full story spread quickly through the castle town.[9] In official circles the report did not stir very much enthusiasm. Yoshida Tōyō, who still served as first minister, disapproved strongly of the action of the Mito plotters, and felt that the bakufu had no choice but to punish Mito severely. He felt that Mito had fallen into ways of disorder and that the teachings of the great Fujita Tōko were being distorted by advocates of direct action. *Taigi meibun*, one may conclude, could never in Yoshida's eyes provide justification for attack on a bakufu minister. It is interesting to note that Yoshida's concern for obedience also led him to take a negative view of the deeds and morality of the 47 rōnin of Genroku times, an incident that was cited by those who defended the Mito *shishi*. A number of loyalist sympathizers among the upper ranks were critical of this narrow interpretation of duty and obedience.[10]

The younger, lower-ranking swordsmen whose training and sympathies gave them much in common with the Mito plotters were held back by none of Yoshida's inhibitions, and they came to consider the successful assassination a call to duty on the Tosa and, later, national scene. The story of the Regent's death was enthusiastically discussed by groups of Kenjutsu students. Soon they had access to a copy of the statement that the Mito assailants had prepared setting forth their objectives and beliefs. Sakamoto Ryōma spent many evenings with his friend Ike Kurata and other future loyalists in heated discussions of duty and legality. According to

[9] *Ishin Tosa kinnō shi*, p. 61.
[10] See especially Sasaki, *sekijitsudan*, pp. 120-121.

the usual accounts Sakamoto, whom the Mito men had considered so uninformed a few years earlier, was now most outspoken in his approval of the course the Mito *shishi* had taken, and he predicted that he and his friends would have to take similar steps in the future.[11] One wishes for more information about the activities of these months. It seems clear that the stage was being set for the process whereby friendships of the fencing academies were beginning to deepen into political brotherhoods as young enthusiasts, students of kenjutsu under Takechi Zuizan and of book learning with Mazaki Sōrō, began to see themselves as agents of ideological and political change. Unfortunately there is little or no correspondence for these days, as they were all in Kōchi, and because virtually the entire group met early deaths in the years that followed, there are few memoirs to follow. Still, it is neither difficult nor dangerous to see in the excitement that followed the murder of the Regent a setting conducive to articulation and activation of energies and ambitions previously dormant or half awake.

Opportunities grew for the upper ranks as well. Sasaki Takayuki, an umamawari (mounted guard) samurai with official position and loyalist leanings, recreates in his account much of the confusion that followed the death of Ii Naosuke. Great concern was felt in Kōchi for the safety of Yamauchi Yōdō, who was still in confinement in his Shinagawa residence. There had been much indignation among Tosa samurai over Yōdō's punishment, but until the Regent's death little action could be taken. Even thereafter there was still no way of determining whether the bakufu would increase or moderate its severity, and so a small detachment under Sasaki Takayuki was dispatched to Edo. Sasaki's account, written many years later, recreates the uncertainty and misgivings that slow communications and limited information caused.[12] Under him were ten young men—"one was a reading man, but the rest were all warriors"—all of them indifferent to comfort at night or

---

[11] *Ishin Tosa kinnō shi*, p. 62.

[12] One never knew, Sasaki notes, whether a traveller would return from a trip as far as Edo. Custom required that he step on a little stone outside the door. Sixty paces farther he would turn around while the family servants beckoned to him with a ladle to which quince was tied, calling "Master! Master!" Thereafter the ladle and quince were added to the shelf of family gods for daily worship, while the little stone was washed each day to guarantee him a trip without incident. When word of his safe arrival came, the stone would be wrapped, to be used—and washed—again on the return trip. Meanwhile a meal would be set for his empty place each morning. Sasaki's wife, being frugal, offered a dried fish head each day of his absence.

danger at river crossings. The trip coincided with a spring of exceptionally heavy rains, and it was particularly difficult to cross the swollen rivers. While travellers who stood on their dignity had difficulty securing bearers, however (after exasperated retainers of one man hit his porters, they "became angry and threw their luggage down and ran away—we would call it a strike today") Sasaki and his youths travelled with little luggage and made good time. The farther he went the heavier the traffic of emissaries from other han who had been dispatched on missions similar to his; regarding each other, as he says, as men from distant and different countries, the travelling samurai were insistent on their honor and prestige, and chary of help to each other. Sasaki arrived long before he was expected at the Edo quarters in Tsukiji. Bedraggled and ahead of his companions, he had to rouse low-ranking men stationed in the residence to secure his entry. Once there, however, he discovered that Yōdō was in no new danger; instead, the terms of his confinement were gradually relaxed. As a result, Sasaki's time in Edo was spent in political discussion and fencing practice.[13]

But the assassination of the Regent Ii affected the lower samurai who had political ideas most dramatically of all. Some of them, at least, began to see the possibility of changes in their personal and collective position. Many of the Tosa samurai had resented the bakufu's treatment of Yōdō bitterly, and their resentment of that injustice—as it seemed—easily brought them to resentment of the feudal institutions that had made it possible.[14] Their primary motivation, however, seems to have been an obscurantist hatred of foreigners which they related to their veneration for the Kyoto court. Lacking responsibility for negotiation and government, full of enthusiasm for the martial values of their own culture without being encumbered by much knowledge about the strength of the West, these loyalists were willing to trust in the strength of sword and spirit to repel the hated Westerners. Their thought was not yet firmly anti-Tokugawa, but it was becoming fiercely partial to the Kyoto court. In this the Tosa men were typical of their col-

[13] Sasaki, sekijitsudan, pp. 120-127.

[14] Hijikata's biographer drew on his subject's memory for the indignation of young bloods in Tosa who stormed about at the news of Yōdō's enforced retirement, and argued that it was nonsense to force a young, healthy man like Yōdō, whose efforts had been only for the national good, to retire on excuse of illness as though he had done something wrong. Iohara, Hijikata Hakushaku (Tokyo, 1914), pp. 20-21.

leagues in other southwestern han. Unlike some others, however, they had competent leadership under Takechi Zuizan, and in the absence of Yōdō they were able to exploit divisions within the upper brackets of the ruling groups in Tosa.

Takechi Zuizan had established himself as the undisputed leader of the young swordsmen in Tosa. Several months after the murder of the *Tairō* he was authorized by the han administration to tour Shikoku and Kyushu with three followers to survey the state of fencing. He returned in the fall of 1860, and the following spring, now 31, he travelled once more to Edo. The purpose of this trip of Takechi's is not clear, but it seems probable that he went as a fencing master for a survey of conditions in fencing circles at the capital. Certainly he moved and worked with complete freedom and in virtual disregard of han installations in Edo.[15]

Takechi reached Edo a year after the assassination of Ii Naosuke. Since that event a pattern of rōnin assaults and bakufu indecision had been established, and few periods could have been more exciting or stimulating for young swordsmen with a penchant for direct action. In Edo Takechi contacted men from many areas. The Mito samurai who had failed to enter the Tosa border station several years earlier were there to tell him about the upsets in their fief. Takechi also met leading figures from Chōshū. Kusaka Genzui, the fiery disciple of Yoshida Shōin, was there as acknowledged leader of the group of radicals who were terrorizing the foreign legations and who would, a few years later, swing Chōshū itself into the leadership of the extremist anti-bakufu and anti-foreign parties. From Chōshū also came Kido Kōin (at this time, Katsura Kogorō), also a Yoshida Shōin disciple, and a swordsman known in kendō circles all over Japan. Kido was to take over leadership of the Chōshū radicals after the death of Kusaka Genzui and Takasugi Shinsaku in later years.[16]

Through these men Takechi also met Kabayama San'en of Satsuma, a priest who specialized in the tea ceremony. Kabayama had had long periods of residence in Edo, and he knew many of the most strategic Satsuma officials, among them the Meiji leader Ōkubo Toshimichi (at this time, Ichizō). The Satsuma anti-foreign

[15] Hirao, *Takechi Zuizan*, pp. 29f.
[16] For Chōshū politics, Albert Craig, "The Restoration Movement in Chōshū," *Journal of Asian Studies*, xviii, 2 (February 1959), pp. 187-197, and Sidney Devere Brown, *Kido Takayoshi and the Meiji Restoration: A Political Biography 1835-1877* (Univ. of Wisconsin doctoral dissertation, 1952).

extremists were optimistic about their chances for attaining quick supremacy, and they recognized in Takechi a kindred spirit. "At the first meeting," Kabayama wrote in his diary, "I could see he was a courageous character."[17]

Takechi thus had opportunity to meet his counterparts from the other centers of loyalist thought and action. Kusaka and Kido told him about the teachings of their martyred teacher Yoshida Shōin, and wrote for him some of his poems as well. They were a little over Takechi's head, but his new friends explained carefully to him the full import of the Chinese verses.[18] Far from scorning Takechi for his lack of education, they recognized in him a leader and they respected his swordsmanship. Takechi introduced them to other Tosa figures in Edo, among them Ike Kurata, a figure who would reappear frequently in Sakamoto's enterprises later.

In this environment of new friends and new ideas Takechi Zuizan took steps to formalize his leadership of the Tosa swordsmen by securing their commitment to a statement of principles. The Tosa Loyalist Party was formed early in October of 1861. Its members endorsed the following statement of belief:[19]

"It is a source of deepest grief to our Mikado that our magnificent and divine country has been humiliated by the barbarians and that the Spirit of Japan [*Yamato damashi*], which was transmitted from antiquity, is on the point of being extinguished. Despite this calamity, men have become so accustomed to long years of peace and so used to indecision and laziness that not one has tried to stimulate this spirit in order to drive this misfortune from the land. Our former lord [Yōdō], however, was deeply grieved by this, and talked and debated about it with those in power; instead of securing action, he was accused and punished. Why should so noble a heart have drawn chastisement? It is said that when one's lord is humiliated his retainers must choose death. Must we not set even greater emphasis on the present situation, in which the Imperial Country is about to know disgrace? We now join our forces in this brotherhood to reactivate the Japanese Spirit; we will let no personal interests stand in the way, and we will plan together to bring about the rebirth of our nation. We swear by our deities that if the Imperial Flag is once raised we will go through

[17] *Takechi Zuizan kankei monjo* (Tokyo, 1916), I, 53.
[18] Hirao, *Takechi*, p. 34.
[19] *Takechi Zuizan kankei monjo*, I, 36-53.

fire and water to ease the Emperor's mind, to carry out the will of our former lord, and to purge this evil from our people. Should any, in this cause, seek to put forward personal considerations, he shall incur the punishment of the angered gods, and be summoned before his fellows to commit hara-kiri. In seal whereof we each affix our name hereto."

The only membership list of the Loyalist Party is one which was presented to Yamauchi Yōdō in March of 1863; the names of 192 men, among them that of Sakamoto Ryōma, were signed in blood.

As their pledge shows, Takechi's loyalists saw, as yet, no real conflict between their feudal duties to their "former lord" and their loyalty to the Emperor. If such a conflict should arise, however, it was probable that the claims of the Imperial Country would outweigh those of conventional loyalty to lord. In the meantime their dedication to a future whose outlines were only vaguely apparent brought into play the most sacred pledges of which they were capable; signatures in blood, a band organized, as "brotherhood," in family cohesion, and the ultimate penalty prepared for those who violated the spirit of the group to pursue "selfish" individual interests or opinions. The evil of which they spoke, described now as a disgrace, now as a disease, was the pollution of Japan's sacred soil by barbarians. In resisting this impurity and setting at rest an agitated Imperial mind they found sufficient authorization to justify breaking the feudal laws against forming parties.[20]

Takechi's list of 192 sworn followers did not by any means complete the roll of Tosa loyalists. It did, however, include men from all parts of Tosa. From Aki district in Eastern Tosa there was Nakaoka Shintarō. The learned and popular teacher of loyalist traditions in Kōchi, Mazaki Sōrō, was a signer. A few Takechi followers were not listed, presumably because their actions had become displeasing to the han administration by the time Takechi showed Yōdō his list. In this category was Yoshimura Toratarō, a *shōya* who became famous for his part in loyalist putsches outside of Tosa. The list did include almost all of the 83 Tosa loyalists who met their death in the next few years. It is clear, however, that loyalism was widespread throughout Tosa, and that Takechi's

[20] Hence Yōdō's characteristically jocular reaction when Takechi presented him with the signed pledge in 1863. "Hampeita," he first said, "do you like sake? Let me pour you some." And then, after a bit, "Your intentions are fine, but it's wrong to form a party. Let's burn the pledge." Hirao, *Yōdō Kō*, pp. 126-127.

was only the most important, most cohesive, and most active group of young men dedicated to this cause. In each part of Tosa, as can be seen from the map on pp. 4-5, there were loyalists, usually teachers, who had their own following. In Hata district Higuchi Shinkichi had trained nearly a thousand students in his school; in Takaoka district there was a vigorous group among the retainers of the Fukao family, and in Aki district Kiyooka Michinosuke had a generous following. Takechi's party was thus the visible evidence of a much more numerous group of confederates and sympathizers throughout the fief.

Who were the Tosa loyalists, and what did they represent? To their contemporaries they seemed to embody insurgent and disruptive social elements. Among the upper samurai Tani Kanjō, future general and statesman, and Sasaki Takayuki were in substantial sympathy with the stated purposes of Takechi's group. But, however sympathetic, their first loyalty was to their lord and to the feudal order of which he was the apex, and this kept them from associating themselves with their inferiors. As Sasaki later put it, "We tended to agree with Takechi for the most part, but since our relationship to our lord was quite different from Takechi's we could not approve entirely of what he did. And while his arguments seemed entirely peaceable and quite reasonable, nevertheless the dangerous thing was that the men behind him were almost all very low-ranking bravos."[21] In Sasaki's eyes, clearly the loyalist movement of Takechi was associated with, and bore the stigma of, lower-rank aspirations. Elsewhere he notes that all ranks from gōshi down were loyalist, and in one passage he goes so far as to say that while the gōshi loyalists talked a great deal about revering the Emperor they were more concerned with resisting their feudal superiors.[22] Tanaka Kōken, who participated, also described the Tosa Restoration scene as a struggle between ranks.

The official history of the Tosa loyalist movement speaks of the group as made up chiefly of gōshi and shōya. A recent effort to clarify the make-up of the loyalists shows that of one hundred twenty-seven men whose antecedents are reasonably clear there were fifty-four gōshi, fifty-one lower-ranking samurai (footsoldiers, etc.), fourteen village officials (shōya and elders), two upper samurai, two declassed gōshi, and one farmer, one doctor, one artisan, and one priest. The breakdown of twenty-three loyalists involved in a demonstration in Aki district in 1864 shows even more clearly this rural base; nine village officials, four *gōshi*, three farmers, two declassed *gōshi*, a footsoldier, a merchant, an artisan, a doctor, and a priest complete the list.[23]

It may be accepted, then, that leadership was provided by *gōshi* and *shōya* to a group for the most part rural-bred, trained in the private schools that were to be found all over Tosa, and barred from official preferment and subject to the decrees of the castle town. This, however, had been the case since early Tokugawa rule. The coming of the foreigners had provided a specific complaint that could be held against the feudal rulers, but for many, Sasaki suspected, more personal aspirations outweighed such generalized complaints.

The bête noire of the Tosa loyalists was Yoshida Tōyō, the minister of Yamauchi Yōdō who had done so much to improve preparedness in the fief. Some of this hostility, it may be suggested, derived from Yoshida's reforms. Designed as they were to increase the fief revenue and further military preparedness, these reforms had brought in their train more effective measures for control of the domain. Additional officials (*bugyō*) had been assigned to supervise coastal areas, steps had been taken to collect metal everywhere for the manufacture of modern weapons, intensified han monopolies had been designed to bring more commercial profit into the fief treasury, and new bureau offices were planned to send the paper, camphor, and other products so purchased to the new treaty ports for sale to the foreigners. These measures meant less profit and less autonomy for the rural leaders, and they could readily be opposed by calls for expulsion of the foreigners, for an end to the corruption of official enterprise, and for fief unity in the face of national crisis. Many of the rural leaders clearly had specific grievances, and several of Yoshida's measures had failed in the face of their protests. A strengthened paper purchasing system instituted in 1860 had to be abandoned because of protests, and *gōshi* in seven villages had protested a reform in the silver tax. Yoshimura Toratarō, a hereditary *shōya* who served ably in several posts and who quoted in his correspondence home some of the language of the Shōya League of the 1840's, may be taken

[23] Ikeda, "Tosa han ni okeru Ansei kaikaku to sono hantai ha," *Rekishigaku kenkyū* (Tokyo, 1957), No. 205, p. 27.

as illustrative of the way in which the self-confidence gained in local affairs could encourage intervention in large-scale problems. Thus resentment of the measures taken by the han under Yoshida Tōyō may have been an important element in the surge of sympathy which Takechi's loyalists inspired. The han administration later hesitated for over a year before disposing of Takechi's case in court, and one reason was precisely this consciousness of widespread support for him, support that might at any time flare up into rebellion. Indeed, the plans of Higuchi Shinkichi in Hata District for a revolt were stayed largely out of fear of endangering Takechi's life.

One point on which Yoshida Tōyō and his loyalist critics should have been able to agree was in their constant call for office for "men of ability" rather than for men or rank. It is clear that the loyalists saw themselves as beneficiaries of such policies, and their call for a domain united as one in furthering the anti-foreign war to ease the Emperor's mind implied a good deal less emphasis upon "selfish" considerations of hereditary position and privilege. Yoshida was himself no less eager to secure men of ability, but by his definition more such were to be found in the middle groups of the upper ranks. In this Yoshida and his critics were at least united against the very highest echelons of the feudal strata in Tosa, which was made up of the families and ranks which had traditionally reaped the greatest advantage from economic and social privileges. Yoshida's reforms had removed them from office and had lessened their autonomy in administering their large estates. Yoshida had not, however, gone so far as to seek administrative talent very far down in the feudal hierarchy, and as a result a combination gradually formed between Takechi's low-ranking loyalists and a few of the highest ranking of the old groups; Takechi was upset because Yoshida had not done more, the others were irate because he had done so much.[24]

Although there were these economic and social bases for the Tosa loyalist groups, one other, smaller group was indebted to Yoshida but not disposed to defend him. These were men who, like Sasaki and Tani, owed official positions to him, but disapproved of his commercialism and plans for exporting to the West as a form of grasping selfishness. They were intellectually pro-loyalist and anti-foreign although socially and politically conservative. How-

[24] Ikeda summarizes the evidence for these problems.

ever, it must be emphasized again that there were great differences between the economic interests of an urbanized *gōshi* like Sakamoto Ryōma and a rustic *shōya* like Nakaoka Shintarō. It must be remembered that many of the loyalists were clearly true to their pledge, fanatically intent on an anti-foreign war to cleanse the country of its Western stain, and anxious for the office and position from which they could carry out these purposes. For many, self-interest must have been involved, but the dangers and dedication of the times suggest that the force of ideas and idealism played as great or greater a part for most of the leading *shishi* who risked their lives for "the highest purpose of all."

His group formed in Edo, Takechi discovered that his new friends from Chōshū, Mito, and Satsuma were planning violent measures to show their disapproval of bakufu policy. They were particularly outraged by the impending marriage of the Emperor Kōmei's sister, Princess Kazu, to the young shogun. One group planned to intercept her cortege as it proceeded to Edo and return her to Kyoto, while another planned an assault on the Tokugawa Councillor Andō who had promoted the marriage.[25] Takechi, however, advised strongly against such measures. They would achieve nothing permanent, he felt, and they would be ruinously expensive in the lives of *shishi*. Far better, instead, for the confederates to return to their fiefs and organize samurai opinion there. If an entire han took a strongly anti-foreign stand, and if other han echoed this, a change in bakufu policy must inevitably follow. There was some disposition on the part of Kusaka Genzui and the Chōshū extremists to remain in Edo and proceed to direct action, but Takechi finally won his point. It was agreed that the *shishi* would try to persuade their respective lords to meet in Kyoto the following spring. Before leaving Edo Takechi was also able to convince Ike Kurata that he should disassociate himself from the plot on the life of Councillor Andō. The attack on Andō, which came early in 1862, failed of its purpose; the principal *shishi* of Tosa, Chōshū, and Satsuma had already returned to their fiefs to prepare for greater things to come.[26]

After his return to Tosa, Takechi devoted his first efforts to the conversion of Yoshida Tōyō and the han administration to his

---

[25] *Ishin Tosa kinnō shi*, pp. 68-74.
[26] *ibid.*, pp. 76f.; Hirao, *Takechi*, p. 42.

views. In several interviews with Yoshida, he explained the plans to which he had been party in Edo. Now was the time for Tosa to appoint men of ability, to adopt a firmly anti-foreign stand, and to prepare to join the Satsuma and Chōshū forces that were to be sent to Kyoto. Takechi also carried his message to several of Yoshida's assistants, among them Fukuoka Kōtei. It seemed to him that since the young daimyō Yamauchi Toyonori was due to go to Edo for his regular period of attendance at the shogun's court, the occasion for a procession to Kyoto was at hand; until the forces stopped in Kyoto, they would seem to be on the shogun's business.

Takechi found that his fief superiors did not welcome political advice from inferiors and that they considered him rash and extreme in his suggestions. Their major concern was still to avoid danger for their former lord, Yōdō, who had not yet returned to full bakufu favor. To reassure the shogunate of Tosa's dependability Yoshida Tōyō was planning to ship large amounts of lumber to Shinagawa to rebuild Yōdō's mansion there. Yoshida and his colleagues also wanted to delay the procession of young Toyonori until they had clear indication that Yōdō would be allowed to return to Kōchi. They did not want both symbols of feudal legitimacy out of Kōchi at the same time.

Most frustrating of all for Takechi was the scorn Yoshida showed for his stories of agreement with men from Chōshū and Satsuma. Takechi's assurance that those great fiefs would be mobilized by spring in accordance with the plans made by the swordsmen in Edo brought only condescending reproaches from Yoshida for taking a rōnin plot so seriously. If plans were really under way in Chōshū and Satsuma, he assured Takechi, the Tosa administration would have heard of them through regular channels. But in any event, the Tosa relationship to the Tokugawa was a special one, and it had been so since the battle of Sekigahara; Tosa could not lightly associate itself with the great fiefs of the southwest. Yoshida was even harder on Takechi's goal of cooperation with loyalist nobles in Kyoto; those "long sleeves," as he called them, knew nothing of politics. It would certainly be unwise to jeopardize relationships with the bakufu and endanger Yōdō for the doubtful advantages of working with men so politically immature as the court nobles.[27] In these talks one sees dramatized all the

---

[27] Takechi's talks with Yoshida are recounted in Hirao, pp. 56f.; and *Ishin Tosa kinno shi*, pp. 86-87. In his scorn for the political potentiality of the Kyoto nobles

contrasts between the responsible feudal official, conscious of the historic and strategic interests of his realm, and the emotional loyalist. Each was conscious of the need for reforms to build strength, but each operated from very different premises and on a very different schedule.

With the han administration fully aware of Takechi's plans and out of sympathy with them, it became more difficult for Takechi to leave Tosa. Still, since it was necessary for him to keep in touch with the confederates in Chōshū and Satsuma, he sent some of his assistants on liaison missions. His selection of Sakamoto Ryōma for an important assignment of this sort indicates how much confidence he had in his young admirer. Sakamoto's reputation as a swordsman made it relatively simple for him to secure travel permits to visit swordsmen and participate in tournaments in other areas.

Sakamoto was sent to Chōshū early in 1862. After a visit to the castle town of Hagi, he returned to Tosa by way of Ōsaka in March. The news which he brought back from Hagi was not very encouraging. The Chōshū administration had launched a policy of mediation between the shogunate and the court, hopeful that its role as sponsor of kōbu-gattai would improve its position relative to that of other fiefs. Kōbu-gattai, furthermore, was still weighted in favor of the bakufu and was designed to secure only modest gains for Kyoto, with the result that the Chōshū loyalists were bitterly opposed to the policy, although as yet unable to secure its modification or the dismissal of its symbol, the minister Nagai Uta.[28] It seemed unlikely, therefore, that the cooperation of Tosa, Chōshū, and Satsuma that had been anticipated could be achieved in Kyoto. But the Chōshū loyalists seemed prepared to risk a revolt to secure a change in their han's policy. Kusaka Genzui indicated this determination in a letter which Sakamoto carried back to Takechi in Tosa: "Ultimately it isn't enough for us to rely on our lords, and it isn't enough for us to rely on the court nobles. It is our opinion that we have no alternative to assembling

---

Yoshida must have resembled Yamauchi Yōdō himself. In later years Itagaki Taisuke, who first attained public office under Yoshida, wrote, "At the time I didn't know these kuge people,' and believed in them blindly. But as I look back now I see that many of them were shallow-brained and stupid. Yōdō, with his wisdom and intelligence, must have considered the nobles to be like children." Quoted by Hiraga, p. 147, from *Itagaki Taisuke Kun den.*

[28] For this stage of Chōshū policy, *Ishin shi*, III, 7ff.

our rank and file *shishi* and rising in a righteous revolt. Forgive me for saying this, but even if your han and our han should be destroyed, it would not matter so long as our cause is just."[29] As in Tosa, then, the emotional loyalists were prepared to risk regional security in the advancement of national—and, to be sure, personal—interests, but they found little response among their bureaucratic superiors.

Another messenger who travelled for Takechi was the *shōya* Yoshimura Toratarō who returned in the spring of 1862 from a trip to Kyūshū and Chōshū. He had contacted Satsuma and Chōshū loyalists as well as men in Kurume and Fukuoka, across the Straits of Shimonoseki from Chōshū. Yoshimura also brought news that revolts were imminent. Loyalists in Kurume and Fukuoka, he announced, were preparing to rise together with those in Chōshū. Satsuma men had assured him that the Satsuma Regent, Shimazu Hisamitsu, was about to advance on Kyoto with a large force of men to provide leadership for the loyalist cause. Yoshimura himself had promised to return to Chōshū later in the spring to join in the fighting, and he urged Takechi that if an insurrection could not be organized in Tosa the loyalists should flee the han to join their friends in Chōshū.

News of this sort found a quick response among Takechi's followers, many of whom urged him to lead them across the Inland Sea. But Takechi was reluctant to take direct action. He still hoped for a favorable han decision. Yamauchi Yōdō he thought, would be partial to his plans, and there seemed little need to alienate him by direct insubordination. Takechi's reluctance was also related to his strong feelings of loyalty and obligation to his fief. What would become of his lord and of Tosa if the loyalists fled or revolted? It seemed clear to him that the path of duty lay in correcting his fief's policy rather than in abandoning it to plunge into national politics with his followers.[30]

As Takechi refused to lead his partisans out of Tosa, and as the anticipated date of the Chōshū and Satsuma actions neared, the Tosa loyalists became more and more impatient. Their resentment of the limited political and social importance their status afforded them grew, and they were more prepared to denounce their superiors as hopelessly conservative and pro-Tokugawa. There were

---

[29] *Takechi Zuizan kankei monjo,* I, 60.
[30] *Ishin Tosa kinnō shi,* pp. 101ff.

a number of incidents of disrespect shown *gōshi* by upper samurai, incidents usually triggered when one or both parties to the insult were in their cups.[31] The official history of the Tosa Loyalist Party, *Ishin Tosa kinnō shi*, is a lengthy lament of upper-rank stupidity and inflexibility. In the numerous memorials which were submitted to the authorities urging the selection of han officials according to "ability," it is not difficult to see the personal interests and prejudices of lower-class *shishi* at work. And as these failed to have effect, numbers of loyalists, unable to stand the inaction any longer and fearful of missing out on the great events that lay ahead, slipped past the border stations and took up the rōnin life in Chōshū or in Kyoto. Yoshimura Toratarō, who had failed to convince Takechi of the necessity for forceful measures, left Tosa after hearing that Chōshū confederates were gaining the upper hand in their fief. Takechi saw him go reluctantly, but persuaded him to leave behind a friend who had access to the han administration's police plans.

Sakamoto Ryōma also became impatient with Takechi's inaction. In the latter part of April 1862, a few weeks after Yoshimura's flight, Sakamoto heard that Chōshū and Satsuma *shishi* were gathering at the Teradaya, an inn south of Kyoto near the Satsuma station in Fushimi. Determined to be a part of the rising that seemed imminent, Sakamoto fled together with a friend named Sawamura. Sakamoto's flight distressed his friends, who saw his departure as a serious blow to their party in Tosa. It dismayed his elder brother Gompei, who had tried to keep him at home. Sakamoto had bypassed Gompei by borrowing money to finance his trip from another relative. He had also consulted another of the loyalists, Hirai Shūjirō, about contacting Hirai's sister who was in service with the Sanjō family in Kyoto. But Hirai was not prepared to sacrifice his sister for Sakamoto's schemes. Instead, he wrote her to warn her against becoming an accomplice in any plans that Sakamoto might develop.[32]

It is of considerable interest to observe the way in which the *shishi* saw their own actions, and Sakamoto's views of his depar-

[31] It is clear from the memoirs of upper class samurai like Sasaki and the accounts of lower-class figures like Tanaka Kōken that tensions mounted in the late 1850's and 1860's as political change intensified social strains. For an account of such an incident in which Sakamoto Ryōma was among those involved, Sasaki, pp. 131-138.

[32] *Sakamoto Ryōma kankei monjo*, pp. 59-60.

ture from Tosa are probably best revealed by further reference to the letter he wrote the parents of Ike Kurata in 1863 to explain why their son had just fled from Tosa. In it one sees mirrored the strains on filial and feudal loyalty that his action caused. Sakamoto criticized the daimyō for thinking only of their own interests: "Truly," he wrote, "loyalty to what we call the Divine Country has no influence on them. They do not understand the idea of returning the Emperor to a position of power, and yet it is the thing that needs most to be done. In such a case, what are men of low rank to do to ease His Majesty's mind? You know that one should hold the Imperial Court more dear than one's country, and more dear than one's parents. The idea that in times like these it is a violation of your proper duty to put your relatives second, your han second, to leave your mother, wife, and children—this is certainly a notion that comes from our stupid officials. And yet confused parents take their cue from them, talk of 'our country' and 'our home,' until their sons do not know what stand to take."[33]

Two weeks after Sakamoto's flight Takechi, who had seen some of his best men leave Tosa, decided that it would be necessary to take action against Yoshida Tōyō. The action seemed necessary in order to make possible Tosa participation in the *shishi* plots that seemed to be coming to fruition. Rōnin were gathering at Fushimi, the Satsuma host was approaching, and the Chōshū men were preparing to overthrow their conservative administration. If the Tosa administrators were allowed to defer the sankin-kōtai trip of their young daimyō indefinitely, the best opportunity for adding Tosa strength to the contingents gathering in Kyoto would be lost. Furthermore it seemed probable that action against the fief's first minister would not be very dangerous. Yoshida was sufficiently aloof and unpopular to have little support among the main body of Tosa samurai, and he had alienated completely the retainers of top rank whose posts, incomes, and authority he had weakened. A number of scurrilous pamphlets were circulating in which Yoshida was denounced as a "Wang An-shih." When Takechi consulted with some of Yoshida Tōyō's most eminent enemies, he found that they were not willing or able to take direct actions themselves—they had already requested his resignation and

[33] See above, n. 6.

failed—but he received the clear impression that they would not be horrified if others were to do their work for them. Many of them were in any case bitterly anti-foreign, and prepared to sympathize with the loyalist criticism of Yoshida's plans for trade with the outside world. These same groups were likely to be the basis of an administration after Yoshida's fall. Thus fear of investigation and punishment was not a major deterrent to direct action. Takechi made his decision and organized a squad of assassins.

On May 8, 1862, Yoshida Tōyō was returning to his home from the Kōchi castle, where he had just lectured to his young lord from Rai Sanyō's *Nihon Gaishi*.[34] It was raining, and Yoshida was carrying an umbrella. With him were five of his men, among them Gotō Shōjirō and Fukuoka Kōtei. Suddenly the little party was assailed by swordsmen. One of these, Nasu Shingo, struck Yoshida down from the rear and took his head. From Chōshū, where he had fled to the house of a merchant who was a loyalist sympathizer, Nasu wrote his father about his achievement.[35]

"We made up our minds to strike on the first day of the fourth moon, and thereafter we met every night. Our chance finally came on the eighth. We made a pledge together to take his head and expose it at the execution grounds. There were just ten of us, carrying parcels and waiting around at the fourth bridge; we were apparently heading for the Goddess of Mercy Pavilion. Just before midnight Yoshida returned from the castle, and we were waiting for him at the Obiya intersection. I was all set to strike him from the rear and take his head, and expected to do it with one blow, but my sword struck his umbrella and was deflected. Then the men with him drew their swords and we had to do a little parrying. But soon I had a chance and took his head. Now I had to take it to the Goddess of Mercy Pavilion. First I stopped to wash my sword and the head in the ditch by the roadside, and then I wrapped up the head in a cloth I had brought for the purpose. I rushed to the west from Obiya machi along the southern street of special tradesmen. Along the way the dogs barked wildly at me; and as they were snapping at the head I wasn't sure what to do. Finally, though, I somehow got to the Goddess of Mercy

---

[34] Yoshida's choice of this celebrated loyalist work as subject shows that he was not by any means blindly pro-Tokugawa as his enemies charged.

[35] The merchant Shiraishi played a prominent role in the politics that lay ahead. His diary is in *Ishin nichijō sanshū* (Tokyo, 1925), 1, pp. 1-146.

Pavilion, and there I was able to hand the head over to my friends. Now it was peaceful again, and I could pack for my trip."[36]

Nasu's friends mounted Yoshida Tōyō's head at the Kōchi execution grounds over a wooden sign on which were written for all to see the crimes of the executed leader. It is significant that the charges made no reference to national politics, but played on the issues which would evoke the greatest response in Kōchi. Yoshida, the sign charged, had abused his high office and responsibility. He had manipulated han finances to his own advantage, and his vigorous economic policies had produced a wild and reckless extravagance which had impoverished the commoners, denuded Tosa timber stands, and weakened the han fiscal structure at a time when it had desperately needed strengthening. He had been punished in order to ease the distress of the people and to atone for his great crimes.[37]

The fires that had been lighted outside the shogun's castle by the Mito rōnin who murdered the Regent Ii had now spread to the very gate of the Yamauchi keep in Kōchi. The fruits of the fencing academies had proved to be not so much protection against the foreigners as direct action against statesmen who refused to heed the extremists.

As Takechi had anticipated, the murder of Yoshida Tōyō was not vigorously investigated. Yoshida was not popular, and his death was greeted with a wide variety of derisive jests. The three men directly concerned in the assassination made their way to Chōshū and thence to Kyoto, where they received protection from their Chōshū and Satsuma friends. For a time it seemed possible that the investigation of the affair in Kōchi might implicate Takechi Zuizan, and the *shishi* prepared to resist such a development with force. Their efforts proved unnecessary largely because of the cooperation with some of the more highly placed enemies of Yoshida Tōyō, especially Yamauchi relatives whose privileges and income had been jeopardized by Yoshida's reforms. Friendly let-

---

[36] Original in the Sakawa, *Seizan bunko*, and quoted in part in *Ishin Tosa kinnō shi*, p. 116. The assassins next fled to Kyoto via Osaka, where they were in touch with Tosa sympathizers. In Kyoto they received sanctuary first from Kusaka and his Chōshū men and then, after Shimazu Hisamitsu left for Edo, confident he had crushed his own extremists, they were sheltered in the Satsuma yashiki. For their doings see *Ishin Tosa kinnō shi*, pp. 136-141.

[37] Text, *Ishin Tosa kinnō shi*, p. 118, and summarized in Hirao, *Takechi*, p. 78.

ters from Yamauchi Toyotaka to Takechi succeeded in stopping the loyalists' preparations for war, and while calm continued the han administration was reformed.[38]

Yoshida's death was followed by a complete overturn of personnel in high administrative posts. The changes were arranged by the long-retired daimyō Yamauchi Toyosuke (ruled 1809-1843, d. 1872), a man who had thwarted the Tempō Reforms of Mabuchi Kahei, and who had never approved of Yoshida Tōyō's measures. With Yamauchi Yōdō still in Edo there was no one to defend the reform group, and as a result the Yoshida appointees were almost all dismissed from office. For the most part the new officials represented a return to the old guard. They had opposed Yoshida's radical measures for strengthening the fief, and they preferred the old order with its guarantees for family and tradition. Some of them were inclined to look with some favor on the loyalist movement, but for the most part their conservatism far outweighed any loyalist sentiments they might profess. In high posts only two men, Kominami Goroemon and Hirai Zennojō, were partial to the loyalists; both of them served as Ōmetsuke, or Great Inspectors. As a result the lower echelons of the police service came to be staffed by Takechi men. Most sectors of the administration, however, were strongly affected by the conservatism of the Yamauchi branch families. The most influential person in the new regime was an arch conservative, Koyagi Gohei. Collectively, the administration leaned toward the position that was to become known as sabaku, or "support for the bakufu." The loyalists had not, in other words, come a great deal closer to positions of power. Takechi, by any measure the most dynamic figure in the Tosa political scene after the death of Yoshida Tōyō, could not hold office in the new regime because of his low rank. Instead the posts went to uninspiring conservatives of impeccable lineage whom Sasaki, who had disliked Yoshida and who was willing to see him go, had to admit were nonentities.[39]

It should have occasioned no surprise that the new administration was no more willing than the old to let the young daimyō (Toyonori was 16) go to Kyoto and Edo, there to be drawn into political whirlpools. Takechi found, however, that there was more

[38] For the derisive comments that greeted Yoshida's death, Hirao, Takechi, pp. 80-82. Yamauchi Toyotaka (Mimbu) was Yōdō's younger brother, the seventh son of Yamauchi Toyoaki.

[39] Sasaki, pp. 182-183.

time than he had at first thought. The rōnin plot his men had gone off to join collapsed when Shimazu Hisamitsu of Satsuma, from whom the plotters in the Fushimi inn had expected assistance, instead sent his troops to crush them on May 21. The first rōnin plot since the seventeenth century had failed. Numbers of participants were captured and handed back to their fief police. Among these was Yoshimura Toratarō, who was returned to Tosa jurisdiction. Sakamoto Ryōma, who had planned to join the Teradaya rising, had instead gone on to Edo, so that he was not involved.

As a result there was less urgency for Tosa participation in national politics, and Takechi had time to wage a careful campaign to force his young lord to leave the fief. The impending sankinkōtai duty in Edo still seemed to offer the best occasion for the trip. At Kyoto loyalist nobles, no doubt on the prompting of their rōnin confederates, approached Sanjō Sanetomi to have him urge his Yamauchi relative to visit Kyoto on his way to Edo. In Kōchi Hirai Shūjirō, a Takechi follower, memorialized to the same effect. Satsuma and Chōshū, he pointed out, had forces in Kyoto; Tosa should not allow itself to be left behind others who were working to effect a closer relationship between Kyoto and Edo. The sole loyalist among the Yamauchi branch families also added his opinion in a document which referred to the presumed wishes of Yōdō, and warned of the folly of forgetting national duties because of personal obligations to the Tokugawa. In answer, however, the cautious mediocrities in Kōchi had their young lord respond that because of his youth he could have no opinion on public matters until he had had the opportunity to proceed straight to Edo, there to consult with Yōdō.[40]

Through their friends in Kyoto, the Kōchi loyalists were able to get word to Sanjō asking for an Imperial request to Toyonori to stop in Kyoto on his way to Edo. This request resulted in the dispatching of a special han messenger to Edo to consult Yōdō. Takechi had already sent his chief lieutenant, Mazaki Sōrō, to Edo, so that the cause was well represented there. Yōdō advised respectful attention to the Imperial request. The Kōchi officials, however, were still afraid that they would be drawn into political eddies not to their liking, and they ruled that their young lord should go directly to Edo to consult Yōdō before making up his mind about Kyoto.

40 Hirao, *Takechi Zuizan*, pp. 100-103.

Toyonori's procession, which had been held up since April 6 by excuses of illness and disturbance, finally left Kōchi on July 22, 1862. It was the largest Tosa mission in many years. The reasons were not entirely of Toyonori's making. As the cortege was being formed, large numbers of *gōshi* appeared in Kōchi clamoring for permission to accompany their young daimyō. They were reluctantly added to the procession and its costs. There were some six hundred samurai of all ranks with Toyonori, and if service personnel is included the procession, according to some accounts, numbered over a thousand men.[41]

The plans for the Kyoto stop were still not definite when nature took a hand. Near Ōsaka an epidemic of measles hit the young daimyō and his train and brought the ungainly movement to a dead halt.[42] The month-long halt in Ōsaka provided time for further maneuvering by the loyalists. Messages were speeded back and forth to Edo. New evidences of growing bakufu weakness helped to make the Edo visit less essential, while from Kyoto came messengers with new requests from the court itself pressing for a visit there before going on to Edo. The daimyō train was mired in indecision for fully a month before another message from Yōdō approving the visit to Kyoto decided the issue.[43]

On September 18 Toyonori's train finally entered Kyoto to add its numbers to the confusion and disturbances there. Takechi, who was one of the procession, could now resume his plotting with his friends from other fiefs. The Tosa loyalists had finally forced their superiors to enter national politics. Immediately after the Tosa entry, an Imperial rescript urged young Toyonori to remain in Kyoto to help defend the court from the foreign threat.[44] It required no rescript to turn Takechi's efforts to this task.

[41] Hirao, p. 105; Sasaki, p. 184; *Ishinshi*, III, 233-234. Osatake, I, 288, gives the figure 500 men for the subsequent mission to Edo.

[42] The daimyō processions had, in this manner, long been a force for spreading disease and pestilence the length of the country. Several smallpox epidemics in late Tokugawa Japan swept along the sankin-kōtai routes.

[43] During the wait the loyalist bravos were able to assassinate one Inoue Sashirō, a former *yokome* ("side glance," police investigator) under Yoshida Tōyō who had aroused their fear by his efficiency during the investigation that followed Yoshida's death. Hirao, *Takechi Zuizan*, p. 110.

[44] "Now we have heard that you, Matsudaira, Tosa-no-Kami, who have been in charge of the Ōsaka defense, are about to pass by Fushimi. So we have hereby determined to ask you to help protect the palace by staying in Kyoto for some time to come." *Ishin Tosa kinnō shi*, pp. 156-157.

3. The Shishi in National Politics

The Kyoto scene on which the Tosa contingent appeared was one of great political confusion, and in order to understand the actions of the Tosa loyalists it will be necessary to make brief mention of developments in national politics after the murder of Ii Naosuke. Those politics were complicated by the economic dislocations that had accompanied the opening of foreign trade. The combination of international markets and domestic economizing had tended to lower samurai stipends and to raise the cost of living at the same time, and dissatisfaction with these conditions helped to exacerbate samurai anger and focus it against the foreigners. As was to be expected, it was particularly the lower samurai with modest stipends who felt these changes most acutely. For rōnin who had fled to Kyoto, of course, the uncertain price level was only another indication of the wrongs which had followed the opening of the country. These considerations helped to increase the flow of armed, desperate, and angry men whose thoughts turned easily to violence against the foreigners and the authorities who had admitted them to Japan.

National politics were also confusing because the great tozama lords seized issues and changed their stands in accordance with the likelihood of self-advancement with the shogunate or court. Within each fief there was, as in Tosa, a sharp debate as to whether prudent adherence to traditional restraint in national politics (which came down to *sabaku*, support for the bakufu), efforts to mediate between court and bakufu (kōbu-gattai), or sponsorship of the loyalist and anti-foreign cause (sonnō-jōi) would best serve the fief interest. As in Tosa the first, or sabaku, stand was associated with the traditional holders of fief power, the second, of kōbu-gattai mediation, with more energetic reformers and planners, while the third, which smacked of radicalism, was the natural refuge for low-ranking and more discontented groups. Factional and bureaucratic rivalries prevented these categories from being exclusive ones, but the main pattern was sufficiently prevalent to justify a distinction among conservative, moderate, and radical solutions to the problem of fief policy. These factions could profit from external situations and internal pressures. Internal pressures consisted of the obvious preponderance of the lowly in rank and emotionally anti-foreign, so that at key points mention of "general opinion" could be made to justify shifts in policy in their direction. External situations showed a constant rivalry between the great lords, especially between Shimazu of Satsuma and Mōri of Chōshū, who were at least as distrustful of each other as they were of the bakufu. The Tosa daimyō, conscious of weakness relative to his more powerful neighbors, would consistently avoid recourse to force, in which he could hope only to be an auxiliary and never a leader, and showed a preference for mediation, in which his role could be central. Chōshū led with mediation until Satsuma seemed to be winning out at the same tactic, at which Chōshū shifted to sponsorship of loyalist extremism. Each such shift, in turn, meant an internal bureaucratic shift from one faction to another, not infrequently accompanied by execution or assassination of the proponents of the conflicting position. And since all of this was influenced by and acted upon bureaucratic rivalry within the shogunate itself, the kaleidoscopic political changes of the loyalist years were of such complexity that they need concern this narrative only so far as they affected the principal Tosa figures.

After the murder of the Regent Ii the bakufu councils showed little imagination or initiative. Ii's departure brought to the fore Andō Nobumasa, a fudai appointment of Ii's who planned to continue the regent's policies in foreign affairs, and Kuze Hirochika, a man previously dismissed and now reappointed in hopes of restoring some contact with the Mito faction. These men symbolized the two conflicting positions and parties, but they lacked imagination or institutional security sufficient to make possible combining the two or eliminating either. There was no determined purge of Mito supporters. The new Mito daimyō was forbidden access to the shogunal palace and his rebellious retainers were rounded up and executed or hounded into suicide, but there the punishments for the Regent's murder ended. On August 25, 1860 Tokugawa Nariaki, the Mito ruler who had played so large a part in the politics of the past few years, died, and thereafter Mito han politics were dominated by a fierce internal strife between those who favored continuation of Nariaki's policies and those who preferred a closer alignment with bakufu leaders. Although a Mito party continued in being around the person of Nariaki's son, Hitotsubashi Keiki, Mito power as an institutional factor would not again loom large.

The new bakufu administration devoted its first efforts to improving relations between Edo and Kyoto. One of the principal steps that were projected to bring this about was the marriage of an Imperial Princess, Kazu no Miya, to the young Shogun Iemochi. This measure, which was opposed by the Emperor Kōmei (because the princess was already affianced to Prince Arisugawa, who later would lead the Imperial armies against the Tokugawa holdouts) was carried through only after vigorous debate at court. One of the most effective arguments in support of the move came from the pen of Iwakura Tomomi, who had become one of the emperor's trusted advisers. Iwakura urged the match on grounds that the way was not yet prepared for a full struggle with the bakufu. It seemed to him unwise and dangerous to place full reliance on the tozama lords, who had their own interests in view, and that the court therefore had no real alternative to approving the bakufu request. It would be best, he wrote, to "concede in name what we retain in substance," grant the shogunal request, and use it for leverage to influence future bakufu policy. As a result the court urged the Tokugawa government to prepare steps to expel the foreigners, and the bakufu agreed to cancel the treaties by negotiation or expel the foreigners by force "within from seven or eight to ten years."[45] The agreement was made in the late summer of 1860. The princess was brought to Edo in November of 1861, and the marriage took place in January 1862. It was for his part in these negotiations that Takechi's *shishi* friends proposed to assassinate the bakufu councillor Andō Nobumasa. They failed to kill him, but the wounds he received in the attack of February 13, 1862 resulted in his retirement from office. *Shishi* distrust extended to Iwakura, who had supported the marriage, and they secured his dismissal from his court posts in September of 1862.

Next came the gradual relaxation of the controls that Ii Naosuke had placed on the daimyō who had opposed his policies. Yamauchi Yōdō of Tosa was allowed somewhat greater freedom in August of 1860, but it was not until May 23 of 1862 that Yōdō, together with Matsudaira Shungaku of Echizen and Hitotsubashi Keiki, was given full freedom to communicate with others again. Thereafter the three were gradually restored to honor and im-

[45] The texts can be found translated in Beasley, *Select Documents*, pp. 198-206.

portance. This was particularly important in the case of Matsudaira Shungaku and Hitotsubashi Keiki, whose relationship to the Tokugawa family qualified them for office. In June the two were received by the shogun, and then efforts began to persuade them to accept advisory positions. The fudai traditionalists in Edo were less prepared to admit them to the decision-making process, however, fearful that Keiki, whose nomination for shogunal heir they had opposed so vigorously a few years earlier, might regain in substance what he had been denied in name.

With reconciliation in the air, the great lords of the southwest did their best to act as spokesmen for it. The first to act was Chōshū which, although it had contributed more than its share of loyalist *shishi*, had not incurred suspicion through official action. The Chōshū councillor Nagai Uta was the leading advocate of this policy for his fief. In 1860 he submitted a memorial, "A Far Sighted Plan for Navigation," which advocated opening the country and promoting reconciliation between Edo and Kyoto. Since his position on opening was clearly in line with that of the shogunate, his reconciliation plan necessarily involved winning Kyoto over to support of the shogunal acts, and this early version of kōbu-gattai was as a result weighted heavily in favor of the bakufu. Nagai Uta won his daimyō's support, and he was authorized to travel to Kyoto and to Edo to work for his proposals there. His lord, Mōri, followed him to complete the work begun by his councillor, but while he was in Edo in February of 1862 the *shishi* attack on Andō Nobumasa removed Andō from office. Rising currents of extremism in Kyoto and in Chōshū doomed further efforts by Nagai to promote his version of kōbu-gattai. Since he could not deliver a settlement as proof of the wisdom of his policy, he was discredited. Within Chōshū both the archconservatives and the activist loyalists had opposed his stand vigorously—indeed, Chōshū *shishi* had figured importantly in the attack on Andō—and as a result, Nagai's efforts ended in failure, and his life ended with an order to commit suicide in 1863.[46]

An important and perhaps the central element in the Chōshū shift of policy is to be found in the fact that its position had been eroded by Shimazu Hisamitsu of Satsuma, who had come to the fore with a version of kōbu-gattai far more to the liking of the Kyoto court and who, as a result, seemed to have appropriated

[46] *Ishin shi*, III, 7-40.

for himself the only version of mediation that had any chance of success. It was now associated with exclusion of the foreigners, and hence weighted in favor of the position favored by the Kyoto court. Hisamitsu left Kagoshima on April 14 with a large host of over one thousand. It was from this body of men that the *shishi* wrongly expected help in their plans, and much of the agitation in Tosa took place against a background of expectation that these troops, together with the rōnin who were gathering at the Tera-daya in Fushimi, would reap the victory alone unless Tosa loyalists were allowed to participate. The *shishi* had, however, misread Shimazu intentions; the Satsuma ruler was firmly conservative. He first sent some of his chief trouble makers back to Satsuma, then urged the court to take steps to control the obstreperous rōnin, and finally did his own part by crushing the Teradaya plotters on May 21, 1862. This action drove the *shishi* to look to Chōshū for help in their future plans, and it ruled out any possibility of Satsuma-Chōshū cooperation for several years.

Shimazu Hisamitsu came with a set of plans designed to imple-ment kōbu-gattai in such a way as to improve both the position of the court and that of the great lords of the southwest. When refined and sharpened in accordance with the thinking in Kyoto, these gradually became three major points. The first was that the shogun should come to Kyoto to consult on national policies with the court, thereby rendering him in some measure responsible to the Emperor for his actions. The second called for a greater role for the lords of the great coastal fiefs, somewhat as in the days of Hideyoshi in the sixteenth century. The third called for the ap-pointment of two men in whom those lords had confidence as high shogunal officials. Matsudaira Shungaku was to be Political Di-rector (*seiji sōsai*), while Hitotsubashi Keiki, who had been denied the shogunate by Ii Naosuke, should be named heir and Shogunal Guardian (*kōken*). When this program was worked out an Im-perial messenger was sent to Edo to communicate this to the sho-gun. The court noble Ōhara Shigetomi was selected for this as-signment, and as escort Shimazu Hisamitsu accompanied him with his impressive body of troops. Nothing could better have drama-tized the change in court standing, for while previous court emis-saries had been sent with few attendants for ceremonial occasions, Ōhara now found himself protected by the most powerful daimyō of western Japan. The Ōhara-Shimazu mission reached Edo on July 6, 1862.

The Edo fudai daimyō resisted some of the suggestions of the mission, and they were particularly reluctant to grant Hitotsubashi Keiki and Matsudaira Shungaku policy-making positions in the shogunate. But persuasion and fear of assassination, plus the hope that it would be possible to sabotage the new offices that had been forced upon them, led to capitulation on August 1, when Matsudaira Shungaku and Hitotsubashi Keiki received their appointments. Other reforms followed. On September 24 the lord of Aizu, Matsudaira Katamori, was appointed Protector of Kyoto (*Kyoto shugoshoku*), and placed above the Tokugawa *shoshidai* who had traditionally supervised all contacts with the court. The family and partisans of Ii Naosuke were punished in order to atone for Ii's misdeeds against the court. Reforms in military, official, and clothing regulations were announced. And, under the influence of Matsudaira Shungaku and his adviser Yokoi Shōnan, the sankin-kōtai regulations were drastically revised on October 15, 1862. Family hostages were permitted to leave Edo, and the time period for daimyō duty there was changed to reduce it to one hundred days in three years. The announced purpose of this change was to permit the lords to utilize the economies that would result in fortifying their realms. Most of them, after extricating their families from Edo, headed for Kyoto. It was also there that Shimazu Hisamitsu, his mission apparently successful, returned in September. On the way, at Namamugi, came the celebrated murder of the Englishman Richardson who, the Satsuma samurai claimed, tried to cross through their procession.[47]

Shimazu Hisamitsu found the situation in Kyoto very different from the one he had left a few months earlier. After his departure from Kyoto Chōshū had changed its stand, dismissed Nagai Uta, and adopted a much more fervently pro-Kyoto position—one that

---

[47] Pompe van Meerdervoort, the instructor of Medicine in the early school set up for that purpose at Nagasaki, adds an intriguing footnote to the Richardson affair in his memoirs. "When I boarded train in The Hague on my return on December 31, 1862, I met by coincidence an uncle of Richardson's who was, as I recall, on his way to Texel as an expert for Lloyd's to inspect a ship which had stranded there. We struck up an acquaintance and he asked me about the incident involving his nephew. After I had told him everything which I have written above, this unassuming, gray-haired old gentleman answered me, 'That's just the way Charles always was, incredibly reckless and stubborn; I always said something like that would happen to him. He had to leave England because of crazy stunts, too.' " *Vijf Jaren in Japan* (Leiden, 1868), II, 143.

resulted in a shift of court support from Satsuma to Chōshū again. Then, on September 18 the procession of the young Tosa daimyō Toyonori had added hundreds of additional samurai to the Kyoto scene. Takechi and the loyalists, who were part of that procession, immediately set about adding their efforts to swell the tide of extremism and anti-foreignism. It was apparent that kōbu-gattai, if anything at all remained of it, would now be much more court-centered than Shimazu Hisamitsu had anticipated or intended, and that to be court-centered would mean being *shishi*-inspired and influenced. The *shishi*, whose friends had so recently felt the edge of Satsuma swords at the Teradaya, were in no sense partial to the Satsuma effort. The Satsuma ruler, therefore, left Kyoto for Kagoshima. His presence there was in any case required by the growing crisis with Great Britain, which was pressing for satisfaction for the death of Richardson.

Kyoto now became the undisputed center of national affairs. The shogun was preparing to come to consult with the Emperor in accordance with the Imperial request conveyed by the Ōhara-Shimazu mission, and daimyō were taking up residence in increasing numbers. But the principal influence and impression that the city gave was that of disorder and violence which resulted from the large numbers of *shishi* and rōnin loyalists. Thanks to their efforts, the influence of anti-foreign court nobles was growing; Anenokōji Kintomo and Sanjō Sanetomi were in positions of influence, while Iwakura Tomomi, whose view of political possibilities was a more rational one, had been forced into retirement as punishment for his earlier advocacy of the match between the shogun and the Princess Kazu. Iwakura, who feared assassination, went into seclusion at the Saihōji Temple outside Kyoto, and there he meditated and commented on the news which reached him from the capital until such a time as it was safe for him to return.[48]

Kyoto belonged more and more to the kuge-zamurai and rōnin who thronged its streets. They had the company of old friends who reappeared as influential persons in the trains of the daimyō of the great southwestern han. With inadequate policing and with a swollen population of warriors, the Kyoto streets were un-

---

[48] Iwakura was under great pressure and in constant danger of "punishment" from loyalist extremists. For the details of his flight, see Tokutomi Iichirō (Sohō), *Iwakura Tomomi Kō* (Tokyo, 1932), pp. 98-104.

safe for any who were suspected of preferring the old order to the new.

The *shishi* collected naturally around some of the court nobles whose views were known to be anti-foreign and anti-bakufu, and none fitted this description better than Sanjō Sanetomi. Sanjō soon achieved a considerable influence and following among the low-ranking swordsmen. They were dazzled by his social eminence, his proximity to Imperial councils, and by his vigorous views. Furthermore, since he was related to the Yamauchi family, he was in a logical position to become the lodestar for the Tosa loyalists. Takechi and his friends had utilized the Sanjō connection earlier to secure the Imperial request for a visit from Toyonori. From 1862 on through the rest of Tokugawa rule, Sanjō would have a following of faithful Tosa *shishi*. They would accompany him on his flight to Chōshū later, and watch over him while he was in political exile.[49] At this time Sanjō Sanetomi was 25. Also popular with the *shishi* because of his readiness to listen to their extremist councils was Anenokōji Kintomo, a young nobleman 23 years of age.

The Tosa *shishi* now worked smoothly with extremists from Chōshū and a few from Satsuma; together they controlled and terrorized Kyoto. Within han administrative echelons, the Tosa loyalists also improved their position relative to the conservatives who had opposed entry into Kyoto. With a flood of Imperial requests and commissions coming to the sixteen-year old daimyō, the conservatives lost ground to Takechi and his partisans. Koyagi Gohei, in fact, soon gave up hope and returned to Kōchi.

The weeks that followed were weeks of unparalleled effrontery and violence. Shortly after Takechi arrived in Kyoto, he composed a memorial which he passed on to friends in the court and to which he affixed his young lord's name. This sought to advance the cause of the court one step farther than had yet been done, and it was perhaps the boldest call for restoration of power to the throne that had yet been made. Takechi proposed three basic steps. First, he suggested that the entire Kinai plain around Ōsaka and Kyoto be brought under direct rule of the Court, that daimyō with holdings there should be moved, and that the area should be garrisoned with troops under the control of court nobles and the

---

[49] Hijikata and Tanaka, in particular, were members of the small group which stayed with the refugee kuge.

court itself. Ōsaka merchants, he felt, could be ordered to pay for whatever expenses were involved. Once the court was safe in this manner, the order could be given to drive out the foreigners. Secondly Takechi proposed that the sankin-kōtai system be revised sharply so that daimyō would need come only once in three or five years. In the third place, Takechi proposed that the court resume responsibility for all political decisions. "All political orders," he wrote, "should come from the Court and the daimyō should come to Kyoto instead of Edo for sankin-kōtai duty." Takechi's memorial did not expect much in the way of bakufu resistance to a strong court stand. Let the Court make a military display by mobilizing seven or eight more large han, he argued, and the bakufu would take a respectful attitude.[50]

As the *shishi* grew in power and confidence bakufu prestige and police power waned in Kyoto. Shortly before the Tosa entry into Kyoto a wave of violence had begun. With the arrival of new recruits from Tosa, it grew in violence. Enemies, real and fancied, and officials with a real or supposed connection with the purge conducted by the Regent Ii in Kyoto three years earlier were struck down. Within a short time some eight men were killed, and in the boldest strike a party of twenty-four Tosa, Chōshū, and Satsuma loyalists overtook and ambushed a Kyoto magistrate and his party who were returning to Edo. The term *tenchū*, Heavenly Punishment, began to appear on placards and sheets distributed by the *shishi*. Scurrilous charges, denunciatory signs on walls, and tear sheets scattered in the streets brought the threat of heavenly punishment to many more than the number actually struck down. The *shishi* succeeded in terrorizing and intimidating many by their tactics. The great merchants of the area were natural targets of the campaigns, and they frequently had to pay to ward off the punishment of heaven. For these who doubted or scorned the threats, the sight of heads of the swordsmen's victims, exposed on the principal streets of Kyoto with placards explaining their crimes, served as somber warnings.

During this same period pressure skillfully applied at the court resulted in the ouster of high court officials who were considered pro-Tokugawa in favor of others more closely identified with the Sanjō-Anenokōji group. For the young court nobles, as for their military allies, virtue was equated with loyalist extremism, and opposition conservatives were "evil officials."

[50] *Takechi monjo*, I, 109f.

In this atmosphere was developed the project for another embassy to Edo. As a result of the Shimazu-Ōhara mission, the shogun was planning to come to Kyoto, and Hitotsubashi Keiki was coming to make advance arrangements. The *shishi* and their *kuge* friends felt that their position would be stronger if they could avoid the possibility that Keiki, by being reasonable, would lessen the tension. Instead, they decided to present the shogun with another Imperial demand. To this end there was devised the plan for a second embassy headed by Sanjō Sanetomi and Anenokōji Kintomo. Takechi and his Chōshū allies worked in close harmony with their court contacts in the appointment of the embassy. It was appointed November 12, 1862, and it got under way on December 3. With it as escort and protector went sixteen-year-old Lord Yamauchi Toyonori with five hundred men. The letter that the mission carried was an Imperial request for an immediate campaign to expel the foreigners from Japan. Thus the anti-foreign fanatics had succeeded in forcing the shogunate into a position of very real embarrassment. Some of them may have been using the foreigners as a stick with which to strike the bakufu, but there is every indication that Takechi and his Tosa men were fully sincere in their demand for an immediate and desperate struggle against the foreigners.

The mission also had some portentous signs of things to come. Takechi, who had come to Kyoto in his lord's train as a *gōshi*, was now a member of the mission which his lord was escorting to Edo, in the retinue of the court noble Anenokōji. Instead of his old name he now bore the honorary title Yanagawa, Lord of Chikugo. He had exchanged the long blade with which he had become famous for the dainty sword of a court noble, and instead of striding along in the dust he rode in a palanquin. It is not difficult to see what a satisfactory outlet activities of this sort must have been for the low-ranking samurai who, a year earlier, had not been able to get a respectful hearing from his han officials. "When we arrive in Edo," Takechi wrote his wife, "I'll get to enter the castle, and I am to see the shogun. We will also offer gifts. And the Lord Shogun will give us gifts of clothing. Truly, it is astonishing." And, of the men assigned to him, "I'm followed everywhere I go by these fellows; it's really just like a *kyōgen*."[51]

The mission reached Edo on December 18, 1862. Its demands

[51] *Ishin Tosa kinnō shi*, pp. 189f.; *Takechi monjo*, I, 138.

precipitated a serious crisis for the new bakufu reform administration under Matsudaira Shungaku and Hitotsubashi Keiki. Shungaku, immediately discouraged and indignant at the turn of events, promptly tried to resign his position. Keiki was not long behind him, but both were persuaded to reconsider. In the complicated maneuverings that followed, Yamauchi Yōdō played an important role. Yōdō thought he saw in the Kyoto demands for exclusion a political trap, and advised the bakufu to stay out of that trap by making a general commitment of exclusion without giving specific guarantees of when it would be done. To reject the demand outright, he feared, would only bring civil war. Through his relationship to Sanjō, Yōdō was able to restrain his impatience, while he also worked to have Shungaku and Keiki reconsider their resignations. When the Chōshū *shishi*, impatient with the time the talks were consuming, decided to improve their leisure hours by exterminating the foreigners in Yokohama in order to start the anti-foreign war, Yōdō heard about this from Takechi in time to send his own men to Yokohama to try to stop them. In turn, he very nearly precipitated violence between his men and those from Chōshū.[52] Thanks to Yōdō's moderating influence, the Sanjō-Anenokōji mission returned to Kyoto toward the end of January 1863 with the bakufu's formal acceptance of the order to drive out the barbarians. No clear date was set, however, and the coming conferences of the Shogun and his officials in Kyoto were presumably designed to settle the details.

From Takechi's point of view the mission must have been an unqualified success. He had gone in the train of a court noble. On his return to Kyoto, his young daimyō promoted him a grade, to rusuigumi, so that he finally became an upper samurai. The Yoshida Tōyō followers were out of office, scattered, and, in some cases, murdered. Yamauchi Yōdō had reemerged into political activity, and could, he thought, be expected to counteract whatever continuing conservatism would come from the old guard in Tosa.

A few days after Takechi left Edo with the Sanjō mission, another detachment of Tosa loyalists came into Edo. Its development furnishes a good example of the disruption which the confusion of the times made in the conventional feudal pattern.

---

[52] Chōshū samurai spoke ill of Yōdō's caution, ascribing it to cowardice, and thus incurred the wrath of their Tosa colleagues. A Tosa plan to kill the Chōshū leader, Sufu Masanosuke, misfired. *Ishin Tosa kinnō shi*, pp. 220-225.

In Kōchi there had been continuing fears for the safety of Yamauchi Yōdō. It was known that he had reemerged as a bakufu
councillor, and it was known that he had used his influence to
effect the changes that had been made to lessen daimyō obligations under the sankin-kōtai system. Slow communications produced exaggeration, and garbled tidings in Tosa convinced some
of the loyalists that their former lord was now in danger of physical violence at the hands of bakufu conservatives. Others undoubtedly used the rumors of Yōdō's unpopularity in Edo as an
opportune excuse to enable them to leave Tosa and engage in
national politics. Whatever their reasons, a party of fifty men,
mostly *gōshi*, gathered in Kōchi and demanded permission to go
to Edo to save Yamauchi Yōdō.

One of the most important members of the group was Nakaoka
Shintarō; and for him the trip marked the entry into national affairs. Nakaoka, the eldest son of a *gōshi* in eastern Tosa, ruled an
area which produced approximately 1,520 koku in late Tokugawa
times. He had had schooling with Mazaki Sōrō and fencing with
Takechi Zuizan, and he was a charter member of Takechi's loyalist
group. As a *shōya* he had also had experience which contributed
to independence and responsibility. In his area he had sponsored
terracing and reforestation, and in emergency he had borrowed
money in Kōchi to help his people through a year of famine. Despite his early interest in the loyalist movement of Takechi, Nakaoka had not been able to leave because of his commitments as
an eldest son; he had succeeded to his father's position in 1857. In
the excitement of 1862, however, he could restrain himself no
longer, and he was among those who organized the party of 50
gōshi.[53]

The group, of which Nakaoka was an officer, petitioned for permission to leave Kōchi, and received its request on December
seventh. It had a stormy trip to the capital. The swashbuckling
swordsmen hoped for an Imperial rescript authorizing an attack.
On their way to Edo they managed to settle a few scores with
some old enemies who had served under Yoshida Tōyō, and their
arrival in Edo can hardly have had a calming attitude on the political situation. The arrival of the party of 50 in Edo balanced

[53] Ozaki, *Nakaoka Shintarō*, pp. 19f.; Nakaoka's development and entry into
the loyalist circles is more reliably detailed by Hirao Michio, *Rikuentai shimatsuki*,
pp. 6-9; for the group of 50 *gōshi* and *shōya* and Nakaoka's participation, *ibid.*,
pp. 19-25.

shishi strength in Kyoto with loyalist contingents in Edo. The new recruits first of all went on record with an emotional pledge to work for Yōdō's welfare.[54]

Like their counterparts in Kyoto, the *shishi* in Edo adopted a dress and behavior which they considered appropriate to their idealistic, non-materialistic values. They let their hair grow long and scorned to shave or wash. They wore thin and informal clothing in the Edo winter, and strode around on wooden clogs in their bare feet. Careless of appearance and improvident, they were not above borrowing or extorting funds from merchants as seemed necessary.[55] They were full of "Japanese spirit"; several considered hara-kiri to stimulate their colleagues to greater heroism, and were talked out of it only with difficulty. They were, as they were dubbed, children of the storm, bravos, and toughs. Revolutionaries without a program and followers in search of a leader, they were groping toward a society in which their chances for eminence would be better than they had been in the past. Yet there was also a genuine patriotism in their make-up, and they acted on the belief that their land was in danger. The foreigners were upon them, and it was much more important to do something immediately than it was to carry on a logical and rational discussion of the content and significance of that danger. The vague, shifting, and often contradictory slogans of Restoration days suited these revolutionaries perfectly, for they required no adherence to a program not yet in sight.

Still, it should not be concluded that all of the loyalist *shishi* were swashbuckling swordsmen and that their thought was centered solely on slaughtering real or fancied enemies. It is true that the political thought of many of the Tosa comrades was rather rudimentary. Kamioka Tanji, when asked by Takechi if he did

[54] The pledge, given in Hirao, *Rikuentai*, pp. 19-20, stressed elements of loyalty, fearlessness, and obedience to the instructions of their leaders. It was the sort of statement the han authorities could not possibly censure, and they had little alternative to allowing the 50 to proceed to the capital, the more so since they were going at their own expense. But actually the trip was self-willed by loyalists anxious to join in the activity on the national scene, and after their exit and its results the han government adopted new rules to block similar plans in the future.

[55] The attire, and some of the spirit, of the *shishi*, survived into modern times in the attitudes of students of the special higher schools (*kōtōgakkō*); perhaps it was also a basic element in earlier samurai schools; Fukuzawa's account of his Ōsaka student life is strongly reminiscent of this. And certainly the attractive and unattractive features of *shishi* life were sedulously cultivated by members of the recent ultra-right wing groups, who tended to support themselves in more or less the same casual manner as well.

not have some suggestion to finance han needs at this time when opportunity was so great, could do no better than to suggest that they point out to the Osaka wealthy that since Osaka would immediately be ruined if war should come, they would be well advised to lend Tosa 200,000 ryō immediately. Should the merchants resist, Kamioka went on, the *shishi* who approached them should commit hara-kiri to show his intense sorrow and sincerity. He predicted that no merchant could stand the sight of more than three such suicides. Takechi saw merit in the plan, but other *shishi* were less concerned for han finances.[56] But others had better plans. Mazaki Sōrō thought that Tosa leaders, like those of Chōshū, should purchase foreign steamships to engage in trade. A han office was set up at Yokohama to market Tosa products to raise money for arms. Takechi favored setting up a school to train young samurai in Western science, and Hirai Shūjirō engaged in negotiations with Ōsaka merchants to increase the flow of Tosa commodities to that market center.[57] Thus the Tosa enthusiasts, faced with the need to recoup han finances after the heavy drain to which they had subjected them, were turning to some of the devices which Yoshida Tōyō had sponsored earlier and which Tosa would pursue again in three or four years under new leadership. There was, however, an important difference to be discerned: while Yoshida Tōyō's policies had been motivated above all else by a desire to strengthen the position of the han, the *shishi* usually thought first of larger goals and concerned themselves with han needs only as a preparation for more intense activity on the larger, national scene.

4. The Decline of Loyalist Extremism

The loyalist successes in national politics just described were the result of cooperation between *shishi*, backed by the Chōshū han, and young court nobles; together they capitalized on the foreign relations problems to reverse the trend toward cooperation between Kyoto and Edo. But the loyalist ascendancy was of short duration. There were several reasons for this. One was that the *shishi* overplayed their hand, working for powers not even the court was eager to accept. Furthermore the foreign powers demonstrated that expulsion of the barbarians could not be taken literally and thereby invalidated a basic premise of the primitive ob-

---

[56] *Ishin Tosa kinnō shi*, pp. 294-296.
[57] *ibid.*, pp. 166-167, 241, 259-262.

scurantism of the early *shishi*. In the third place the prominence of Chōshū in Kyoto affairs and the extremist course brought down the wrath of Shimazu Hisamitsu of Satsuma and resulted in a brief period of military cooperation between Satsuma and the bakufu. These events had a direct bearing on Tosa policy and the fate of Takechi's loyalist party.

The Sanjō-Anenokōji mission had produced the promise of a shogunal visit to Kyoto, and this came about in the spring of 1863.[58] Not since the seventeenth century had the Edo ruler visited Kyoto, and although Iemochi's suite consisted of over three thousand men this could not conceal the weakness that his visit signified. With the shogun came Matsudaira Shungaku and Hitotsubashi Keiki. At Kyoto they found a political setting hostile to them. Bureaucratic changes at court had shifted personnel and offices to put more power into the hands of Sanjō and Anenokōji, thereby consolidating the anti-foreign power. New violence in Kyoto was accompanied by rōnin decapitation of statues of the Ashikaga shoguns as symbol of what the *shishi* had in mind for their successors.

Steps were now taken to deal with rōnin and *shishi* violence. The Aizu lord, Matsudaira Katamori, who had assumed the title Protector of Kyoto in September of 1862, decided to utilize rōnin to control rōnin. Instead of ordering his retainers to fight or avoid the Kyoto activists he encouraged them to mix with them and report on their doings, and he ended by organizing a number of special rōnin corps to fight for the bakufu. The *Shinsengumi* and several similar groups were thus prepared, drilled in complete obedience to the corps commander, and trained to strike in the same terrible manner that the loyalists had adopted.[59] Several years later Sakamoto would fall victim to members of a unit of this sort.

In the political discussions held between the shogunal party and the court, the bakufu was commissioned, for the first time, to

---

[58] Osatake, *Meiji Ishin*, I, 314-344, gives a good account of the visit and its significance.

[59] One of the few studies of this is that of Hirao Michio, "Bakumatsu rōnin to sono hogo oyobi tōsei," in Shigakkai, ed., *Meiji Ishinshi kenkyū* (Tokyo, 1930), pp. 552f.

"conduct civil government as heretofore." This interesting authorization, which had never before been issued, was evidence of the Tokugawa need for legitimization of its power and authority. Equally significant was the ritual discourtesy shown the shogun by members of the Imperial court when he was taken to visit Kyoto shrines. When a second tour of shrines was planned, both the shogun and Keiki excused themselves on grounds of illness. Most important of all was the reluctant acceptance by Hitotsubashi Keiki of June 25, 1863 as the date for expulsion of the foreigners from Japan. This unrealistic promise, which Keiki hoped to be able to change or weaken, would soon serve as authorization for individual action by Chōshū, while in Edo it brought denunciations of Keiki by traditional fudai officials who claimed he had put them in an impossible position. Matsudaira Shungaku had meanwhile resigned his commission, although he retained much of his importance in future negotiations between Edo and Kyoto.

The Satsuma ruler Shimazu Hisamitsu was full of indignation at the Chōshū and rōnin dominance in Kyoto. In the spring of 1863 he returned briefly to Kyoto again to attempt to sponsor kōbu-gattai as he understood that much-interpreted term, but he found the court totally under the influence of the extremists. Chōshū showed the vigor of its anti-foreign position when the date set for expulsion arrived. Without bakufu authorization, Chōshū interpreted the June 25 promise to mean the opening of a general anti-foreign war, and shelled foreign shipping in the Straits of Shimonoseki. Then, on July 8, the young court noble Anenokōji Kintomo was killed in Kyoto by assassins who tried unsuccessfully to strike down his companion Sanjō Sanetomi as well. Chōshū loyalists seized upon the uncertain evidence that Satsuma men were guilty to secure the expulsion of Satsuma troops that provided part of the guard service at the Imperial palace.[60] Next, the loyalist allies pushed for a further step in their plans by suggesting that Kyoto should take over full responsibility for foreign affairs. Friends at court produced an Imperial Edict authorizing a campaign against the barbarians led by the Emperor. All of this was done despite the known reluctance of the Emperor Kōmei to accept such responsibility, and it produced a worried request to Satsuma's Shimazu Hisamitsu to restore order.

[60] Osatake, II, 367f.; *Ishin shi*, III, 428-432.

The stage was now set for a dramatic reverse of loyalist fortunes. On September 30, 1863 a swift coup on the part of Aizu and Satsuma units seized the gates to the Imperial palace and barred Chōshū troops from entering. Chōshū units retired from the capital in confusion, and with them went a group of seven loyalist court nobles. Sanjō Sanetomi, the idol of the Tosa *shishi*, was one of the seven. The loyalists' chief support, Chōshū, was now in trouble with the foreigners over its shelling of Shimonoseki and it had lost all opportunity to plead superior knowledge of the Imperial intention. The loyalists' favorite court nobles were in exile. Suddenly there seemed little hope or likelihood of gaining the goals that had seemed so near a few months earlier.

The loss of the Chōshū foothold in Kyoto doomed several putsches that the loyalist extremists had planned; deprived of support, they now became acts of desperation. In Yamato a Heavenly Loyalty (or, written differently, Punishment) Band (*Tenchūgumi*) included the Tosa *shōya* Yoshimura Toratarō among its leaders. Confederates in the Kyoto court had planned an Imperial procession to the Nara shrines, and a rising was planned to coincide with the procession, thereby establishing Imperial loyalty and producing risings of sympathizers in other parts of the country. The main force of seventy-five men under the nominal leadership of the nobleman Nakayama Tadamitsu, a youth closely identified with Yoshimura and his Chōshū friends, sailed from Kyoto to Sakai and then moved inland to the office of a bakufu bailiff. This man was murdered together with four assistants, and their heads were exposed with denunciatory placards pronouncing the region under the direct rule of the Emperor. Promises of a 50% cut in taxes and general permission to assume family names and swords were held out to attract support. Among the leaders men from Tosa were most numerous; there were three lower samurai, two *gōshi*, three *shōya*, and seven others not clearly identifiable. Many *gōshi* of the Yamato area, which was one with a traditional attachment to the court, joined in and recruited participants in the villages; according to some sources the number of those participating reached nearly two thousand. The September 30 political change in Kyoto doomed the attempt. The Imperial procession was cancelled, help from Chōshū was not forthcoming, and the neighboring han obeyed bakufu commands to send troops to crush the rebels. Yoshimura Toratarō was wounded and afterwards commit-

ted suicide in a farmhouse; a number of leaders, including Nakayama Tadamitsu, made their way to Chōshū.[61]

Related to the Yamato putsch, and designed to help it, was a
rising at Ikuno, near modern Kobe, where a group of enthusiasts
under the nominal command of Sawa, one of the nobles who had
fled the court in September, tried to set up an area under direct
court rule. Actual command lay with Hirano Kuniomi, a veteran
loyalist agitator. The plans called for *gōshi* in the area to recruit
several thousand farmer-soldiers. When it became clear that the
Tenchūgumi had failed, Hirano tried to cancel the revolt, but he
was overruled. As in Yamato, a bakufu bailiff station was occupied,
and then manifestoes to the inhabitants of the neighboring areas
made the customary charges and promises. The area would come
under direct Imperial rule, and taxes would be halved for the next
three years. Unlike Nakayama in Yamato, however "Commander"
Sawa fled as bakufu troops approached from Himeji, and when
the villagers saw the discomfort of their leaders they turned on
them instead of fighting the bakufu samurai. The rising ended
ignominiously as a result.[62]

The principal chapter of loyalist violence came in Kyoto, where
Chōshū elements tried to regain the position at court which they
had lost to their Satsuma competitors. Feelings of bitterness toward the bakufu and Aizu were eclipsed by the resentment against
the intervention of Satsuma forces. Late in 1863 a notice to all
Chōshū retainers still stressed loyalty to the bakufu, but pointed
to Aizu and Satsuma elements as han enemies. On February 1,
1864, a Satsuma ship was shelled in the Straits of Shimonoseki.
Shortly afterwards Chōshū men burned a Satsuma ship in the

[61] An excellent account is that by Hara Heizō, "Tenchū-gumi kyohei shimatsu
kō," *Tosa shidan* (March 1938), No. 62, pp. 1-31, and (June 1938), No. 63, pp.
14-36. See also the succinct account of Osatake, *Meiji Ishin*, II, 485-501.

[62] The Ikuno revolt is summarized in Osatake, II, 502-519. There is also a concise analysis in *Rekishigaku Kenkyū*, p. 127 (1947), by Tōyama Shigeki and Hara
Heizō, "Edo jidai goki ikki kakusho," pp. 27-29, which seeks to trace the motiva-
tions of the *shōya* and wealthy peasants (*gōnō*) who led and lost in the rebellion.
The authors show that the Ikuno area was one directly controlled by the bakufu,
that it had a long record of revolts, and that the *shōya* and wealthy peasants were
consistently the sufferers in riots directed against money lenders and sake brewers.
They also trace the business ventures of representative local leaders in Meiji times
to buttress their case that these were the emerging petty bourgeoisie, able to arouse,
but not to effectively channel, popular discontent of the "people." On the other hand
the biography of one of the Ikuno revolt leaders, *Hirano Kuniomi den*, p. 152,
which ascribes the swift loss of popular support to inconsiderate behavior on the
part of drunken leaders.

Beppu harbor. Chōshū tempers were rising, and they snapped when the bakufu's rōnin troops, the Shinsengumi, surprised a group of Chōshū and Tosa *shishi* in the Ikedaya in Kyoto on July 8, 1864. Word had reached the bakufu of a proposed coup, and to head off large-scale trouble the Ikedaya plotters were surrounded and attacked with a loss among them of seven dead, four wounded, and twenty captured. When word of this reached Chōshū, han units were moved to the Osaka area by ship. That the Chōshū troops, divided into several units, were able to enter Kyoto without difficulty illustrates better than anything else could have done the way in which the bakufu had lost the military initiative. In times of crisis and fear, it was no longer an act of automatic rebellion to move troops into the once-forbidden capital without the shogun's permission.

The tension in Kyoto exploded when a Kumamoto xenophobe killed Sakuma Shōzan on August 12 as the great Westernizer rode along on his Western-style saddle and trappings. A week later the ancient capital was the scene of bitter fighting as Chōshū troops drove for the gates of the palace. At the Hamaguri gate, the focal point of the struggle, the issue was for some time in doubt, but the Aizu, bakufu, and Satsuma troops finally prevailed. Numbers of important loyalist leaders, including Kusaka Genzui, were killed. Sympathizers like Maki Izumi also met their end, and Nakaoka Shintarō, who had remained with the Chōshū forces, was wounded. The bakufu followed its military victory with the execution of the prisoners from the Ikuno and Yamato risings who were still in prison.

Immediately after this the violent discontent and hatred that had long smoldered between the loyalist and conservative factions in Mito erupted into a civil war whose end, with the conservative forces victorious, left that han so drained in leadership and resources that Mito ceased to figure in national politics thereafter.[63]

[63] The general collapse of discipline is illustrated by the expedition of about 800 Mito insurgents to Kyoto to put their case before Keiki who was, it will be remembered, the son of Tokugawa Nariaki of Mito. Although the rebels had to fight their way past bakufu troops at the outset, they had little or no difficulty along the inland road thereafter. The han along their route reported to the bakufu their "resistance" to the "rebels," who invariably "escaped." Often the "pursuit" was not launched until the group had passed the han borders. The group finally surrendered to Kaga forces, who handed them over to Tokugawa "justice" as supervised by their Mito foes. 353 were executed, and 137 banished. Osatake, II, 555-580. There is also a brief account by E. W. Clement, "The Mito Civil War," in *Transactions of the Asiatic Society of Japan*, XIX, 1891.

Against this background it is instructive to follow the fate of the Tosa loyalists within their own fief. The return of Yamauchi Yōdō from confinement in 1862 would in any case have cost them much of their freedom of action. Yōdō was not a free agent, however, for like other daimyō he had to take account of opinion among his retainers and at the capital. Unlike most of his fellows, however, he did so skillfully and in such a manner as to maintain his own counsel and position. Yōdō deserved the appraisal of the British interpreter Mitford, who wrote of him that "He was a far-seeing man of the highest intelligence . . . gifted with that magnetic attraction which is so rare even amongst the greatest men and which fully accounted for his influence among his peers."[64] His influence among his inferiors was even greater, and he took full advantage of this to keep himself aware of their plans. Like Matsudaira Shungaku, Yōdō took time to listen to rōnin and *shishi* in an effort to gauge the state of "public" opinion. In an age before mass communications, it was prudent to check with men who voted with their swords. Yōdō flattered them, wined them, and encouraged them to tell him of their plans. His own fondness for wine endeared him to the *shishi*, and they came away from such encounters with profound veneration for their lord.[65]

The loyalists were long confident that Yōdō was on their side. He had been punished by the Regent who had approved the treaties which opened Japan to trade, and it was logical to suppose that he had opposed those treaties. Furthermore, he had more recently advised the bakufu to give in to the demands of the Sanjō-Anenokōji mission for expulsion of the foreigners. The young daimyō Toyonori had, to be sure, been a useful front for loyalist activities, and his recent marriage to a daughter of the Chōshū daimyō could be expected to keep up the Tosa standing in the loyalist cause.[66] Still, young Toyonori could not possibly exert the leadership of which Yōdō was capable, and the Tosa partisans wanted a strong leader to enable them to maintain equality with their Chōshū friends. It is certain that they had no idea, as yet, of removing or by-passing their lord altogether.

[64] *Memories by Lord Redesdale* (New York, n.d.), II, 483-489.

[65] For a Nakaoka interview with Yōdō, see Hirao, *Rikuentai*, pp. 38-39.

[66] When the hostage provisions of the sankin-kōtai system were repealed early in 1863, three generations of Yamauchi wives left Edo together: Toyosuke's wife, a Shimazu from Satsuma; Yōdō's wife, and Toyonori's new Chōshū bride. *Ishin Tosa kinnō shi*, p. 239.

The loyalists were therefore anxious to have Yōdō back in Kyoto, and they arranged with their friends at court to have him summoned to the capital in the fall of 1862. The call came just as Yōdō was beginning to exert his influence in Edo again, and since he played an important role in the reception given the message of the Sanjō-Anenokōji mission he was able to secure a delay before going to Kyoto.

In the meantime he had to face the problem of the party of fifty gōshi and shōya who had rushed to Edo to "protect" him in December of 1862. Yōdō was concerned by the violence of his low-ranking retainers, and when he first received word of the coming of this group he considered taking steps to try to stop them in the Osaka area. After their arrival in Edo, Yōdō ordered the creation of a special group of fifty upper samurai to counter the threats of their feudal inferiors. The commander of the new unit, an umamawari (mounted guard) member, was Itagaki (then Inui) Taisuke, later Restoration hero and founder of Japan's first political party. After Itagaki had organized his group of stalwarts, the loyalists had the assurance that violence would be met with violence.[67] Thus in Edo and, later, in Kyoto and Kōchi, Yōdō utilized class lines to strengthen and bolster policy plans. Itagaki himself and many of his men were personally anti-foreign and increasingly pro-Kyoto, but they could not bring themselves to join their social inferiors who were disturbing the established order. Itagaki, moreover, had entered government service as a protégé of Yoshida Tōyō.

Having checked the violence of the party of fifty, Yōdō had contacted some of its more responsible members. Early in 1863 he entrusted to Nakaoka Shintarō, the shōya from eastern Tosa, a mission to Matsushiro to approach Sakuma Shōzan, the expert on things Western, with a request to consider employment in Tosa. Nakaoka went together with Kusaka Genzui, the leader of the Chōshū radicals. They first travelled to Mito, presumably to contact shishi there, and then headed north into modern Nagano prefecture to consult the famous scholar. It would seem that Kusaka also carried with him a request for Sakuma to enter Chōshū employ. This strange procedure, if known to Yōdō, may reflect the fact that he was using the invitation as a device to remain au courant with developments among his loyalists. He may also have rea-

[67] Gekai suikō, p. 185.

soned that the contact with Sakuma would prove educational for Nakaoka. It would seem, however, that Sakuma Shōzan dazzled his visitors with such a display of logic and learning that they failed to mention the purpose of their visit. Sakuma talked of the power of the West, of the excellence of Western weapons, and of the nature of Western science.[68] His warnings of the necessity to utilize Western techniques to withstand the West found the two loyalists at a loss for arguments. For Sakuma, who had taught himself Dutch and who had experimented with a wide variety of scientific ideas, was at the same time a loyalist whose fervent nationalism could scarcely be questioned, least of all by Kusaka, a student of Sakuma's friend Yoshida Shōin. Kusaka and Nakaoka continued their journey to Kyoto, arriving there February 26, 1863. There is unfortunately no clear indication of any lasting influence on Nakaoka as a result of his talk with Sakuma, but one is tempted to ascribe to it some significance as an early incident in the education of the young Tosa *shōya* to the necessity of learning from the West.[69] Sakuma Shōzan's final influence on the lives of both Nakaoka and Kusaka came in the summer of 1864, when his assassination in Kyoto touched off the fighting at the palace gates between Chōshū and bakufu forces in which Kusaka was killed and Nakaoka wounded.

When Yōdō did go to Kyoto in February of 1863, it was to lend his weight to the men who preceded and accompanied the shogun in his visit to the ancient capital. Yōdō approved highly of the efforts of the new bakufu regime, under Matsudaira Shungaku and Hitotsubashi Keiki, to work out a compromise program. He was also in close touch with bakufu moderates of lower rank like Ōkubo Ichiō and Katsu Rintarō. Before advancing from Osaka, where he landed March 10, to Kyoto, Yōdō issued instructions to all Tosa samurai that should have indicated where his sympathies lay:

Never for a moment forget sincerity of heart.
When you meet people from other han, do not criticize
    your own officials.
Avoid unnecessary contacts.

[68] Hirao, *Rikuentai*, pp. 31-33.
[69] Hirao, *Rikuentai*, pp. 34-35, reproduces a letter to a friend which justifies doubts that Sakuma's influence was very great. Nakaoka speaks much about his experiences in Mito, and marvels at the way loyalism has spread to the commoners, but fails to mention Sakuma Shōzan.

Do not try to intimidate people with the strength
of our forces in Kyoto.[70]

And after arriving in Kyoto Yōdō consulted with leaders of the
kōbu-gattai cause, including Shimazu Hisamitsu himself, to see
what could be done to head off the loyalist extremists who dominated the court.[71]

Yōdō devoted his principal efforts in Kyoto to the promotion of
a compromise between the court and the bakufu. He was aware
of a number of suggestions that had already been made by Matsudaira Shungaku and others. Yōdō seems to have envisioned
some sort of council of daimyō which would tend to unify national opinion. He found, however, that the court was dominated
by those who refused to cooperate, and that these men in turn
were—until September 30 and the Chōshū expulsion from the
palace—influenced by Chōshū and *shishi* opinion. When the date
for the expulsion of foreigners was set, Yōdō realized that his plans
had failed and returned to Kōchi, which he had not seen for eight
years, at the end of May.

While Yōdō worked for kōbu-gattai he was presented with one
memorial after another by the loyalist leaders in Kyoto. Mazaki
Sōrō, Hirai Shūjirō, and above all Takechi Zuizan tried to persuade their lord of the urgency of the situation, the timeliness of
his action, and the necessity of a strong loyalist stand. These memorials invariably asked for reforms in the Tosa administration.
The basic point envisaged here was selection of officials by "ability" instead of by rank. Specifically Takechi, for instance, hoped
for central positions for some of his more highly placed sympathizers. He and his friends clearly expected that their own influence
in han councils would increase once such steps were taken. The
memorials spoke also of the "highest duty of all" that faced the
Tosa leaders, and continued to hold out the possibility of a Satsuma-Chōshū-Tosa alliance along this path of "morality and righteousness." Focus on the greater duty instead of lesser aims would
also, as can be seen in Takechi's memorials, make the Tosa administration less concerned with bakufu commands and more concerned with Imperial safety. Troops stationed at Sumiyoshi at
Tokugawa desire could be brought into Kyoto, thereby increasing

---

[70] *Ishin Tosa kinnō shi*, p. 269.
[71] Already before leaving Edo, Yōdō had ordered Itagaki to get in touch with
Hisamitsu's able young retainer Ōkubo Toshimichi. *Gekai suikō*, p. 189.

the Tosa influence there. Expensive luxuries and institutions could be abolished and the wealth of Tosa dedicated to measures exclusively designed to promote military preparedness. And the han, instead of fortifying its borders against entrants and runaways so carefully, should be more concerned with the national borders instead. Of what use to defend Tosa border points and let the foreigners enter the national borders? And what danger could a few runaway rōnin cause? How much better, instead, to adopt a virtuous and loyalist position, and become a refuge for rōnin instead of fearing their flight.[72]

Before his own departure from Kyoto Yōdō responded to these requests by sending three of Takechi's men, Mazaki Sōrō, Hirose Kenta, and Hirai Shūjirō, to Tosa to take up posts in the fief government. They went gladly, expecting posts of importance for the implementation of the reforms they had proposed. With them they also took a rescript which they had extracted from a high court noble addressed to the former daimyō, Toyosuke, endorsing the sort of personnel reform they wanted. But to their disappointment they returned to a Tosa in which the conservatives under Koyagi were still dominant. Far from returning to new seats of power, the loyalists found themselves farther from authority than ever before.

The *shishi* who remained in Kyoto fared little better. When Mazaki Sōrō returned to Kyoto after several frustrating months in Kōchi he found Hirai Shūjirō under indictment for his part in obtaining the court rescript; the two confessed their guilt and threw themselves on Yōdō's mercy. Takechi himself, despite signs that all was not well, had continued to urge his program and ideas on Yōdō. On the second of May, Takechi was appointed director of the Tosa Kyoto residence. His new duties prevented further visiting and intrigue with his friends. The Tosa loyalists had thus lost their freedom of maneuver.[73]

The *shishi* now began to realize that their appraisal of Yōdō had been erroneous. Threats of violence once again endangered the peace of the capital, and Itagaki's upper samurai became so aroused that they considered exterminating fifty lower samurai in order to have done with their intimidation. Talks between Ta-

---

[72] Text given in *Ishin Tosa kinnō shi*, pp. 370-378.
[73] *Ishin Tosa kinnō shi*, pp. 323f. Takechi was immobilized just as Shogun Iemochi made his first visit to Kyoto.

kechi and Itagaki convinced each that the other was in deadly earnest, and they also averted the proposed vendettas.[74]

Even when Yōdō decided to return to Kōchi from Kyoto at the end of May 1863, the Tosa loyalists still had some hopes of having their way. They accompanied Yōdō willingly, hoping to be able to influence han policy at home. Nakaoka Shintarō, of whom Yōdō had formed a good opinion, was even promoted to metsuke for purposes of the trip. Once in Kōchi, the loyalists reasoned that the han regime would in all probability feel bound to obey the Imperial decree calling for exclusion of foreigners. Even if Tosa failed to join in the battle at first, once the foreign war was begun by other han Tosa would have to join in. Their judgment proved erroneous. Yōdō disapproved of the action which Chōshū precipitated in the Straits of Shimonoseki, and he stood firm against those who wanted to go to the aid of Chōshū.[75] No general anti-foreign war resulted.

Instead, Yōdō set out to investigate the murder of Yoshida Tōyō of the previous year. Inevitably, the *shishi* came under suspicion. Some, who had foreseen this, fled from Tosa to join their Chōshū friends in Kyoto. Takechi himself had been advised by his Chōshū friends to do this earlier but he refused. In Kōchi Takechi had several further interviews with Yōdō, and he continued his insistent requests for selection of able officials and basic reforms. "In extraordinary times," he memorialized, "extraordinary ability is required"; the han and the nation were in danger, and it was desperately urgent to upset old precedents and strike out anew.[76]

In the weeks that followed Yōdō showed his agreement with Takechi's sentiments, but the two proved to have differing estimates of "ability." As soon as Yōdō felt han opinion had quieted sufficiently for him to take action, he installed a new slate of officials in han offices. Most of these men were drawn from among the disciples of Yoshida Tōyō. This done, Yōdō was prepared to act against the loyalists. Mazaki Sōrō, Hirai Shūjirō (who had been sent to Kōchi under guard), and Hirose Kenta were the first to receive punishment. Their crime lay in having extorted the rescript

[74] *Ishin Tosa kinnō shi*, p. 298.

[75] When Chōshū envoys came to Tosa seeking assistance Yōdō prevented them from seeing Takechi and his partisans, and in a letter to Date Munenari he was strongly critical of the rash action of their fief; far better for Chōshū, he thought, to unite with Satsuma instead of alienating it. Hirao, *Yōdō Kō*, pp. 134-38.

[76] *Ishin Tosa kinnō shi*, pp. 382-383.

addressed to the former daimyō Toyosuke. Yōdō had heard of this from the Kyoto noble in question, and the trio were ordered to commit hara-kiri in July. To the last, the low-ranking *shishi* were conscious of their class status and anxious to show their feudal and moral worth. Their gratification at being permitted an honorable end instead of being executed as criminals, and their eagerness to perform the rites smoothly and decorously, so that their names might be honored, make curious reading and remind one strikingly of the force of feudal values among all brackets of the ruling class. At such a time the *shishi* seem revolutionaries for a return to antiquity, and not for a bright new world.[77]

Then, after the political change of September 30, 1863 forced Chōshū units together with their loyalist friends among the court nobles out of Kyoto, Yōdō felt that the time had come to strike against the leading Tosa loyalists. There was no further prospect for loyalist supremacy at court, and it was possible to act against the loyalists whose violence or insubordination had threatened the fief in recent years. Three days after the Kyoto change, Takechi and the remaining leaders of the Loyalist party were arrested. At the same time, numbers of *shishi*, including Nakaoka Shintarō, fled the fief. Nakaoka fled to Mitajiri, in Chōshū, and for the next three years he became a member of the Chōshū group of military figures.

There followed a long and drawn-out investigation of Takechi's earlier activities. Numerous efforts were made to implicate him in the murder of Yoshida Tōyō, but this was not successfully done. Instead, Takechi was tried for the crime of forging his young lord's name to the memorial in Kyoto. In the summer of 1865, after long delay and investigation, Takechi too was ordered to commit *seppuku*.[78]

---

[77] The description of the seppuku may be found in *Ishin Tosa kinnō shi*, pp. 365f. Organization of the suicides is credited to Hirose Kenta, who had had close contacts with the Chōshū *shishi*, had studied the method of hara-kiri, and impressed upon his fellows the urgency of living up to their names and to the ideals of bushidō.

[78] Copious details of interrogations and final end can be found in *Ishin Tosa kinnō shi*, pp. 514-814, and *Takechi Zuizan kankei monjo*, II; sentence in monjo, II, 258-259. The full catalogue of his crimes were: having taken advantage of the political situation to form a party, agitating people's minds, instigating plans among court nobles, presenting plans disrespectfully to his former lord, losing sight of his proper place, despising higher authority, disrupting order, and using disrespectful language. Years later Yōdō summed it up by saying that Takechi had assassinated his minister Yoshida Tōyō, and that if he had let him live the realm

There was much talk in Tosa of a rebellion to free Takechi from prison. Meetings of *gōshi* and *shōya* loyalists decided against a general rising lest it shorten Takechi's life at the hands of his jailers. A group of twenty-three loyalists in eastern Tosa did, however, organize a demonstration of discontent in October 1864. They prepared a statement setting forth their grievances and moved out in a joint demonstration. They anticipated little violent retribution, and planned a retreat across the border into Awa han if it proved necessary. But they were mistaken. Han units attacked them, and the pass station refused to allow them passage into Awa. As a result the demonstrators were killed in action or executed after their capture.[79]

From Chōshū, Nakaoka Shintarō, who had been wounded in the Chōshū attack on Kyoto in the summer of 1864 and who had done his best to incite protests among the loyalists in Tosa earlier, now wrote of caution. Nothing could be done at the time, he pointed out; it would be necessary to wait and plan for the future.[80]

The loyalist years had taken a heavy toll of lives. Men of all persuasions and ranks, including, in Takechi Zuizan and Yoshida Tōyō, two of the most impelling personalities in Tokugawa Tosa, had fallen. But the violence had not been without its benefits. Some youthful extremists had come to see the folly of unorganized and poorly prepared *émeutes*, and henceforth they would prove better politicians. They would also, after the Chōshū and Satsuma experiences with foreign gunboats, have a healthier respect for the armaments of the foreigners. Indeed, hereafter anti-foreignism, however fervently held by individuals, would function chiefly as an issue with which to reproach the bakufu.

Despite the effrontery of the *shishi* and *rōnin*, it would be wrong to conclude that law and order had collapsed completely in Japan. The violence in Kyoto was possible only because Chōshū military strength could temporarily render Tokugawa police measures ineffective; individual heroics and acts of terrorism might intimi-

---

would have disintegrated. Ōmachi Keigetsu, *Hakushaku Gotō Shōjirō* (Tokyo, 1914), pp. 141-142. Sasaki, too, felt that order could not be restored in Tosa until Takechi was removed. *sekijitsu dan*, p. 308.

[79] The Noneyama Incident is chronicled in *Ishin Tosa kinnō shi*, pp. 649-660. For breakdown of participants, see above, p. 111.

[80] Hirao, *Sakamoto Ryōma . . . Nakaoka Shintarō*, p. 198. For letters showing Nakaoka's earlier efforts to spark protests, *ibid.*, pp. 183f.

date, but they could not negate, the holders of traditional political and administrative power. For every retainer who took the rōnin path of defiance, many others like Takechi, Mazaki, and Hirose refused to flee despite the certainty of punishment and probability of death; Takechi's obedient seppuku, like that of Nagai Uta, testifies to the strength of traditional values and controls.

It was this traditional loyalty and obedience, skillfully manipulated by Yamauchi Yōdō, that made possible the Tosa return to the course which Yoshida Tōyō had originally set. The ability and prestige of Yōdō, and the respect in which his men held him, remained an important element in the years ahead.

Equally striking, however, was the evidence of sharp conflicts within the samurai class. In the Tosa political scene positions of loyalism and caution were so affected by class status that some could later describe the Tosa Restoration movement as a struggle between ranks. One can see a considerable basis for such a statement in the recollection of Sasaki Takayuki and Tanaka Kōken. By 1864 there was a sharp, easily combustible antagonism between the upper samurai and the low-ranking loyalists. Only after the loyalists were put under control was the way open for upper samurai like Itagaki Taisuke to espouse a loyalist and anti-foreign position.

Perhaps more significant still than this evidence of gōshi and lower samurai resentment was the clear indication of a far-reaching gulf between those who controlled the countryside—shōya, village leaders, and gōshi—and those who made policies in the castle towns. In Tosa the loyalist strength in the countryside seems to have been directly related to discontent with the centralization policies that accompanied the reforms of Yoshida Tōyō. Elsewhere closer to Kyoto the loyalist putsches were premised on the ability of leading village leaders and gōshi to recruit and influence their farmer neighbors. In fact, however, failure and danger showed that that influence was limited and easily strained. It may be too much to deduce national crises from these isolated instances as many writers have done. But there can be little doubt that a profound discontent and insecurity characterized several vital areas of interclass relationships in Japan, and that the resulting instability was in some measure comparable to that which has characterized periods of revolutionary change in other countries. It was this social insecurity, which was the setting for talk of a worried emperor, that made the foreign crisis so difficult and so dangerous for the feudal rulers.

In focusing chiefly upon the political struggles and violence of the loyalist years, however, one inevitably runs the risk of exaggerating the degree to which the loyalists differed from their fellows in the realm of ideas. Aside from a very few firebrands among their number, the *shishi* were far from ready to question or reject the basic features of their society. It is well to remind ourselves of the large areas of agreement between all the groups. The *shishi*, when close to power, tended to utilize more and more of the ideas and techniques of the Yoshida Tōyō men whom they had murdered, while the upper class samurai later remembered, with Sasaki, that the thing that had kept them from espousing full loyalism earlier was that it seemed to be associated with lower samurai. The position we have designated as "loyalist"—thoroughgoing opposition to foreigners, and insistence on a maximum political role for the throne—was as yet an unstable one, and subject to change through experience or responsibility. It would require flexibility and sophistication of outlook before a program with broad appeal could be worked out, and to trace the manner in which this could take place it is necessary to turn next to the activities of Sakamoto Ryōma.

IV. SERVICE WITH KATSU

ONE of the remarkable things about the late Tokugawa period is the way numbers of young men trained in duty, loyalty, and obedience took it upon themselves to know better than their elders and strike out on their own. As they did this they usually managed to combine ambition with idealism, and they justified sharp breaks in the patterns of obligation in which they had been educated by citing a higher duty to country and sovereign. Many writers have rightly pointed to the willingness of the *shishi* to sacrifice their status and their lives for the newly found Imperial cause; but this readiness to risk everything needs to be set beside the hope of fame and power that helped to make the risks worth while. No better instance of this can be found than in the case of Sakamoto Ryōma in the years after he fled Tosa in April of 1862. His impatience with the conservative course the han authorities were following had already led him to join fencing companions who were anxious to do great things for themselves and for their country. When his new companions proved unable to influence the Tosa administrators, Sakamoto, like many others, fled his home and domain in order to take a personal part in the national drama.

In the months that followed Sakamoto showed how little he and others like him had realized the complexity of the problems that Japan faced. At first, with the simple logic of the swordsman, he was convinced that differences over policy could be traced to cowardice or subversion in high places, and therefore he set out on a path of direct action, in the belief that assassination and terror might succeed where polite requests had failed. When brought face to face with evidence that he had been wrong about this, however, Sakamoto proved willing not only to reconsider his charges and his threats, but even to accept employment in the service of one he had planned to kill. This shift from enemy to disciple was not without its roots in the behavior pattern of feudal Japan, but in Sakamoto's case it was accompanied by a growing sophistication and maturity which made it possible for him to substitute for the simple solutions of his early extremism a much better view of the political steps that might be required to bring about Imperial rule. The new orientation required no sacrifice of

Sakamoto's hopes of personal fame and importance, however; indeed, the possibilities of new and exciting contacts undoubtedly did their share in persuading him of the wisdom of his new program. But whatever the balance of ambition and idealism in his make-up, there is no doubt that Sakamoto was unusually fortunate in the selection of his intended victim. Katsu Rintarō was a man of exceptional experience, training, and insight into the problems of his day and country. He had a wide circle of friends and supporters within the Tokugawa administration. And, through personality and outlook, he was peculiarly able to appeal to Sakamoto's prejudices and likes. The study of Sakamoto's conversion to a new program must therefore begin with the man who became his mentor for the next two-and-one-half years.

1. Katsu Rintarō

Katsu was born in Edo in 1823, the son of an obscure and impoverished Tokugawa retainer. Although his status and outlook were improved considerably by a fortunate adoption, his early difficulties illustrate the economic hardships possible within even the hatamoto rank.[1] Katsu's boyhood years were devoted to enthusiastic study of fencing. He was probably better able to understand the feelings of his later disciples, most of whom were graduates of the fencing schools, than most officials would have been. Katsu's fencing master encouraged him to take training in Zen discipline, and to this, with its emphasis on mental and physical alertness, he later credited his good fortune in escaping from a number of assassination attempts.[2]

Up to this point there was little in Katsu's background to differentiate him from many of his fellows. At the age of fifteen or sixteen, however—during the later years of the Tempō period—he embarked upon the study of Dutch learning. After some convincing displays of industry he was introduced to the lord of Fukuoka, Kuroda Narihiro, who took him under his patronage.[3]

---

[1] W. G. Beasley, "Councillors of Samurai origin in the Meiji Government 1868-9," *Bulletin of the School of Oriental and African Studies*, University of London, xxx, 1957, p. 102, gives Katsu's family income as 41 koku.

[2] "Shosei Shūyōdan," *Kaishū Zenshū*, Vol. x (Tokyo, 1929), p. 297.

[3] Thanks to the patterns of adoption, the upper levels of the ruling class were often closely related. Thus this lord of Fukuoka was an elder brother of Shimazu Nariakira, the progressive daimyō of Satsuma who had done so much to sponsor Western studies in Kagoshima. The Fukuoka lord was responsible, together with Nabeshima of Hizen (Saga), for defence of Nagasaki, and Nagasaki duty pro-

Housed in the Fukuoka billet in Edo, encouraged as a student, and adequately provided for, Katsu prospered in his studies. This experience was to make him less provincial and less narrowly Tokugawa-minded in the years that lay ahead.

By 1850 Katsu was becoming known as a student of Dutch learning. He had started his own academy of Western learning, and he was in close contact with leading students of the West. Takano Chōei, for instance, while in hiding from the bakufu authorities for his temerity in publishing a booklet critical of the way the Morrison incident had been handled, visited him to request his assistance. Takano's strong views on the necessity of coastal defence may have figured in the development of Katsu's own position.[4]

The coming of Perry and the problems that resulted produced a dramatic change in the bakufu's estimation of its specialists on the subject of the West. As noted earlier, Katsu was among the Dutch scholars who were consulted by the shogunate when it circulated requests for advice. The invitation to him to participate was extended by Ōkubo Ichiō, an official who was to be of great importance for both Katsu and Sakamoto in later years. Katsu responded to the invitation with a memorial which was sharply critical of the antiquated state of Japan's defences. He urged the development of a competent corps of interpreters and foreign-affairs experts as well as the training of military specialists. This document played a significant role in the bakufu's decision to set up the school for the preparation, control, and dissemination of Western knowledge which became known as the *Bansho Shirabesho*. Katsu also forwarded a memorandum concerning coastal defence in which he enlarged on the need for producing warships. He proposed a shipbuilding program to be financed by the promotion of trade, and which would be preceded by purchases of foreign ships and training in their navigation and handling. He recognized that there would be difficulties at first because of the lack of experience on the part of the Japanese, but argued that the native spirit and wisdom of the Japanese race would suffice to make up for these before long. The thoroughness with which Katsu spelled out his

---

vided his retainers with abundant opportunity for access to Dutch learning. Thus Katsu received auspicious sponsorship.

[4] A brief account of Takano can be found in G. B. Sansom, *The Western World and Japan*, New York, 1950, pp. 260-263.

ideas about the school of Western learning, the provision of foreign-style armaments, and the manufacture of commodities like glass, gunpowder, and iron, showed that his response to the Western impact was one which had been long in preparation. For him the crisis was of value chiefly in making legitimate and patriotic views that otherwise might have been considered subversive and dangerous.

Katsu now became considered an expert in a field which was, by general agreement, vital to Japan's safety. He was given official status, and he served on the committees that planned for the new institute of foreign knowledge. Service of this sort brought him into contact with the most progressive and enlightened Tokugawa officials; he accompanied Ōkubo Ichiō on a trip to inspect coastal defence positions along the Osaka and Kii coasts.

Most important of all was Katsu's assignment to the group of men who were sent to Nagasaki to be trained in naval matters by the contingent of Netherlands officers and men who had come from Java to serve as instructors. Katsu left Edo late in 1855 for this mission, and he spent the next few years in Nagasaki. He later wrote, "The naval science we studied in those days was basically no different from what we have today. We had to take six subjects, such as navigation, transportation, mechanics, arithmetic, and so on. Of course we studied astronomy, too. Besides, everything had to be studied in Dutch. This was not so bad for those of us who had studied the language before, but the men who had to depend on Chinese characters had a difficult time."[5]

Katsu remained after the first group of Japanese students was replaced by a second, and he was undoubtedly among the better officers. He himself wrote that he assisted in the instruction of the second group of students, and the Netherlands reports show that he was in command of a ship which sailed to Edo in 1858 or early 1859.[6]

Katsu's account of the years in Nagasaki tells of talks with foreigners who told him of developments in international relations and military techniques. Already predisposed to slight fief barriers from his student years in Edo, he must have noted the abilities of

[5] "Keireki seihendan," *Kaishū Zenshū*, x, 332. Katsu gives a longer and fuller account of the training and personnel involved in his *Kaigun rekishi; Kaishū Zenshū*, vIII, 36f.

[6] van der Chijs, p. 467, and *Kaishū Zenshū*, x, 329-330.

the delegations sent by the feudal lords to learn seamanship from the Hollanders. Like most of his countrymen, however, Katsu was greatly opposed to the unequal treaties the shogunate had signed. When he learned about them, he wrote, "I could hardly restrain my resentment. But, since I was a person of low estate, all I could do was to sigh and deplore the situation."[7]

Katsu returned to Edo early in 1859. The Regent Ii was now in command. He had already begun punitive measures against the Court nobles and Mito supporters, and he now moved to lessen the danger of disaffection in distant places like Nagasaki. The Nagasaki training school was ordered closed in March 1859, and shortly after that the shogunal students were recalled.[8] In Edo, Katsu was distressed to find that Ii's police methods had made his former friends afraid to converse with him; he deplored, both now and after the fall of Ii, the insecurity of official life under Tokugawa rule.

Katsu's reason for wanting to return to Edo had been his desire to join the first embassy to the United States. He found the bakufu opposed to sending a Japanese ship because of the risks involved, but he was able to persuade the authorities of the desirability of a compromise whereby the official mission would travel on board the U.S.S. *Powhattan*, while the *Kanrin Maru* would follow under his command. It required considerable seamanship and courage to cross the Pacific in this small vessel, designed as it was for coastal waters. Fukuzawa Yukichi, a member of the party, later wrote proudly of the thirty-seven day voyage: "As I consider all the other peoples of the Orient as they exist today, I feel convinced that there is no other nation which has the ability or the courage to navigate a steamship across the Pacific after a period of five years of experience in navigation and engineering."[9] Fukuzawa thought poorly of Katsu's performance on the voyage, however; he noted that Katsu, a poor sailor, kept to his cabin while at sea and reemerged to take charge again only after they had made port.

Katsu and the *Kanrin Maru* remained in San Francisco Bay while the official party, which included Fukuzawa, went on to

---

[7] *Kaki no ibara no ki, Kaishū Zenshū*, IX, 190.

[8] For a time a few students from Hizen, Chōshū, and Fukuoka continued to be instructed in Deshima. The Netherlands commandant speculated that the change in policy derived from an extremely conservative regime in Edo which was pursuing a reactionary policy justified in the name of economy. Van der Chijs, p. 490.

[9] *The Autobiography of Fukuzawa Yukichi*, p. 119.

Washington. For Katsu the period spent in California was full of demonstrations of the strength of Western civilization. He made many notes about the naval installations, ships, and armaments he saw there, and he was eager to learn about the problems encountered in organizing a navy. He also visited mines and industrial plants in the San Francisco area, and his careful and detailed notes show the diligence and earnestness with which he seized his opportunities.[10] For Katsu, as for Fukuzawa, the trip with its opportunities for firsthand information about the West provided many new arguments for hastening the process of change in Japan. Two hundred years earlier the Tokugawa rulers had concluded that national seclusion was prerequisite to the perpetuation of their political system, and now that that seclusion had been sacrificed, Japan's first ambassadors to the West realized that the political system itself would require modification. There remained room for argument about the direction and extent of those modifications, however, and the ambassadors discovered their countrymen and superiors were not prepared to listen uncritically to the advice with which they returned.

Upon his return to Japan, Katsu discovered that the Regent, Ii Naosuke, had been murdered. National policy changes were temporarily at a standstill pending the emergence of new leaders in the bakufu. Discouraged and uneasy, Katsu retired to obscurity for a time. He recorded his feelings in a little work, at once a history and a document of opinion, which he did not publish until much later. *Kaki no ibara no ki* ("An account of the vine on the fence") was written during the winter of 1860 and 1861. Katsu wrote that the regime in Japan had been overdue for change even before the pressure of foreign nations made that change inevitable. He saw a general decline in moral standards, a tendency to waste public funds, widespread bribery, and a government indisposed to listen to those who were alarmed by this. Much of this, he thought, was true of Asia as a whole and not Japan alone; static

[10] Among his less scientific but highly readable impressions were his report of an evening at the theater, where he apparently saw a minstrel show ("We would consider it a rather low form of theater") and a social occasion at which he was startled to note that "one man took a *biwa* and began to play it. Hearing this, the guests seized their women by the hand and danced; some held several by the hand in succession while they danced, while others clasped women by the loins and by the shoulders while dancing." Katsu's impressions have been recorded in *Kaigun rekishi; Kaishū Zenshū*, vɪɪɪ, 120-176.

technology and declining morality were everywhere apparent. To this he contrasted the scene he had just visited in America. There, every effort was being made to master new techniques and methods. That these were far superior to those of Asia had been demonstrated by the Opium War in China. Katsu went on from this to argue the necessity of opening Japan fully to the outside world. He pointed out that this did not mean approving of the barbarians or slighting Japan's own tradition, but that it was the only way to strengthen the country while also avoiding a disastrous war with a consequent loss of prestige. Thus Katsu's education and experience were beginning to be put together to produce a constructive synthesis whereby Japan might retain independence and integrity. He was far from being "pro-foreign," but he was no longer a zealot conscious only of the superiority of his own tradition.[11]

When the bakufu, after a period of hesitation, turned again to programs of technological modernization and political reform following the murder of Ii Naosuke, Katsu's sponsors and friends came back into prominence. In May, 1861 Katsu was among a group appointed to study military systems. His own part of the work concerned the navy, and in the study papers his group produced there was a steady insistence on the necessity of combining and pooling the beginnings of modern naval strength that had been made in all the fiefs. From now on Katsu was recognized as an expert in naval matters; in the summer of 1862 he was appointed to represent the new navy in bakufu councils, and in 1864 came his appointment as *gunkan bugyō*, or Naval Commissioner. In this capacity he finally had the opportunity of taking action along some of the lines he had advocated. Katsu's conviction of the desirability of a single, national program still could not be implemented, but he used every chance to utilize the enthusiasm and patriotism of similarly minded men, regardless of their status or origin.

Katsu's outlook and experience were likely to make him view the *shishi* as something more than upstarts. In turn, his own training in swordsmanship and in Zen and his undoubted appreciation for the distinctive features of the Japanese spirit and way of life made him acceptable to the young chauvinists of his day. Conscious of his own abilities and proud of his growing importance, Katsu had

---

[11] *Kaishū Zenshū*, IX, 173-253, contains the full text of *Kaki no ibara no ki*.

a jaunty air that inspired admiration and trust among the young swordsmen who graded their contemporaries according to courage and verve.

Katsu's success with young swordsmen depended upon his ability to persuade them that he was by no means pro-foreign. He could, with all sincerity, assure them that although he thought the country had to be opened, he did not for a moment consider this desirable or permanent. He tended to hold out the hope that by uniting with other nations in Asia Japan might yet best the foreigners. Korea and China, he thought, had everything to gain and nothing to lose by close cooperation with Japan. If it made sense for the fiefs to act together against the foreigners, it was equally desirable for Asians to act together against the West. The forced opening of the country could be turned to profit by building commercial strength which could in turn be utilized to build military strength. Then, one day, Japan would no longer have to make concessions to the West. With arguments like these Katsu was able to convince many of the leading Restoration heroes that he shared their goals. Japan's modern ultranationalists, in fact, later rewarded him by listing him as a forerunner of twentieth century expansionism.[12]

2. Sakamoto and Katsu

Sakamoto had fled his home and fief on April 22, 1862. As has been noted, he was impatient with Takechi Zuizan's failure to win ascendency in Tosa and afraid that his domain would lose out if it did not join in the ambitious plans that were being prepared by the Chōshū and Satsuma extremists. A final impetus to Sakamoto's resolution had been provided by Sawamura Sōnojo, a man who had fled earlier with Yoshimura Toratarō. Sawamura slipped back across the border to report that a putsch was being prepared near the capital, and that Shimazu Hisamitsu, the regent of Satsuma, was going to provide the armed force the rōnin had lacked. When Takechi failed to take advantage of this news, Sakamoto fled with Sawamura.

Sakamoto had earlier discussed his plans with his elder brother, Gompei, the family head, who disapproved strongly. But this

---

[12] For example, Kuzuu Yoshihisa, *Tōa senkaku shishi kiden* (Tokyo, 1935), I, 10-11, and III, 230-232. This work is the official history of the Kokuryū Kai (Amur, or literally "Black Dragon" Society).

failed to deter him. He borrowed some money from a relative, and his older sister Otome quietly handed him a sword which had been in the family for several generations.

The two fugitives went first to Shimonoseki in Chōshū, where they were housed by the merchant Shiraishi Seiichirō, a man whose loyalist sympathies and financial resources made his house a frequent meeting place for refugee *shishi*. They had expected to find Yoshimura Toratarō there, but he had already left for the excitement scheduled for the capital. Then word came that Shimazu Hisamitsu, instead of sponsoring the rising, had crushed it by attacking the headquarters of the conspirators at the Teradaya Inn in Fushimi on May 21. There was now no longer need to hurry; Sakamoto travelled in Kyushu before proceeding to the Osaka area, where he arrived some two months later.[13]

His friends in Kōchi were aware of his movements and expected him to take an active part in political agitation. Some of them thought him rash and irresponsible. The loyalist Hirai Shūjirō wrote his sister, who was serving in the Sanjō mansion in Kyoto, to stay clear of any schemes Sakamoto might broach to her. "Sakamoto Ryōma fled at night on the twenty-second," he wrote, "and he will probably come your way. Ryōma and I talked about his plans the day before he left. Whatever fine schemes he may have, be sure you have nothing to do with them. Your job now is to carry out your parents' wishes in that house, and you shouldn't let yourself serve other people's purposes. Although Ryōma is a splendid fellow, he doesn't have any learning, and therefore he sometimes makes serious mistakes, so be very, very careful. I beg of you to put first things first; do not leave the path of loyalty and filial duty."[14]

But Sakamoto was not to spend much time in Kyoto as yet. Tosa men soon told him of the successful attack on Yoshida Tōyō; there was every likelihood that anti-loyalist measures might result in his arrest for interrogation and possible punishment. So Sakamoto decided to continue on to Edo, where he arrived late in the summer of 1862. By the time he reached there, his associates among the Tosa loyalists were reaping the advantages of their assassination of Yoshida Tōyō; they were dominating the scene in Kyoto, and

---

[13] The chronology of Sakamoto's flight and movements can be followed in Chikami, *Sakamoto Ryōma*, pp. 51f.; and Hirao, *Kaientai shimatsu ki*, pp. 37f.

[14] *Sakamoto Ryōma kankei monjo*, I, 59-60.

plans were beginning to take shape for the Sanjō-Anenokōji mission to Edo. That mission, it will be remembered, reached the Tokugawa capital in the middle of December.

Sakamoto's movements to and in the capital cannot be traced exactly. After he realized that the search for the murderers of Yoshida Tōyō was not being pressed vigorously, his initial fear of apprehension must have lessened. Undoubtedly he was in touch with the loyalists who won posts in the han administration, and it is known that he renewed his friendship with his old fencing master, Chiba; possibly he also received protection and housing from him.

There is no indication that Sakamoto had changed any of his opinions since his initial emotional reaction to the foreign threat. His convictions had been strong enough to persuade him to leave his home and fief, and he had undoubtedly been chagrined to find himself unable to take part in the rōnin revolt that had been crushed by Satsuma troops in the summer of 1862. After some eight months of semi-fugitive existence on the borderline of respectable samurai society, Sakamoto must have been eager to make his name known and to establish himself in the front ranks of loyalist heroes through some striking act of merit. Quite possibly he was led to this by the new tide of violence that had followed the intervention of the Chōshū and Tosa loyalists in Kyoto politics, and it may be that the Sanjō-Anenokōji mission to Edo, which included so many Tosa loyalists among its number, played an important part in Sakamoto's decision to enter the path of violence.

At any rate, Sakamoto decided to assassinate Katsu. Katsu's vigorous advocacy of opening the country had brought him to the notice of the *shishi*. It is not difficult to imagine the way Sakamoto must have catalogued his proposed victim's crimes. A student of foreign learning, a man who studied under the Dutch at Nagasaki, a man who had accompanied the embassy sent to America to ratify the treaties signed by Ii Naosuke, and a man who now had increasing opportunity to implement his views on opening the country to foreign technology and trade—surely here was an ideal target. Not a few officials had been struck down for reasons less compelling.

Sakamoto prepared to strike during December of 1862. He decided to gain access to Katsu through Matsudaira Shungaku, lord of Fukui (Echizen) and friend of the Tosa lord Yamauchi Yōdō. Shungaku had emerged from punishment by Ii Naosuke to become Political Director of the new bakufu administration. Like Yōdō, he was highly esteemed by the *shishi*. He kept on his staff men whom the loyalists trusted, and he often flattered the loyalists by listening to them in order to sound out the opinions of this volatile group. Even so, it remains astonishing that a lonely rōnin like Sakamoto was able to make his way into the presence of one of Japan's most important political leaders with such apparent ease.

In later years Shungaku described the occasion in a letter to Hijikata, a Tosa loyalist who survived the Restoration violence to become a high court official. He was about to leave for the shogun's castle, he recalled, when two samurai suddenly entered his grounds and asked for an interview. Shungaku referred them to an assistant,[15] and later invited them to return and heard them out. The two were Sakamoto Ryōma and Okamoto Kenzaburō.[16] They proved, he wrote, "inspired by the purest desires of imperial reverence and exclusion of the foreigners. I listened to their friendly warnings and was very favorably impressed by them. It turned out that the two of them had come to Edo because they believed the popular opinion that Katsu and Yokoi[17] were exercising an unfortunate influence on the political scene by advocating wrong views." Shungaku granted their request for introductions to Katsu and Yokoi, and saw them depart. The two went straight to Katsu's house. Katsu had been forewarned, for "As soon as they entered his house, he called out, 'Did you come to kill me? If you did, you ought to wait until we've had a chance to talk.' The two were astonished and quite cast down. But," continued Shungaku, "after hearing Katsu's explanations they were deeply impressed and full of admiration." From hatred to devotion; within a few days, when new rumors of possible assaults on Katsu spread, Sakamoto and

---

[15] Shungaku's account is given in *Sakamoto monjo*, I, 60-61. His assistant was Nakane Yukie (1807-1877), a vigorous loyalist of the Hirata Atsutane Shintō school of thought who was perfectly suited to allay *shishi* misgivings about his master's loyalty.

[16] But Katsu, *Kaishū Zenshū*, x, 261, identifies the second as Chiba Jūtarō, the fencer. Hirao, *Kaientai*, p. 51, also notes the discrepancy.

[17] Yokoi Shōnan, Kumamoto samurai who was Shungaku's counsellor. He became a friend of Sakamoto's, and his son a follower of Katsu. For a sketch of Shōnan, Sansom, *Western World*, pp. 266-269.

Okamoto quietly stood guard and patrolled around his house.[18]

This account has much to puzzle. Men do not usually procure formal introductions to those they plan to kill, and unless Katsu was better guarded than Shungaku it seems difficult to explain Sakamoto's procedure. Moreover, Shungaku had clearly put Katsu on his guard. Undoubtedly Shungaku himself had begun the work of reassuring the two rōnin as to the character of their intended victims. Thus it is clear that Sakamoto must have been in some measure prepared for the arguments with which Katsu was to persuade him. Katsu himself, however, expected an assault and reported Sakamoto's confession: "He said to me, 'My secret intention this night was to kill you, whatever you might say; but now that I have heard what you have to say, I am ashamed of my narrow-minded bigotry and beg you to let me become your disciple.' "[19]

What was there about Katsu's explanation that impressed Sakamoto so deeply? The details of the conversation cannot be reconstructed, but we can safely assume that the discovery of Katsu's patriotism and resentment of the Western demands helped to stay the assassins' swords. Then, the idea that the opening of Japan could be utilized to strengthen the country, and that creative utilization of Western techniques would open up new possibilities for national power and greatness must have revealed to Sakamoto how inadequate his own "narrow-minded bigotry" had been.

Although we lack an account of Katsu's talk with Sakamoto, we can see how he approached the Chōshū loyalist Kido Kōin a few months later, and there is little reason to think the arguments he used on Sakamoto were very different. A revealing entry in Katsu's diary for June, 1863 shows how he suggested the possibilities for leadership in Asia to Kido and a friend. "We talked about the state of Korea," Katsu notes. "I said that just now, all through Asia no one is offering any resistance to the Europeans; everybody is just imitating them in a petty manner, and none of us is pursuing a far-sighted policy. What we ought to do is to send out ships from our country and impress strongly on the leaders of all Asian countries that their very existence depends on banding together and building a powerful navy, and that if they do not develop the

---

[18] One is reminded of the 1932 assassination of Premier Inukai, who might have talked the first group of officers out of their deed had not another man burst into the room and shouted "Fire!" Hugh Byas, *Government by Assassination* (New York, 1942), p. 25.

[19] *Kaishū Zenshū*, x, 261.

necessary technology they will not be able to escape being tram-
pled underfoot by the West. We should start with Korea, our
nearest neighbor, and then go on to include China. The two
agreed with me completely."[20]

Sakamoto had now found a leader whose program made sense
to him. His swift turn-about may, at first sight, seem a sign of
fickleness or superficiality, or of a prior lack of resolution. But it
would probably be wiser to ascribe it to the limitations of his previous experience and thinking. As with most of his fellow *shishi*,
Sakamoto's experience and knowledge had been contained within
rigidly bounded, customary patterns. Fencing, which makes only
limited demands on the mind, had been a major part of that experience. When faced with the first indications that all was not
well within his society and country, Sakamoto's reaction had been
emotional and violent. The early anti-foreign frenzies and fears
had been a turbulent and irrational impulse, while affiliation with
the Tosa loyalists had provided the excitement of intrigue and conspiracy. Reason had not been required or employed in these early
paroxysms. But a concrete and rational plan of action was quickly
acceptable to Sakamoto, for he had not been operating on that
level at all. As a result he was prepared to learn that the most
effective way of strengthening the nation and expelling the foreigners lay through a utilization of some of their techniques and
institutions. And no one could have been better fitted to demonstrate this to him than the quick-witted Katsu.

Moreover, service with Katsu did not by any means rule out
continued cooperation with his old friends. Katsu's projects, as
will be noted below, required the service of many young enthusiasts, and Sakamoto proved an efficient recruiting agent. Furthermore, Matsudaira Shungaku, one of Katsu's contacts, continued
close to Yamauchi Yōdō, and Yōdō still carried the hopes, albeit
mistaken, of the Tosa loyalists. Sakamoto could therefore think
that he was furthering the cause of his friends in Tosa. Late in
January of 1863 Sakamoto took several of his loyalist friends to
visit Matsudaira Shungaku. A month later he departed for the
Osaka area with his new mentor, Katsu.

Katsu was known to Yamauchi Yōdō, and at the first opportunity
he interceded with Yōdō for Sakamoto. Early in March, 1863
Katsu and Shungaku were on their way to Kyoto by ship to pre-

[20] *Kaishū Zenshū*, ix, 17.

pare for the shogun's trip. Yōdō had finally decided to obey the requests from Kyoto that he come to the capital, and the ships carrying Yōdō and Katsu anchored in Shimoda harbor on the way. Yōdō invited Shungaku and Katsu to come to see him. In the course of a long and jovial talk Katsu put the case for "eight or nine of your fellows, including one named Sakamoto Ryōma, who have come into my camp" and who "do not have an evil thought." Yōdō, who was usually in a good mood when in his cups, freely agreed to pardon Sakamoto for having left the han. Katsu feared that a promise made over sake might be of short duration and pressed for a formal statement of pardon. On April 19 the Tosa administration formally pardoned Sakamoto.[21]

Sakamoto knew that he had found his cause and leader, and his exuberance is reflected in a buoyant letter he wrote his sister Otome a few months later:

"I must say that it's beyond me the way things work out in a man's life. Some fellows have such bad luck that they bang their privates on getting out of a bath tub and die as a result. When you compare my luck with that, it's really remarkable. Here I was on the point of death, and I didn't die. I really thought I was going to, and instead I am to live. Now I have become the disciple of the greatest man in Japan, Katsu Rintarō, and every day I can spend on things that I've dreamed about. Even if I should live to be forty, I wouldn't think of leaving this to return home. I've told elder brother about this too; he's in good spirits, and gives his approval. I'm giving everything I have for the province and the country."[22]

Katsu's enthusiasm for his convert was equally apparent. In his *History of the Navy* he later wrote, "Fortunately a Tosa man, Sakamoto Ryōma, entered my following. He was most energetic about the project, and added much enthusiasm."[23]

3. The Hyōgo Naval Academy

The project for which Katsu needed Sakamoto's energy and enthusiasm was a new naval training institute and shipyard which

[21] Documents in *Sakamoto monjo*, I, 66-70.

[22] *Sakamoto monjo*, I, 71-72. Letter dated May 7, 1863. Sakamoto had been able to communicate with "elder brother" Gompei because that worthy was serving in the han office in Osaka at this time.

[23] *Kaishū Zenshū*, VIII, 342.

was established at the coastal village of Hyōgo, near modern Kōbe, in the spring of 1863. The school was an outgrowth of the visit of the shogun Iemochi to Kyoto from April 21 to July 31 of that year. Katsu's trip to Kyoto that spring (during which he secured Yōdō's pardon for Sakamoto) had been made to prepare for the shogun's visit, and Katsu took full advantage of Iemochi's presence in the Kyoto area to show him the inadequacy of coastal defence points in that part of the Inland Sea.[24] Katsu followed this up with memorials which pointed out the vulnerability of Osaka and Sakai, and the shortage of ship-building and maintenance plants in the Osaka area. His urgings bore fruit in a directive of May 11, 1863, which ordered the establishment of a naval training academy and shipyard at Hyōgo. The facilities earlier set up at Nagasaki were to be transferred to this new center, and Katsu was put in charge of the project.[25]

Katsu had need of an assistant like Sakamoto for this charge. The bakufu coffers were very nearly empty, and it was clear that individual han would have to be called upon to contribute money and to pool their naval resources. Personnel was to be drawn from Tokugawa retainers in the Osaka area, supplemented by recruits from other han. It would require negotiation to bring compliance with requests for contributions the bakufu was powerless to enforce. Equally pressing was the need to recruit men at all levels to man and staff the new center. The policies that Katsu followed showed the sincerity of his stand in favor of a national, cooperative effort instead of a narrowly bakufu-centered institution. He asked few questions about origin or status of the men he took under his care; indeed, he aroused such uneasiness in the minds of conservatives in the bakufu that they were able to have him dismissed for sheltering rōnin in November of 1864.

Until then, however, Sakamoto was well suited to help Katsu. As a loyalist trusted by his fellow *shishi*, he was able to recruit men of high purpose and low status like himself. In addition his fidelity to his new mentor, together with his sincerity and ability, made him an ideal diplomatic agent for the negotiations that Katsu had to carry on.

More important for Sakamoto's own development was the fact

---

[24] *Kaishū Zenshū*, IX, 9. Katsu had gone on ahead in a futile attempt to keep costs of the shogun's trip down, but the traditionalists overruled him.

[25] *Kaigun rekishi, Kaishū Zenshū*, pp. 340f.

that his duties for Katsu brought him into contact with some of the most enlightened Tokugawa councillors. It was, in fact, from these men that he first heard of the possibility of a peaceful transfer of power from shogun to Emperor.

Early in March of 1863, Sakamoto and some Tosa friends he had recruited for Katsu's service had an interview with Katsu's friend and sponsor Ōkubo Ichiō. As an administrator of the Institute for the Study of Barbarian Books and as Commissioner of Foreign Affairs, Ōkubo had been able to gain wide knowledge of the West. He had profited from what he had heard and read about Western systems of government to develop the idea that it would be a useful move for the sake of national unity for the shogun to resign his special powers and office, retaining only his domains in the provinces of Surugawa, Tōtomi, and Mikawa. With these he would still figure as one of the chief men involved in the organization of a new and more truly national government. In his thinking about such a government Ōkubo was inclined to favor a council of major lords, meeting in Osaka or Kyoto every five years, and a council of lesser nobles which would meet in Edo. This crude bicameral suggestion is certainly one of the earliest forms of constitutional thought in modern Japan, and it is significant that it originated in bakufu councils. Recent studies have sought to trace the spread of this idea from Ōkubo to Matsudaira Shungaku, and to Katsu.[26] On this route it reached Sakamoto Ryōma also. On March 7 Sakamoto noted that he had heard that Katsu himself had proposed, to the consternation of the traditionalists present in the central audience hall (*Ōhiroma*) in Edo, that the shogun should resign his office and title. Thus it is clear that Sakamoto, who did much to advance the peaceful transfer of power a half decade later, first heard about such possibilities while in the service of Katsu.[27]

As Katsu entrusted more and more important missions to him, Sakamoto's enthusiasm for his new life grew. In June, while the shogun was still in Kyoto and subject to heavy pressure from court nobles like Anenokōji to adopt a thoroughly anti-foreign and exclusionist position, Katsu had Sakamoto take young Anenokōji

---

[26] Osatake, *Meiji Ishin*, I, 318. Although Ōkubo was not the first with such suggestions. Shungaku's adviser Hashimoto Sanai, executed by Ii Naosuki's orders in 1858, had also groped toward such a solution.

[27] *Sakamoto monjo*, II, 76.

some of his own writings on coastal defense as well as translations of a Dutch work on Sevastopol. It may be imagined that Sakamoto, whose friends Takechi and Mazaki had worked so closely with the young noble, was a peculiarly well-qualified ambassador to send to him. Anenokōji received the works cordially. The young nobleman was assassinated shortly afterwards, however, so that Katsu's effort came to nothing.[28] Still, it is not difficult to imagine Sakamoto's elation at being assigned missions of this importance.

The turbulence and danger of the loyalist frenzy could not fail to affect Katsu's *shishi* followers. Katsu noted in his diary how restless some of his Tosa followers became as the excitement grew around them: "I hear that last night five or six men were murdered. Tadokori Shimatarō, a Tosa man in my following, came, and told me that his companions were upset because they weren't achieving their loyalist goals, and that they had formed a secret plan to gather 300 men."[29] But Sakamoto continued to enlist support for Katsu's project from among his fellow rōnin, and especially from the Tosa group. On at least one occasion, one of the Tosa men saved Katsu's life when assassins dogged his steps.[30] Thus service with Katsu provided Sakamoto with a sense of importance and excitement, while for Katsu the Tosa loyalists provided much-needed assistance and even safety.

By June of 1863 Katsu was entrusting Sakamoto with more responsible and difficult missions. The Hyōgo institute was to be financed by contributions from the daimyō, but few of them would greet requests for funds with much sympathy. Naturally Katsu looked first to his friend and supporter, Matsudaira Shungaku, who had returned to his castle in Fukui. On the first of July Katsu sent Sakamoto to Fukui, the first of two trips that summer for him. Thanks to these missions Sakamoto had opportunity to meet some of the most able young feudal administrators in Japan. One of these, whom he had first met a half year earlier when he planned his death, was Yokoi Shōnan, Shungaku's gifted adviser. Together they had numerous discussions about national affairs. Sakamoto also established himself among the Fukui samurai as a drinker and bon vivant. In the course of this fraternization he met another

[28] *Kaishu nikki; Kaishū Zenshū*, ix, 9.
[29] *Kaishū Zenshū*, ix, 12.
[30] *Kaishū Zenshū*, x, 334. This was in June-July 1863, and the Tosa man was Okuda Izō, a rōnin who, as was noted earlier, came to a bad end.

outstanding figure among Shungaku's retainers, Yuri Kimimasa (then Mioka Hachirō). It is possible that Sakamoto discussed the suggestions of shogunal abdication he had heard about with these men, for Yokoi himself favored such a pacific solution. At any rate the visits brought Sakamoto close to men who would have great influence in the days ahead, and it broadened his view of national politics and possibilities. He was also able to collect for Katsu the sum of five thousand *ryō*.[31]

In the months that followed, Katsu showed his trust and affection for Sakamoto more and more. Early in December of 1863 he took Sakamoto to Edo with him, and later that same month Sakamoto was appointed head of training at the Hyōgo school. During this brief visit to Edo the Tosa administration tried to reclaim Sakamoto's person and services. A letter from Katsu to the Tosa police officials in Edo makes it clear that the han had tried to claim its man again, and also that he did not choose to return. Katsu's letter explained that Sakamoto was engaged in important work with him, and that his trip to Edo was actually in connection with his tasks as head of training in the Hyōgo naval academy. Katsu had, he reminded the *metsuke*, discussed Sakamoto's status with Yōdō personally, and hoped that there would be no further difficulty.[32] Despite Katsu's efforts, however, the Tosa authorities persisted in their efforts to recall Sakamoto. When he failed to comply, he was once again listed as a rōnin.

Sakamoto served as Katsu's assistant in the Hyōgo project for approximately eighteen months. This period marked a decisive turning point in his development. Much of the swordsman's bravado remained, and the protestations of loyalty to the throne rang as insistently as before. But to these had been added a new political outlook that reflected the broadened contacts and greater sophistication of men in the Katsu and Ōkubo pattern.

The many letters that Sakamoto wrote Otome are full of revealing indications of the way he saw his new role, and they leave little room for doubt about the part ambition and bravado played

[31] Hirao, *Kaientai*, pp. 70-71; for Yuri's reminiscences, *Sakamoto monjo*, I, 62-66; for Yokoi and Sakamoto, Yamazaki Masatada, *Yokoi Shōnan den* (Tokyo, 1942), II, 274-283; for Katsu's notes of these assignments for Sakamoto, *Kaishū nikki*; *Kaishū Zenshū*, IX, 21.

[32] Mr. Michio Hirao kindly provided me with a copy of this letter, dated January 14, 1864. It was discovered in Kōchi in 1958 and later published in *Tosa Shidan*, No. 93 (April 1958), pp. 11-12.

in his make-up. He announced his new position to her in these terms:

"Recently I've become a disciple of a student of military matters who has no equal in the country, Katsu Rintarō. He is a wonderful man, and a real pioneer. Before long we are going to set up a big naval training place at a spot more than ten *ri* from Osaka named Hyōgo, and we'll build ships two or three hundred feet long there. We have collected four or five hundred men, mostly younger sons. Along with fellows like Takamatsu Tarō, I am going to get training in the new techniques, and once in a while I'll get to practice on board a ship too. Before long I'll come to Tosa on our training ship. Wait till you see me then! . . ."

Sakamoto's satisfaction was evident throughout this letter, and he even felt obliged to apologize for it. "I seem to have something of an 'Ahem!' look about me, but that's just in private. The look outsiders see is quite severe."[33]

With greater responsibilities came greater satisfaction, and by August 1863 Sakamoto was a good deal less discreet in a letter to his sister. A long letter he wrote at that time tells so much about him at this stage that it is quoted in full.

"Don't show this letter to a soul, and do not chatter about it; treat it very carefully. I can't remember whether I wrote you on the twentieth. But yesterday I got your letter from Sugi, and many thanks for it.

"My things are coming along nicely just now. One of the big han is really letting me in on things. If trouble should start now, I would have two or three hundred men I could use as I thought best. And as for money, I have ten or twenty *ryō* at the least. This certainly eases my mind. But it really is too bad that Chōshū started a war last month by shelling ships six times; that doesn't benefit Japan at all, and I don't like it a bit. The boats they shot up in Chōshū are being repaired in Edo now, and when they're fixed again they'll head right back for Chōshū. This is all because those rascals in Edo are hand in glove with the barbarians. But although those scoundrels have a good deal of power, once I get

---

[33] *Sakamoto monjo*, I, 74. The "Ahem!" is Sakamoto's *ehen*, and seems to convey his joshing note of self-importance reasonably well.

together with two or three daimyō they'll have to think about their country. Then we will be able to do something. Once I join with my friends in Edo (you know, daimyō, hatamoto, and so on) and go after those wicked officials there we'll kill them. It is my firm desire to clean up Japan. Now this big han I mentioned is fully agreed with me, and their representatives are telling me all their secrets. Still, I haven't really been appointed to anything; it's really a shame there aren't more characters like mine around the country.

"From the letter I got from you yesterday I gather that you want to become a religious person and retire into the remote mountains somewhere. (Well, well! Ahem!) An interesting idea, that, but you've had it before. Things are pretty hectic these days, but if you go through with it, put on some old faded priest's robes and start wandering around like a pilgrim, it probably won't be too much trouble. You can get from Nagasaki to Matsumae on Hokkaido without spending a single silver coin. Still, if you're going to do that, you've got to read Shingon sutras, Kanon sutras, Ikkō sutras, and Amida sutras first. They are rhythmic and quite difficult. Still, there are a lot of Monto sect people around here and you've got to be able to do it, so you'd better get on with the job. This is really going to be delicious. You see, if you go to a Shingon place as a Shingon nun, you've got to read a Shingon sutra; if it's an Ikkō temple, it has to be an Ikkō sutra (the places you stop you really ought to preach, the way Saint Shinran did; that would be a story). If, when you get to a town, you read, read, morning, noon, and night, you'll get lots of coins; so be sure you do that. That really will be most interesting. After all, this world doesn't count for much. So let's give it a try, now, with all you have! When you die, what's left in the fields will look like white stones (dear, dear!).

"But you know, this isn't a thing you can do alone, without checking with people (for instance, poor old Ryōma is likely to die and haunt you any time); if you're thinking about things like this, you have to think of others and respect their wishes and thoughts. It occurs to me that you really are a little too young, you know. When you look for a mate, you don't just want some pretty fellow who looks good on the outside; you've got to be a vigorous, tough woman with some spunk. If, for instance, you go out with one or two friends of an evening and meet robbers, go after them and don't let go until you have them where it hurts. "I don't expect I'm the sort that's going to be around very long. But I don't expect to die like an average man either. Still, if while I'm alive I can't do any good for the country—but in any case I don't expect I'll be quite worthless. And since I'm fairly cagey, I'm not likely to die immediately either. But seriously; although I was born a nobody, of low rank in Tosa, I'm hardly likely to change the country much by myself. Certainly I'm not going to get all puffed up. Quite the reverse; I'm going to stick to the bottom of the pool, and keep my nose in the sand, so don't be worried about me."[34]

Ryōma

An interesting letter, this, full of the rough, earthy humor which characterizes the popular heroes of Japan. The doings of priests are fit for weaklings, and not even a courageous woman should seek solace in them. The times call for greatness and for courage, and these Sakamoto is quite sure he has in abundance. And despite the closing disclaimers of self-importance, there is far too much self-esteem here to dismiss it all as humor. Takechi Zuizan had once called Sakamoto a *hora fuki*, or braggart, and one suspects that Otome would have agreed. Still, this very exuberance serves to indicate how much he preferred his new life to the old, where station and rank would have ruled out his coming to prominence unless he had chosen the path of violence and desperation. A few years later Sakamoto put this quite succinctly in a letter to Otome. Writing from Nagasaki in 1865, he pointed out that "in a place like home, you can't have any ambition. You waste your time loafing around, and pass the time like an idiot."[35] Small wonder that service with Katsu proved such an acceptable alternative.

The Hyōgo assignment was the more welcome in that it required no commitment to the life of peace-loving student or bureaucrat. Sakamoto and his friends kept up their cordial relationships with loyalists from Tosa and other areas, even when, as noted in his letter to his sister, they disapproved of their rashness and grieved for their failures. They continued to consider themselves loyalists and *shishi*. Indeed, at one point the affairs of the Hyōgo academy went into temporary recess as Sakamoto, with

[34] *Sakamoto monjo*, I, 83-87.
[35] *Sakamoto monjo*, I, 136.

Katsu's cooperation, helped a friend find, and then avenge himself on, his father's assassin.[36]

The letter to Sakamoto's sister just quoted contains some evidence of the continuing insistence upon the Imperial cause. The Edo officials are "scoundrels," and Sakamoto and his friends are determined to "clean up" the country. A more carefully reasoned statement of the *shishi's* "high purpose" is to be found in a letter written July 31, 1863 to the parents of Ike Kurata, a friend who had just fled Tosa to join the ranks of loyalists in Kyoto. This letter, which has already been cited in part, contains such an excellent statement of Sakamoto's loyalism that it is useful to give it in full. It was written just after Yōdō had returned to Tosa; the cooperation of the great lords in Kyoto had failed to make any basic changes in the political structure, and even the shogun's visit had come to an end without apparent result. Who could blame patriots for deciding to take a hand in things themselves? Sakamoto put it this way.

"Ike's flight came about in this manner: Just now the activity on behalf of the court is not meeting success. All the daimyō, beginning with our own Lord of Tosa, have returned to their realms. Kura, from the bottom of his heart, felt that Lord Yōdō was exaggerating the difficulties and just temporizing in Edo and then in Kyoto, with much talk of his fears about the safety of the nation. Then, when things began to get difficult, he retreated to his own realm on some excuse or other. And then even the shogun returned to Edo.

"I must say that loyalty (*giri*) to what is called the divine country seems to have no influence; these men do not understand the idea of returning His Majesty to a position of power, and still that is the thing that has to be done. Well then, what are we men of low rank going to do to ease His Majesty's mind? Surely you realize that one ought to put the Imperial Court before his own province, and ahead of his parents. The idea that putting your relatives second, your province second, and abandoning your mother, your wife, and children—that this is a violation of your proper duty—is certainly, considering our times, something that comes from the stupid officials. And confused parents take their

[36] Hirao, *Kaientai*, pp. 63-68. Katsu's help consisted in a letter which gave the plaintiff free passage while he sought for his intended victim.

cue from them, talk about 'our own province' and 'our own house,' until their sons don't know what stand to take. If at such a time as this, you and Kura's wife take up your brooms and wave them about in petty discussions, and sob and weep, he will certainly be ashamed of you. . . ."[37]

Here one finds a staunch insistence on more power for the Emperor; Sakamoto is prepared to renounce every other consideration to that end, and the notion that feudal or family loyalties should come first seems outrageous to him. Service with Katsu had certainly not dulled his loyalism.

The period Sakamoto spent with Katsu did, however, educate him in national politics. This was particularly the case during the late summer and early fall of 1864, when Sakamoto was very close to Katsu. Their travels found them taking more and more of a part in national politics. Katsu, as Naval Commissioner, was an important Tokugawa official, and his assistant received a good introduction to national affairs. Already in the summer of 1863 Sakamoto had written his sister to deprecate the impatience of those who did not wait for the proper time before acting. The swordsman who had sought to kill Katsu had clearly learned a great deal, but his opportunities for education were also unusual.

Sakamoto's education continued during the foreign flotilla's moves to punish Chōshū for having fired on foreign shipping in the Straits of Shimonoseki. The politics of the affair provided abundant material for reflections on Tokugawa depravity and Chōshū imprudence. The bakufu envoys, who had been sent abroad in response to the promises made the court in the summer of 1863, had not only failed to persuade the Western powers to renounce their treaty rights, but had actually agreed to French demands for indemnities for the ships that had been shelled by Chōshū, and they had promised that action would be taken, with French help if necessary, to reopen the Shimonoseki Straits. When the shogunate refused to honor these agreements, a combined Western flotilla of seventeen ships entered the Straits early in September of 1864.

It was apparent to most informed Japanese that the bakufu's attitude toward the proposed shelling of Shimonoseki, like its earlier view of the British attack on Kagoshima, was ambivalent.

[37] The letter, dated July 1863, is in the Sakawa Bunko in Kōchi Prefecture.

175

Some officials (among whom Katsu was certainly one) were chiefly concerned by the prospect of a foreign attack on Japanese soil, while others, with a sharper eye to internal advantage, welcomed the convenient foreign assistance against Tokugawa foes. A formal court order for a Tokugawa expedition to punish Chōshū had been issued on August 24, but the expedition was not to get under way until December 16. Therefore it is not surprising that some Edo officials should have thought of dispatching a land force to penalize Chōshū simultaneously with the foreign fleet. The idea was abandoned for fear of unfavorable reactions to Tokugawa-European cooperation, but the consensus of students of the period is that the bakufu ended by deploring openly, and approving secretly, the action of the foreigners.[38]

At the last possible moment the bakufu sent Katsu to Nagasaki to try to arrange a peaceful settlement with the foreigners. Katsu found the leaders of the foreign flotilla unwilling to change their plans.[39] Within Chōshū last-minute negotiations were carried out by Itō and Inoue, newly returned from England, but these too failed to secure the concessions that would have averted the shelling.[40] The resulting humiliation of Chōshū convinced the Chōshū loyalists, as earlier foreign action had convinced their Satsuma counterparts, that the foreigners could no longer be expelled by force.

While Katsu was at Nagasaki he sent Sakamoto to Kumamoto to talk to Yokoi Shōnan. Sakamoto (as his letter just quoted showed) regretted both the Chōshū provocation and the bakufu attitude, and feared the possibility of a foreign seizure of Chōshū ground. Katsu recorded in his diary a talk with Sakamoto which revealed the latter's anger at the Tokugawa willingness to profit from foreign help. "Although Chōshū deserves punishment," he said, "fellow countrymen of our Imperial Country should never use foreign hands to strike them; this is wrong, and a discredit to our *kokutai*" (national polity).[41]

A few months later Katsu noted a suggestion that Sakamoto had made when they were both returning from Nagasaki by ship. It was a new idea for utilizing loyalist enthusiasm; Sakamoto sug-

[38] Osatake, *Meiji Ishin*, II, 448-450.
[39] Shibusawa Eiichi, *Tokugawa Keiki Kō den*, III, 40.
[40] E. Satow, *A Diplomat in Japan*, pp. 97f.
[41] *Sakamoto monjo*, I, 98-99.

gested that several hundred anti-foreign extremists might be recruited to form the backbone for the settlement and strengthening of Hokkaido.[42] It is particularly noteworthy, however, that Sakamoto explained that the Councillor Mizuno (Tadakiyo, who became rōjū in 1862) had already been informed about the idea. Clearly Sakamoto's channels to the highest authorities in the Tokugawa administration were now quite good.[43] But the project was already impracticable when Sakamoto suggested it on July 20. Unknown to both him and to Katsu, bakufu forces had struck against Chōshū plotters in Kyoto ten days earlier and so infuriated the loyalists that they were now interested only in assaulting Kyoto and capturing the Emperor.

Sakamoto and Katsu were at Osaka when the defeated Chōshū forces fled from Kyoto later in the summer of 1864 after the unsuccessful effort, described earlier, to invade the capital. With so many of Katsu's men drawn from the ranks of loyalist *shishi*, it is not surprising that some of them, including several from Tosa, had left the Hyōgo academy to join in the fighting with their friends. Many, if not most, of Katsu's men must have been in sympathy with the Chōshū attempt, and it is understandable that the Edo officials should later have suspected Katsu of assisting the Chōshū fugitives.[44] Nor was Katsu's sympathy limited to Chōshū loyalists; his diary notes show lively interest and concern for the Tosa scene, where Yōdō was proceeding to punish the Takechi group with increasing severity.[45]

With such excellent opportunities to study the dangers of impetuous action, Sakamoto was able to refine and moderate his own political thinking under Katsu's stimulus without in any way sacrificing his loyalist convictions. There are many indications that his thinking had begun to show a maturity and that he was beginning to put forth as his own ideas which were current in the circles in which he moved. Thus after Chōshū guns shelled foreign shipping in the Shimonoseki Straits, Sakamoto, in talks with the Fukui leaders, warned that only a sweeping reform of the bakufu organization could prevent foreign infringement of Japan's territorial integrity. He felt that reforms of the order that were required could

[42] A few years later Restoration leaders used the same idea by recruiting former partisans of the Tokugawa cause to develop the northern island.
[43] *Sakamoto monjo*, I, 98.
[44] Chikami, *Sakamoto Ryōma*, p. 74.
[45] *Sakamoto monjo*, I, 94.

only come through the determined cooperation of men like Matsudaira Shungaku, Yamauchi Yōdō, and Ōkubo Ichiō. Thus he was
already envisaging a situation in which the work of mediation and
negotiation would be central.[46]

Sakamoto's concept of a new political organization gradually
took the form of a conciliar system, and it followed the lines he
had heard suggested by the bakufu minister Ōkubo Ichiō. He concluded that the bakufu should share its principal decisions with a
council of feudal lords. By this means decisions and responsibilities would be more widely shared, and greater unity and support
would result. The early steps toward realignment of Tokugawa institutions which had resulted in appointments for Matsudaira
Shungaku and Hitotsubashi Keiki had run afoul of the jealousy
and conservatism of the regular bakufu councils. The few gatherings of the lords of Satsuma, Tosa, and Fukui had also proved unprofitable, as there was no institutional structure within which
their meetings could operate.

Sakamoto seems to have concluded that effective leadership in
the formation of a new and better council could best be exercised
by Matsudaira Shungaku of Fukui, a man who was trusted by most
Tokugawa supporters and esteemed by the tozama lords and *shishi*
alike. Sakamoto discussed these hopes several times with the Fukui
councillors of Shungaku, and with Yokoi Shōnan as well as with
his nephew, who was among those Sakamoto recruited for Katsu's
Hyōgo academy. These ideas were extremely congenial to Yokoi,
who had long hoped for some structure of cooperative decision-
making, or, as he termed it, *kyōwa seiji*.[47]

In the spring of 1864 hopes of this sort still seemed far from
fruition. Matsudaira Shungaku showed little eagerness to take the
lead in pressing for such a new order. Katsu, writing in his diary on
May 18, deplored the failure of the lords to realize their "great
duty," and there is no reason to think that his lower-ranking assistant Sakamoto thought more kindly about Shungaku's reluctance
to take the initiative. But true stability, in any event, would require more than a willingness on the part of the great lords. It
would be essential to get the support of the loyalist circles which
had done so much to make political reorganization difficult and

---

[46] *Sakamoto monjo*, I, 88-92.
[47] Shiomi Kaoru, "Sakamoto Ryōma no Ganji gannen," *Nihon Rekishi*, No. 108
(June 1957), p. 84.

dangerous. The next step therefore required Sakamoto's return to the ranks of the rōnin, in order to influence them, and this was made possible and necessary by the loss of his support from Katsu.

4. *The Dismissal of Katsu*

The dismissal of Katsu from his Tokugawa post, and the consequent loss of support for his rōnin followers, came as the result of a period of shifting bakufu policies and purposes. Many of the conservative fudai in Edo councils had never been content with or confident of the wisdom or loyalty of either Hitotsubashi Keiki or Matsudaira Shungaku. It was only a few years since the two had been put under the ban by Ii Naosuke, whose support had been strongest among the Edo traditionalists, and the sweeping changes the new administration had made—new talks with the outside lords, shogunal trips to Kyoto, pardons for Ii's enemies, punishment for Ii's heirs, and relaxation of the sankin-kōtai system—made them very uneasy about the future. An impression had been created that Keiki and Shungaku were far more reformist than they actually were. Shungaku's reluctance to agree to a full opening of Japan, and his consequent hesitation to become the front for any new political organization, were aspects of his ambivalence and desire to appease the doubters. Keiki, for his part, was far from happy with any trend that seemed likely to replace Tokugawa influence with that of Satsuma or Chōshū, and he did not work smoothly with Shimazu Hisamitsu of Satsuma at all. This, plus the pressure he was under from Edo, made his role equally uncertain and cautious. As a result the conversion of Satsuma to a position previously taken by Keiki and Shungaku went far toward making them reevaluate their earlier position.

Most of this became clear during 1864, which witnessed the second visit of the shogun Iemochi to Kyoto. With Keiki accompanying and directing him, Iemochi entered Kyoto on February 22 and remained until June 23. During this period a series of meetings with the Court and with the tozama lords, who now served as palace advisers, was devoted to the problem of foreign relations. The palace councils were temporarily dominated by Shimazu Hisamitsu, who had been summoned to Kyoto immediately after his city of Kagoshima had been virtually destroyed by the bombardment of a British squadron in August of 1863. After that encounter the Satsuma leaders, among whom Ōkubo Toshimichi,

Saigō Takamori, and Komatsu Tatewaki were now most prominent, had begun energetic measures to increase their foreign trade with a view to gaining foreign weapons. Their encounter with the British, moreover, despite its destructive outcome, had served to convince them that the foreigners were not necessarily evil and that contact with them could strengthen their fief as well as the bakufu. Thereafter, as has been described, Satsuma troops assisted Aizu forces to drive Chōshū extremists out of Kyoto. In the Kyoto discussions which began in March 1864 Satsuma opinion swung the court spokesman toward a position which emphasized rearmament and strengthening the national defences far more than it did exclusion. Yamauchi Yōdō, a participant in the discussions, took the same stand. Thus the Kyoto scene, for the first time free of the influence of the loyalist nobles and their Chōshū friends, had changed radically.[48]

The shogunate, however, had already dispatched a mission to Europe to try to gain French approval for closing the port of Yokohama. And Keiki, whether to gain the confidence of the conservative fudai councillors in Edo who doubted his fidelity, or to offset the influence of Satsuma in Kyoto councils, now insisted that for the sake of consistency and national confidence decisions which had been previously affirmed could not be renounced. He maintained his position in some very violent and angry scenes.[49] Keiki's announced intentions of implementing exclusion were of course doomed to failure, and when his envoys returned from Europe in August it turned out that they had made further concessions to the West instead of gaining Western concessions—a failure for which they were summarily dismissed and punished. But the violence of the argument served to lessen any expectations the great lords might have had of a closer liaison with the bakufu under the program of kōbu-gattai, and it convinced them of the bakufu's determination to consider its own immediate interests paramount at all times. The disgruntled lords of Satsuma and Tosa returned to their fiefs.

The confusing course of these negotiations gave unmistakable evidence of basic conflicts of purpose within the bakufu leader-

---

[48] Osatake, *Meiji Ishin*, II, 410.

[49] Osatake quotes Keiki to the effect that the bakufu could not turn around simply because Satsuma, instead of Chōshū, was now feeding ideas to the court. For a contemporary description of Keiki's tirade, Beasley, *Selected Documents*, pp. 268-273.

ship. The "reform" faction of Matsudaira Shungaku and Keiki, under whose aegis Katsu and Ōkubo Ichiō had come to prominence, seemingly had the choice between changing its positions or losing its influence.

Shungaku, in fact, resigned his post. It was the failure of leadership in a quarter from which so much had been hoped that made Katsu and Sakamoto take a dim view of the readiness of their leaders to accept their duty. Keiki, too, gave up his office in 1864. He accepted a new commission to look after coastal defences, but chiefly, it would seem, to prevent Shimazu Hisamitsu from receiving the appointment.

As Shungaku and Keiki reconsidered their plans and retreated from responsibilities, the conservatives in Edo strengthened their position. Many of them, it must be noted, were conservative not so much in terms of exclusionist policies as in a determination to retain political leadership during a period of change within firmly Tokugawa, fudai hands. Among these men a vigorous exponent of a firm policy toward the tozama daimyō was rising in importance and power. Oguri Tadamasa had visited the West in 1860 on the same mission as Katsu's. Like Katsu, he had been convinced of the need for changes in Japan's political structure. While Katsu returned anxious to work toward a more moderate and cooperative organization, however, Oguri chose instead to work toward a more autocratic structure in which the bakufu would gradually take over from its feudatories essential functions of defence and government and thereby construct a unitary state under Tokugawa auspices. Oguri rose rapidly through the orthodox channels of Tokugawa bureaucracy. A hereditary Tokugawa retainer of considerable family influence, he moved through the offices of *koshōgumi bangashira, kanjō bugyō, machi bugyō*, and, in 1863, *rikugun* bugyō. Thus a career in military, finance, civil administration, and finally army leadership gave him powerful support for the political debates of the final years of Tokugawa rule.

The errors in judgment that the Chōshū loyalists made in 1863 and 1864 created a setting in which it seemed possible that the firm policy men like Oguri desired had some chance of success. Chōshū's precipitate action in shelling foreign shipping in the Straits of Shimonoseki had brought the whole nation close to danger, and in September Aizu and Satsuma troops combined to drive Chōshū forces from the Imperial palace. In July 1864 bakufu troops surprised a group of Chōshū plotters and foiled their plans, and in August the Chōshū attempt to invade the capital was thwarted by renewed bakufu-Satsuma cooperation. Chōshū was now branded an "enemy of the court" (*chōteki*), and the court ordered the bakufu to punish its recalcitrant vassal.

The Tokugawa traditionalists naturally thought they could now resume their old ways. There was no longer much danger of a Satsuma-Chōshū alliance such as the *shishi* had dreamed of earlier. Hatred between the two great domains was running strong, and the old techniques of divide and rule gave at least some promise of regaining their former effectiveness. If Satsuma could be prevented from moving into the spot from which Chōshū had been driven, bakufu hegemony seemed assured.

After the foreigners had chastised Chōshū, the fudai traditionalists in Edo decided the time had come to adopt a more self-confident course. In October of 1864 an effort was made to reestablish the system of alternate attendance (sankin-kōtai) on its original lines. The crisis was past, it was explained, and the lords should by now have been able to rebuild sufficient military strength with the economies that have been possible. The attempt failed completely—even fudai daimyō were unenthusiastic—but nothing could have served better to illustrate the determination of Edo conservatives to return to the conditions of an earlier day.[50]

Then, on November 10, 1864 came the order dismissing Katsu from his post as Naval Commissioner. His enemies in Edo had finally convinced the top bakufu administrators that a new policy of firmness, built on Western technological advances and designed to buttress a more, rather than less, authoritarian administration, was the need of the day. The plans for a military expedition against Chōshū were about to be set in motion. In such a setting, Katsu's strange collection of rōnin and loyalists seemed suspicious. Katsu was dismissed, and his Hyōgo following was disbanded completely. The building of a modern navy was to be entrusted to Oguri Tadamasa.[51]

The new developments placed Sakamoto and his friends in im-

[50] Tsukahira, "The *Sankin-Kōtai* System of Tokugawa Japan," p. 186.

[51] For Katsu's own account of his dismissal, *Kaishū Zenshū*, x, 336-337. For Oguri's advance, the brief biography in *Dai Nihon Jimmei Jiten*, i, 653, and the longer but totally uncritical Abe Dōzan, *Kaigun no senkusha: Oguri Kozuke no Suke den* (Tokyo, 1941), 420 pp.

mediate danger. They had ignored orders from their han authorities to return home. As fugitives before the law, they changed their names in order to escape detection.[52] But safety in the face of the new Tokugawa posture would require powerful protection, and Katsu was no longer able to provide this. He did, however, provide some very useful requests to Satsuma friends.

Both Sakamoto and Katsu had recently become acquainted with several of the leaders of the Satsuma domain. Already in September, a letter to Yokoi Shōnan from his nephew (a colleague of Sakamoto's) told about a meeting Sakamoto had had with Saigō Takamori in the Satsuma headquarters in Kyoto.[53] Sakamoto had been acting as representative for Katsu, who first met Saigō two weeks later. With this meeting began the contacts with Satsuma that led to protection for Sakamoto after Katsu's dismissal. After he received notice of dismissal, Katsu wrote to the Satsuma leader Komatsu Tatewaki to ask his assistance in helping his former employees. The Satsuma men had use for people able to sail the new steamships which they were buying from Western traders. Since they had also met Sakamoto personally, they responded with friendly assistance. Komatsu wrote to the Satsuma representative Ōkubo Toshimichi,

"A Tosa man attached to Katsu in Kōbe is anxious to borrow a foreign style ship and operate it. His name is Sakamoto Ryōma. We have been talking about having him go to the Edo area and arrange for the use of one of our ships there. Another man from the same han, Takamatsu Tarō, has come too. It seems that just now the political situation in Tosa is so bad and that they are carrying on in such an extreme manner there that these men would lose their lives if they went back. It is true that even if a ship is available it would be some trouble to hide this man until he can board it, but since Saigō and others who are in the capital have talked it over and think it would be a good idea to make use of this rōnin in sailing, we are putting him up in the Osaka residence.[54]

[52] Henceforth Sakamoto used several names, but usually Saitani Umetarō. It will be remembered that Saitani was the name under which his forebears had operated as merchants.

[53] *Kaishū Zenshū*, ix; Shiomi, p. 81. Elsewhere Katsu described the report Sakamoto brought him on Saigō. "He's a real character (*jimbutsu*)," he assured Katsu; "if you speak softly he replies in kind, and if you make more noise, he roars in reply." *Kaishū Zenshū*, x, 261.

[54] *Sakamoto monjo*, i, 99-100, and *Ishin Tosa kinnō shi*, pp. 676-677.

The Tokugawa dismissal of Katsu had now brought a Tosa rōnin into the Satsuma fold with ideas of conciliar government and co-operation among the fiefs, ideas which he had first heard from bakufu ministers. Thanks to these, Sakamoto was far better fitted to play a part in the Restoration movement than he had been two-and-a-half years earlier when he set out to murder Katsu.

V. THE SATSUMA-CHŌSHŪ ALLIANCE

*I*N THE 1860's only two domains were capable of providing a direct political and military threat to Tokugawa hegemony. Satsuma and Chōshū were the two strongest realms in southwestern Japan. They had gone to great effort and expense to modernize their military establishments. Although punitive shelling by Western ships in 1863 and 1864 brought temporary setbacks in their programs of self-strengthening, they also resulted in new determination to build greater strength. Neither han could achieve this alone, however, for the September violence in Kyoto had shown that the Tokugawa leaders would utilize the assistance of one rival to block the exaggerated claims of another. Suspicion and jealousy between Satsuma and Chōshū retainers grew as each side suspected the other of aspiring to the direction of a new bakufu. Distrust between the two sides had contributed to their kaleidoscopic policy changes in the fevered years of the loyalist ascendancy, for Chōshū insistence on exclusion had helped bring about Satsuma preference for a reconciliation between court and shogunate. This distrust had erupted into violence in 1863. Chōshū guns shelled a Satsuma ship in the Straits of Shimonoseki, and Satsuma troops helped Aizu units drive Chōshū out of the Imperial capital. The Chōshū leaders habitually referred to the "Satsuma bandits" in their letters, and their Satsuma contemporaries were not accustomed to returning good for evil.

The only thing that could have brought these jealous contenders for national supremacy together was a new threat from the shogunate or from the foreigners. The shogunate provided both. The same conservatives who pressed for the dismissal of Katsu Rintarō as Naval Commissioner wanted more striking humiliation for Chōshū. They gave every indication that they were no longer interested in soliciting the advice or help of the great tozama lords in national policy, and they seemed likely to seek a new formulation of the powers the Imperial court had delegated to the shogun. To achieve this they were also prepared to consider a program of military and technical assistance from the France of Napoleon III. Thereby they made it patriotic, as well as prudent, for the great fiefs of the southwest to seek other sources of arms in the West to counter the new Tokugawa threat. And, as will be seen, that search could best be undertaken cooperatively.

This situation made some sort of working arrangement between Satsuma and Chōshū logical and, perhaps, inevitable. Nevertheless it required a great deal of preparation and much mediation. This role fell to the Tosa rōnin who had fled to Satsuma and Chōshū for protection after the collapse of their hopes in Tosa. Sakamoto, who had been referred to Satsuma leaders by Katsu in 1864, was thereafter perfectly situated to win them over to the ideas he had developed; he is best known for his work in bringing the alliance to completion. He did not, however, work at this alone. His friend Nakaoka Shintarō joined the Chōshū loyalists during the same period that Sakamoto turned to Satsuma and prepared the way with leaders there. Still others from the Tosa Loyalist Party were close to the Kyoto nobles who had been driven from the capital together with the Chōshū troops in September of 1863. The work of Sakamoto and his friends, particularly Nakaoka, thus provides an excellent opportunity to see the way in which the lessons of the decade were being absorbed in Satsuma and Chōshū. It will be seen that what was at work was much more than the illumination of an occasional *gōshi* or rōnin, for a good number of alert young samurai were awakening to the opportunities of their time.

1. Saigō Takamori and Satsuma

The Satsuma leaders who sheltered Sakamoto in the fall of 1864 were representatives of a domain whose antiquity and resources made it one of the most remarkable baronies of Tokugawa days.[1] The family of Shimazu could trace its residence in Kagoshima to 1185, when its founder Tadahisa was appointed representative of the first Kamakura shogun. Much of the area had earlier been held by the great court family of Konoe, with the result that rela-

[1] A basic compilation of documents, with commentary, for part of the Satsuma realm is that of K. Asakawa, *The Documents of Iriki* (second edition, Tokyo, 1955), pp. 442, 323. A brief summary of Satsuma institutional structure is that of Robert K. Sakai, "Feudal Society and Modern Leadership in Satsuma-han," *The Journal of Asian Studies*, XVI, 3 (May 1957), pp. 365-376. Some further details can be found in William E. Naff, "The Origins of the Satsuma Rebellion" (unpublished M.A. thesis, University of Washington, 1959). I have also been able to profit in my consideration of Saigō by many discussions with Professor Robert K. Sakai, who is preparing a full-length study, from which he drew a report to the University of Washington Japan Seminar on August 27, 1958. Of the tremendous volume of literature in Japanese on Satsuma and Saigō, I have made most use of the standard *Kagoshima Ken shi* (Tokyo, 1939-43), 5 vols., and the correspondence and biography found in Ōkawa Shigeyoshi, ed., *Dai Saigō Zenshū* (Tokyo, 1926), 3 vols.

tions between the Shimazu and the Konoe were also of great antiquity and intimacy. In the warfare of the fifteenth and sixteenth centuries Shimazu power had for a brief moment extended to all of Kyushu, but defeats by Hideyoshi in 1587 and Tokugawa Ieyasu in 1600 ended hopes of larger dominance. Nevertheless its lands were vast. The barony included an area larger than present-day Kagoshima Prefecture and its tax base of 770,000 Koku was augmented by trade and tribute from Okinawa. The Satsuma daimyō's income was second largest among Japan's feudal lords; only Maeda of Kanazawa, in Kaga, exceeded him in income and honor.

The secluded and distant location of Satsuma made possible a security that Maeda's more central location could not afford. Satsuma border patrols made entry into Kagoshima all but impossible for outsiders during Tokugawa times. Word of this reached even the Dutch, as seen in the report of the Chief Factor H. Doeff in 1833 that one Tokugawa police post involved spying on the great lords. There were, however, no cases, he noted, in which such a person had returned alive from Satsuma; "all who have been discovered there have been executed, so that those who are sent to that province consider themselves doomed."[2] There is room for doubt as to the existence of the unpopular post Doeff described, but his story can serve as example of the difficulty of violating the Satsuma borders. Satsuma's proportion of samurai to commoners (one to three) was the highest in Japan (the over-all average was approximately one to seventeen), and the large samurai population was employed to restrict popular consumption and enforce compliance with feudal decrees. No realm in Japan was more closely policed, and none knew such order.

Within the large samurai group, however, patterns of privilege and favor at times aroused resentment and concern. A group of seventy-one enfeoffed households monopolized high office within the han. These, the families of "Great Status" (ō mibun), preferred to continue the policies of a conservative past and avoid antagonizing the Tokugawa power, while many of the more junior ranks tended to deprecate the wisdom of their betters and ascribed their caution to self interest. Still, it must not be thought that the rank line resulted in automatic political antagonisms; at least one of the Satsuma leaders in late Tokugawa times, Komatsu Tatewaki, was very high on the status scale. Nevertheless, there

---

[2] H. Doeff, *Herinneringen uit Japan* (1833), p. 20.

remain numerous indications that in late Tokugawa and early Meiji times the opinions of the young, lower-ranking samurai were at variance with those of their betters, that they sought to encourage a more decided and, in their eyes, courageous stand by the han administration in national politics, and that representative spokesmen of this opinion acquired an importance and fame that would normally have been unattainable for those of low rank. The best example of this is to be found in the career of Saigō Takamori, Sakamoto's friend and sponsor in 1864, who was universally acknowledged to be the leader—and, at times, the captive —of the dissident groups.

Saigō was a heavy-set, intense, enigmatic individual who is often considered a perfect repository of the samurai tradition. Around him so many tales have collected that it is difficult to distinguish the figure from the symbol. His popularity has proved equal to the requirements of Japan's changing climate of opinion, with the result that he has been eulogized as a forerunner, first of ultranationalism, then of Lincolnian democracy. A glance at his career will show how this can be, and how remarkably his intellectual development had paralleled that of Sakamoto.

Saigō was thirty-six when he extended to Sakamoto the protection of the Satsuma barracks in 1864. His career had already seen sharp alternation of favor with danger, with the result that he no longer set great store by praise or safety. His schooling had included training in the teachings of Zen and of Wang Yang-ming, and from both sources he had absorbed a belief in the identity of knowledge and action. His approach to any problem was direct and intuitive. Careful analysis and tactical planning did not interest him, for he believed that "sincerity" would succeed, if only by stirring men who witnessed a noble failure, while "trickery" and artifice would accomplish nothing. Saigō's learning was of some depth, and he may have been motivated in his efforts by an injury he suffered in a fight (at the age of 13) which limited his feats of arms. His intensity and his great and powerful frame, however, had combined to give him great fame as a true samurai swordsman.

His early career was not military; he spent nine years as a minor official in a rural tax office. In this post he submitted courageous memorials denouncing administrative corruption and proposing measures for alleviating peasant distress, and it may be these that brought him official notice. These protests of Saigō's, together with his later efforts to give instruction to illiterate villagers during his banishment, furnish the basis for his repute as a warm-hearted, conscientious samurai who knew and sympathized with the difficulties of the commoners. His other characteristics—quick temper, a coarse and earthy humor, provocative silences that could pass for contempt or wisdom—combined to make him an excellent representative of the traditional Japanese popular hero, known for his courage, intractability, and sincerity.

Saigō's prominence began with his selection by Shimazu Nariakira (daimyō from 1851-1858) as one of the promising young men suitable for intelligence work and other assignments requiring discretion. From 1854 to 1858 Saigō carried out his lord's missions; plans for the substitution of Keiki for Iemochi as shogunal successor in 1858, for a more representative, conciliar power structure, and closer relations with the Kyoto court. These missions required constant travelling, and they provided opportunities to know and be known by some of the most forward-looking individuals in the political scene of the time. During these years Saigō also developed a measure of leadership among the groups of young samurai who waited for an opportunity to strike against the foreigners and those who favored them. Han surveillance ruled out organizational devices like the Tosa Loyalist Party, but it is significant that when Satsuma *shishi* vowed their loyalty to their new lord in 1859 Saigō's name led all the rest.

Saigō's lord, Nariakira, died shortly after Ii Naosuke thwarted the hopes for which he had worked. To Saigō's dismay the new han administration was unwilling to take any chances with the new bakufu regime. Not only were no protests against Tokugawa policy mounted or allowed, but representatives of Nariakira's policies were shunted to one side. Saigō himself was sent into exile on an island off the Satsuma coast; here he stayed for three years and two months. He had been exiled partly for his own protection against bakufu reprisals, and was treated with great leniency.

Saigō was reinstated in 1862. Nariakira's brother, Hisamitsu, was acting as regent for his own son, daimyō Tadayoshi. Hisamitsu dominated Satsuma until the abolition of feudalism in 1871. He professed to follow his brother's plans and policies, but he showed himself a good deal less imaginative and resourceful intellectually and politically. In particular, he was more concerned with control than he was with utilization of samurai opinion and energy. Saigō got into Hisamitsu's bad graces almost immediately by loose construction of commands he had been given to precede Hisamitsu on the latter's trip to Kyoto in 1862. When Hisamitsu concluded that Saigō had not only disobeyed him but also associated with the rōnin who dominated Kyoto in that summer, he banished Saigō once again, this time to a smaller island off Satsuma. This banishment lasted until March of 1864. It was a period of strict control and imprisonment, for Saigō had now incurred Satsuma, as opposed to Tokugawa, displeasure. Saigō was thus inactive politically during the key years of Satsuma reorientation from exclusionism to moderation. But it did not take him very long to absorb the lessons his countrymen had learned; indeed, it is probable that under Nariakira's tutelage he had already absorbed some of them. Certainly he showed a quick awareness of the possibilities for the new weapons and techniques that became available.

Saigō's recall was arranged by friends in the bureaucracy who pressed upon Hisamitsu assurances as to his loyalty and ability. Of these friends the most important was Ōkubo Toshimichi [then Ichizō]; together he and Saigō now came to dominate Satsuma policy and thought.[3] After his reinstatement he was stationed in Kyoto, where he was in charge of the Satsuma residence and troops. His powers in this post were considerable, for distance prevented close control from Kagoshima. Saigō refused compliance with instructions he felt unwise, and at several points he personally determined the tactics Satsuma should follow. He reported regularly to Ōkubo in Kagoshima his impressions of the Kyoto scene, and these letters—one of the most remarkable treasures in a period rich in documentation—make it possible to trace his ideas in the days when Sakamoto first came to know him.[4]

Saigō assumed this important post at a time when Satsuma policy was beginning to point toward a much stronger position. It will be recalled that Hisamitsu had worked, in Edo as in Kyoto, for Kōbu-gattai in 1862 and 1863. His hopes had come to nothing. At the meetings of the great lords in Kyoto in the spring of 1864, Keiki had insisted on continuing to try for abrogation or modifica-

---

[3] There is a useful but little-used Western-language biography of Ōkubo, Maurice Courant, *Ōkubo* (Paris, 1904). The standard biography is Katsuta Magoya, *Ōkubo Toshimichi den* (Tokyo, 1911), 3 vols.

[4] The more significant of these are compiled with commentary in Ōkawa Shigeyoshi, ed., *Dai Saigō Zenshū* (Tokyo, 1926), 3 vols.

tion of the treaties with the West because of his unwillingness to accept the moderate stand which Hisamitsu had persuaded the court to adopt. The bakufu seemed to have a new confidence in its ability to have its own way in national affairs, and it was evident that by kōbu-gattai it meant little more than court support for policies determined in Edo. Hisamitsu had returned to Kagoshima, and henceforth when he used the term kōbu-gattai he would project a change whereby the Tokugawa, as the first among equals, would join with their peers in councils designed to give all the lords equal opportunity to serve the Imperial cause. But in fact the term was heard much less frequently in Satsuma, for it was being replaced by talk of bringing down the shogunate—expressed in the term *tōbaku*. Such talk was much more to the liking of young and restless warriors, and Saigō, returned in triumph from an unjust banishment, was their hero.

When Saigō took up his post at Kyoto the first subject that concerned him was the threat from Chōshū. The previous September Satsuma units had helped exclude Chōshū from the palace gates. By the time Saigō arrived in Kyoto rumors were spreading about Chōshū plans to invade the capital and seize the Emperor. Saigō saw to it that Satsuma had no part of bakufu defence preparations —he refused a Tokugawa request for troops—until he was convinced that the Chōshū plans did indeed concern the person of the Emperor. He reported to Ōkubo that the bakufu might use the help of foreigners against Chōshū, and also that Chōshū itself seemed to be negotiating with the Westerners.[5] But when the Chōshū attack on Kyoto did come, he led Satsuma forces to defend the palace gates against the assault, himself receiving a foot wound in the battle. Satsuma troops had helped to tip the scales against Chōshū, but they had done so in response to a court, and not a bakufu request. It is, however, understandable that this incident did not endear Saigō—or Satsuma—to the Chōshū loyalists.

At the same time that Saigō was immersed in this effort to keep Chōshū from upsetting the balance of power of Tokugawa feudalism, he was showing a lively interest in ways to improve the financial position of his han. The classical, "Confucian" pattern of Tokugawa days was to avoid all contact with commerce (numbers were, as Fukuzawa's father told him, "the tools of shopkeepers"). As a result han commercial dealings were often delegated to spe-

[5] *Saigō Zenshū*, I, 330, 345.

cially favored "official merchants." Strong political leaders, on the other hand, periodically tried to divert some of the profits from private to official channels by establishing han monopolies. This was also true in Satsuma. Saigō's experience as tax official and in banishment had familiarized him with some of the injustices that could develop under a monopoly system operated by licensed merchants, and he now moved in the direction of having the authorities take trading functions into their own hands completely.

The problem concerned Satsuma efforts to buy foreign ships, which were so expensive that normal han resources quickly proved inadequate. Saigō's letters to Ōkubo discussed the problem of getting the currency required for these purchases, and he began by suggesting that more Satsuma goods be shipped to the Ryūkyūs for sale to foreigners there. Soon he decided it would be better to ship them to Osaka, and then came a startling suggestion that he himself be authorized to use Satsuma cash reserves to buy up goods, especially silk, when the market was glutted in order to hold them for sale at a later, more advantageous time. It was true, he wrote, that foreign merchants were clever, but he would gladly try his hand at outwitting them. Profits were certain and they could be used to pay for the much-needed warships.[6] By the time he met Sakamoto, in other words, Saigō had left all simple antiforeignism behind him; he was in favor of open ports and foreign dealings, and looked to these as a way of strengthening his Satsuma vis-à-vis the Tokugawa. Indeed, shortly afterward he and his friends complained to Ernest Satow that the main trouble with the bakufu was its desire to monopolize all the profitable trade for itself.[7]

Besides these ideas for commercial gain, Saigō was learning to think in terms of cooperative action between han. His service under Nariakira undoubtedly helped to prepare him for this, as the maneuvers of 1858 involved close cooperation between several domains. But in the fall of 1864 a meeting with Katsu Rintarō introduced new ideas of conciliar organization. It was this meeting, which took place on October 16 in Osaka, that Sakamoto had prepared for Katsu in his first encounter with Saigō. The talk, as reported to Ōkubo by Saigō, provides significant detail both for his own development and as explanation for the distrust in which

[6] *Saigō Zenshū*, I, 483, 498.
[7] See a conversation with Saigō reported by Sir Ernest Satow, *A Diplomat in Japan*, pp. 183-184.

Tokugawa conservatives held Katsu. Although it took place at a time when Satsuma-bakufu cooperation seemed promising, there was more in the discussion to distress than to reassure orthodox Tokugawa councillors.

According to Saigō, Katsu, who was on his way to Edo, told him of his plans to talk to a member of the Senior Council, Abe Masato. He had some hope, he said, of persuading him to dismiss reactionary officials and arrange a new administrative system under which four or five of the great daimyō would hold office. Katsu went on to talk about defence measures. He felt it desirable to combine Tokugawa strength with the naval forces of four or five lords in order to be able to repel foreigners in the Inland Sea area. Yokohama and Nagasaki, he thought, could well be left as open ports without danger or shame, but the Inland Sea ports were in a different category. Katsu seemed to feel that the foreigners were reasonable people, and could be won over to give up their plans for a port in the Inland Sea if there was evidence of united defence action in case they should refuse. These were, on the whole, new ideas to Saigō, and they were the more attractive because they came from an important Tokugawa official.[8] Saigō hoped that his lord would see the value such an arrangement would have for Satsuma; he was particularly attracted by talk of the new "cooperative government" that was to come after the immediate danger was past. Thus Saigō, like Sakamoto, was won over for ideas of political change he heard from a member of the Tokugawa regime.

Saigō's full emergence into national politics came during the Tokugawa expedition of chastisement for Chōshū's attempt to invade Kyoto in 1864. He began the enterprise full of determination to humiliate Chōshū, only to moderate his views as he became aware of the danger his own han would incur if it permitted and assisted in the complete destruction of its great rival. Saigō left Kyoto to join the expedition, in which he held a high post. As leader of the Satsuma contingent, he had much influence in the dispositions and plans that were made. His initial inclination was to make sure that Chōshū would be punished severely. Prompt pursuit of Chōshū, furthermore, would have deprived the foreigners of their excuse for taking on themselves an action against the Shimonoseki batteries that had shelled their ships. On the other

[8] *Saigō Zenshū*, I, 490-504.

hand, Saigō wanted it to be very clear that the cooperation which Satsuma was extending the bakufu was one between equals, and that it was in response to court, and not shogunal, requests. He altered plans for the utilization of the Satsuma troops that took part, he criticized Tokugawa dispositions, and he rejected indignantly a bakufu request to station three military observers in Satsuma; it was difficult, he wrote Ōkubo, to hold his stomach, so full-bellied was his laughter at the thought.[9]

Saigō gradually became convinced of the desirability of a compromise settlement; there was no reason to help the bakufu crush Chōshū completely. He put more effort into political than military dispositions, and he prepared a bridge over which the Chōshū leaders could retreat with some dignity. First through Chōshū men who had been captured by Satsuma forces in Kyoto, and then in person, he suggested terms that were accepted. Three Chōshū *karō* were to be ordered to kill themselves, the defences of Yamaguchi castle were to be levelled, and the refugee Kyoto nobles were to be moved to Kyushu.[10] The program was one that was acceptable to the conservatives in Chōshū, who now tried to consolidate their power by pointing to the dangers to which the extremists had brought their han.

The expedition ended amicably on January 24, 1865. The heads of the three *karō* were delivered to the Tokugawa commanders, and all seemed in order. Saigō had gained greatly in political stature and repute. He visited Shimonoseki with no thought of his own safety to explain the details of the settlement, and he personally arranged for the transfer of the court nobles to Dazaifu, near Fukuoka, on Kyushu.[11]

But the weeks that followed found all Saigō's hopes of political betterment frustrated. Edo conservatives showed no inclination to moderate the Tokugawa prerogatives. For a while Saigō and his colleagues carried on their efforts to convene a council of their lords. Saigō urged Hisamitsu to come to Kyoto, Ōkubo travelled to Fukui to encourage Matsudaira Shungaku, and a third Satsuma man went to Uwajima in search of Date Munenari. When these efforts failed, partly through the caution of lords who were wary

---

[9] *Saigō Zenshū*, I, 512.

[10] *Saigō Zenshū*, I, 570-613. The compromise was also partly the work of the Fukuoka *karō* Katō Shisho, and is described by his biographer, Shisho Kai, ed., *Katō Shisho den* (Fukuoka, 1933), pp. 52f.

[11] *Saigō Zenshū*, I, 618f.

of seeming to grasp powers that had not been offered to them, Saigō began to conclude that a sweeping, and probably violent, political change would be required. He now began to suggest closer relations with the British, with an eye to trade and military assistance. He urged that the Satsuma residences in Edo be virtually emptied of their official residents; Kyoto had now become the political capital, and there was no reason to contribute to Tokugawa dreams of grandeur.[12] It was inevitable that he would also begin to think differently about the Chōshū enemy whose utter destruction was now being planned by the Edo councils. He had, in other words, been well prepared for the arguments for cooperation with Chōshū that Sakamoto Ryōma was going to use. Fortunately for Sakamoto, a Tosa confederate was performing a similar role with the Chōshū leaders.

2. Nakaoka Shintarō and Chōshū

The contribution that the Chōshū domain made to the Restoration was greatest of all. From the time of Yoshida Shōin on, Chōshū loyalists led in the extreme anti-foreign movement. They provided more than their share of martyrs and heroes for later patriotism, and they arranged sanctuary for rōnin who had fled other areas. In no other domain were the disputes between conservative and radical factions so sharp and violent; each major turn in han policy was preceded by an overthrow of han administrators. By the latter half of the 1860's, leading figures in both the radical and the conservative camps had been lost through battle, sickness, and hara-kiri. The foreign bombardment of Shimonoseki had served to rule out simple anti-foreignism as a program, while bakufu insistence on full humiliation had also lessened the attraction of slogans like kōbu-gattai. Nevertheless, the suspicion and hatred which the Chōshū men bore their Satsuma competitors for national leadership made an alliance between the two seem remote.

It would require a lengthy digression to trace the Chōshū scene in any detail, and even brief description of the leaders' intellectual development would involve the retelling of much of the story already told.[13] It will be more appropriate to treat that scene as it

---

[12] *Saigo Zenshū*, I, 687.

[13] The Chōshū story will be the subject of a forthcoming work, *Chōshū in the Meiji Restoration* by Albert Craig; part of it has already been presented by him

contributed to the education of Nakaoka Shintarō, the Tosa rōnin who shares with Sakamoto the credit for having realized the necessity of an alliance between Satsuma and Chōshū. He performed with Chōshū the role that Sakamoto played in Satsuma.

Nakaoka Shintarō appeared earlier in this narrative in the account of the Tosa Loyalist Party.[14] The eldest son of a village head in eastern Tosa, he was one of the party of fifty shōya and gōshi who demanded permission to go to Edo to protect Yamauchi Yōdō in 1862. It may be recalled that Yōdō, who proved to be in no danger whatever, was favorably impressed by Nakaoka, sending him on several missions, using him to keep abreast of shishi opinion, and even appointing him metsuke in the retinue with which he returned to Tosa in the spring of 1863.

During this period Nakaoka gave on the whole the impression of having a rigid, dogmatic cast of mind. With little of Sakamoto's humor and balance, he maintained a firm position of thoroughgoing anti-foreignism. As a result Yōdō's decision to ignore the imperial authorization to expel the barbarians by June of 1863 dismayed Nakaoka. His sense of the urgency of the situation led him to take counsel with members of the upper samurai group. Itagaki [then Inui] Taisuke, a member of the "mounted guard" (umamawari) rank who had been ordered by Yōdō to form a group of fifty warriors to discourage violence by the party of fifty rustics (of which Nakaoka was one) in Edo earlier, was also fiercely opposed to the treaties with the West. Between Itagaki—who lost his official post for his position on the Imperial authorization to fight—and Nakaoka there now developed a friendship that paved the way for cooperation between their rank groups a few years

---

as "The Restoration Movement in Chōshū," *The Journal of Asian Studies*, XVIII, 2 (February, 1959), pp. 187-197. Studies of Chōshū leaders include Roger F. Hackett, *Yamagata Aritomo: Soldier-Statesman of Modern Japan*, forthcoming from Harvard University Press, a revision of a dissertation entitled "Yamagata Aritomo: A Political Biography" (Harvard University, 1955), and Sidney D. Brown, "Kido Takayoshi and the Meiji Restoration" (unpublished Ph.D. dissertation, University of Wisconsin, 1952), which forms the base for the same author's "Kido Takayoshi, Japan's Cautious Revolutionary," *Pacific Historical Review*, XXV, 2 (May, 1956).

[14] For Nakaoka the principal sources are Hirao Michio, *Rikuentai shimatsu ki* (Tokyo, 1942), 324 pp., and the less reliable Ozaki Takuji, *Nakaoka Shintarō* (Tokyo, 1926), 378 pp., which includes, however, Nakaoka's diary, pp. 329-372. Part of the diary and much of Nakaoka's corrrespondence and other writings have been compiled and discussed by Hirao Michio, in *Sakamoto Ryōma-Nakaoka Shintarō* (Tokyo, 1942), pp. 174-358.

later.[15] Itagaki's feudal loyalties were strong enough to keep him in Tosa. Nakaoka's, however, were not; in the fall of 1863 he visited Chōshū secretly, and when, on his return, he saw the indications that the Loyalist Party was on the decline, he fled to Chōshū. From late November of 1863 on, Nakaoka was a rōnin refugee with Chōshū. His family, it is interesting to note, approved of his course. When his father sickened and died in 1866, they kept the news out of their letters to Nakaoka lest his loyalties as eldest son should weaken his resolution in the Imperial cause.

At the Chōshū port of Mitajiri, Nakaoka joined a contingent of Tosa men (among them Hijikata Hisamoto) who had joined the cause of the court nobles who had taken refuge there. From Mitajiri appeals went out to recruit others for the cause. From Kurume came Maki Izumi, who was soon to lose his life in Kyoto. The seven court nobles (soon reduced to five with the departure of one for the Yamato putsch and the death of a second), were naturally the center of attention for they symbolized the loyalist cause; Sanjō Sanetomi, who was now 26, was the leader of the group. In the Mitajiri center life was organized in the pattern followed by ultranationalist academies of later times. The *shishi* rose at six and worshipped to the east. After breakfast came work in *bumbu* (letters and weapons); the afternoon hours were spent in military exercises, while evenings were "free" for recommended tasks like books on war. There was a regular schedule for drill, examinations, and group activities.[16]

The Tosa administration was aware that many of its men were at Mitajiri and it sent the father of one *shishi* to try to persuade them to return. The comrades considered assassinating this emissary, but Nakaoka kept them from doing so. They decided to hear the messenger out, but they paid no attention to his requests. There was, however, a certain ambivalence in the Tosa official attitude. The emissary himself showed respect and moderation in his talks with the *shishi*, and no formal negotiations were undertaken to attempt their extradition. Indeed, Nakaoka was personally assured that no steps were being taken against his relatives to punish them for his defection. The Kōchi administrators probably felt that the men who had left their inheritance to help

[15] Itagaki has been studied by Cecil E. Cody, "A Study of the Career of Itagaki Taisuke (1837-1919), A Leader of the Democratic Movement in Meiji Japan" (unpublished dissertation, University of Washington, 1955).

[16] *Rikuentai*, pp. 56f.

protect the exiled court nobles had given evidence of considerable moral courage, and in any case they could not have moved against them without further antagonizing the restless loyalists in Tosa.

Shortly after his arrival in Mitajiri, Nakaoka was sent to Kyoto as an intelligence agent. While there he was in close touch with a number of extremist rōnin; he lived with Takasugi Shinsaku, leader of the Chōshū Kiheitai, and other Chōshū stalwarts. Until Chōshū troops invaded Kyoto later in the summer in their attempt to seize the emperor, Nakaoka was at the center of extremist activities. During the spring of 1864 his hopes of an early loyalist putsch were high. The great lords had left Kyoto as their plans for kōbu-gattai failed. For a time Nakaoka thought he saw in Shimazu Hisamitsu the chief bar to a loyalist movement, and together with Takasugi he even tried to plan his assassination. Hisamitsu proved too well guarded, however; when rumors of the plot reached him he hastened his departure for Kagoshima.[17] Curiously enough, these plans seem to have come shortly after Nakaoka first met Saigō Takamori in Kyoto. Whatever the details of that meeting (and none are available), it is clear that Nakaoka and the Chōshū men saw little hope of an understanding with Satsuma.

Nakaoka's thinking can best be learned from the analyses of the political situation which he sent to his loyalist friends in Tosa. In the summer of 1864 he thought victory for the loyalists in most of Japan was at hand. From Mito came news of the desperate civil war that had broken out there; for a time it was conceivable that the "Party of Righteousness" would succeed in its plans to overthrow the fief government and march on Kyoto. Early in June, 1864, Nakaoka sent a long letter to his friends in Tosa in which he set forth the possibilities. On the discouraging side was the predominance of moderates at the court. Conservatives and "evil" councillors had promoted Hisamitsu to a new court rank, and conservative court nobles had risen in office. On the other hand, there was the obvious discomfiture of the kōbu-gattai faction reflected in the departure of the lords from Kyoto. Now, thought Nakaoka, was the opportunity for *shishi* from all areas to arise, seize control of Kyoto, and restore the extremist nobles to power. A quick coup in Kyoto would prepare the way for the Chōshū return to the capital, and once that was accomplished the tide

17 *Rikuentai*, p. 70.

would turn. Nakaoka urged his Tosa comrades to do their share in this task. He held out the hope of cooperation from upper samurai in Tosa like Itagaki Taisuke. Nakaoka saw no problem of feudal loyalty in disobeying han orders. "A time of opportunity like this," he wrote, "will not come again in a hundred years. It is true that we will seem to be out of step with our Tosa in this noble work, but after all it will have the result of making Tosa prosper; can it then not be considered loyalty and filial piety? And in any case, if we fail to grasp this occasion there will never be another. . . ." As a final argument Nakaoka reported the latest word that had come to him from Nagasaki: in China a second war had ended with the foreigners in Peking itself; the very center of the empire had fallen. In truth, there was no time to be lost. Would the confederates in Tosa do their part? An immediate insurrection was essential.[18]

This letter reached Tosa during the days in which Yōdō was dealing with the Takechi adherents. It was directly responsible for a petition addressed to the han regime by thirty *shishi* asking for Takechi's release, and when that was not effective twenty-three loyalists in eastern Tosa, Nakaoka's homeland, rose in the demonstration at Noneyama that cost them their lives.[19] Nakaoka's advice had thus had the effect of deepening antagonisms in Tosa and hastening the demise of the Tosa Loyalist Party.

In June of 1864 Nakaoka returned to Chōshū to help prepare the details of the *shishi* revolt he had wanted his Tosa friends to join, and a month later he returned to Kyoto. Before he reached there, however, he received word that a group of plotters had been surprised at the Ikedaya Inn and that the conspiracy had been found out. This was followed by the decision of extremist groups in Chōshū to launch a full attack on Kyoto. Maki Izumi, of the Mitajiri rōnin, was a leader in the plot; he and his "Loyal and Brave Company," the *Chūyūtai*, were to deliver one attack. Nakaoka was among those who prepared to fight. Their goal, they thought, was to rescue the Emperor from the evil hands of the Aizu-Satsuma traitors. In the bitter fighting that took place at the gates of the palace on August 19 Nakaoka was wounded, but he made his escape. A letter that he wrote the night before, taking leave of his family, shows his emotions at this time. "In view of

---

[18] *Sakamoto-Nakaoka*, pp. 185-188.
[19] The fullest account of Noneyama is in *Ishin Tosa kinnō shi*, pp. 560-572, 644-650.

father's advancing age," he wrote, "this coming battle is a very unfortunate thing, and I will probably be thought very unfilial. But be that as it may; although I was born a poor, ignorant rustic in the mountains of Tosa, I have always, from my earliest years, done my best to follow the path of loyalty and righteousness, and if I should come to lay down my life for the Imperial Country and for the Son of Heaven I will have nothing to regret."[20]

But Nakaoka survived the fighting. He spent some days in hiding recovering from his wound, and then he returned to Chōshū. When the foreign gunboats shelled the Shimonoseki emplacements on September 5, Nakaoka was again one of the "Loyal and Brave Company" which tried to thwart the allied landing parties which spiked and captured the shore guns. This fight, too, was lost. Shortly thereafter the Chōshū loyalists, twice defeated, were being blamed by their compatriots for the disasters that had befallen Chōshū. The bakufu was about to launch a punitive expedition, the foreigners had already done their part, and the court had branded loyalist Chōshū an "enemy of the court." Not only were the Chōshū upper classes disagreed on the proper course to follow. The commoners had shown themselves quite uninterested in all the fuss. They had watched the battles with the foreigners from a safe distance, and thereafter obligingly helped the foreigners load the guns they took as booty. Satow, who noted that the Japanese were "very friendly," thought they were "not improbably glad to get rid of the toys that had brought them into so much trouble."[21]

Small wonder, then, that Nakaoka now was chastened and contrite in a letter he wrote his Tosa friends on November 9. He had received word from Tosa of the twenty-three shishi lost in the Noneyama Incident; but for his advice, they might still have been alive. He told his friends of the failures in Kyoto and Shimonoseki. The court seemed committed to opening the ports, and worse outrages were sure to follow. Foreign hulls could soon be expected to mar the smooth surface of the Inland Sea. Despite all this, Nakaoka felt that nothing could be done. There was nothing to be gained by creating new disturbances or fleeing the han. All that could be done was to restrain one's tears and remain silent. As for the Imperial permission to open the ports and the entry of foreign

[20] Sakamoto-Nakaoka, pp. 191-192.
[21] Satow, Diplomat in Japan, p. 118; Osatake, Meiji Ishin, II, 456.

ships into Inland Sea, it would be proper for the Tosa lord to ask the throne to think on these matters. To this sage advice Nakaoka added a list of questions about political conditions in Tosa. Were the loyalists still being prosecuted? What was the state of public opinion? Who was in prison? Who had been punished? What about affairs in Eastern Tosa?[22] Nakaoka had now learned that individual or regional heroics could only complicate, and never solve, Japan's pressing problems.

After the Shimonoseki failure Nakaoka was used for a time as scout for the Chōshū militia units. He went to Tottori to see whether there was any chance that the Chōshū sympathizers there might be able to swing the han into official support. And he travelled again to Kyoto to survey the situation. Nowhere did he find any basis for optimism. Everywhere conservative, "vulgar view" factions seemed to be gaining in power over the loyalist, "righteous" parties. Young Yamauchi Toyonori, the young daimyō of Tosa had even put aside his Mōri (Chōshū) bride of a few months to avoid possible charges of sympathy.[23]

When he returned to Chōshū on December 16, Nakaoka was given joint command of the "Loyal and Brave Company" of militia together with a younger brother of the impetuous Maki Izumi who had lost his life in the Kyoto battle. It was not an easy assignment. The company, made up of rōnin and *shishi* from all over Japan, was depleted in number and spirit since the recent defeats. Chōshū conservatives were beginning to blame all their han's troubles on the undisciplined and erratic rōnin who had been recruited by the loyalist han officials. Those officials, moreover, were about to lose power completely for a time. Kusaka Genzui had been killed in Kyoto. Inoue Kaoru [then Bunta] was very nearly killed by a conservative partisan and forced into a lengthy retirement,[24] while Sufu Masanosuke, one of the outstanding loyalist leaders, committed suicide to take responsibility for the unfavorable course of events. As the bakufu's first punitive expedition against Chōshū neared the borders, the conservative faction was so far in control that the surrender terms that Saigō suggested were quickly accepted. Early in 1865 the Chōshū administration agreed to the death of the policy-making *karō*, apolo-

---

[22] *Sakamoto-Nakaoka*, pp. 199-200.
[23] *Ishin Tosa kinnō shi*, pp. 625.
[24] There is an account by K. Tsudzuki, *An Episode from the Life of Count Inouye* (Tokyo, 1912), p. 189.

gies from the daimyō, destruction of the defences of Yamaguchi castle, and transfer from Chōshū of the five remaining Kyoto nobles who had fled with the Chōshū forces in September of 1863. The punishment of the guilty advisers was speedy, and in the aftermath of the ceremonial suicides of the han leaders many lesser lights in exclusion and loyalist movements lost place and influence. Nakaoka's "Loyal and Brave Company" was disbanded, as were the other militia units.

The only part of the loyalist dream that could still be salvaged was to assure the safety of the refugee court nobles. To the loyalists these men became increasingly important, for they served as reminder and hope of court support and legitimacy. They would have to leave Chōshū, which was now atoning for having given them shelter. The bakufu would have liked to take them into custody, but this would constitute betrayal by Chōshū. An alternative —which was adopted—was to transfer them across the straits to Fukuoka, where loyalist confederates in the han administration would welcome them. Unfortunately, no one could be sure of the political future of these loyalists (again, a "Party of Righteousness" —Seigi-tō), for the Chōshū disasters had discredited loyalism everywhere.

What was required, then, was some agreement with other han about a guarantee of sanctuary for the Kyoto nobles. To this end Nakaoka crossed the straits to Kokura in January, 1865, to discuss the problem with Saigō Takamori. Saigō sent a Satsuma friend, Yoshii Kōzuke, back with Nakaoka to Shimonoseki. Gradually, a plan was worked out. More important, the way had been prepared whereby Nakaoka—and the Chōshū loyalists—could begin to put some trust in Saigō as a man of honor and patriotism.[25]

While the discussions for transfer of the nobles were still under way, the political situation in Chōshū underwent a sharp change. The militia units, of which Takasugi Shinsaku's Kiheitai was to become the most famous, were restive under the capitulation of the han administration. There were rumors that the court nobles might be surrendered to Edo, and there were signs of a general purge of loyalists. The militia units came to life. Takasugi, who had fled to Kokura, reappeared with a handful of followers, among them Itō Hirobumi [then Shunsuke] and Yamagata Aritomo on January 12, 1865. Beginning with a handful of twenty men, he

[25] *Rikuentai*, pp. 108f.

rallied support and seized the initiative. Soon his old militia units were forming around him. For some weeks the outcome was uncertain. The determination of the small number of loyalists contrasted to the caution and inertia shown by their conservative opponents, however; a series of quick strikes found them everywhere victorious. On March 19, after it had become apparent that the will and strength of the radicals was sufficient to make it impossible for the conservatives who had agreed to the capitulation to govern, the Chōshū lord, after penitential prayers to his ancestors, consented to do the will of his new masters. Thereafter Chōshū received its direction from Takasugi and his courageous group of radicals.[26]

In view of the uncertain and troubled state of han politics, however, it seemed more desirable than ever to remove the Kyoto nobles from Chōshū soil. The Tosa rōnin, and especially Nakaoka and Hijikata, played an important role in the move, which came on February 9, a month before the Chōshū lord gave in to the will of the loyalists. Nakaoka was among the group who accompanied the nobles to the Fukuoka domain of Kuroda Nagahiro.

It soon proved that the misgivings of the loyalists about Fukuoka were well grounded. The Kuroda administration was plagued by the same divisions between loyalists and conservatives that plagued every major han in these years. A group of loyalists, led by the rōjū Katō Shisho, had been in charge during most of the year 1864. Katō represented his lord in the discussions at Hiroshima among the thirty-six han which sent troops for the first Chōshū expedition, and he and Saigō had worked out the plan of compromise under which Chōshū had agreed to return to the fold. Now he arranged with Saigō and with Chōshū emissaries, among them Takasugi, the terms and guarantees under which the nobles would be sheltered in his han. Unfortunately, the revolution in Chōshū alarmed the Fukuoka conservatives, who foresaw a second and possibly successful bakufu expedition of punishment; they wanted no part of the rebel cause, and began a movement to oust Katō and his followers. Their work bore fruit late in 1865, when Katō was ordered to commit suicide and his party driven from office. Even before then, however, the stay of the nobles in the domain had been precarious.[27] For a time the five refugees

---

[26] *Ishin shi*, IV, 428f.
[27] For Katō's death, *Katō Shisho den*, pp. 157f.

were kept in virtual imprisonment, prevented from having contact even with each other. The *shishi* who had accompanied them were quick to report this outrage to their sponsors, and it required the personal intervention of Saigō with Satsuma troops to secure for the nobles better accommodations and treatment at Dazaifu.[28] There the nobles were housed until the eve of Restoration.

Despite the ambivalent and reluctant attitude of the new Fukuoka regime, Satsuma protection sufficed to give the nobles security. Dazaifu became a major center of command and intrigue in the months that followed. The release of the nobles from Chōshū protection now made them national figures. Sakamoto, Nakaoka, Saigō, and the others almost always visited Dazaifu on their way to Nagasaki or Kagoshima. In Dazaifu, Sanjō, the strongest of the nobles, had his devoted rōnin followers with him, and these he could send to Kyoto and to Chōshū. Despite the lack of position or power, Sanjō exerted a good deal of moral authority, and he and his four colleagues provided visible evidence of Kyoto support for the loyalists.

The principal actors were now assuming their places for the final acts of the Restoration drama. The Chōshū regime was securely in the hands of Takasugi Shinsaku and his party. National politics dominated their attention, and because they sought military strength and modern weapons the European experience of Itō and Inoue proved invaluable. For a time, the former anti-foreign fanatics even discussed the possibility of opening Shimonoseki as a port for foreign trade. In Satsuma, the team of Ōkubo and Saigō worked smoothly to keep han policies on even keel, and their sympathy with the anti-bakufu extremists of Chōshū grew as it became clear that Edo was becoming insistent on a full restoration of its old authority. Within the bakufu the moderate and enlightened policies of Katsu Rintarō were being replaced by the dreams of a new despotism in the mind of Oguri Tadamasa, and before long these plans would receive the support and encouragement of Napoleon III's minister, Leon Roches.

3. From Shishi to Statesmen

There is a good deal of evidence that the dangers and turbulence of the loyalist years left the activists more attractive per-

[28] The Fukuoka daimyō, Kuroda Nagahiro was the son of Shimazu Shigehide of Satsuma, and hence perhaps particularly responsive to Satsuma suggestions.

sonally and wiser politically. The *shishi* no longer believed that individual heroics would help their cause, and they had a new understanding of the complexity of the problems their country faced. They begin to emerge from their papers and letters as confident and dedicated men, tempered by danger. They had shown and seen enough courage to take it for granted, and they were now concerned with other qualities—generosity, foresight, prudence. Not, of course, that they became ascetics. An encounter with danger was still prepared for with sake if possible; Nakaoka, the night before the nobles were moved to Fukuoka, suggested to his friends that before risking their lives they might well make one last visit to a brothel. The *shishi* were still *jimbutsu*, "characters," with a light-hearted attitude toward danger that endeared them to each other and to posterity. What was new was a softening of the arrogance that had made them so contemptuous of their enemies; they had come out of their experience sobered and more responsible.

There is a letter from Sakamoto to the parents of Ike Kurata written in 1865 which illustrates some of these changes. Ike had fled Tosa in 1863, and at that time Sakamoto had written his parents the stern reminder of the superiority of loyalist duties that has already been cited. Ike had joined Chōshū militia units, he had been in the Yamato putsch of Yoshimura Toratarō, and he was a member of Nakaoka's "Loyal and Brave Company" in Kyoto.[29] Sakamoto's warm, human account of this reunion shows the ties of affection that bound the *shishi* by this time. He had come to "a place called Shimonoseki," as he wrote to Tosa, hoping to see "Kura." Then, on hearing it would take three days to reach him, he had thought the better of it. Suddenly, without warning, Kura showed up at his inn.

"We clapped our hands and exclaimed about this amazing coincidence and wonderful luck. Kura is just fine, and he looks very well. He was particularly eager to hear about his family. We spent the whole day talking about the state of things; he was in fine shape. We agreed on practically everything:—that there won't be another useless war, and that even if there is neither of us will get ourselves killed. So far eighty of those who have left Tosa have been killed in the fighting. Kura has been in battle eight or nine

<hr />

[29] Hirao, *Nakaoka-Sakamoto*, pp. 34-35.

times, and hasn't a wound despite the bullets, arrows, and rocks that flew around him. What he's particularly proud of is the fact that he proved he could take it. He faced the enemy at a distance of about two hundred feet, and with shells flying in all directions and bullets whizzing all around him he stood right up and sang out his orders, his own gun smoking as he fired at the other artillery carriages. Most of the men hit the ground as soon as they saw the flash of the enemy guns, but Kura says that since they were at such close quarters he saw no point in ducking. He is quite proud of this.

"As you know, Kura has always been very self-assertive, quick to run others down, and not very generous. It seems to me that a man improves when he goes through a war. Now Kura loves everybody. We had a wonderful time talking together. . . ."[30]

How far superior this exciting life must have seemed to the drab existence the Tosa men would have known if they had been obedient to the traditional values and remained at home as filial sons! We have no outside testimony to Sakamoto's growth in grace and generosity, but it may be remarked that it required some measure of these qualities for him to recognize them in his friends. His letters, in any case, are no longer as full of the kind of self congratulation that filled them a few years earlier. And his experience under Katsu had trained him to be on the lookout for ability and honesty in the ranks of the opposition.

The evidence of growing political perception which can be found in the papers of Nakaoka Shintarō is particularly arresting. The extremist who had urged his Tosa friends to rise in revolt in 1864 had reluctantly adopted a counsel of caution later that same year. His further experiences with Chōshū militia units acquainted him with the advantages of Western technology. In 1865 Nakaoka also had his first trip on a Western steampowered ship, and he was greatly impressed by its speed and efficiency.[31] The path of xenophobic opposition to Westernization was no longer tenable for him, and in his diary and in his writings to Tosa he showed

---

[30] *Sakamoto monjo*, I, 131-134. A postscript reinforces the point of danger: "That *Shōya* Shima Yo's second son Namima, who became famous because he knocked a man down during a battle, was surrounded with some other rebels the other day (there were two hundred in all) and committed hara kiri."

[31] *Rikuentai*, p. 137.

the shift clearly. He even considered a trip to the West for himself, but decided he could not be spared.[32]

Besides Nakaoka's correspondence, there have been preserved his fragmentary diary for the years 1865-1867 and a number of general discussions of the political situation which he sent to his comrades in Tosa. From these sources it is clear that Nakaoka's importance in the Tosa loyalist movement rose steadily after the imprisonment and punishment of Takechi and his lieutenants. Only a man of stature within the movement, and a man out of the reach of the han authorities, could have had the moderating influence on it that Nakaoka did. Nakaoka's activities with Chōshū and Satsuma gave him the authority of a man who spoke with detailed knowledge of trends outside the fief. In fact, he could also tell his friends in Chōshū of doings elsewhere. Thus in September 1865, Nakaoka could write to Kido Kōin, who was then in political difficulties in Chōshū because of his rumored plans to open Shimonoseki to foreign trade, that Satsuma had also shifted to a stand favoring opening the country.[33] He was even better qualified to report to the *shishi* in Tosa, who were cut off from almost every source of outside news, the developments in national politics. Most of the Tosa loyalists were still living in the shadow of Takechi's recent ascendancy in Kyoto. Many were still prepared to believe in the physical and political possibility of driving the foreigners out of Japan, and they distrusted persons who might have changed their positions as traitors and turncoats.

Nakaoka could understand this position perfectly well, for he had held it very recently. But his travels and dangers since leaving Tosa had served to broaden his view. No doubt, part of this new sophistication he owed to the Chōshū men whose education he had shared. But he also found time to read in those busy years. For every day of activity and travel there were several of waiting and hiding, and Nakaoka put them to good use. In his diary we find him recording his reading habits. There is a consistent emphasis on the wisdom of the past, one which speaks well for the quality of this *shōya*'s education. He speaks of "classics," and at

[32] Hirao, *Rikuentai*, pp. 148-149. It is impressive to note that many of the first-line *shishi* seriously considered going abroad at one time or another. Takasugi considered going to Europe after his early victories (partly because he feared assassination at home), but was dissuaded by the Nagasaki merchant Glover. *Ishin shi*, IV, 440.

[33] *Sakamoto-Nakaoka*, pp. 229-231.

other times itemizes the *Ta Hsüeh*, the history of the Former Han Dynasty, the *Chung liang* commentary, and Sun Tzu. There is mention of Commissioner Lin Tze-hsü and China's disastrous attempt to deal with the English by force, and references to "news from Nagasaki" and "Nagasaki newspapers." And, significantly, there is mention of Fukuzawa Yukichi's *Seiyō jijō* (*Conditions in the West*), the little work which Fukuzawa published serially in late Tokugawa days and which did so much to acquaint Japanese of all walks of life with knowledge of the West.[34]

The best statement of Nakaoka's political views is one which he addressed to his friends in Tosa shortly after the victory of Takasugi Shinsaku in Chōshū. The one surviving copy, in the collection of Tanaka Kōken, bears an inscription to Itagaki Taisuke, and it is possible that Nakaoka had hopes of affecting han policy by addressing his important friends. Whatever the specific purpose of his document, however, it is clear that he wanted his friends in Tosa to realize the general meaning of what was happening on the national scene.

Nakaoka begins with the observation that some significant new personalities have arisen on the national stage, men of whom his countrymen should be aware. The first of these is Saigō Takamori. He describes Saigō as a stocky figure, who might be compared to Abe Sadatō, a celebrated rebel leader in north Japan in the eleventh century. Saigō is wise and learned, courageous, and usually quiet; but while normally he speaks little, when he does utter a few words they have a depth of thought which penetrates directly to the hearer's heart. A man of great virtue who overcomes others, Saigō is rich in experience as well. Indeed, in the way he combines knowledge and action he is comparable to Takechi Zuizan himself. After Saigō, Kido Kōin and Takasugi Shinsaku of Chōshū deserve mention as new heroes; they too have courage, wisdom, and profundity, and they have shown their capacity for action.

From this discussion of personalities, Nakaoka goes on to discuss the deeper aspects of the national crisis by asking whether the feudal divisions are advantageous or disadvantageous. As a result of three centuries of peace, he notes, fighting spirit has declined and no one has the stomach for action. Fief divisions have given rise to different approaches, with each area going its

[34] Diary as reproduced in Ozaki, *Nakaoka*, pp. 348, 349, 351, 352, 354, 362.

own way. Some advocate a war to the death against the foreigners, while others argue this is impossible. Certainly this sort of bickering must be considered a drawback of feudal disunity. Nakaoka goes on to note that others advocate opening the country in order to learn from the foreigners. They suggest building up strength and learning about modern weapons and machinery so that, after the process is completed, it will be within Japan's power to open or close the ports as seems best. A "rich country, strong defense," many men of wisdom warn, must be achieved before war with the West is possible. Nakaoka's exposition of this thesis outruns, in length and vigor, the space he allots the exclusionists, and it is hardly necessary for him to add, as he does, "Formerly I could not accept this position, but now I am convinced of its truth." Nakaoka explains that he draws this conclusion from the men from Mito, Satsuma, and Chōshū who tried to take direct action. They failed but they also contributed toward an ultimate solution. The Mito civil war, the murder of Richardson, and the shelling of foreign ships in the Straits of Shimonoseki helped by eliminating alternatives and suggesting new answers. They were by no means failures, but the work of farsighted men who were in touch with the national deities.

Among these farsighted men, Nakaoka goes on, was Kusaka Genzui of Chōshū, who lost his life in Kyoto. A disciple of Yoshida Shōin and a student of English, Kusaka knew the barbarian spirit well. He had often pointed out that when one looked at the work of men like Peter in Russia and Washington in America, he could see that even in barbarian countries heroes arose in times of crisis to unify and lead their nations. He used to say that if you were not willing to resort to direct action at some point you would never get anywhere, for otherwise you would spend all your time estimating the chances of success. Nakaoka endorses Kusaka's view completely.

As proof of its correctness, he cites two incidents. The first of these, in which Richardson was killed, seemed a disaster, for it led to the bombardment of Kagoshima. Still, this served as nothing else could have done to unify Satsuma men in a determination to revenge their shame. Men of ability, regardless of their rank, were summoned—Saigō was recalled from his banishment—and fundamental reforms in the Satsuma armed services and government were set in motion.

The other incident affected Chōshū. The shelling of foreign ships in the Straits of Shimonoseki had led to the Kyoto disturbance; after peace was restored with the barbarians, shogunal armies converged on Chōshū. Then came capitulation and civil war, after which Kido and Takasugi, together with Inoue and Itō, who had returned from England earlier, became the new leaders. They had now unified Chōshū opinion. The han had assumed a determined stand in military matters, its spirit was rising, and it had progressed from discussion to action. Nakaoka explains that the Chōshū modernization was not simply a matter of a company of men armed with Western guns. Chōshū was now using Minier guns, modern artillery, and cavalry units. Every day large units were drilling and forty-six companies of militia were working together regularly. All of this was the result of war; nothing could have been achieved without the initial violence and danger. Satsuma, too, had refused to know defeat, and was building naval yards, artillery, and a navy.

Nakaoka now reaches his point:

"As far-sighted men will see, Satsuma and Chōshū are the two han that will be able to stir the realm in the future, and they have reached their present position because of the benefits of war. In my opinion any one can see, as though looking in a mirror, that in the near future we will all be following the orders of these two han. Any hope of establishing our national way of life [*kokutai*] some day and wiping out the barbarian insults, must rest on these two han. The fact that this has become a possibility must be scored as a benefit of our feudal order.

"But, however much we promote our warrior spirit and push our defense measures, unless we establish our national policy we will never be able to become stronger than the enemy. What, then, is the basis of this policy? It is first of all, that we carry out the highest duty of all [taigi meibun] by returning all power to the throne and establishing a unity of government and worship. [*saisei itchi*]. It is a matter of the most desperate urgency that we establish this throughout the whole country. If all, both high and low, study to see how they can best meet the great opportunity that is ours today, we can still convert failure into fortune. Some day we will look back on these days and recognize the foreign disease as a purgative that really did a great deal for our country. If this is so, we will have put it to good use."

Nakaoka's letter ends with a final injunction to his friends to work together without undue emphasis on differences of rank.[35] The *shōya* who had rushed to Edo in 1862 to save his lord was now devising programs to save his country. He was aware that the progress toward that goal would have been more difficult without the multi-centered feudal society in which he moved so freely, but he was also beginning to realize, as did Tokugawa leaders, that the divisions of feudal society posed a formidable bar to true national unity of purpose. Real national unity, he thought, would require the cooperation of the two great han of the southwest. Together with Sakamoto, he now devoted his efforts to speeding that cooperation.

4. The Alliance

The agreement between Satsuma and Chōshū was not so much offensive as it was defensive in origin, and the setting in which it was worked out is to be found in the fears of Tokugawa resurgence and foreign intervention that consumed the loyalists in 1865.

A number of bakufu conservatives remained dissatisfied with the settlement that had been reached with Chōshū. They wanted the Chōshū daimyō and his heir, together with the five court nobles at Dazaifu, to be sent to Edo, and they wanted more drastic measures taken within Chōshū to punish loyalist extremists.[36] These bakufu officials made their position known just as the armies of the thirty-odd han which had combined to send troops against Chōshū were being disbanded. It was too late to change the terms of the truce agreement. Soon thereafter, however, came the revolt of Takasugi Shinsaku and his loyalist militia. Now it became clear that even the initial settlement terms would not be carried out, and there was new reason to complain.

But the Chōshū issue, important as it was, was only one aspect of the broader problem of bakufu relations with Kyoto. On this issue the split between the bakufu traditionalists, largely old-line fudai diamyō who wanted a "hard" line followed, and the conciliary "outsiders" like Hitotsubashi Keiki and Matsudaira Katamori of Aizu, men whose exposure to national politics in Kyoto had taught them the futility of attempts to return to tactics of an earlier day, was most striking. Soon one group was forced into using the Kyoto court to counter its adversaries.

---

[35] Text in *Sakamoto-Nakaoka*, pp. 314-320.
[36] Osatake, *Meiji Ishin*, ɪɪ, 598.

Many Tokugawa supporters had hoped that the young shogun Iemochi would lead the first attack against Chōshū in person, and the Imperial court had indicated its desire that he at least come to Kyoto. Edo conservatives, however, opposed; they were suspicious of Keiki and Katamori, who would have the shogun's ear in Kyoto, and they felt little good had come of the earlier trips to Kyoto in 1863 and 1864. After the compromise settlement had been reached with Chōshū, Keiki and his friends at court continued to hope the shogun would come to his Osaka castle to make his final disposition of the Chōshū affair. The Edo conservatives instead sent two rōjū, Abe Masatō and Matsumae Takahiro, to Kyoto. They had orders to replace the troops which guarded the Imperial palace with the regular bakufu levies which accompanied them to Kyoto, and they were to bring back the resignations of Keiki and Katamori. Keiki was aware of the game, however, and secured an Imperial rescript that ordered the shogun to come to Kyoto immediately. To add point to its order, the court directed that the Edo councillors who had come to Kyoto, Abe and Matsumae, be ordered to commit hara-kiri. The sentence was not carried out, but its audacity showed how seriously the Edo councillors had misjudged the situation. The two men were dismissed from their posts.[87]

For Edo, the revolt of the Chōshū loyalists offered a face-saving way of getting out of this dilemma. The traditionalists decided that the shogun's Kyoto trip, which could no longer be deferred, could be combined with a second expedition against Chōshū, one he would lead himself. This would, they thought, regain for them the initiative. They were confident that Chōshū conservatives would regain the upper hand once the bakufu armies approached their borders, and the resulting surrender would improve Tokugawa prestige everywhere in Japan and particularly at the court.

Thus the second expedition against Chōshū was designed to strengthen the Tokugawa position at court. Originally it was announced that the shogun would call at Kyoto after, and not before, dealing with his recalcitrant vassal; but plans were changed. The expedition was announced on March 6, 1865, and the shogun set forth on June 9. (Because of difficulties discussed below the armies did not move on to the southwest until December, however, and fighting began only in the summer of 1866.) The sho-

[87] Osatake, *Meiji Ishin*, II, 608, 640.

gun's reception in Kyoto, which had been prepared by Keiki, was favorable beyond most expectations. Not only was the expedition formally authorized, but the shogun was especially named Imperial Commander for its duration. This elated bakufu circles, but it also alarmed leading tozama lords.[38]

The great lords realized that the second punitive expedition was begun for partisan reasons, and they gave it a partisan reception. They saw that it was designed to crush the possibility of resistance to the Tokugawa, and they reacted according to their own interests. The lord of Owari, who had accepted—albeit reluctantly—command of the first expedition, refused to cooperate with the second. The lord of Fukui (Matsudaira Shungaku's successor), who had been vice-commander of the first expedition, worked in court circles to try to block the second. Ikeda (Okayama) and Asano (Hiroshima) felt that the project could not possibly work to their interest. Kuroda of Fukuoka, who cooperated during the period his conservative counsellors first came to power, later tempered his initial promises of help. Satsuma, thanks to the work of Saigō, first remained aloof and then took a hostile attitude. Tosa too rejected the request to send troops with the explanation that compliance would surely lead to a rebellion by the still restive loyalists who had worked with the Chōshū men in earlier years.[39]

The uneasiness of the great lords about bakufu purposes was heightened by a general suspicion that Edo administrators were seriously considering getting French support in the erection of a centralized, "modern" despotism. These fears had a good deal of substance to them, and the danger was magnified in the anticipation.

Oguri Tadamasa, the man who had replaced Katsu, was an important figure in the plans to accept French help. A crushing victory over Chōshū, he thought, followed by dismemberment or absorption of the entire Chōshū realm, would prepare the way for similar action against other possible centers of resistance to bakufu authority. With French help to the Tokugawa, a program of military and technical modernization would lead to the abolition of feudal decentralization in favor of a unitary, Tokugawa-run state.

[38] Osatake, *Meiji Ishin*, II, 627.
[39] For the reactions of the han, *Ishin shi*, IV, 414-425; for Tosa, Sasaki, pp. 327-333.

The full development of these plans came after the second Chōshū expedition, but the background had already been prepared shortly after the arrival of French minister Leon Roches in the spring of 1864. This servant of Napoleon III, fresh from service in North Africa, was determined to win for his Emperor leadership over British diplomacy in Asia.[40] After 1865, Roches' efforts were spurred by his British counterpart, Harry Parkes, who leaned increasingly toward support for the Satsuma and Chōshū men who had proved so cooperative after the bombardment of Shimonoseki and Kagoshima. Roches found the bakufu more and more willing to talk about details. Late in 1864, when a bakufu diplomatic mission visited France, the ambassadors were greatly impressed by the advice given by a Belgian nobleman, the Count of Montblanc, that the bakufu should crush the feudal lords and create a central government. Montblanc compared Japan to the France of four centuries earlier, and he stressed the need for forceful action. The bakufu ambassadors began preparations for formal agreements, but their initiative was later repudiated by Edo. Still, the ideas thus planted were not without fruit. Military officers, manuals, arms, and the Yokosuka shipyard and arsenal began the swing to French tutelage that characterized late Tokugawa days. Even Fukuzawa Yukichi was to memorialize urging complete reliance on French aid.

This increasing readiness of the bakufu to utilize foreign assistance could not remain secret, and it loomed large in the intelligence reports that came to the eyes of the great lords in 1865 and 1866. It was not calculated to make them more enthusiastic about helping the bakufu crush Chōshū, for they realized that by so doing they would be preparing for their own destruction.

But the foreigners were a danger as well as potential help for the shogunate. Just as the shogun's procession reached Kyoto, a foreign flotilla entered Osaka Bay, and the waters nearest the capital had been "polluted" for the first time. Chōshū policy had to take second place until this intrusion was brought to an end.

The Western powers had come to demand full Imperial approval of the treaties that had been signed; on hearing that the shogun and his councillors were in Osaka, they had decided to

---

[40] Osatake, *Meiji Ishin*, II, 625, 697f. The basic sources for the negotiations with France are Ōtsuka Takematsu, "Fukkoku kōshi Leon Roches no seisaku kōdō ni tsuite," *Shigaku Zasshi*, xlvi (1935), 809-850, 982-1001, and Ishii, *Meiji Ishin no kokusaiteki kankyō* (Tokyo, 1957).

beard him there. They now had new ability to threaten, for Parkes influenced his associates to warn that they were prepared to go directly to Kyoto if necessary. The shogun's hopes of a new ascendancy over Kyoto never recovered from the appearance of the foreign ships. There was more talk, and new hope of a council of feudal lords to share key decisions. Some, like Saigō, thought the court should take foreign affairs out of the shogun's hands altogether.[41] As the impasse heightened, Iemochi resigned his powers as shogun to force the court to responsible action. Keiki lobbied vigorously to make sure that the resignation would be rejected, and after prolonged argument the Emperor approved the principal treaties and ports (excluding, however, Hyōgo). The foreign fleet left Osaka.[42]

During all of this the Chōshū crisis deepened. The loyalists who controlled the han were by no means inclined to surrender. Takasugi Shinsaku and the new administration had strengthened their defences and their stand, while the bakufu's revelations of its purposes by the proposal to entrust to Tokugawa troops the defence of the Imperial palace had alienated what few partisans the expedition might have had. While the Chōshū will to fight was strengthened, Tokugawa morale declined. Most of the soldiers who had come to the Tokugawa headquarters in Osaka had not really expected to have to fight to secure Chōshū capitulation. The discovery that Chōshū would not capitulate created a situation in which the bakufu was forced to undertake an expedition it would not afford and was not prepared to prosecute vigorously. Forced loans from all possible contributors in the Osaka area, including even the pariah *eta* community, increased popular distrust and discontent. The armies had no will to fight, and the bakufu tried desperately for some way of combining peace with face. Not until July 18, 1866, after several "final" missions had shown Chōshū determined to resist and united in its refusal to compromise, did the military action begin.

During all this delay, Sakamoto had not been idle. It will be recalled that his Satsuma sponsors had planned to put him in charge of a ship and to use the knowledge of sailing which he

---

[41] *Saigō Zenshū,* I, 618.
[42] For a good summary of the negotiations and problems, Beasley, *Select Documents,* pp. 80-83.

had gained in Katsu's service. This they did, giving him independent status as head of a simple organization first known as *Shachū*, "the company," and later as *Kaientai*, "Naval Auxiliary Force." Satsuma funds and Satsuma protection were essential in this, and headquarters were established near the Satsuma trading station in Nagasaki. This was indicative of the purpose kept in mind for the little firm: it could buy from the Western traders in a Tokugawa-run port city without implicating its Satsuma sponsors in its activities. Sakamoto posed, however, as a Satsuma samurai. He described his arrangements in a letter to his sister in October 1865 as follows:

"I've come to Nagasaki with twenty men . . . we're all here getting good experience. There's another fellow studying at the western, English, study place who was sent from Tosa. There are also about thirty men here from all parts of Japan, all getting experience, and this is really a very busy place. I travel about a good deal now, and I'm having a very interesting time. I've organized my men in a temporary commercial company. I'm writing you from Kyoto today, but in five or six days I'll go back to the west. If you send me anything, send it to the Teradaya Inn, in Fushimi, at the Orai bridge . . . near the Satsuma residence. Nearby there is also a Ninoya, at Kyōbashi; these inns are completely home to me. . . . Have the messenger ask for Mr. Saigō Isaburo, of Satsuma, and address things to him, also your letters, and they'll get to me."[43]

The new enterprise was clearly to Sakamoto's liking, and he contrasted his activities to "a place like home," where "you can't have any ambition, and you spend your time in stupid ways like an idiot." Sakamoto's "twenty men" were old friends, rōnin from the Katsu school in Hyōgo. (Among them was the future Mutsu Munemitsu, Foreign Minister in 1894.) In Nagasaki, Sakamoto's dealings were largely with foreign merchants. Of these the most important was Thomas Glover, a Scottish merchant who played a large role in importing weapons and exporting students for the anti-Tokugawa han in late Tokugawa days.[44] In time, Sakamoto's firm extended its ambitions and activities to deal with several han

---

[43] *Sakamoto monjo*, I, 136-138.
[44] Glover's role, which was an important one, is described in Chapter VI, 4. *The Nagasaki Scene.*

which lacked facilities for selling their goods on the foreign market.

Sakamoto's firm began by helping Chōshū to by-pass the bakufu blockade on foreign weapons. Chōshū representatives sent to Nagasaki had been so closely watched that they were unable to deal with foreign merchants, but it was possible for Sakamoto, with, of course, the approval of Saigō Takamori, to work out a solution for this. After some preliminary negotiation the Chōshū leaders sent Itō Hirobumi and Inoue Kaoru to Nagasaki, where they put up at the Satsuma residence. They had the job of stage-managing the negotiations with Thomas Glover, who had, incidentally, been the merchant who smuggled them both to England earlier in the decade.

With Sakamoto's help Itō and Inoue were able to buy seven thousand rifles in Nagasaki.[45] In September Inoue accompanied a Satsuma karō to Kagoshima to bring formal thanks from Chōshū for the Satsuma help. Greater help for Chōshū was to come. On December 4, 1865, the steamship *Union* was purchased from Glover for the sum of 37,500 ryō. For a time it was not clear whether her title belonged to Chōshū, Satsuma, or Sakamoto's company—each took the most favorable view possible of the affair —but it was finally decided in favor of Chōshū. The ship, renamed the *Otchō Maru* was the most spectacular fruit of the Satsuma cooperation to date.[46]

Next, Sakamoto's good offices were utilized to provide Chōshū grains for Satsuma troop needs. Since Kagoshima was a rice-deficiency area, Saigō was anxious to have sources of supply for his forces on Honshu. Kido proved amenable to this arrangement, and by fall of 1865 trade was resumed between Satsuma and Chōshū. It is not without significance that Sakamoto and other Tosa *shishi* often lodged at the Shimonoseki house of Shiraishi Seiichirō, a merchant who had a considerable stake in the Satsuma trade.[47]

[45] A number of documents from Itō and Inoue, in Nagasaki, to their Chōshū superiors and instructions to them from Yamaguchi are included in *Sakamoto monjo*, I. See especially pp. 121-129, dated September 15, 1865, in which Itō and Inoue report their progress and expenditures.
[46] For the contracts, including renegotiated contracts when ownership changed from Satsuma (*Sakurajima Maru*) to Chōshū (*Otchō Maru*), Hirao, *Kaientai*, pp. 113-119, and *Sakamoto monjo*, I, 173-177. Many traders realized good profits by selling obsolete vessels worn out in the China trade to fiefs anxious to gird for future war in late Tokugawa days.
[47] Hirao, *Rikuentai*, p. 132. Nakaoka on at least one occasion carried money for

By now the desirability of a more permanent agreement was apparent to both Satsuma and Chōshū leaders. There was a third group anxious to see it come about. The exiled court nobles at Dazaifu had a direct interest in seeing a powerful coalition form to lay claim to the loyalist cause. They had been "saved" by Chōshū and they were receiving protection from Satsuma. Their rōnin followers were eager to help bring an alliance about. While the commercial relationships between Satsuma and Chōshū were beginning to take shape, both Sakamoto and Nakaoka travelled to Dazaifu to see if they could interest the nobles there in lending their prestige and authorization to a formal agreement. Sakamoto had twenty-four talks with Sanjō Sanetomi, and as many with Higashikuze, and both he and Nakaoka did their best to persuade the nobles that they should judge Satsuma intentions not so much by the troops that had helped drive them out of Kyoto as by the units Saigō had sent to protect them at Dazaifu. In this they succeeded, although it was apparently not easy to persuade the nobles to overcome their antipathy to the Satsuma leaders. This done, however, Sakamoto and Nakaoka both turned to the Chōshū leaders to try to assure them of the depth of Satsuma sincerity.

It comes with some surprise, in view of the commercial cooperation already established between the two realms, and in view of the distrust they both bore the Tokugawa conservatives, that Sakamoto and Nakaoka needed so much effort and time to convince the Chōshū leaders that Satsuma could be trusted.[48] Their difficulties in making their point should serve as reminders of the depth of hostility between the two areas, as well as of the new confidence that was beginning to animate the Chōshū leaders. Their revolution accomplished, these men distrusted the Satsuma figures whose break with their conservative betters had not been equally dramatic.

Shiraishi on his travels. (p. 139.) Shiraishi's diary has been published in the Restoration papers compiled by the Shiseki Kyōkai, in *Ishin Nichijō Sanshū* (Tokyo, 1925), pp. 3-146, but it is disappointingly cryptic and uninformative.

[48] It must be granted that grounds for rumor were many. As late as November 1865 officials of Aizu han approached Ōkubo Toshimichi with proposals for an Aizu-Satsuma agreement which would have revitalized the cooperation of 1863. Ōkubo, who was afraid of compromising his position with Chōshū, declined to discuss the matter. *Kagoshima ken shi*, III, 420. More promising was an arrangement discussed with Fukuoka, but this came to nothing after the removal and execution of the leaders of the "Party of Righteousness" there.

The work was begun by Chōshū agents in Dazaifu, who sped home to report to their leaders proposals Sakamoto had aired with the nobles. In June, 1865, Sakamoto himself went to Shimonoseki, where he stayed for nearly a month.[49] As word of the possibility of an alliance spread in Chōshū, Kido Kōin came from Yamaguchi to discuss the matter with Sakamoto. Sakamoto was able to explain to him the campaign Saigō was carrying on in Satsuma against participation in the Chōshū expedition, and to assure him that the Satsuma loyalist faction had a good chance of victory in fief politics.

Meanwhile Nakaoka was doing his part. In the spring of 1865 he was in Kyoto, attentive to rumors and stories about bakufu intentions and capabilities. By late June 1865, he had decided with Hijikata, the Tosa rōnin attached to the entourage of Sanjō Sanetomi, that it was their duty to promote an alliance between Satsuma and Chōshū. They left Kyoto together. Hijikata went to Chōshū, while Nakaoka continued on to Kagoshima to speak to Saigō. Saigō agreed to stop at Shimonoseki on his way back to Kyoto, and Kido Kōin came to meet him there. When all was in readiness for diplomatic talks, Saigō proved unable to keep his appointment. Nakaoka arrived alone and did his best to explain this to Kido, but it was not an easy task, for the Chōshū emissary felt that his fief and his cause had been insulted once again by the Satsuma foe.

Early in 1866 Sakamoto persuaded Saigō and Ōkubo to send Kuroda Kiyotaka to Shimonoseki to resume talks with Kido. On February 22, 1866, Kido himself journeyed to the Satsuma headquarters in Kyoto prepared to negotiate with the Satsuma leaders. His decision to go had aroused a good deal of antagonism in Chōshū, for many of the militia leaders, including Takasugi, were still distrustful of the Satsuma leaders.

Kido met with Komatsu, Saigō, Ōkubo, and other Satsuma leaders for ten consecutive days. While this was going on Sakamoto, together with Ike Kurata and a Chōshū samurai named Miyoshi Shinzō, also came to Kyoto. In Osaka he decided to visit his former bakufu friend, Ōkubo Ichiō (Katsu's former sponsor), who was now serving in the important post of Keeper of the Castle. Sakamoto ignored this man's warning that his life would be forfeit

---

[49] See Hirao, *Sakamoto-Nakaoka*, p. 168, for an excellent chronology of Sakamoto's movements.

if bakufu police should apprehend him, and boldly went on to Kyoto, identifying himself and his friends as "Satsuma samurai" at guard stations. Thus the two Tosa rōnin and their Chōshū friend, all three prize catches for bakufu police, were able to enter the capital safely.

Sakamoto reached Kyoto March 6, 1866, and proceeded immediately to see how the talks between Kido and Saigō had progressed. To his astonishment, they had not gone forward at all during the ten days of "meetings." Neither side was willing to appear the suppliant. Kido was furious that Saigō had not once mentioned an alliance, and he was prepared to return to Chōshū. But Sakamoto, who had no face or prestige to lose, could mediate and promote the project, and under his stimulus the conferees pushed on to conclude the talks.[50] The next day, March 7, 1866, the terms of the agreement were hammered out by Kido for Chōshū and Saigō, Komatsu, and Ōkubo for Satsuma. Sakamoto Ryōma was present as witness. Kido's letter to Sakamoto summarizing the agreements has remained the official text for the terms.

The Satsuma-Chōshū agreement was designed to reinstate Chōshū in the favor of the court and to block bakufu plans to crush Chōshū politically:

Article I pledged Satsuma to act if war broke out between the bakufu and Chōshū. Satsuma was to restrain the bakufu by adding two thousand men to its forces in Kyoto, another thousand in Osaka, and investing the capital area.

Article II provided that, in case of a Chōshū victory, Satsuma would use all its influence at the court to secure reinstatement for Chōshū.

Article III was to hold in the event of a Chōshū defeat. Chōshū, it held, would in any case not be destroyed for a period of six months to a year, and during that interval Satsuma would do everything within its power to aid Chōshū.

Article IV covered the possibility of continued peace. If the bakufu armies returned without fighting, Satsuma would approach the court and do its best to obtain a pardon for Chōshū.

Article V envisaged the possibility of Satsuma's joining in the war. If, it read, Hitotsubashi, Aizu, Kuwana, and other pro-

---

[50] Saigō explained to Sakamoto that he had only been testing Kido's sincerity. Chikami, *Sakamoto*, p. 92.

bakufu han tried to oust Satsuma from its position as guardian of the court in Kyoto, Satsuma would join in the fight.

Finally, *Article VI* was a pledge for united action in the future. Once the Imperial pardon was granted, the two han would exert themselves to the fullest extent for the sake of the Imperial Country, and thenceforth they would use whatever power and influence they had for the restoration of the Emperor to power.[51]

Thus the long period of hostility between the two great han had been brought to a close. Bakufu intransigence and the logic of common interest had provided the need and the setting. Sakamoto Ryōma, Nakaoka Shintarō, and their fellow exiles from Tosa had provided the mediation and the persuasion. Kido professed particular gratitude to Sakamoto, and wrote him that his fame would deservedly be spread in years to come.[52] His prediction was borne out; it is for his share in bringing the alliance into being that Sakamoto is best known.

The alliance sealed, Kido sailed for Chōshū on a Satsuma ship together with Kuroda. Ōkubo returned to Kagoshima to report his activities to Shimazu Hisamitsu. Kuroda Kiyotaka proceeded from Chōshū to Dazaifu to tell the exiled court nobles of the progress that had been made. Shortly afterward Satsuma sent an official party to Chōshū, which in return sent Kido with a party to Kagoshima.

The alliance between Satsuma and Chōshū meant that the bakufu's chances of retaining national leadership had dwindled, and it made it most unlikely that any attempt to crush the han in favor of a new centralization could succeed. To be sure, it was still too early for men to begin to talk in terms of destroying the shogunate as such. For the most part discussions were still along lines of correcting, restraining, and reorganizing the shogunate. Effective utilization of French help could still have made the Tokugawa sufficiently powerful so that their prerogatives would at least have received careful attention in any new political order that was

---

[51] Good accounts of the negotiations and the agreement can be found in *Kagoshima ken shi*, III, 410-417, and in *Sakamoto monjo*, II, 299-344. Part of the latter is an account by Hijikata, pp. 299-312. Hijikata's principal record of his Restoration experiences, *Kaiten jikki*, appeared in 1900. 2 vols., pp. 236, 264.

[52] *Sakamoto monjo*, I, 186-191, gives the letter in which Kido summarizes the agreements reached.

designed. As has been shown, however, the bakufu was far from united. The greatest ability and intelligence lay with men who, like Keiki and Katsu, were unsure of the goals for which they ought to strive. Theirs was to be a failure of will rather than of money or materials. They would hold back from full recourse to foreign aid because, as patriotic and responsible figures, they saw the dangers and the accusation to which that could lead.

The Satsuma and Chōshū allies, for their part, having successfully defied Tokugawa leadership in the first alliance between domains since the seventeenth century, easily went on to new acts of disobedience. Their relations with the British improved as the bakufu thought about French aid. In the summer of 1866 Harry Parkes himself visited Kagoshima, and he and his interpreter Ernest Satow found the young leaders of Satsuma and Chōshū far more to their liking than the reticent bakufu officials who, never quite sure of their backing, could never deal openly and efficiently with them. Parkes and Satow began to think that British power should be directed toward eventual negotiation with the court itself.

The Satsuma-Chōshū alliance was an important step in the decline of Tokugawa power, and in helping to bring it about Sakamoto and Nakaoka had made a significant contribution to the eventual Tokugawa overthrow. Having brought the two fiefs together, they would now busy themselves in trying to add Tosa into the coalition as a third power. To this end they continued to work, through Sakamoto's Kaientai, at the exchange of goods between the areas, and began too the exchange of ideas pointing toward a new, conciliar pattern of political organization.

VI. THE KAIENTAI

*T*HE months after the completion of the Satsuma-Chōshū alliance brought many changes for Sakamoto Ryōma. He began the period as a hunted rōnin, and he narrowly escaped with his life an attempt by Tokugawa police units to capture him. He owed his life to the timely warning brought by a favorite maid in his hotel, a woman he afterward married. A vacation in Kagoshima preceded participation in a naval action in the Straits of Shimonoseki during the Tokugawa-Chōshū war. Thereafter he was occupied with the affairs of his firm, now named the Kaientai, in Nagasaki.

The alliance Sakamoto had helped to bring about enabled the Chōshū leaders to stand firm in their refusal of Tokugawa demands for submission. When military action against Chōshū came in the summer of 1866, the bakufu forces suffered humiliating setbacks. It then began to be clear that a new stage in the Tokugawa decline was at hand. Henceforth there was little talk of reconciliation between Kyoto and Edo. The question was no longer whether the shogunal institutions should be changed, but how, and what role should be reserved for the Tokugawa in the new order. This change in the political climate affected the leadership of all the fiefs, and it was also felt in Dazaifu, where the stock of the refugee court nobles rose rapidly as emissaries from important feudal centers sought them out.

During 1866 and 1867 rapid efforts for military and economic strengthening were taking place everywhere. There were new and intensive efforts to utilize the possibilities of Western trade and Western support. Some of the most important of these centered in Nagasaki, Sakamoto's base. That port had always been most difficult for Tokugawa administrators to control, and resourceful Western traders there helped fiefs anxious to modernize to accumulate shipping, armament, and even direct experience in the West. These efforts helped to confirm the policies of the Western powers; the British strove for more contacts and more trade for their merchants, while the French, who opposed all dealings with feudal lords as contrary to the spirit of the treaties with the Tokugawa, gained near-monopoly privileges with their pledges of support to the Tokugawa cause. Nagasaki was undoubtedly one of the most exciting and stimulating places in Japan for the restless and the ambitious, and Sakamoto's experiences there contributed to his new maturity.

The political reorientation that was taking place everywhere in Japan was especially marked in Tosa, where the disciples of Yoshida Tōyō came to power again. A vigorous program of self-strengthening prepared the fief for the warfare and diplomacy that lay ahead. Political alternatives now seemed fewer, and old hatreds ebbed. There was no longer much reason to fear the violence of the loyalists at home, and their warnings of cooperation between Satsuma and Chōshū had now been borne out in fact. The han leaders discovered that some of the rōnin they had long despised had the keys of friendship with Satsuma and Chōshū leaders. They forgave them their insolence and disrespect, and the rōnin, who had new need of fief allegiance and status, gladly entered the service of their newly converted superiors.

These changes were particularly dramatic in the case of Sakamoto Ryōma and Nakaoka Shintarō, who were pardoned by Tosa for their disregard of previous orders. Sakamoto received official support from his fief for his maritime ventures, and he was befriended by Gotō Shōjirō, the disciple of the Yoshida Tōyō the loyalists had slain five years earlier.

1. The Attack in the Teradaya

By 1866 the bakufu police organizations were sufficiently alert to the doings of troublesome rōnin to ask no questions in dealing with suspects. The rōnin had no official sponsorship, and unless they had the temporary hospitality of a han residence their residences and meeting places—inns and houses of pleasure—were easily invaded by the units set up to deal with trouble-makers.

The inns and pleasure haunts also provided their share of women whose participation in the activities of the decade made them fitting subjects for later chroniclers of screen and fiction. Many a *shishi* owed his life to a timely warning brought by a geisha or maid. Kido Kōin, who was sheltered by his favorite geisha after the disastrous Chōshū battle in Kyoto in 1864, later made her his wife. In 1866 the Fushimi inn maid who saved the day for Sakamoto not long after became his wife.

There are few details about Oryō, as Sakamoto's wife was named. She was, Sasaki Takayuki once noted, "a famous beauty, with unimaginably perfect features."[1] But there is plenty of evidence of courage, for this is the quality that Sakamoto stressed in his letters home. Already before his life was endangered, he is found singing the praises of Oryō. There is a loyalist connection dating back to the purge of Ii Naosuke in 1858. The hardships that followed this brought out all her determination and pluck. Writing his sister and old nurse from Nagasaki in October 1865, Sakamoto reminded them of:

"Rai Mikisaburō, Umeda Genjirō, Yanagawa Seigan and Kasuga Senan, who lost their lives for the Imperial court. At that time there was a doctor, Sosaku Ki, a colleague of theirs. He recently became ill and died, leaving a wife, three daughters, and two sons. Of the sons, Tarō is fairly bright, and Jirō is only 5. The oldest daughter is 23, the next 16, and the youngest 12.

"Now this was a good family, trained in flower arrangement, perfume, the tea ceremony, and so on, but they have nothing to eat and no one to look to. It seems the doctor inherited nothing, and he had no relatives. Sometimes they have been so hard up that they have had to borrow household implements and return them after using them. They sold first their house, then their belongings, and then the oldest girl began selling her clothes so that her mother and younger sisters wouldn't have to do the same thing.

"But then the youngest girl, who is unusually beautiful, was duped by some scoundrel and sold into the Shimabara as a *maiko*; the same villain, without saying anything to the mother, took the girl who is 16 and sold her to an Osaka brothel. The five-year old boy entered a Shibataguchi temple as an acolyte."

This was the setting in which Oryō had shown her courage:

"When the eldest sister realized this, she sold her last good kimono, headed for Osaka, and confronted the villains there. She didn't care if they killed her, and she carried a dagger. When they saw how determined she was, the scoundrel showed her the tattoo on his arm and shouted threats at her. But she had come prepared to die, and so she flew at him, grabbing his clothing, striking him in the face, and exclaimed that if he didn't return the younger sister he had brought to Osaka with him she would

---

[1] Sasaki, *sekijitsudan*, p. 453.

stab him. The wretch shouted, 'Look out, woman, or I'll kill you!'
They went at each other with shouts of 'Kill!' and 'Do your worst!'
After all, though, he couldn't very well murder the woman who
had come to Osaka, and so she was finally able to get her younger
sister back and take her to Kyoto with her again. Isn't that a story?
The youngest daughter in the Shimabara is in no danger immediately, so she has left her there for now."

Sakamoto's letter went on to detail the help which Oryō and
her family had provided for Tosa loyalists in plots in the past, and
explained the hardships which police inspection and confiscation
of property had caused the little family. Addressing his sister, he
assured her that

"The woman I've been talking about is really a very interesting
woman. She plays the zither, but of course in times like these she
can't do very much with it. Since she did so much to help us when
we were in danger, I would certainly like to do something for her
and for her brother. I am helping to get her younger sister back
for her. And she is very anxious to meet you, Otome, and acts as
though you were her own elder sister. So you see you are famous
in many places."

Elsewhere in the letter, Sakamoto asked his sister and nurse to
send along for him a "book on etiquette by Ogasawara," which
"somebody asked me to get." He also wanted a book of poems
called "Shin'yōshū, which was compiled in the time of Kusunoki
Masashige," and he hoped Otome would be able to send his favorite "an obi or a kimono; she's anxious to have one again. Her name
is Ryō, like mine; when I asked her about it, I learned that her
father had given it to her when she was born." At the end of his
letter, Sakamoto itemized his requests all over again, lest his intentions should be misunderstood, and added the ultimate in
praise of Oryō: "I must say, she has more strength than I do."[2]

At the time of the negotiation of the Satsuma-Chōshū alliance,
Oryō was in the Teradaya, the inn next to the Satsuma residence in
Fushimi. Fushimi was the port immediately south of Kyoto. It had
its own bakufu commissioner [bugyō], since it was an important
communication point on the north-south route. In earlier times
lords on their way to Edo had been expected to stop at Fushimi,

[2] Sakamoto monjo, I, 136-143.

and hence they could keep residences [*yashiki*] there, but they were to go no closer to the capital. By the last decade of Tokugawa rule these earlier restrictions had gone by the board, and Fushimi had gained a new importance as the port of entry to Kyoto and the place which, one step removed from Kyoto, could best serve as center for the planning and organization of *shishi* plots. The Satsuma residence at Fushimi could house only those sent on official business, and smaller inns clustered about it to house those affiliated with the Satsuma cause. The most important of these was the Teradaya, a hostel specifically authorized to house Satsuma boating personnel who transported official parties and goods to Fushimi. The Teradaya had been used by rōnin on numerous occasions, and the first great plot of the loyalist era had concentrated there in the spring of 1862, only to be broken up by the orders of Shimazu Hisamitsu.[3]

After he received the protection of his Satsuma friends in 1864, Sakamoto was accustomed to staying there; indeed, as he wrote his sister, the inn was as much home to him as if he were at the house of his brother-in-law. Sakamoto was posing as a Satsuma samurai, and therefore subject to Satsuma police and judicial control. He had successfully passed numerous bakufu barriers by this means. It is not surprising that the maids of such an inn should be fiercely partial to their guests' cause and that they should try to shield them from danger. The Teradaya was run by a strong-willed woman whom Sakamoto praised in his letters as one "who helps men who work for Chōshū and the nation . . . she has a good deal of learning, and carries out projects worthy of men. . . ."[4] It was at Sakamoto's urging that she had provided shelter for Oryō, Sakamoto's favorite.

On March 9, 1866, Sakamoto had returned to the Teradaya from Kyoto with the news of the signing of the Satsuma-Chōshū alliance. With him, and waiting for him there, was a Chōshū friend, Miyoshi Shinzō. The two had come up from Shimonoseki together, but Miyoshi had remained in the shelter of the Teradaya while Sakamoto went on to Kyoto. By the time Sakamoto returned to Fushimi, bakufu police forces had been alerted to the presence of one or more trouble-makers at the Teradaya, and a party of men

[3] This is the rising Sakamoto had hoped to join when he fled Tosa. It is well described in *Ishin shi*, III, 86-94.

[4] *Sakamoto monjo*, I, 227.

was sent by the Fushimi Commissioner to apprehend them. Sakamoto's account of this affair was written to his brother in Tosa in the fall of the same year. It is perhaps the best first-hand account of an occasion of which the late-Tokugawa years saw so many, and therefore it is quoted here in full:

"That Fushimi trouble I just mentioned came at 8:30 in the evening on the 23rd of the first month. [March 8, 1866] There was one man, Miyoshi Shinzō, with me. We had come up from the bath and were on the point of going to bed, when we thought we heard something strange; it sounded like the footfalls of someone sneaking around below us (we were on the second floor). Then, in the same way, we heard the clattering of six-foot staves. Just at that time the woman I've told you about earlier (her name is Ryō, and I have since made her my wife), with no thought of her own safety, came running up to us and warned 'Look out! The enemy have invaded unexpectedly, and men with spears are coming up the stairs!' At that, I jumped up, grabbed my hakama and the two swords, along with a six-shooter pistol, all of which I had left in the next room, and crouched down towards the rear of the room. Miyoshi Shinzō had on his hakama, put on his two swords, and grabbed a spear; and then he too crouched down.

"The next minute a man tried to open the *shōji* a crack, and when he saw our swords, he called out, 'Who's there?' As he prepared to come on in, he saw that we were ready to defend ourselves, and so he backed up again. In a moment there was a creaking sound in the next room. At my instructions Yoshii removed the sliding panel which opened into the next room from the rear of our back room, and looked. There were already 20 men lined up with spears; they also had two burglar lanterns, and to top it off there were fellows carrying six-foot staves everywhere. We glared at each other for a minute, and then I said, 'What's going on here? You're forgetting you can't insult a Satsuma samurai like this.' The enemy moved closer, shouting insults; 'Oh, is that so! Get down! Get down!'

"By this time one spear-man was half way up the stairs and coming in my direction. He was on my left. I figured that if there was a spear on my left it could strike me from the side, and so I shifted my position to face to the left. Then I cocked my pistol, and threatened all ten of the spearmen, from right to left. They ran away. Meanwhile, others of the enemy were throwing spears, and also charcoal braziers, and fighting in all sorts of ways. We, for our part, were ducking spears, and you can imagine that it was really a noisy war inside that house. We also hit one man, but I don't know whether we killed him or not.

"One of the enemy managed to come in from the shadow cast by the shōji and, with a short sword, he cut the base of my right thumb, chopped the knuckle of my left thumb, and cut my left index finger to the bone at the knuckle. Of course these were shallow finger wounds, and I quickly pointed my barrel at him, but he darted back into the shadow of the shōji. Since the fellow had advanced on me, I shot another bullet, but don't know whether I got him or not. My pistol was a six-shooter, and since I had shot five rounds I was now down to one shot. I thought I ought to save it for an important target, and as a result the war became a little bit quieter. Then one fellow wearing a black kerchief advanced along the wall holding his spear at the ready. When I saw him, I cocked my pistol again and used the left shoulder of my companion who was standing with his spear as a gun mount, so I could really aim at the man's heart. It looked as though there were dead men all around us. Some were dying while crawling on their stomachs in front of us, and looked as though they were about to fall asleep.

"All this time the enemy was making a terrific racket as though they were tearing shōji and sliding and breaking panels, but not once did they come out into the open. Now I thought I would try to reload my pistol, and took out the cylinder. . . . But although I got two bullets in, I couldn't carry it off as I thought; because my left finger was cut and my right hand was wounded too. The next thing I knew, I had dropped it (the bullet chamber). I looked for it on the floor, and of course felt through the blankets for it, it had apparently fallen into a fire brazier or something, so that I couldn't find it. All the time the enemy were making crashing noises, although none of them came into view. Then I threw away the pistol and said to my companion, Miyoshi Shinzō, 'I've thrown away my gun!' Miyoshi answered, 'In that case, let's rush into the middle of the enemy and fight!' But I said, 'Let's see if we can get out the back way instead.' At that, Miyoshi also discarded the spear he was holding, and we went down the ladder at the back. We found that the enemy was guarding only the part of the building that served as inn, and that there wasn't anyone coming.

"Next we got through the *yasoi* behind the building, and when we had broken through the shutters and entered, the people of the house came out half asleep. We were in a bedroom. It was too bad, but we were determined to get out through the far side of that house into the town if we had to wreck everything in it. It was a very big house, and we had to do a lot of damage. The two of us hacked away with our swords and stomped and kicked with our feet, and we made it. Then when we got through and came out into the town, there wasn't a soul around. That was good luck, and we ran five blocks, although I was becoming ill, not to mention being out of breath. (You know, you're never supposed to go out without a long kimono on underneath, but since I had just come out of the bath I had on a *yukata* and a padded robe over it, with no *hakama*.) My feet were in as wretched a state as my dress, and I fled the enemy looking very disreputable.

"We got to Yokomachi and to a place called New Tosa Moat, and in a place just off the water gate we entered a building from the rear, climbed up on a shelf of lumber, and tried to sleep. Even then a dog began to bay at us and we were still in trouble. There we were. After a bit, I suggested to Miyoshi that he go to the [Satsuma] residence, and he managed to reach there. Then the people from the residence came right away and took me back with them. My wounds were slight, but they must have reached an artery, since the blood was still running without let-up the next day. For three days it was all I could do to go to the bathroom. . . ."[5]

This famous account of Sakamoto's has inevitably drawn to it the talents of popular novelists and film directors. One can sense some of the courage and the strength required in the thought of the two desperate rōnin, half crazed with fear and anger, cutting and kicking their way through an entire house in the darkness. It is little wonder that it is this picture of Sakamoto that has become most firmly fixed in the minds of Japanese today, thanks largely to motion pictures. For those who thrill to violence and action on

[5] *Sakamoto monjo*, I, 226-232.

the screen, the Japanese inn, with its paper and paste construction, has possibilities which easily eclipse those offered by the swinging shutter doors of the Western saloon.

The Fushimi commissioner, unsuccessful in his attempt to capture the two rōnin, continued for a time to guard the Satsuma Fushimi residence in which they were sheltered. But the Satsuma military leaders Saigō and Ōyama were not men to be intimidated by a show of bakufu strength. They failed to hand over their guests as they were requested to do, and a week later Saigō sent Yoshii Kōzuke from Kyoto with a company of soldiers to escort Sakamoto and Miyoshi to the Satsuma Kyoto residence. The bakufu police preferred peace to war, and in the Kyoto residence Sakamoto and Oryō, who now joined him there as his wife, could rest in safety.[6] Sakamoto was the object of much concern from his comrades, and their reaction to the news of his danger shows the esteem in which they held him. Kido wrote him of his concern and his relief at his escape,[7] and Nakaoka Shintarō rushed to Kyoto to make sure that Sakamoto was safe. Saigō secured for him the care of a doctor, and when Saigō left Kyoto on April 14 Sakamoto and his wife accompanied him. Also in the party were Komatsu Tatewaki, a Satsuma karō, and Yoshii Kōzuke; in company like this, bakufu attack was impossible. The party reached Kagoshima on May 24, after a stop in Shimonoseki to drop Miyoshi off. Miyoshi was praised, promoted, and rewarded with extra income by the Chōshū administration.[8]

In Kagoshima, Sakamoto was housed in the home of Komatsu Tatewaki. Thus the Tosa rōnin was now house guest of a Satsuma karō. Komatsu and Saigō had gone home to acquaint Hisamitsu with their success in negotiating an alliance with Chōshū. Sakamoto and his bride, however, had a restful stay which served as honeymoon and recuperation from his Teradaya wounds. Until July 13, when they left Kagoshima for Shimonoseki again, Sakamoto's letters to his sister tell of his enjoyment of the Kirishima hot spring, of mountain hikes, and of new sights and places.[9] For him this was an interlude between periods of action and danger.

---

[6] Chikami, *Sakamoto*, pp. 105f.
[7] *Sakamoto monjo*, I, 242-243. Earlier Sakamoto had written Kido that he owed his life to the pistol, a gift from Takasugi Shinsaku. *ibid.*, p. 241.
[8] Hirao, *Kaientai*, p. 139.
[9] *Sakamoto monjo*, I, 233-239.

2. The Second Chōshū Expedition

Sakamoto's holiday in Satsuma came to an end with the out-break of warfare between Chōshū and the bakufu. He returned to Kagoshima from his hot spring vacation on the fifth of June, and on the thirteenth of July he sailed for Shimonoseki on the old *Union* which had been purchased from Thomas Glover. Still under Satsuma registry, it was now the *Sakurajima Maru*. Satsuma was returning the Chōshū cargo of grain to its donors, together with the ship, which would next become the *Otchō Maru*. The vessel reached the Straits of Shimonoseki just in time for Sakamoto to take part in the fighting of July 28 against Tokugawa naval units.

The bakufu's effort to chastise Chōshū ended so disastrously and had such tremendous effect in Japan that it requires brief descrip-tion. Nothing better serves to illustrate the inefficiency inherent in the Tokugawa effort to crush a militant domain by assembling a conglomeration of reluctant vassals. The outcome strengthened opponents of the bakufu and exhilarated the *shishi*.

It will be remembered that the arrival of shogun Iemochi in Osaka in July of 1865 had been arranged to symbolize his per-sonal leadership of a second punitive expedition against Chōshū. Almost immediately after his arrival a foreign flotilla had arrived to demand Imperial approval of the treaties, and the months that followed were dominated by the pressing urgency of dealing with this threat. After much bickering and maneuvering, Imperial ap-proval had been granted on November 22, 1865. The departure of the foreigners, and the postponement of further measures affecting the opening of the port of Hyōgo, opened the way to action on the problem of Chōshū.

By December of 1865 the Tokugawa administration was caught in a very difficult position in regard to its handling of the Chōshū problem.[10] It had an Imperial mandate to deal with the issue, but it was able to stir no enthusiasm for warfare on the part of its feudatories. Some bakufu leaders, including Hitotsubashi Keiki and Matsudaira Katamori, the lord of Aizu, espoused a "hard line," partly to cover themselves in Edo and partly in the belief that it was necessary to reestablish the bakufu's primacy over any

---

[10] The account of the handling of the Chōshū expedition which follows is based largely on *Ishin shi*, IV, 474-522, and Osatake, *Meiji Ishin*, II, 692f.

possible opponents. But most daimyō opposed such a policy for the reason that its success would threaten them and benefit only the Tokugawa, while the diversion of strength to internal strife might open up the way for foreign attack or domestic disturbances. The bakufu's original assumption, that Chōshū would submit to a further show of force, was proved wrong when a number of missions returned from meetings with Chōshū representatives empty handed. The Chōshū administration, however, was careful to avoid a show of outright defiance that would guarantee prompt military action. They were anxious to gain time in order to improve their preparations, and they realized the need of courting a favorable opinion among other han. As a result the bakufu was denied the excuse to strike at the same time that it was thwarted in its hopes of compromise.

While inconclusive negotiations with Chōshū were being carried on by the rōjū Ogasawara Nagamichi, there were significant signs of discontent and disunity within the bakufu leadership and forces gathered at Hiroshima on the borders of Chōshū territory. Among high bakufu officials, Ōkubo Ichiō, Katsu's friend and Sakamoto's contact, made clear his objections to military adventures. Matsudaira Shungaku's representative, Nakane Yukie, was equally vigorous in his objections. And Katsu himself, although still very much out of favor, was also known to be in opposition to the war, although his political position may have forced him to use caution in saying so. The arguments used by most of those who objected were basically the same: the expedition had already cost a great deal of money; over thirty han had obediently assembled troops whose maintenance was costing hard-won money that should go for defence against the West. Furthermore, it was clear that few of the troops and none of their commanders had much stomach for warfare. They had come expecting that political coercion would suffice, and their preparedness for a real fight was very inadequate. Many of the lords present were anxious to return their forces to their own domains, and concerned lest disorders take place while they were absent. It was clear that they had responded to the call for troops in a purely formal fashion, and that they would hesitate before committing to the bakufu's cause forces they might later be able to use in their own interest. On the other hand, Keiki and the few who agreed with him argued that precisely because so much had been committed in treasure and prestige to the expedition it could not now return empty-handed, and that the total superiority over Chōshū was of such an order that eventual victory was certain.

In Chōshū, on the other hand, the conviction of danger and isolation produced a unity and purpose that had been lacking two years before. It had become clear that the bakufu proposed to force both the (Mōri) daimyō and his heir into retirement and that it planned to decrease the han area and income by more than one hundred thousand koku. These were the sort of threats that could be expected to unite all groups in opposition to the Tokugawa demands, for they affected the honor of all samurai, while the cuts in revenue would imperil incomes of all within the ruling class. There was therefore abundant cause for indignation, which contrasted to the lack of purpose shown within the bakufu councils. Furthermore, the revolutionary leadership of the loyalist extremists had taken extraordinary steps to arouse general enthusiasm and produce unity. Pamphlets and statements were issued so that there could be no mistake as to the purpose and necessity of the fight. The various militia units, of which Takasugi's Kiheitai was the best known, drawn as they were from a variety of social groups, were ideally suited to spread some of this determination and spirit beyond the ranks of the samurai. Chōshū was becoming what its leaders later desired for all Japan, "a nation in arms." A vigorous campaign of purchase and import of Western arms brought important additions to the military potential, while the time bought by negotiation with the bakufu forces was devoted to exercise and drill.

The Chōshū administration carefully lengthened this favorable period during which their strength increased as the bakufu's determination ebbed. It had, indeed, the difficult task of restraining the spirits of those who wanted immediate and all-out war. A group of Kiheitai stalwarts, impatient because of the delay, absconded and crossed the border to attack the enemy without being ordered to do so, and the han administration had to take vigorous police measures to guard against further lapses of this sort.

On June 13 Ogasawara Nagamichi transmitted to Chōshū representatives the bakufu's final terms. Moderated somewhat by Keiki out of a desire to retain his backers, they still represented a decisive change from the arrangement which had brought the first expedition to a close. Besides the arrangements for succession within the Mōri family whereby the grandson would succeed, and the reduction of Chōshū territory by 100,000 koku, they included punishment and guarantees against the branch fiefs which had been active in the earlier loyalist years. It was clear that Chōshū administrators could not accept such terms without first unhorsing the revolutionaries who had seized control in the previous year. They did not, however, reject them either, but instead requested an extension of the time granted them for decision in the ultimatum. When this was granted and proved to make no difference, the bakufu requested and received Imperial permission to chastise its vassal.

As the preparations for attack were rushed to completion, a variety of misfortunes befell the Tokugawa leaders. The increasing costs of the expedition, already immobile for almost a year, had driven food prices up until the urban commoners, as well as the bakufu commissariat, were distressed. Riots broke out in Osaka and quickly spread to other major cities in the Tokugawa domains. Everywhere a temporary loss of authority and prestige faced the shogunate. In its desperate search for money, it called for new forced loans from all merchants and communities under its control. In the Osaka area it even pledged to merchant houses that they would not be troubled again for several years. According to some authorities, the fear of domestic insurrections further hampered the shogunate by forcing it to keep some of its best forces in reserve.

The loss of power and authority which the riots revealed served as convenient excuse for the Satsuma lord to decline to support the expedition. The shogunate did not, of course, know of the Satsuma-Chōshū alliance as yet, although it was beginning to receive information which made some such agreement seem very likely. The Satsuma reply to a call for troops, however, pointed to the dangers at home and abroad and concluded that a domestic war was a risk that ought not to be undertaken. Satsuma's refusal was a portentous one. It was soon known to a number of han for whom its example served as suggestion, and this open defiance complicated the bakufu's expectations considerably. Equally important, it showed the Chōshū leaders that Satsuma was keeping its share of the bargain. Sakamoto, who could be expected to watch over and encourage the friendship he had helped to sponsor, could write Kido in September that Satsuma had sent seven or eight hundred men to Osaka as agreed, and that the Satsuma agent Godai Tomoatsu was vigorously buying munitions in Nagasaki for Chōshū.[11]

The Satsuma refusal was followed by one more striking, from Hiroshima. The staging area for the expedition, Hiroshima had already suffered severely in economic terms as a result of special levies and needs, and the han administration decided that it had contributed all it should to the effort. Therefore Hiroshima also contributed no troops.

Further evidence of Tokugawa impotence came in Fukuoka, where the conservative faction had finally won the upper hand and caused the deaths of a number of the administrators who had worked with the Chōshū men and the refugee court nobles who had come to their realm. When it seemed that the han was about to yield to a bakufu demand that the court nobles be sent to Edo, a company of Satsuma military led by Ōyama Tsunayoshi and Kuroda Kiyotaka came in to protect them.[12] Thereafter it was apparent that attempts to enforce the command would require direct conflict with Satsuma, and the bakufu emissaries were powerless to change the situation. The military action against Chōshū which began in July was thus inaugurated in unpromising circumstances.

The bakufu's original plans had envisaged a simultaneous advance on Chōshū from all sides. On the land frontiers with Hiroshima and Shimane the principal land armies, including contingents from Hikone, Hiroshima, Fukuyama, and Kii would attack. The islands on the southeastern border of Chōshū, called the Kaminoseki entrance for one of their number, would be invaded in amphibious operations by Matsuyama and other Shikoku fiefs. Shimonoseki would be entered from Kyushu by troops from Kumamoto, Yanagawa, Kokura, and other fiefs, while still another amphibious operation was to be carried out against Hagi by Satsuma and Kurume. In the event, the failure of Satsuma and Hiroshima to cooperate caused a slackening of effort on the Hiroshima front and ruled out the Hagi operation, but action on the other sectors was begun as planned. The successful prosecution of a campaign involving the cooperation of thirty-two fiefs, most of

[11] *Sakamoto monjo*, I, 215.
[12] Hirao, *Rikuentai*, p. 173.

them anxious to lose as few of their effectives as possible and determined not to do more than their share, would have required at the least superior leadership and superior equipment. The events were to prove that the bakufu had neither. Only on the sea was its strength markedly superior to that of its opponents, and even there the intrepid and venturesome tactics of the Chōshū defenders made up for the bakufu's preponderance of strength.

The off-shore islands Ōshima and Kaminoseki were shelled and successfully occupied by pro-bakufu units at the outset. Within a few days, however, elements of Takasugi's Kiheitai were put ashore, and Takasugi himself, in command of a small vessel, the *Heitora Maru* (formerly the *Otento*) maneuvered among the bakufu vessels with such boldness as to disrupt the plans of the attack. Within a week most of the bakufu troops had withdrawn. At the Hiroshima borders, where the bakufu's best-trained and equipped troops were deployed, the issue was closely fought, but the bakufu commander, Honjō Masahide, was numbered among those who had little heart for the civil war. He soon set plans for an armistice in motion. Although he was dismissed and Hikone and other units continued the warfare somewhat longer, Chōshū successes produced a Chōshū advance into Hiroshima. The Tokugawa commander-in-chief resigned, and soon a virtual truce was in effect along that sector of the front. The truce was formalized by a private Chōshū-Hiroshima agreement which ended hostilities there. On the Shimane (Sekishū) front on the Japan Sea, Chōshū units commanded by Ōmura Masujirō gave a good account of themselves against a bakufu force whose top commanders were far from enthusiastic about the warfare.[13] Here too, truce talks were soon in prospect, but before they were negotiated the Hamada han army had fled, leaving their castle in flames.

The remaining front was that of Shimonoseki, and it was there that Sakamoto brought the ship he commanded from Kagoshima. At Kokura, on Kyushu, the bakufu forces were commanded by Ogasawara Nagamichi. Under him were units from Kokura, Kumamoto, Kurume, Yanagawa, and Karatsu, as well as a thousand-man Tokugawa force. Their plan was to cross the straits into Chō-

[13] The system of adoption among daimyō families made for numerous lateral ties. Thus on this front the daimyō of Inaba (Ikeda Yoshinori), and of Okayama (Ikeda Shigemasa) were brothers of Matsudaira Busō of Hamada. *Ishin shi*, IV, 512. Among their other brothers, all sons of Tokugawa Nariaki of Mito, were Hitotsubashi Keiki and Tokugawa Yoshiatsu, of Mito.

shū, while Chōshū units, under Takasugi's Kiheitai and captained by Yamagata Aritomo, sought to prevent the crossing and planned one of their own. Nakaoka, who was in Shimonoseki shortly before the fighting began, described the state of affairs as follows:

"Just now the price of foodstuffs here has become very high, as is the case in other areas too. A shō of rice has more than doubled in price, and it is terrible. However, everyone seems to be getting along quite well and to go on with his business, and one doesn't see even lower class people who seem to suffer very much. But this is a particularly wealthy area in both rice and gold, and they say that even if war comes and farming is impossible they will have a three years' supply of food in storage. In this way you can see how the Chōshū han, determined to fight to the death, has taken care of the food supply for the soldiers who are burning to fight."[14]

Sakamoto arrived with the old *Union* just before the fighting broke out. He had stopped at Nagasaki, where he left his wife, and where he also had some discussion and correspondence about the cargo of grain which Chōshū had sent to Satsuma.[15] When he reached Shimonoseki, Takasugi Shinsaku requested his assistance in the naval battle that was shaping up in the straits. Sakamoto accepted gladly, and the rōnin under his command willingly lent their efforts to follow the Chōshū strategy. The bakufu had five ships in the straits, and Takasugi needed the *Union* to help to even the score. The bakufu ships were cautious, however (Sakamoto noted on a position sketch he drew for his brother, "These bakufu ships did not take part, but I can't imagine why"), while Takasugi displayed the same imaginative and adventurous planning that had distinguished his action at Ōshima a few days earlier. His ships boldly shelled the gun emplacements on the Kyushu side of the straits, shelling Moji, Dannoura, and other fortifications, while Kiheitai units were put ashore under cover of the bombardment to attack the bakufu land forces. This first landing was only a raid in force, however. Takasugi's men made a quick

---

[14] Hirao, *Rikuentai*, p. 172.

[15] Satsuma, with exaggerated politeness, had returned the cargo to Chōshū. Kido refused to accept its return, and suggested that Sakamoto use it as capital for his commercial company. Sakamoto accepted it, but not without being amused by the whole affair. "This," he remarked, "is about like making off with somebody else's *fundoshi* (loin cloth)." Hirao, *Kaientai*, p. 152.

strike, destroyed the small ships the enemy might have used to invade Chōshū, and then withdrew to Shimonoseki again. But brief though the action was, Sakamoto was delighted by his participation in it. As he wrote his brother, "This was the most interesting thing I have ever done. If I told you everything you wouldn't believe me, but that's the way a war is." Sakamoto stressed the numerical superiority of the bakufu forces, and wrote that Takasugi had bolstered his men's morale with a ration of sake before the battle. The losses of this initial clash were astonishingly few; as Sakamoto put it, "Before, when we talked about war, we thought of a large number of people killed. But you can have quite a sharp engagement and lose only ten men."[16]

A few days later, after Sakamoto had left the straits again, Takasugi was able to take advantage of bakufu weakness and indecision. The Kumamoto forces, whose commander was opposed to the war, failed to support Kokura, which was the object of a second Chōshū attack. Even the Tokugawa units failed to support their ally, for Ogasawara, secretly informed of the fatal illness of the shogun Iemochi in Osaka, deserted his sector of the front in favor of the political front in Osaka. Thus the weaknesses of feudal disunity were again strikingly apparent. The Kokura troops, however, refused to give in, and a pointless and hopeless struggle with Chōshū units ended with the Kokura castle in flames and Chōshū in unchallenged control of both sides of the straits. Tosa rōnin, among them Tanaka Kōken, were in the attacking forces.[17]

To Nakaoka, who was at Dazaifu, the outcome was no surprise. He reported to Tosa that the Kokura landings and victories had taken place despite the fact that Chōshū was outnumbered twenty to one, and that the Chōshū forces had fought with such spirit that, in one unit of a hundred and forty men, over a hundred men had become casualties. Thanks to their determination, they had swept the field, capturing large stocks of rice, weapons, and ammunition.[18]

While the bakufu forces, reluctant to risk further involvement, contained in some areas and driven back in others, were everywhere demoralized, the shogun Iemochi died in Osaka castle on

[16] *Sakamoto monjo*, I, 218. Sakamoto's sketch for the letter, p. 217.
[17] Tanaka Kōken later reminisced about the unnecessary destruction. "That was the first time I had ever set fire to people's houses, but after all I was a hot-blooded young fellow of 23 or 24. . . ." Quoted in Ozaki, *Nakaoka*, p. 200.
[18] Letter in Hirao, *Sakamoto-Nakaoka . . . sensho*, p. 245.

August 29, 1866. The grand expedition which he had come to lead in person and which was to restore the fortunes of his house had thus ended with his own death, at a time of general defeat and frustration. His death was not announced until September 28. It then provided the justification for a general truce. Katsu was sent to arrange the terms of the cease-fire with Chōshū representatives on the Kokura-Shimonoseki front, and reached agreement on October 10.

The second Chōshū expedition thus ended in complete disaster for the Tokugawa. It had begun with hopes of new victories and powers, and instead it had made the Tokugawa weakness and disunity apparent to all. Hereafter either thoroughgoing compromise or outside help in large quantities would be required.

For several months, however, bakufu energies were necessarily concentrated on the problem of the shogunal succession. Keiki, who was appointed deputy to command the expedition, should it be continued, preferred now to stop it completely, thereby alienating the few who had supported his original advocacy of the war.

For the *shishi*, the bakufu disaster and the shogun's death opened up a new era of confidence and hope. As low-ranking activists showed their optimism and self-importance, order in Kyoto declined once again. The day for individual heroics was past, however; more able figures began to think in terms of construction.

Sakamoto now began to see new possibilities for his commercial company. He had need of more assistance; his capital and resources were fast running out. A schooner that had represented his chief capital investment had sunk with a loss of nine men, among them his old friend Ike Kurata. Chōshū, with much greater opportunity for direct commerce with the West than before, was no longer as dependent upon the help of men like Sakamoto, and neither it nor Satsuma needed to sponsor Sakamoto's efforts at a time when open defiance of Tokugawa rule became possible. Logically, therefore, a new form of help and sponsorship was needed, and this could best come from Tosa itself.

Sakamoto therefore spent the months after the Chōshū war trying to restore an understanding with the fief he and his friends had fled. He followed the trends in Tosa official policy closely, and he saw in them signs that he might find a favorable hearing.

Nakaoka Shintarō too, who had now established himself as an authority in land tactics as Sakamoto had in maritime interests, was able to write to makers of han policy and to argue with them the necessity for sweeping changes that would bring Tosa policy into line with that of Chōshū, and, as he now saw, with that of most of the Western world as well. The Tosa administration, no longer afraid of domestic insurrection from the loyalists, and conscious that Yōdō's old councils of reconciliation between court and camp had little further chance of success, was prepared once again to reenter national politics. In doing so, it would have good use for the excellent channels to opportunity and influence which its former retainers had developed.

3. Changes in Tosa

The return of Yōdō to Kōchi in 1863 to resume personal direction of Tosa affairs had ended the indecision that had characterized politics there since the death of Yoshida Tōyō. Yōdō returned to Kyoto for the conferences to rebuild relations between the bakufu and the court in 1864, but after these meetings failed he returned to Tosa, where he remained for several years. Officially unavailable for further counsel because of illness, he actually devoted his time to hunting and to directing the changes within his fief. His advice and participation were, in any case, less sought during the period of bakufu intransigence which led to the second Chōshū expedition. Like his counterparts Shimazu Hisamitsu and Matsudaira Shungaku, Yōdō preferred to absent himself from the national scene in order to be able to return to it as the leader of a realm whose administration, military, and finances had been restored to solvency and efficiency.

The first task he had undertaken was that of political consolidation. This had involved, most obviously, the suppression and punishment of the low-ranking loyalist leaders who had murdered Yoshida Tōyō and done their best to subvert the administration thereafter. Yōdō was equally displeased with the ineffective leadership that the traditional houses had provided thereafter, however, and he moved to replace them by men drawn from the middle ranks, men who were of the persuasion and, indeed, of the clique of Yoshida Tōyō.

These steps had to be undertaken cautiously and slowly, because signs of favor for the Yoshida group, coupled with the open suppression of the popular loyalists, threatened to bring to flame the resentment of the *gōshi* and *shōya* groups throughout the realm. The han administration was conscious of its widespread unpopularity, and this insecurity was in part the reason for the elimination of Takechi, who was considered the cause. It was also a convenient excuse for failing to provide full support for the second Chōshū expedition.

Until the loyalists were under control, the han administration moved cautiously. It issued statements to its low-ranking retainers, principally the *gōshi*, who were assembled for words of restraint and caution from the young daimyō Toyonori.[19] It also avoided antagonizing them by vigorous participation on the national scene. More than usual caution was shown in the manipulation of administrative personnel whose sympathies were believed to be ambivalent. Sasaki Takayuki, who was widely criticized by his comrades in rank for his emotional and intellectual preference for the cause (but not the tactics) of the loyalists, was shifted frequently lest he develop contacts with or encourage confidence among the low-ranking loyalists who were everywhere to be found.[20]

But gradually, as order returned, a need for talented and vigorous administrators to direct the program of rebuilding and reform made Yōdō seek out again the disciples of Yoshida Tōyō. The principal figures who returned to action had gained from Yoshida a vision of Tosa strength and wealth through policies of official trade and commerce. They also believed in tapping the sources of Western technology and science to strengthen their fief. Necessarily, this brought them into opposition with the conservatives who, like Koyagi Gohei, advocated a policy of support for the bakufu and the exclusion of foreigners. Nor could they look for support from the loyalists, who still used the slogan sonnō-jōi.[21] Convinced of the necessity of a firm policy of opening the country (kaikoku), the Yoshida men worked until the progress they could demonstrate convinced the loyalists that power for the

19 Sasaki, p. 222.

20 Thus Sasaki was sent to Hata as bugyō, only to be reassigned a few days later because the han officials, on second thought, remembered that there were many loyalists there. Sasaki, p. 249.

21 There were of course many factions in Tosa; as many, in fact, as could be assembled from possible combinations of loyalism (*kinnō*), exclusionism (*jōi*), opening (*kaikoku*), and support for Tokugawa (*sabaku*). Thus there was a sabaku-jōi group, profoundly conservative, which contrasted to the usual designation for the Yoshida clique as sabaku-kaikoku.

throne could be based only upon a program that utilized the benefits of open ports.

The official who dominated Tosa policy in the last years of Tokugawa rule was Gotō Shōjirō. A disciple of Yoshida Tōyō, Gotō had accompanied Yoshida on the night of his murder. Conscious of his own danger, he wisely avoided both Tosa and the limelight during the years of loyalist extremism that followed. Instead he spent several years in Edo familiarizing himself with the problems and possibilities of Western-style sailing and navigation. Then, after Yōdō had been able to stabilize the political situation in Tosa, Gotō returned to his home in the spring of 1864. For a period he continued to avoid publicity, and worked quietly with Iwasaki Yatarō, another Yoshida disciple, to develop plans for continuing their master's work. These drawn up, they submitted them to Yōdō during a monthly session which he conducted for considering and reading poems drawn up by his retainers. It is an interesting commentary on the abilities of the traditionalists and conservatives then in power that Gotō decided to couch his opinions in Chinese (*kambun*) in order to evade the scrutiny of his political enemies.[22] Now and later, Gotō proved to have the elasticity of mind and tactics which enabled him to see ability and promise even in the ranks of the *shishi* who had so recently threatened his life. In person and bearing he was courageous and firm, and he possessed in abundance some of the single-mindedness and humor which made the comrades rate him as a jimbutsu.[23]

Gotō's close friend and fellow protégé of Yoshida Tōyō, Iwasaki Yatarō, came of much lower stock. The son of a *jige* rōnin, or former *gōshi*, Iwasaki had shared some of his father's difficulties with the authorities. For a time he was imprisoned for disrespect to officials. Whether from that period, as is sometimes reported, or from his studies under Yoshida Tōyō during the latter's period of banishment, Iwasaki became convinced that his path lay in ways of business and trade. Yoshida appointed him to several commercial posts, and also sent him to Nagasaki to look into foreign trade in 1859.[24] After Yoshida's murder, Iwasaki's life was in danger, but he prudently avoided all prominence. Thereafter,

[22] Ōmachi, *Gotō Shōjirō*, p. 135.

[23] One of the incidents that made the *shishi* think well of him came one evening when Gotō was assaulted by assassins on his way to a brothel. He fought off his attackers and continued serenely on his way.

[24] Hirao, *Ishin keizai shi no kenkyū* (Kōchi, 1959), p. 6.

as it became safe to reenter public life, he utilized his contacts with officials to try his hand at a lumber enterprise. He soon found he could do nothing in the face of the patterns of han monopoly, however, and shortly afterward he reentered official service under Gotō as a supervisor and agent of the new mercantile enterprises that the han set up.[25] In this manner Iwasaki gained the experience and official contacts that stood him in good stead in later years when he built up the Mitsubishi firm; his Tosa and Nagasaki contacts would provide the political basis of his support in later decades when Gotō became a leading figure in the Meiji government and a founder of the early democratic parties.

Gotō was appointed to the central policy board on August 10, 1864. His rise thereafter was one of the most striking of the many who rose during those years of rapid change. Beginning as a member of the mounted guard (umamawari) with an income of 150 koku, he advanced to senior elder (karō), with lands delivering 1,500 koku.[26] Others of his group who soon took office with him were Fukuoka Kōtei, Ogasawara Tadahachi, and Itagaki Taisuke. They were all "Yoshida men," all of upper-middle rank, and all men of considerable ability. There was room for disagreement between them. Itagaki, who was to lead the Meiji liberal movement, was the most military-minded and anti-foreign of the group, and hoped for an early war to drive out the barbarians. Ogasawara's position was more favorable to the bakufu, and until he was converted to the loyalist cause he tended to deprecate any forms of anti-Tokugawa maneuver. After his conversion, however, he espoused the new cause so warmly that Yōdō dismissed him, and he died as a soldier in the Tosa armies that besieged the Aizu keep in 1868. Fukuoka, a scholar and organizer, was close to Yōdō. It was he who would prepare the final suggestion to the shogun that he resign and then pen the initial Charter Oath for the Meiji Emperor. But it was Gotō, a skillful tactician who developed the bridges with the loyalists like Sakamoto over which the han entered the final loyalist movement, who was the center and organizer of the group. This was as able a group of leaders as any han could show in late Tokugawa days. It combined literary, adminis-

[25] Tanaka Sōgorō, *Iwasaki Yatarō den* (Tokyo, 1940), p. 55.
[26] W. G. Beasley, "Councillors of Samurai Origin in the Early Meiji Government, 1868-9," *Bulletin of the School of Oriental and African Studies* (London, 1957), xx, 98.

trative, and military distinction, and it developed the policies whereby Tosa entered the Meiji period as a full partner of its larger neighbors.

Domestic and international dangers put an immediate premium on military reforms and strengthening, and this was the task assigned to Itagaki. It was not an easy one, for the traditional formations were the basis of the system of samurai ranks. Modern weapons and tactics required the concept of the training of masses of men in maneuver and movement, and this could be done only at the cost of the individual glory upon which the feudal samurai set such great store. Sasaki Takayuki, who was assigned to military training for a time, records the discontent of the bowmen at being changed to guns, which had previously been reserved for the least honored ranks of ashigaru, or foot troops.[27] Any change in military formations would involve, therefore, a change in the samurai ranks, and an effort to simplify these and restore them to at least the logic of the seventeenth century was made in 1867.[28] But it remained difficult to build a modern military structure on an outworn social order; Itagaki found himself recruiting rōnin in Edo, and organizing within Tosa the Mimpeitai (People's Corps) that had been begun when an early war with the foreigners was expected in the 1850's.

Modern military strength required the import of weapons and techniques, and Tosa lacked both the economic and educational background for ready appropriation of what the West had to offer. Efforts to overcome this had, to be sure, been begun under the administration of Yoshida Tōyō. In 1863 Tosa's first Western ship, the *Nankai Maru*, had been purchased. Its efficiency and speed had ushered in a new era of han transportation.[29] Iron foundries had also been contemplated, but a shortage of money had brought the decision to try to utilize bronze and copper which could be gathered by reclaiming bells and implements. Yoshida had also had ambitious plans to extend Tosa's commerce to other parts of Asia as well as to the rest of Japan. These plans had been shelved during the period of loyalist ascendancy. With the coming of Gotō to power, however, Yoshida's type of thinking returned to the fore.

[27] Sasaki, p. 296.
[28] Sasaki, p. 347.
[29] Hirao, *Ishin keizai*, pp. 48-87, presents a full-scale study of the ship's use and importance.

The immediate and most pressing need was for money. The extravagance in troop movements during the loyalist period had drained the treasure of its reserve; toward the end of their period of influence even the loyalists themselves had been casting about for some way of marketing Tosa products in the Osaka area in order to realize the money they lacked.[30] The suppression of the loyalists, who had the sympathies and appreciation of so many of the most influential groups in the countryside, further meant that the han faced difficulties in increasing and even maintaining its rate of income from the normal channels. Sasaki notes repeatedly that there was a virtual loss of faith in the administration. Forced loans were announced but could not be collected, and only the samurai could be effectively squeezed by special levies which deprived them of half of their salaries. Special economy regulations sought to prohibit unnecessary luxuries and to regulate spending. These might help the administration, but they did not win it popular support; as a restaurant owner told Sasaki, "These economy measures are all very well for you gentlemen with fiefs, but they make it very difficult for us townsmen."[31] So the han, unable to persuade or force its subjects to make special contributions of the size it needed, had once again to go into business itself.

Gotō's solution was an institution called the Kaiseikan, one which had been conceived earlier by Yoshida Tōyō. Opened in the spring of 1865, this bureau was designed to centralize and direct all han enterprise in Tosa. Departments were set aside for naval development, for a medical school in which English and French were taught, an industrial department which would promote the production of camphor, paper, sugar, tea, and other domestic products, a mining division to seek out and exploit reserves of gold, silver, copper, iron, lead, and lime, a division to promote the whaling industry, and a purchasing agency to market such goods and to purchase needed foreign ships, machines, weapons, and books, with offices in Nagasaki and, later, in Osaka. Such measures, it was felt, would solve the economic problems. The new institution was also designed to provide money for Tosa industries in need of capital, thus freeing them from dependence on Osaka money lenders.[32]

[30] Hirao, *Ishin keizai*, p. 51.   [31] Sasaki, p. 225.
[32] Egashira, "Kōchi han ni okeru bakumatsu no shinseisaku," *Bakumatsu keizai*

On the other hand, such a direct entrance into official trade alienated many. Sasaki felt, as he memorialized, that it was a serious error to sink to the foreigners' level and seek for profits. What he and others found most objectionable, however, was the cost entailed in the erection of the Kaiseikan headquarters. Objections of this sort had always been made against the plans of Yoshida Tōyō, and as far as Sasaki was concerned the new administration was now well on its way to increasing instead of lessening the burdens upon the people. This was particularly the case because the headquarters of the new organization was constructed by *corvée* labor at no benefit to the villagers whatever. This, he felt, was no way to try to win and unify popular support.

In answer the han issued a statement to the samurai explaining the intrinsically moral purpose of the Kaiseikan as a device for *fukoku-kyōhei*, enriching the country and strengthening its defence. It is interesting to note that the argument was pitched on loyalist grounds as well; this would by no means benefit the Tosa house alone, it made clear, but the Imperial country as a whole. The document went on to say that other changes could be expected to follow; it should not be thought that the usual techniques would suffice any more. Indeed, it was contemplated to expand to some of the islands to the south, and to conquer and develop them to further the han purposes.[33] Thus profit, when in a proper cause, need be no source of shame.

Profit required markets, and in order to open direct contact with the foreigners Gotō wanted a Nagasaki branch for the Kaiseikan. It was here that his path crossed Sakamoto's. Gotō went to Nagasaki in the late summer of 1866, taking with him Nakahama Manjirō ("John Mung"), the Tosa fisherman who had been educated in Massachusetts.[34] At first, however, Gotō did a good deal more purchasing than selling, and his vigorous measures to import needed goods caused such a storm of criticism in Tosa that he

---

shi kenkyū, p. 119, and Hirao, *Ishin keizai*, pp. 1-47. Tanaka, *Iwasaki*, p. 58, adds that one of the functions envisaged for the *Kaiseikan* was to provide capital for domestic enterprise in order to end the dependence on Osaka capital and thus gain the interest for the han.

[33] Sasaki, pp. 320, 336, and for the han reply, Egashira, pp. 116-117, and Hirao, p. 5.

[34] The chronology and ambiguities of the *Gotō Shōjirō* have been corrected by Hirao Michio in "Gotō Shōjirō no Nagasaki Shanghai shuchō to sono shimei," *Tosa shidan* (1935) No. 52, pp. 25-31.

would have been sacrificed if he had not enjoyed Yōdō's full confidence. In Nagasaki Gotō dealt with Thomas Glover, the firm of the Prussian consul, L. Kniffler & Co., and the English firm of Alt and Co. Gotō was not content to buy in Nagasaki, but he went on to Shanghai. Expected to buy one ship there, he was so impressed with the possibilities open to him that he dealt with Jardine, Matheson and Co. to buy a gunboat as well. He also contracted for numbers of the new Armstrong guns. The substantial debts and obligations Gotō incurred did little to endear him to conservatives in Tosa,[35] but they made of the Nagasaki branch a busy place for fief plans in the next years.

The Tosa changes that have been described were accompanied by diplomatic and intellectual shifts in which the han adjusted to the fact that one partly modernized fief had successfully defied the shogunate and some thirty of its vassals. Yamauchi Yōdō turned to consider the possibility of cooperation with the newly formed loyalist coalition, and Nakaoka Shinarō contributed a policy paper that skillfully united the themes of loyalism, exclusion, and Westernization.

Yōdō, who had refused to receive ambassadors from Chōshū before the fate of the expedition was settled, counseled Keiki to give up all thought of conquest after the disasters of the summer of 1866. He also began to think once again of the possibility of working with his powerful neighbors, and sent Gotō to Satsuma to talk to Shimazu Hisamitsu.[36] More interesting still, he felt it advisable to send a small group to Dazaifu to talk to the exiled court nobles and to take a reading on the political climate outside of Tosa.

Sasaki Takayuki was one of those who went to Dazaifu. Also in the party were several lower-ranking loyalist partisans who requested permission to accompany their rivals. The fact that Sasaki, known to be loyalist in his sympathies, was chosen to go, and that others found it possible to go at their own request, indicates that a change was taking place in the political scene. Indeed, with conditions changing so rapidly outside of Tosa, and with the likelihood of an early shift so much in the air, the old antagonisms between the loyalists and the Yoshida faction were beginning to

[35] *Ishin Tosa kinnō shi,* pp. 1017f.
[36] Hirao, *Yōdō Kō ki den,* pp. 179f.

lessen. Both groups were beginning to realize that they had more in common with each other than they did with the conservative traditionalists who had, successively, allied with Takechi's wing and then with their enemies. Sasaki describes this gradual shift. In his case it was crystallized by his rapprochement with a Yoshida clique official named Nakayama Saieishi, a man with whom he served as bugyō, after he decided it might be well to cultivate this person. He found to his surprise that it was both easy and rewarding.[37] On the larger scene, there developed a comparable willingness of the leaders like Gotō and Ogasawara to see possible merit in the loyalists whom they had so recently feared. And even if there had been no identity of thought whatever, the fact that those loyalists had such excellent contacts with the great fiefs of Satsuma and Chōshū would probably have sufficed to make for some sort of rapprochement.

But in fact there were large areas of agreement that had developed. Anti-foreignism in the simple form in which Takechi had espoused it was a dead issue for almost everyone of any intelligence, and unquestioning support for the bakufu in the form that the traditionalists had earlier felt obligatory was no longer tenable for realists.

In Dazaifu Sasaki heard for the first time from Hijikata of the Satsuma-Chōshū alliance. His own convictions of the need for a loyalist position and of the impossibility of salvaging the power and prestige of the bakufu strengthened as the Tosa rōnin told him of the victories they had won and the support they had gained. He returned convinced that Tosa would have to change its course. Not all of his fellow-travellers were equally convinced, however, and the han had its choice of two very different reports. Indeed, one man was even able to report Satsuma support for the bakufu.

The han administration decided to try to resolve this by sending a party to Kyoto. There Ogasawara Tadahachi met Nakaoka Shintarō, and the former shōya overwhelmed him with the evidence of the concerted anti-Tokugawa movement, one that was not likely to be stopped. Ogasawara was not the only one of the top leadership group to be so persuaded. Itagaki, too, was now fully convinced of the need for a loyalist position.[38] More than most, Itagaki was still inclined to the view that a war against the

---

[37] Sasaki, p. 355.
[38] Hirao, *Rikuentai*, pp. 220-221.

foreigners was likely. But even should this fail to come about, he was prepared to consider steps against the bakufu, and his new contacts with Saigō, to whom Nakaoka would shortly introduce him, were not likely to lessen this martial predisposition.

For many others the abandonment of the naïve assumption that the foreigners could and should be driven out was an essential element in the new resolution of internal differences in favor of a united front. Sasaki Takayuki, recovering from an illness that prevented him from being a member of the group that travelled to Kyoto, received from his doctor, a loyalist who had studied in Fukuzawa Yukichi's school of Western learning in Edo, a copy of Fukuzawa's Seiyō Jijō—the first, he writes, to circulate in Tosa. From it he could discover that the Western world had things worthy of emulation as well as of repudiation, and that it was not necessary to reject all contact to maintain Japan's proper course.[39]

Most striking, and probably most persuasive for the remaining exclusionists among the Tosa loyalists, was the argumentation of Nakaoka Shintarō. Nakaoka had read Fukuzawa long before, and would soon present a copy of that important little book to Iwakura Tomomi in Kyoto.[40] In the fall of 1866 Nakaoka wrote, probably for the perusal of the han officials who had come to Kyoto to sound out the political situation there, a document which restated his views on the necessity of sweeping changes in military, administrative, and policy for Tosa.

Extraordinary times, he wrote, required extraordinary measures. It was essential as never before that all groups in Tosa be united and that the old system of self-centered measures by daimyō and lesser figures be changed. Under the old system, the people feared authority and cringed before it instead of identifying themselves with the larger purpose. What was needed was a government that would protect the people, develop them, and act as father and mother to them. At present, he thought, only Chōshū was following such a policy. Abroad, countries like England and France followed it too. It was not enough to have policies of force. Nakaoka quoted with approval Katsu's statement that an army that did not know the Way was not strong. True strength required justice and law as well as force. Today there was in the world a concept of international law, and a country was sound to

[39] Sasaki, p. 363.
[40] Diary entry for May 26, 1867; Ozaki, Nakaoka, p. 362.

the degree that its Way, its human abilities, and its laws were good, its spirit strong, and its customs beautiful. Nakaoka called therefore for a broader and more imaginative program of unification and activation.

Succeeding paragraphs spoke of the need to develop a navy in conjunction with maritime enterprise of all sorts. It should be possible, Nakaoka thought, to ally with the merchant princes of Osaka, and by following the commercial law of the West to trade with Shimonoseki, Osaka, Nagasaki, Shanghai, and Hongkong; in that way the country would be made wealthy and strong. Military strength, in turn, could be developed only by scrapping the rank and status divisions of the old military order, and weapons and methods should be brought in from other countries.

Toward the close of this extraordinary document, Nakaoka bethought himself of his first principles.

"When I talk about military matters in this way, it will seem that I like only the Western way, and that I am no longer in favor of expelling the barbarians. [Jōi] People may think this, but actually this is the real form jōi has to take. . . .

"This jōi we talk about is not by any means a term exclusively ours. In times of necessity, it has been practiced in every country of the world. America used to be a colony of England. The oppression of the English king became more heavy every day, and the American people suffered. At that point a man named Washington complained of the people's hardships, and thereafter roused the people of the thirteen colonies of America to expel the English. He carried out exclusion [jōi] and drove out the barbarians. This war lasted seven years, and the English, realizing they had lost, sued for peace. American thus gained its independence, the thirteen colonies united, called themselves the United States, and became a strong country. This was eighty years ago."

It would be desirable, Nakaoka agreed, to rise up at this time and smite the foreigners to make up for the shame and humiliation which the Tokugawa officials had foisted upon the country by their shameless behavior in negotiating unequal treaties with a view to their convenience and interest. But the country, as a result of three hundred years of peace and softness, was weak, and to attempt to hurry history now would result in defeat and suffering. What should be done, therefore, was "to yearn, in long-range terms, for the august conquests of the sacred Emperor Jimmu. In short range terms, we should carry out the jōi of Yoshida Shōin by crossing the seas, learning of the strong points of other peoples, and adopting their spiritual unity; we must join together to master their technology, and study their military science, in order to bring about true exclusion as soon as possible; then we can reform the treaties, conquer the countries of distant seas, and plan to wipe out this disgrace of ours. Shall we let death keep us from carrying out this resolve?"[41]

Jōi had thus changed radically. It no longer meant exclusion and obscurantism, but began to signify independence, equality, and strength. Who would oppose such goals?

4. The Nagasaki Scene

The loyalists talked and wrote a great deal about the shame and humiliation that the unequal treaties had brought to their country. The provocation to nationalism which the West provided was certainly real enough. The original copies of letters submitted by the Nagasaki consuls to the bakufu's commissioners have been preserved in Nagasaki, and these yellowed papers provide abundant evidence of the inequality of the treaty era. A few samples serve better than pages of analysis to illustrate the tone that both parties were expected to maintain. "I have a very important communication to make to your Excellencies," British Consul Morrison could write the Nagasaki Governors in 1863, "and request you will send both Vice Governors with Interpreter Shinagawa to this Consulate at one o'clock this day, in order to hear what I have to say."[42] Foreigners thought guilty of wrong received all the protection that their consuls could give them under their own law and through evasion and blusters, while high Japanese officials were expected to be meek and submissive. This was certainly the reverse of the time-honored pattern in Nagasaki, where the lowliest samurai had been as superior to the Dutch merchant as honor was to greed.

Nevertheless the unequal treaties also provided tremendous opportunity for political and technological change, and the loyalists took full advantage of them. Gotō's ability to trade in Nagasaki, and even to travel to Shanghai, serves as example of the oppor-

---

[41] Text in Hirao, *Sakamoto-Nakaoka . . . sensho*, pp. 325-333.
[42] Nagasaki Prefectural Library. Dated June 28, 1863.

tunities that were now open. The traders as a whole were indifferent to Tokugawa sensibilities, and the enormous impact their work could have on political stability was succinctly shown by a reply of J. G. Walsh, the American consul (and trader), to a bakufu protest in 1864. "I will," he agreed, "give the notification you request, but must again say that I consider it useless and that it will have no effect. So long as Japanese propose to buy, foreigners will try to sell and as there is no penalty provided by the Treaty for selling munitions of war to the agents of Daimios and the Merchants, it will not be in my power to prevent such sales."[43] It is appropriate here to look at the Nagasaki scene to see the way in which foreign trade and contact affected the politics of the period.

Until 1865, the foreign powers, though not always their merchants, tended to observe the letter and spirit of the treaties, trading in Tokugawa-approved channels. The shelling of Kagoshima and Shimonoseki introduced them to new elements and ideas, however, and their views of Tokugawa efficiency and integrity declined with the confusion which attended bakufu efforts to chart a course in those years. Even before then, important merchants saw the possibility for profit and broke the line. Prominent among these was Thomas B. Glover, of the firm of Glover and Company, a man—and firm—with earlier experience in the China trade. On the whole, the China hands like Glover seem to have come to Japan with a low opinion of the "central" government, and they were quick to scent the possibilities for gain in trade with outside lords. As early as 1862 the Yokohama representative of Jardine, Matheson and Company reported a visit from a so-called "anti-foreign" lord who had expressed his anxiety for trade and urged traders to come to his realm. The dating suggests that this was Shimazu Hisamitsu, and his visit probably came just before his retainers struck down the Englishman Richardson.[44] Whatever

[43] Dated August 6, 1864.

[44] Ishii Takashi, *Meiji Ishin no kokusaiteki kankyō* (Tokyo, 1957), p. 388. For above-board sales the Tokugawa could be informed, as when in May 1867 British consul Flowers enclosed the text of a contract made on 29 March "between Gotō Sogero acting for and on behalf of His Excellency The Prince of Tosa of the one part and Glover and Company of Nagasaki, Merchants of the other part. The said Gotō Sogero hereby contracts and agrees to purchase from the said Glover and Company the "Gunboat 'Nankai' as she now lies in Nagasaki Harbour with all fittings and armaments as set forth in the specification hereunto annexed for the sum of Mexican dollars seventy five thousand ($75,000) payable as hereinafter

scruples Jardines may have had, Glover had none. He sold to any who could pay, and helped to smuggle Itō Hirobumi and Inoue Kaoru of Chōshū to Britain as he later did Godai Tomoatsu and Matsuki Kōan of Satsuma. Gotō Shōjirō also made the trip to Shanghai in a vessel of Glover's. Glover was not alone in this trade —an American merchant, Drake, helped Chōshū come by ships, guns, and rifles—but he was certainly the most important figure in it, and his subsequent decoration by the Meiji Government suggests that his protégés thought highly of his services.[45]

In 1865 a new British Minister, Harry Parkes, arrived from China. For a time he was prepared to give the bakufu full recognition as Japan's treaty-making government, but before long he agreed with Glover in the view that British interests lay in broadening trade as much as possible, and Tokugawa attempts to control and channel trade should be resisted or sabotaged. Thus precisely during the period when Chōshū was desperately seeking arms for its stand against the bakufu, British policy was inclined to favor such trade. There was never any doubt about Glover's position; in talks with Kido, who complained about the Tokugawa blockade, he explained that it might be difficult to send goods to Shimonoseki directly, but that if shipping from Nagasaki could be arranged no one could prevent his selling. Hence when Itō and Inoue came to Nagasaki, the cooperation of Satsuma and Sakamoto made it easy to buy a ship with Satsuma funds, man it with Sakamoto's followers, and use it to run arms to Shimonoseki.[46] As the trade developed, Harry Parkes, who was increasingly impressed by the vigor and ability of the Chōshū and Satsuma leaders he met, did everything he could to obstruct ba-

---

mentioned, viz.: Mexican dollars $10,000 on signing this agreement, the receipt of which sum is hereby acknowledged by the said Glover and Company. . . ." $14,379.37 was due within twenty days, an identical sum before the end of seventh Japanese moon, and the balance within twelve months, with 12% interest per annum added. A month later, however, the consul was protesting, for Glover, at Gotō's report that the "governor of Nagasaki" had somehow withheld permission for Gotō to take possession.

[45] A biography of Glover in Japanese, *Garaba den*, has not been available to me. His career seems little studied, and might repay careful treatment. A short and unsatisfactory piece is that of W. B. Mason, "Thomas B. Glover, A Pioneer of Anglo-Japanese Commerce," *New East* 2 (February 1918), pp. 155-167. Glover married a Japanese wife and settled in Nagasaki. In recent times enterprising promoters have shown his Nagasaki mansion, with its sweeping view of the bay, to tourists as the "Madame Butterfly House."

[46] Ishii, p. 411.

kufu efforts to end or lessen this kind of contact. While the Chō-shū war was being prepared he visited Kagoshima, together with Glover, who had prepared the way in an earlier visit to the Satsuma capital. Glover added help in the form of a large loan to Satsuma, and Parkes received a warm welcome. He returned enthusiastic about free trade relations with tozama lords. Indeed, he saw fit to add injury by complimenting the bakufu on the magnificent reception he had received in Satsuma (some estimated its costs at 30,000 ryō) and suggested Edo might well hold up such courtesy as a model to be followed by other vassals Parkes might visit.[47]

Opportunities opened by Glover were not restricted to his firm, as can be seen from the Satsuma agents who made their way to Europe and bargained vigorously in Belgium and France as well as Great Britain. The Satsuma Nagasaki representative, Godai To-moatsu, provides a useful parallel to the developments in Tosa under Gotō; like Iwasaki and Gotō, he became an important figure in the world of finance and business in later Meiji years.

Godai had been assigned the study of navigation under the Netherlands instructors who came to Nagasaki in the 1850's. There-after, disguised as a coolie, he made his way to Shanghai. Godai went with the tacit permission of his lord, and in Shanghai he made some unsuccessful efforts to convince European traders that he had the backing necessary to buy a steamship that was for sale. He returned to be assigned a post in Nagasaki, and in 1864 Glover made it possible for a group of nineteen Satsuma men, among them Godai, to learn first-hand of the West. A period of study in England was followed by shorter periods of observation in several other countries of Europe; two of the group returned by way of the United States. These experiences, gained with the per-mission and knowledge of Shimazu Hisamitsu (who is sometimes described as conservative and anti-foreign) equipped Godai with the first-hand knowledge which made it possible for him to reject any suggestion of thoroughgoing anti-foreignism thereafter. His letters from Europe were full of praise for Western law, which he considered more fair and moral than that of Japan, for the effi-ciency of Western script (the Japanese language could perhaps be retained, he thought, provided that Chinese loan words were dropped), and for the necessity of an immediate arrangement to

[47] Ishii, pp. 441, 454.

tap the springs of Western science and technology.[48] An eighteen-point program he drew up on his return included the suggestion of a league of Japanese lords, like the North German Confederation, and the employment of "Indians and Chinese" to develop the resources of Japan and Asia.[49] He was able to report that Westerners considered Chinese little better than slaves, and that Japan, through projects like the Yokosuka arsenal, was becoming known as a progressive corner of Asia.

In England Godai took part in negotiations that brought to Kagoshima the equipment for Japan's first modern spinning plant. On the continent, he arranged with the Conte des Cantons de Montblanc, Baron of Ingelmunster, a plan whereby Satsuma and Ryukyuan products would be sent to Europe; the Paris Exposition of 1867 was to be the first occasion at which these goods were fully shown and made available. The contracts and letters of introduction and attorney which were drawn up left little doubt of the readiness of Godai and, in turn, his Satsuma superiors, to engage in large-scale commercial arrangements with the West. All of this, it must be remembered, was done in the name and on behalf of the daimyō, who bore in the documents the title "Matsudaira Shurinodaibō Minamoto Motsihisa, by the Grace of God King of all the Liu Kiu, Prince kokshi of Satsuma, Osmi and Hiuga," and who extended "to all to whom these presents shall come Greeting."[50] This from the nominal head of the coalition that would drive out the Tokugawa under slogans calling for exclusion of foreigners and a return to power for Japan's sacred Emperor!

Experience in the Western world produced intellectual as well as technological changes. Godai's suggestion from England that a league of daimyō might be set up to approximate the North German Confederation illustrated the way foreign examples could be suited to the Japanese experience. There is evidence, however, that the process worked both ways, and that the Japanese emissaries' suggestions affected European, and in particular British, policy.

In the spring of 1866 Matsuki Kōan, one of the Satsuma men Glover had helped to get to England, had an interview with a

[48] Tomoatsu kai, ed., *Kindai no ijin: ko Godai Tomoatsu den* (Tokyo, 1921), pp. 327-341 for excerpts.

[49] Godai Ryūsaku, *Godai Tomoatsu den* (Tokyo, 1936), p. 56.

[50] *ibid.*, pp. 73-74.

former secretary of the British Ministry, Laurence Oliphant, in London. Matsuki assured Oliphant that the foreigners were hated only because the Tokugawa were able to monopolize the trade, and he assured him that once a new government, more broadly representative of daimyō opinion and centered around the emperor, was set up, Japan would accept its international commitments and be faithful to them. This intelligence was transferred by Oliphant to Lord Clarendon, who personally talked to Matsuki twice; the same sentiments then formed the substance of a dispatch to Harry Parkes in Japan, with the suggestion that he might well try to interest the shogun in broadening the political process in this manner if the occasion permitted. Thus Satsuma's ideas formed the substance of Foreign Office dispatches to Harry Parkes.

For many Japanese there was another index to English policy in the form of two substantial essays published by Parkes's able interpreter, Ernest Satow, as "English Policy" in the *Japan Times* of December 1865 and May 1866.[51] A translation which Satow worked out with his language instructor found its way to Japanese printers and had wide currency as a pamphlet; most readers accepted it as an official statement of British policy. Satow himself writes that this was done without the knowledge or permission of his chief, but his healthy respect for that chief's ability and temper makes one suspect that he was not likely to have stepped so far out of line without reasonably good knowledge of Parkes' mind. The Japanese language text of *Sakuron* that has been preserved makes a number of points with great emphasis. First, it says, the powers were wrong in negotiating and signing with the shogun, giving him the title Great Lord (Taikun); he holds power only at the Emperor's will, and to overlook this is to take part in the wrong of the usurpation the Tokugawa family has perpetrated. The real rulers of Japan are not the shogun, and not the Emperor, but the feudal lords. What is desirable, therefore, is a policy for Britain that will recognize these facts, and try for agreement with those who hold real power. Satow suggested the possibility of a council of the principal lords (of whom, as he put it, the

---

[51] The conversation is described in *Tokugawa Keiki Kō den*, p. 367, and the sequence of dispatches is noted by Ishii, p. 428. Ishii, writing before the date of Satow's first essay was known, credited Satow's pamphlet to the London dispatch. "Hakken sareta '*Eikoku sakuron*' no gembun ni tsuite," *Nihon Rekishi* No. 149 (November 1960), pp. 7-14.

shogun was only the greatest) under the Emperor; with such a group, the treaties could be revised, and agreements thus reached would be carried out.[52] Thus in writing, as in act, the British drive for wider markets and free trade had the effect of reinforcing the demands and satisfying the needs of the great fiefs of the southwest. It is clear that the "humiliation" the loyalists deplored had its practical uses for their cause. Parkes' visits to Satsuma, his warnings to the bakufu against blockading Shimonoseki in the event of further war with Chōshū, and his continual urging, in private talks with men like Saigō Takamori, that a "unified government" and "council of lords" be established, left little doubt where the British stood on the major questions of internal policy that Japan faced.

In view of this British partiality, the bakufu representatives saw little reason to turn a deaf ear to the offers of help that the French Minister Leon Roches offered. Roches believed that Japan's future lay with the Tokugawa, and he believed the great fiefs of the southwest were predominantly anti-foreign; he made few efforts to establish first-hand contacts with their leaders, and as a result he was much less informed than Parkes was on what was being prepared. Roches was firmly convinced of the bakufu's ability to punish Chōshū, and offered a good deal of advice on how this might best be done. In contrast to Parkes' insistence that Shimonoseki should not be blockaded, Roches urged that foreign arms be denied the Chōshū loyalists at all cost. French representatives helped keep the bakufu abreast of British doings. Thus the Nagasaki consul reported to Roches that "the English commander has come here on the *Princess Royal* and is expected to stay here, at the home of Glover, for a month. The Minister is also due. Chōshū is receiving many weapons through Satsuma assistance in Nagasaki, and they are being imported through Glover and other Englishmen. The small steamer *Otento Maru*, with English officers aboard, has headed for the Ryūkyūs, but it is now speeding here again. It is probably going to be handed over at Nagasaki for Shimonoseki."[53] Roches quickly followed to Nagasaki to see what

[52] Ishii, pp. 375-385, gives the Japanese text. Satow, *Diplomat in Japan*, pp. 159-160, describes his tract. That it had influence can be seen from a letter from Kido to Sakamoto, September 1867, which states that it is a shame for every man in the divine country to have to hear such words from the mouth of an Englishman. *Sakamoto monjo*, I, 380-381.

[53] Otsuka, "Fukkoku Kōshi Leon Roches no seisaku kōdō ni tsuite," *SZ* (July, 1935), p. 833.

Parkes was up to, arriving there after his departure for Kagoshima; he refused an invitation from Satsuma officials to visit their domain, however, on grounds that it was contrary to the spirit of the treaties. By 1865, the bakufu leaders were beginning to believe that Roches was as disinterested as he claimed to be, while their doubts about British purposes multiplied.

In February of 1865, the Tokugawa minister Kurimoto Joun submitted a detailed plan asking for French assistance in technical and military matters, and even broached the possibility of stationing more French troops in Yokohama to offset growing Satsuma strength near the Imperial capital.[54] Beginning in January, 1865, special economic programs were worked out with Oguri Tadamasa; French interests were to receive a virtual monopoly on certain goods for export to Europe, notably silk worm cards and cocoons, and in return French money and technical advice would be put at the disposal of the Tokugawa. A Société de Commerce Française was established with five or six merchants of each nationality, with a French representative in Edo and a Japanese in Paris. In February 1866, the organization was completed with the appointment of the Parisian banker Paul Fleury Herard as Special Consul General of Japan, with powers to negotiate and contract for the required goods and services. Transactions rose in number and amount, particularly after the Chōshū disaster, and French munitions, uniforms, shoes, and blankets were ordered in large quantities. In all, it is estimated that equipment for some 25,000 infantrymen, 500 cavalrymen, and 1,250 artillerymen was obtained from the French in the months that followed. Meanwhile Roches, in person and through his contacts within the bakufu like Oguri, emphasized the need of reorganization to lessen the autonomy of the lords and increase the efficiency of the government and army.[55]

5. Reinstatement and Support for the Kaientai

After the bakufu's failure to crush Chōshū the import of arms through Nagasaki increased steadily. The fiefs no longer had much reason to fear Tokugawa displeasure, and they could carry on their own transactions without resorting to Sakamoto's group of rōnin who had served as middlemen. As a result, by the time Tosa

[54] Ishii, pp. 553ff.
[55] Ishii, p. 558.

policy makers were prepared to reconsider their course in national politics, Sakamoto too was ready to seek reconciliation with the men whose authority he had fled five years earlier. For the Tosa leaders rōnin like Sakamoto, with their ability to give information about developments elsewhere and to serve as intermediaries, promised to be very useful. For the rōnin, reinstatement in official favor brought hope of new and direct assistance in their projects; they might, as a result, participate in the events that lay ahead as representatives of a major fief. In any event, Takechi Zuizan's old dream of a common front of Satsuma, Chōshū, and Tosa remained to give such proposals a stamp of loyalist legitimacy.

Sakamoto found the opportunity to make the first move in this direction through a Tosa samurai named Mizobuchi Hironojo who had been assigned to study Western military science in Nagasaki toward the end of 1865. Mizobuchi and Sakamoto had been students of fencing in Edo a decade earlier, and although they had chosen different political courses they had remained friends.[56] It was logical for Sakamoto to choose this old companion as a channel through which to indicate his readiness to receive official help, while Mizobuchi was well qualified to describe changes in official policy to Sakamoto.

Late in 1866, Sakamoto addressed Mizobuchi in these terms:

". . . I was born a second son, and until maturity I followed the wishes of my elder brother. When I was in Edo, I became conscious of the shameful way in which obligation to the ruler was construed. I had a deep interest in naval matters, and I pled with the han officials and struggled painfully to gain experience in those matters. But however I tried, I failed to achieve my goal, for I had little talent, my knowledge was shallow, and I was poor and without resources. However, as you know, I have managed to make a beginning towards the building of a small navy. For some years now I have been on the go in all parts of the country, and I have often had to treat old acquaintances like strangers when we met. Who is there who does not think of the land of his father and mother? Despite this, I endured it, and forced myself not to think about it, forbearing to turn around in my path in order to gratify my heartfelt desire. But since, after all, I have failed to carry my hopes through to completion, I have somehow come to

---

[56] Hirao Michio, "Mizobuchi Hironojo," *Tosa shidan*, No. 29 (1929), pp. 59-65.

wish that I might again see my ruler's face. I seek no rank after the long period during which I have travelled and wandered, and I am not deserting the goals towards which I have devoted half of my life. But since you know and respect me, I have given you this outline of my efforts in the hope that you will be so kind as to reflect on it. . . ."[57]

This interesting letter shows Sakamoto confessing nostalgia for his homeland and failure in his hopes for acting on his own. It is in sharp contrast to his earlier letters to his friends, and yet it offers no excuses, no flattery, and no regrets. Sakamoto clearly must have felt that, despite his past and present, he had a good deal to offer his fief.

Mizobuchi thought so too. He visited Sakamoto several times, heard from him of developments in Satsuma and Chōshū, and told him of the changes in Tosa. Sakamoto's change of heart may also have become known to Tosa officials through the reports of the captain of a Tosa ship, the *Yugao Maru*,[58] named Mutō Hayame. Mutō himself, of the umamawari class, had also known Sakamoto in earlier Edo days. Sakamoto described his meeting with him in the same letter to his brother which included the account of the Fushimi fight. "The other day," he wrote, "I had occasion to meet Mizobuchi Hironojo, a man from Enoguchi, and had a talk with him. Thereafter I happened to meet the captain of a steamship, Mutō Hayame. Since he was an important officer, and since I was afraid he would report everything when he returned to Tosa, I was going to pass him without recognizing him. But then I thought that Mizobuchi had come two or three times and had listened to my thoughts, and I decided I would see Mutō too. I had known this Mutō earlier in Edo, and since he is really an easy-going man it was very pleasant to see him again. It is good to take up again relations with former friends."[59]

Sakamoto derived great satisfaction from the news these men brought him of a change of heart among Tosa policy makers. Gotō's plans for a Tosa navy were of particular interest to him.

[57] Hirao, *Kaientai*, p. 174, gives the text of this letter, which is not included in other compilations.

[58] If the chroniclers are correct, it was the American missionary Guido Verbeck, in Nagasaki, who suggested to Tosa representatives that they select names for their steamships from *Genji Monogatari*.

[59] *Sakamoto monjo*, I, 226.

He began to hope, as he wrote Miyoshi, that Takechi's old dream of a Satsuma-Chōshū-Tosa common front might be established after all.[60] For this it was essential to establish contacts between responsible Tosa emissaries and the Chōshū leaders, and to this end he arranged for Mizobuchi to go to Chōshū to talk to Kido Kōin. Kido was not slow to see the advantages of a new tie with Tosa, and from his enthusiastic reference to Mizobuchi's visit in a reply to Sakamoto his interest in the project can readily be seen.[61]

Through Mizobuchi the Tosa administration reestablished for the first time direct contacts with Chōshū. On his way back from Chōshū, Mizobuchi also visited Dazaifu, the headquarters of the exiled court nobles. His reports from the loyalist centers, added to those that had already reached Tosa, provided material on which decisions could be made. There was indeed reason to think that Tosa policy might make a complete turnabout, and that Sakamoto would be reinstated by the han.

Sakamoto's own projects were also involved in his hopes of reconciliation with Tosa officialdom. His commercial company was in difficult financial straits, and it seemed likely that unless new sources of aid opened up he would have to give up his activities. He was having difficulty keeping his group together. He lacked ships, and he lacked money. At one point he even considered moving his headquarters to Shimonoseki, a move that would have made him a Chōshū auxiliary instead of an independent with considerable opportunity for maneuver.

The first ship that had been purchased from Thomas Glover, the old *Union*, had been transferred to full Chōshū control after its participation in the battle in the Shimonoseki Straits. As the *Otchō Maru*, the *Union* was now part of the Chōshū navy, and it was lost to Sakamoto's company. The second ship to come into the firm's hands, also purchased through Glover, was a schooner. As with the *Union*, the purchasing was done through Satsuma channels, and the vessel was to have sailed for Kagoshima with the *Union* on its first run. When both vessels encountered stormy seas, however, the schooner, which lacked steam power, foundered. The

<hr>

[60] *Sakamoto monjo*, I, 249-250.

[61] Kido to Sakamoto, *Sakamoto monjo*, I, 241. See also *ibid.*, p. 471, for a letter from Sakamoto to the Shimonoseki merchant Itō Sukedayu asking his help for defraying the costs of Mizobuchi's trip to Shimonoseki.

ship was lost with its entire complement. Sakamoto's old friend Ike Kurata was among those lost.[62] This disaster came during the time that Sakamoto was in Kagoshima recovering from the attack made on his life in Fushimi.

It is interesting to note that during these days morale remained high; the rōnin bound themselves to a strict code which ruled out self-interest. When an old friend of Sakamoto's, Kondō Chōjirō, was discovered to have discussed a trip to Britain with Thomas Glover, his comrades' criticism of his "selfishness" was so severe that he committed suicide to redeem his good name.[63]

After the end of the bakufu war with Chōshū, Sakamoto discussed with Godai Tomoatsu and with Chōshū officials a new plan whereby his company would serve trade between fiefs on a more regular basis. A charter was drawn up consisting of six brief and general provisions which envisaged traffic through the Straits of Shimonoseki for distributing on the main island of Honshu the products of the fiefs of the south. The charter made clear that fief names would not be used in contracts, but that merchant firms would be substituted for the real negotiating parties. The contracting parties would honor each other's notes. The Satsuma flag would be used for the cargo vessels, and the straits would be kept open for all traffic carried on under the plan provided the Chōshū authorities were given advance notice. Here, then, Sakamoto was trying to develop a commercial, profitable trade which would break through the bakufu-imposed barriers; the operations would be camouflaged as purely merchant in origin, and they would weaken the feudal restrictions by promises of free passage and mutually honored notes of exchange. This was quite obviously designed to help the Satsuma-Chōshū allies. In spirit it was also close to the British ideal of free, open trade. But since Sakamoto and his firm had no shipping, the new venture came to little.[64]

Sakamoto's next project was one that revived his earlier ideas about exploiting the possibilities of the northern island of Hokkaido. A plan was formed to buy a vessel from a Prussian mer-

[62] Hirao, *Kaientai*, p. 149, mentions only Glover in connection with this ship, while *Ishin Tosa kinnō shi*, p. 891, quotes a Sakamoto diary fragment which mentions a Prussian merchant. This last is applied by Hirao to the next venture, and since his research is more recent I am following his distinction between the two. The name of the ship, given in syllabary as *Wairu uefu* [Weir wolf?] I cannot identify.

[63] *Ishin Tosa kinnō shi*, pp. 885-894, and Hirao, *Kaientai*, pp. 120-122.

[64] Chikami, *Sakamoto*, pp. 129-130, *Kaientai*, pp. 160-163.

chant. It was to be named the *Daigoku Maru*. Foreign technical assistance was to come from two Americans, Nye and Onkins, while part of the capital was to be raised from Osaka merchants. The principal sponsorship and guarantees were to be provided by Sakamoto's Satsuma sponsors. Unfortunately, their credit with the Osaka capitalists was not very good, and although the project began ambitiously with enthusiastic letters and optimistic predictions, it failed through difficulties of financing.[65] Abortive as it was, however, the plan illustrates again how consistent were Sakamoto's interests in projects of this sort. Indeed, shortly afterwards he was to discuss the development of Hokkaido with a member of the Tokugawa Junior Council. His Satsuma friend and counterpart, Godai, was to be involved in the ambitious plans for the development of Hokkaido in Meiji years, and would have benefited from a projected sale of those assets into private hands; a deal which, when exposed, brought about the political crisis of 1881.[66] Sakamoto's Hokkaido plan, in its boldness of conception and deficiencies of backing, illustrated once again that he could not continue without support more dependable than any he had so far enjoyed. He was responsible for the behavior and support of his men, and the Satsuma channels of aid were apparently becoming less dependable. Furthermore, bakufu police measures in Nagasaki, though imperfect, made it very important for him to have official sponsorship. Hence Sakamoto's consideration of a move to Shimonoseki.

In the course of these difficult times, Sakamoto's contacts with merchants in Nagasaki and Shimonoseki were very important to him. His Nagasaki headquarters were in the residence of a well-to-do operator of a pawn shop, Kosone Eishirō. Kosone sympathized with and helped the *shishi* a great deal. He also had connections with trade in Satsuma goods, so that he could conveniently serve as nominal purchaser or guarantor in some of the complex transactions that were carried on. Sakamoto also, on at least one occasion, entrusted him with a mission to Shimonoseki.[67]

[65] Hirao, *Kaientai*, pp. 164-170.

[66] John Harrison, *Japan's Northern Frontier* (Gainesville, 1955), treats the incident in considerable detail.

[67] Hirao, *Kaientai*, pp. 160-161. See also the discursive comments of Nagami Tokutarō, "Nagasaki jidai no Sakamoto Ryōma," *Tosa shidan* (1929, No. 29), p. 71. A letter in *Sakamoto monjo*, I, 473, shows Sakamoto using Kosone as a messenger, while a ship contract given in *Ishin Tosa kinnō shi*, p. 891, shows Kosone acting as surety.

At Shimonoseki there was the important Shiraishi, whose friendship has been mentioned earlier. In addition, when Sakamoto sent Mizobuchi to talk to Kido, Kido suggested as lodging the residence of the merchant Itō Sukedayu.[68] Sakamoto's correspondence thereafter includes a number of letters to Itō, showing that he became a respected member of the *shishi* group. Indeed, as Sakamoto's consistent interest in commercial ventures shows, there was no longer much reason to expect from him any animus against a merchant. That part of his Confucian-samurai heritage had made way for the new order that was coming into being. It is not without significance that Sakamoto used during this period the name Saitani Umetarō as his alias. The merchant house from which his grandfather had entered *gōshi* ranks almost a century earlier, the Saitaniya, had produced in him a worthy successor.[69]

But merchant friends by themselves could only cushion the hardships and disappointments that Sakamoto was meeting. Assistance of the order he needed could be extended only by someone with access to tax money. And this came through the hands of Gotō Shojirō.

Gotō had arrived in Nagasaki on September 4, 1866. He had paused before going on to Shanghai with a party of twelve, and he returned to Nagasaki on October 14. His mission, it will be recalled, had been to purchase ships. It was one in which he succeeded, and the large sums he spent roused vigorous criticism in Kōchi. But Gotō knew that he had the full support of Yōdō. In discussions with him before his departure they had agreed that Tosa's role in the difficulties that lay ahead would be a minor one unless the han prepared a vigorous policy of ship acquisition and, thus fortified, extended its realm to "distant islands."[70]

These were ideas very much like Sakamoto's. Mizobuchi had told Sakamoto about Gotō's plans for naval expansion, and now

[68] *Sakamoto monjo*, I, 243, 471. Also see n. 61 above.
[69] A letter to the Teradaya early in 1867 shows Sakamoto still using the Satsuma affiliation: "address me as Saitani Umetarō of Satsuma." *Sakamoto monjo*, I, 244.
[70] Years later Gotō recalled that when Yōdō had asked him for his opinion on the course to follow, "I said that he would have to take a chance and reenter national affairs, if necessary to fight the bakufu, and to keep on until they were defeated, even if it meant destroying the realm. But the time had not come for that as yet. In the meanwhile we should buy ships, occupy islands to the south, and enlarge our domain." "But of course," added Gotō, "I was only twenty-six then, and didn't have much sense." Hirao, "Gotō Shōjirō no Nagasaki Shanghai shuchō," p. 28.

he could tell Gotō about Sakamoto's plans for maritime profits. Through Mizobuchi, then, Sakamoto met Gotō early in 1867 in a Nagasaki house of pleasure. Gotō had wisely provided sake, Mizobuchi, and one other guest, and, in addition, Sakamoto's current favorite from the licensed quarter. Unfortunately, neither has given a full account of the discussion that took place over the sake cups.

Sakamoto had been under some pressure from his rōnin companions who wanted to assassinate Gotō for having condemned Takechi Zuizan to death. He resisted this, according to one source, by pointing out to them that it might be possible to "do business with Gotō" and really achieve something. Then, after the talk, he expressed his astonishment and gratification that Gotō, who might after all have looked upon Sakamoto as an enemy of long standing, had not said a single word about the past. Instead they talked only about the big issues. Clearly, Gotō was a man of uncommon ability, and a genuine *jimbutsu*.[71]

To Kido, Sakamoto wrote that "affairs in Tosa have changed radically recently. I am sending Nakajima Sakutarō to tell you about them in detail. But of course even though there be this change, we remain most sincerely grateful for your help and strength. There is a likelihood that Tosa will stop being on the bakufu side. This can be brought about during the summer of this year, and then, to our great joy, the old line-up of Chōshū, Satsuma, and Tosa may materialize."[72]

Gotō also thought well of his new acquaintance. Through Mizobuchi he had already learned of the strength and determination of the anti-bakufu forces. His own ideas on trade and expansion were close to those of Sakamoto, and he was interested in the possibility of utilizing the energies and contacts of the rōnin for the period that lay ahead. Moreover, the decision to support them was not his alone. It was made on the highest levels of Tosa officialdom. A visit to Kōchi by Saigō had helped prepare the way. Gotō's fellow councillor Fukuoka Kōtei came to Nagasaki in April of 1867, bringing with him a document which absolved Sakamoto of his crimes and which restored him to favor as head of his commercial company, now renamed the Kaientai, or naval auxiliary force. The document reads:

---

[71] Hirao, *Kaientai*, p. 177.
[72] *Sakamoto monjo*, I, 248.

NOTICE

Saitani Umetarō,
or Sakamoto Ryōma

"The above named person has been acquitted of the crime of absconding and has been appointed to head of the Kaientai. He has been entrusted with all matters within the organization."

The Tosa support for Sakamoto's company consisted, initially, of money; 15,000 ryō were made available as capital.[73] More important, it brought status, safety, and purpose to an organization that had almost foundered for lack of support. The charter that was worked out by Sakamoto and Gotō made it clear that the organization would tap ability wherever it could be found, that Sakamoto would have full control, that the organization would include educational opportunities, and that funds, if not forthcoming from commercial profits, would come from Tosa. Its text follows:

1. Those who have left our han or other han because of their interest in maritime affairs may join this organization. Its purpose is to help our han in such things as transportation, commercial enterprise, exploitation, and speculation. Hereafter, the selection of members will be made on the basis of the individual's personal aspirations, regardless of his place of origin.

2. All matters of the company will be decided by the head. No one will disobey his orders. If a member imperils the undertakings of the organization and causes disorder, the head will decide whether he is to be executed or not.

3. The members of the company should help each other in time of sickness, protect each other from harm in emergencies, develop their sense of righteousness, and rectify their spirit together. Members should carefully avoid causing trouble for others by narrow judgments or violent deeds, nor should they form factions to force their will on others.

4. The members of the company will specialize in fields of learning such as government, gunnery, navigation, languages, and

[73] *Sakamoto monjo*, I, 274. The same source is used by Tanaka, *Iwasaki Yatarō den*, p. 65.

steam-engines, according to their particular interests, studying together, and in no event being idle.

5. The operating funds of the company will be drawn from its profits. The profits will not be distributed among the members. If the company is short of funds for new enterprises or for training its members, the head may report this to the han official in Nagasaki and await his reply.[74]

Sakamoto's energies and talents had now found an appropriate outlet. His company consisted of some fifty persons in all. The leaders of the group were drawn from several areas. Tosa contributed twelve, Echizen six, Echigo two, Mito one, and Kii one, this last being Mutsu Munemitsu. The provisions for learning and study showed Sakamoto's intention to capitalize on the potentialities of the large number of would-be scholars of Western learning who collected at Nagasaki. There was a surprising range of opinion and talents among the group, for it even included one avowed bakufu supporter.[75] The provisions for study further illustrated Sakamoto's belief in the necessity to follow various paths to achieve the national purpose. "The way to open the country," he wrote Miyoshi Shinzō, "is for those who fight to fight, those who study to study, and those who trade to trade, each doing the thing he is best fitted to do."[76]

The company began ambitiously. Its official Diary notes that "it was divided into sections, such as civil officials, military officers, engineers, surveyors, navigation officers, medical doctors, and so forth. There were about fifty men altogether, including sailors and boilermen."[77] Actually this small number of men in view of their limited resources could hardly hope to become a full-fledged force of such diversity. Still, their publishing and political activities, as will be seen, were considerable in scope, and they provided an important addition to the maritime plans which were paramount.

Sakamoto's was not the only pardon that the han issued. Fukuoka Kōtei brought with him to Nagasaki a parallel pardon and commission for Nakaoka Shintarō, who was authorized to organize

---

[74] *Sakamoto monjo*, II, 81f.; I, 251-253.
[75] Hirao, *Kaientai*, p. 188. Names of the leaders in *Sakamoto monjo*, I, 254-255.
[76] *Sakamoto monjo*, I, 275.
[77] *Sakamoto monjo*, II, 81.

and lead a military auxiliary force. But since this force, the Riku-entai, was activated later, in the summer of 1867, the Kaientai was prior. While Sakamoto was negotiating with Gotō and reorganizing his company at Nagasaki, Nakaoka was travelling. In Kagoshima, in Dazaifu, and in Kyoto, he was doing his best to speed the process of unification against the Tokugawa rule. He too contacted high Tosa officials, in the person of Itagaki Taisuke and Ogasawara Tadahachi, and he added his part in persuading them of the inevitability of the Tokugawa fall.

The *shishi* who remained in Tosa, still oppressed and resentful of the course which Gotō and his friends had followed in suppressing the loyalist party, were understandably confused and suspicious of the friendships their old friends were forming with their enemies. Even Sakamoto's sister Otome, his most faithful correspondent, took him sharply to task. It seemed to her that he was now working for his own profit and status and neglecting his cause.

In answer, Sakamoto wrote an interesting letter which stated his approach to the reconciliation. There was, first of all, the low quality of personnel he found everywhere. His nephew, an adopted son of his brother's, had just joined him. Sakamoto observed that the man had some ability and some dedication. He would be able to sacrifice his life, or follow Sakamoto around, but he would have no real initiative. Still, he was many cuts above the average Tosa official. In Osaka he had recently met some minor functionaries who put on airs that would better fit a chancellor. Gotō Shōjirō, poor fellow, had told him that *he* had to work with such self-important incompetents all the time. Perhaps Sakamoto meant to say that one could not always have his choice of followers.

Then Sakamoto turned to Otome's charge that he was consorting with the rascals who were running Tosa at the present time. It was all very well for her to talk, he wrote, but she did not realize how hard it was for him to support his followers in Nagasaki without any help from home. Each man cost him about sixty ryō per year, and he had fifty followers. Furthermore, he refuted her charge that he was compromising his name and his plans. His every action and trip were motivated by concern for the nation. As for the Tosa men he was dealing with, Sakamoto listed Gotō Shōjirō, Fukuoka Tōjirō, Sasaki Sanshirō (Takayuki), Mōri Arajirō, and Ishikawa Seinosuke. This last, the name being used by

Nakaoka Shintarō, he followed with "(this is a man just like me)."
Of Gotō, he wrote, "Among these men Gotō is a real comrade,
and in spirit and in purpose there is probably no Tosa man who
is his superior." Furthermore, Nakaoka had talked to Gotō about
possible prosecution of the families of the rōnin who had fled the
fief. Gotō had agreed that men like Nakaoka and Sakamoto had
been striving to serve their fief's interests, so that there would be
no trouble for the family. "If you'll think about things like this,"
Sakamoto pointed out, "I wonder whether it won't put an end to
your talk of rascally officials." And, he went on sharply, it might
be beyond her imagination, but wasn't it just possible that he
would be able to achieve more if he were able to bring the whole
realm of Tosa, with its 240,000 koku, into line than if he just collected five or seven hundred followers?[78]

Sakamoto was thus prepared to stand by his actions and decisions. Nor was he ready to take admonishment from his sister.
Indeed, he devoted the rest of the letter to a very sharp reply to
Otome's suggestion that she too leave the fief and follow him to
join in his cause. He poured ridicule and contempt on the idea.
It was absurd for a woman to leave home and take part in national politics. His wife, fortunately, was a proper and devoted
companion, upset during his absences, and busy with her needle-
work. And in any case, it was more than likely that he would soon
return home for a visit on a steamer with Gotō Shōjirō.

[78] *Sakamoto monjo*, I, 301-309.

VII. THE EIGHT-POINT PROGRAM

*A*FTER Gotō Shōjirō began to give official support to the Kaientai, Sakamoto Ryōma thought his difficulties were at an end. He saw a future full of profit and fame, and he looked forward to joint missions with his new patron. "When I come back to Tosa," he wrote his sister, "the bakufu officials will really have to take notice. I'm doing great things with the rōnin I've collected from many areas. I'm also thinking about making a trip to Kyoto with Gotō Shōjirō one of these days. When we do I'm going to stay at the Teradaya in Fushimi, and can't wait for the commissioners there to find out about it."[1] In fact, however, Sakamoto's first return to Tosa was under circumstances quite different from those he had anticipated. Both that trip and the one to Kyoto with Gotō were overshadowed by new problems with the West. Kaientai men had been implicated in the murder of two British seamen, and national politics had to wait until the Tosa men could free themselves from these new charges. Indeed, the West had now become so much a part of the domestic scene that when, as will be seen, a problem of inter-fief responsibility arose in connection with the Kaientai, Sakamoto and Gotō could suggest looking to Western precedents for a solution.

In this preoccupation with the Western presence and problem Sakamoto and his Tosa sponsors were not alone, for the same was true of the national political scene. International problems, in particular those related to the opening of the port of Hyōgo, helped doom a final effort at collaboration between the great lords and the bakufu after the shogun insisted on immediate Imperial approval for his opening of that Inland Sea port.

Fears of Western intervention heightened the sense of crisis and urgency. Hitotsubashi Keiki, upon his accession to the shogunate, gave first priority to the courteous treatment of the Western envoys, and he and his councillors received new help and encouragement from the French minister Leon Roches. On the other side the Satsuma leaders were closer than before to the British representatives, and Ernest Satow's talks with Saigō Takamori left no doubt of where his sympathies lay.

For a brief moment, however, Keiki seemed likely to give the

[1] *Sakamoto monjo*, I, 256 letter dated May 10.

bakufu the leadership and direction it had needed for so long. His presumed willingness to accept French assistance provoked lively apprehension among the Tokugawa rivals, who began to develop plans for war. In this planning a new figure, Iwakura Tomomi, came into prominence as the leading court exponent for force against the Tokugawa. The story of his growing importance in Kyoto and of his ties with the Satsuma leaders is also the story of the formation of the leadership group of the future Meiji government. The death of the Emperor Kōmei, who was succeeded by a fifteen-year-old boy, provided this group with great opportunities.

Among the Tosa men, a number of fervent loyalists shared the Satsuma and Chōshū plans for war with the bakufu. Itagaki Taisuke and Nakaoka Shintarō, whose outlook and talents were martial, enthusiastically prepared for the battle. Sakamoto Ryōma, however, preferred to work for compromise and peace. He worked out a political program which promised to preserve for the shogun some of his power and prestige through a voluntary return of his political powers, and he persuaded Gotō Shōjirō to sponsor this in Kyoto and in Tosa. It was to present this program that Sakamoto and Gotō made their way to Kyoto in the summer of 1867. These eight points of Sakamoto's foreshadowed in intent and wording the first pronouncements of the Meiji government, and their genesis and development are therefore of great importance.

1. The Advantage of Tosa Support

During the spring months of 1867 Sakamoto was fully occupied with the affairs of his Kaientai in Nagasaki. He was far from the centers of political maneuver in Kyoto, and somewhat out of touch —so much so, in fact, that he could write his friend Miyoshi to report a rumor (brought by Kido) that there was some danger of the bakufu's managing a reconciliation with Satsuma.[2] Gotō Shōjirō was also in Nagasaki for much of the spring, doing his best to build up Tosa strength through the purchase of foreign arms and ships. It is of considerable interest to observe the way in which the two combined their efforts to protect the Tosa cause in dealing with other han, and it is equally significant to note the readiness they showed to look elsewhere for precedents and rules that might apply to the new situations in which the fiefs, now

[2] ibid., p. 247.

practically independent principalities, found themselves in dealing with each other.

The Kaientai was far from being a profitable enterprise, and its activities were of more political than economic importance. The first venture that Sakamoto launched after getting official support illustrates this perfectly.

In the spring of 1867 Sakamoto leased from the Ōsu han in northern Shikoku a small ship of 45 horsepower which displaced 160 tons. On May 22 this ship, the *Iroha Maru*, sailed from Nagasaki under Sakamoto's personal command with a cargo of small arms for the Tosa station in Osaka. Four days later, on the twenty-sixth of May, as the ship was proceeding through the Inland Sea off the coast of northeastern Shikoku in a heavy fog, a steamer belonging to the Kii (Tokugawa house of Owari) han bore down on it. The Kii steamer was much larger, with 150 horsepower and 887 tons. As the two neared each other the *Iroha Maru* turned to port while the Kii steamer turned to starboard. As a result it rammed the Kaientai vessel amidships. The battered old *Iroha* listed quickly, and Sakamoto and his men were transferred to the other ship. While the *Iroha* drifted, Sakamoto tried to get help in transferring his cargo or salvaging his ship. His hosts were of no help, however, and while he debated with them the *Iroha* went to the bottom.

Sakamoto now tried to get a spot settlement to cover part of his damages from the captain of the Kii vessel. His charge was that the mishap had been caused by negligence on the part of the Kii ship—there had been no officer on deck, and the evasive actions that were taken had guaranteed the collision. But the officers of the offending ship were not disposed to delay their business by on-the-spot negotiations, nor were they ready to risk losing the 10,000 ryō Sakamoto asked as part settlement. Instead Sakamoto and his men were put ashore with the promise that negotiations in Nagasaki would follow to establish responsibility and work out a settlement.[3]

Sakamoto made careful preparations for the conference that was to follow. He sent the log book of the *Iroha Maru* on to friends in Nagasaki, warning them not to reveal its contents. Conscious that his company of rōnin would not stand much of a chance against one of the three great Tokugawa houses, he sought outside sup-

[3] Hirao, *Kaientai shimatsu ki*, pp. 193f.

port and sent the documents to Saigō Takamori as well. Most of all, he was anxious for the support of his Tosa sponsors. If the conversations could be run on the basis of han to han negotiations, then the Kii men would have to listen to reason. At the same time, Sakamoto had to guard against direct action by some of his crew, who thought that it might be better to take revenge against the Kii officers with their swords.[4]

The Nagasaki negotiations opened on June 17. They were held under the informal jurisdiction of the Nagasaki Commissioner, a Tokugawa official. As was customary in Tokugawa justice, this man did his best to bring about a settlement out of court.[5] This was not reached until the first of July, after a long squabble. At first Sakamoto and some of his colleagues dealt directly with the Kii officers. Later, toward the end of the negotiations, Gotō Shōjirō, who had left Nagasaki in the spring, returned to assist in the debate. As the talks dragged on, Sakamoto's letters contained dark threats of possible war, and in one he reported that there was so much displeasure in Nagasaki over the procrastination of Kii that even the children were hoping for war.[6] Sakamoto also tried his hand at psychological warfare by spreading rumors that Chōshū and Tosa might ally against Kii if a settlement was not reached. And the Kaientai stalwarts, whose contacts in the licensed quarter of Maruyama were undoubtedly excellent because of their prolonged residence there, arranged to have a menacing jingle strummed in the pleasure houses of the area:

> The indemnity for the ship that sank,
> Will be not in money but in land.[7]

More significant than these threats, however, were the efforts to utilize international precedents to settle the problem. Gotō at one point suggested to the Kii representatives that Japan lacked, as yet, precedents for the settlement of a case of this sort. "But fortunately," he wrote, "the commander of the British flotilla is in port at present, and perhaps we ought to ask him about the pro-

[4] *Kaientai*, pp. 198-199; for Sakamoto's letter forwarding the log book, p. 270. For the full documentation of the case, including the negotiations and counterproposals, *Sakamoto monjo*, I, 257f.

[5] Henderson, Dan F., "Patterns and Persistence of Traditional Procedures in Japanese Law" (unpublished doctoral dissertation, University of California, Berkeley, 1955, 514 pp.)

[6] *Sakamoto monjo*, I, 270, 294.

[7] Hirao, *Kaientai*, p. 200.

cedure customary in cases of this sort elsewhere. This would not mean letting him settle the matter, but just having the benefit of his opinion."[8] Sakamoto, too, wrote the captain of the Kii vessel to suggest that they go to see the British commander together. Sakamoto was, in any case, developing a lively interest in international law, and his correspondence includes notes of gratitude for the gift of books on this subject.[9] In this he was fully representative of his times; late Tokugawa days saw a number of best sellers about Western international law.

The Kii representatives finally decided they had the poorer case, and declined to submit to the indignity of a foreign opinion which was likely to go against them. In order to ease their discomfiture at surrendering, the Satsuma commercial representative Godai Tomoatsu offered his services as intermediary. On the first of July the Kii representatives agreed to pay damages in the amount of 83,000 ryō, in installments. Sakamoto was overjoyed. "They are to pay the cost of the ship," he wrote, "the goods aboard, and even the hand luggage of the sailors and the passengers."[10] His Tosa support was proving its worth. As he wrote a merchant friend in Shimonoseki, "the Tosa men stuck together like one big family and did their very best; I must say that I was impressed, as I hadn't expected so much."[11]

The Kaientai's first venture had ended poorly, but it had served to show the solid nature of the support which Sakamoto could expect from the Tosa han. And Sakamoto had developed a new interest in international law; shortly thereafter his Kaientai added some publishing ventures which included a work on the subject.[12]

There is much evidence that Sakamoto enjoyed and profited from the numerous opportunities available in Nagasaki for the open-minded. "I must say," he wrote his Chōshū friend Miyoshi, "that Nagasaki, with all these people here, is as interesting as something from the period of warring states."[13] The people and the influences were certainly varied. The city was, as has been noted, more free of shogunal policing, less subject to anti-foreign

---

[8] ibid., p. 201.   [9] Sakamoto monjo, I, 287, 292.

[10] ibid., p. 296.

[11] ibid., p. 288. The indemnity payment was later scaled down to 70,000 ryō. Writers have charged that it was paid to Iwasaki, who appropriated it for his own purposes. See, for example, Iwai Ryūtarō, Mitsubishi Konzern tokuhon (Tokyo, 1937), pp. 71-72. But this has been disproved by Hirao, Kaientai, p. 204, and Tanaka, Iwasaki, p. 68.

[12] Hirao, Kaientai, p. 189.   [13] Sakamoto monjo, I, 276.

pressures that prevailed in the newer treaty ports, and less diverted by intensive political scheming and gossiping than were other metropolitan centers. The Dutch-American missionary Guido Verbeck was there with a wide circle of samurai acquaintances. The Saga men Soejima Taneomi and Ōkuma Shigenobu, still out of favor with their domain's high officials, were there to begin the contacts with Gotō that later bore fruit in the movement for representative institutions. And numbers of other, younger students (among them Nakae Chōmin, later a prominent figure in the "left wing" of Tosa liberalism) were there to begin the education that would carry them directly to the mainsprings of Western social and political thought.

Nagasaki was equally a center for ambitious schemes of commercial profit. After Gotō's departure in the spring of 1867 the official Tosa enterprises were entrusted to the hands of Iwasaki Yatarō, the future Mitsubishi founder. For Sakamoto and his Kaientai followers, however, the change from the free-spending Gotō to Iwasaki, who followed a "business first" policy, was unfortunate. For the Tosa domain, it was probably not. Iwasaki was not overly conservative or cautious, for his commercial horizons widened as did Sakamoto's intellectual interests. He simply did not feel that Sakamoto's rōnin were a sound investment of han funds, and he kept the connection to a minimum.

Iwasaki inherited a mountain of debts that Gotō had accumulated for the Kaiseikan. Most of them had been incurred in the purchase of ships and small arms; the largest obligation was to the British firm of Alt and Company.[14] Gotō had complicated things by his addiction to the good life, moreover, and his personal profligacy had helped to cause the burgeoning debt of the han.[15] Partly because of this, the Kaiseikan, which had been designed to make money, had instead been losing money consistently.

Iwasaki thus set to work increasing the income of the trading office. His ideas were for the most part those of his old teacher, Yoshida Tōyō: near Japan there must be uninhabited islands that

[14] Tanaka, p. 66, gives a list of debts which total 431,251 ryō, of which he credits Alt with 180,000 ryō. But since Tanaka's totals, which I have corrected, are in error, the individual totals are likely to be questionable also. Hirao, *Ishin keizai shi*, p. 31, gives 180,000 ryō as the total foreign debt. See also Chap. IX n. 8.

[15] Sasaki, p. 377, blames a special tax of half the retainers' stipends on Gotō's spending. For a strong statement of Gotō's personal tastes and costs, Iwai, *Mitsubishi*, p. 56.

would make possible expansion and profit. A Korean in Nagasaki stirred in Iwasaki the hope of exploiting the possibilities of trade with Korea, which was still in total seclusion. Since the Koreans were still ignorant of world markets, Iwasaki reasoned that it should be possible to buy their goods cheaply and sell them to the foreigners at a large profit. As entrepôt for this trade he selected the small island of Ul-lung-do, off Korea's east coast. A ship was outfitted to make for this island, complete with signboard to establish a claim under international law:

"Iwasaki Yatarō, by order of Tosa han in Great Japan, discovered this island."

Unfortunately for Iwasaki's hopes, the island proved to be inhabited by Koreans, and the expedition returned empty-handed to Japan.[16]

This venture, however insignificant in itself, was typical of the optimism with which the Nagasaki men viewed their country's commercial future. Sakamoto had dreamed of developing trade and contacts with Hokkaido. Godai Tomoatsu of Satsuma also developed plans for Hokkaido, and he too wondered about the possibility of developing a trade with Korea.[17] And out of the Japanese astonishment that the Koreans, when finally approached with offers, refused to jump at the opportunities presented to them, came the hurt pride and suggestions for "forcible modernization" that played so large a role in early Meiji thinking about Korea.

Everywhere, then, there were schemes of expansion and belief in miraculous profits which could be gained by exploiting less developed areas for trade with the foreigners—just as it was assumed that those same foreigners had reaped fabulous profits from their exploitation of Japan. There was a readiness to grasp features of Western precedent and organization wherever they might prove applicable, whether in negotiating disputes or in commercial organization. In the opportunity to grasp some of these things piecemeal for regional or private advantage, Japan's decentralization undoubtedly proved a decided advantage for the development of a consensus favorable to the adoption of Western institutions.

Iwasaki was content to limit his interests to profit and commerce. The same was not true of Gotō Shōjirō or Sakamoto Ryōma, whose interests and connections led them back to the Kyoto scene.

---

[16] Tanaka, *Iwasaki*, p. 85.   [17] Godai, *Godai den*, p. 92.

Before following them there, however, it will be necessary to note the developments that had taken place while they were arguing with the representatives from Kii about the *Iroha Maru*.

2. The Shogun Yoshinobu (Keiki)

The shogun Iemochi had died in Osaka castle on August 29, 1866. The announcement of his death was delayed until September 28, so that it could be preceded by a request to the court in his name on September 6 asking that he be excused from his duties because of illness and that Hitotsubashi Keiki be appointed his deputy with the commission to complete the punishment of Chōshū. The court granted this request the following day.[18]

As soon as Keiki received reports from the front and learned how badly things had gone after word of the shogun's death had reached Kyushu, he decided that the fighting had to be stopped. He utilized a sixteenth century precedent to work out an armistice out of respect to the dead shogun, and he sent Katsu Rintarō, newly restored to favor, to Chōshū to work out the terms. Katsu explained to the Chōshū leaders that the bakufu had decided to reform its procedures by taking counsel with the great lords, and assured them that the ultimate disposition of the Chōshū matter would be handled in this manner. As soon as he succeeded in bringing hostilities to a halt the bakufu vassals began to recall their armies. Peace returned to the front everywhere except in Kyushu, where scattered hostilities with Kokura continued for several months.[19]

The immediate problem that the Tokugawa side faced was the selection of a new shogun. It is indicative of the Tokugawa position at this point that although there was little real enthusiasm for Keiki in some very important bakufu quarters, there was no real alternative to his selection. No one else had the experience and contacts that he had developed in national and international politics, and all were agreed that his ability was outstanding. In spite of this, his succession was not announced by court edict until January 10, 1867.

The delay was caused partly by Keiki's own reluctance, for no one was more aware than he of the difficulties a new shogun would face. But Keiki also faced a great deal of opposition within

---

[18] Shibusawa Eiichi, *Tokugawa Keiki Kō den*, III, 385.
[19] *ibid.*, pp. 401-404.

the Tokugawa system. There were still many fudai daimyō who saw him as the son of Tokugawa Nariaki of Mito, the man whose opposition to the bakufu's course in the 1850's had led to the difficulties at the end of the decade. Keiki's friendship with the great lords of the southwest, and his prolonged absences in Kyoto, had also convinced many Edo traditionalists that he did not have the interests of the Tokugawa house at heart. His uncertain course on the chastisement of Chōshū—first for, then against, and, now that he was in charge, for peace—alarmed them; they were also willing to think that he had frequently utilized the Imperial Court to score points against the bakufu conservatives.

Not even the great lords whose friendship Keiki had formerly enjoyed were as much his admirers as they had formerly been. Matsudaira Shungaku of Echizen, who had worked closely with Keiki to reform the bakufu in 1862, had grown progressively less certain of Keiki's intentions and opinions, and he had not approved of the manner in which Keiki had insisted on Imperial approval for the treaties the previous year. Shimazu Hisamitsu of Satsuma, who had felt the edge of Keiki's anger at that time, had abandoned his earlier enthusiasm for kōbu-gattai, and saw no particular reason to second Keiki's efforts at this late date. Others, like Yamauchi Yōdō of Tosa and Date Munenari of Uwajima, found it easier to absent themselves from Kyoto than to take a stand that might prove to be a losing one.

On the other hand Keiki enjoyed the strong support of a number of bakufu men who had cooperated with him in Kyoto and who admired him greatly. The Councillors Itakura Katsukiyo and Ogasawara Nagamichi worked for his appointment with vigor and tact. A Mito follower, Hara Ichinoshin, gained such distinction in the maneuvering of the next months that some historians have treated the last period of Tokugawa rule as a contest between him and Ōkubo Toshimichi of Satsuma.[20]

The four-month interval between Iemochi's death and Keiki's succession encouraged plotting on the part of those who wanted to change the shogunate or end it altogether. Since the Chōshū leaders were still technically under the Imperial ban, leadership in these efforts fell automatically to Satsuma. Ōkubo Toshimichi and Saigō Takamori feared that the accession of an able shogun might set back their hopes considerably, and they did what they

[20] *ibid.*, pp. 372-375.

could to head off the appointment. Their field of operation was Kyoto, and the ancient capital was once again alive with rumor. Matsudaira Katamori, Lord of Aizu and Protector of Kyoto, retired to his fief in displeasure with Keiki's decision against continuing the Chōshū campaign, and order in Kyoto declined once again. Rōnin and *shishi* began to intimidate the conservative court nobles who had worked for better relations with the shogunate. Scurrilous pamphlets, denunciations on walls, and personal threats began to unnerve the ranking court officials.[21]

It required more than violence to change court policies. Under the Emperor Kōmei the chief court officials had gradually built up a considerable confidence in the shogunate. They were displeased with some of the bakufu's dealings in foreign affairs and aware that many daimyō showed little liking for many of the shogun's policies, but the brief interlude of loyalist extremism in 1862 and 1863 had served to convince the senior and most respected nobles of the madness of violent anti-Tokugawa and anti-foreign measures. Furthermore, the bakufu had been quietly increasing the income and respect paid the chief court officials (*kampaku, sesshō,* and *gisō*) to reward them for their support.[22] Since, in addition, those officials held a good opinion of Keiki personally, it would require effective argument and leadership to build support for the Satsuma cause.

The chief figure in the new loyalist movement at court was not Sanjō Sanetomi, who was still in exile in Dazaifu, but Iwakura Tomomi, who had been sent into retirement outside the city ever since *shishi* had threatened his life. It is not difficult to see why Iwakura's development had made the loyalist enthusiasts suspicious of him. In his first statement of opinion, in 1858, he had advised holding off the West while a fact-finding committee could be sent to Europe and America under Dutch help. He warned the court against seeming to oppose the bakufu, and pointed to the dangers of playing to the ambitions of the tozama daimyō. His competitors at court, a group that worked closely with Nariaki of Mito, won out over him at that time. During the rule of the Regent Ii Naosuke, however, Iwakura again came to the fore with convincing arguments in favor of the marriage of the Princess

---

[21] *ibid.,* p. 410.

[22] *ibid.,* pp. 358-360. The climax of this effort came in the summer of 1867, when the bakufu presented the court with the income of the province of Yamashiro.

Kazu to the young Shogun Iemochi. Then, with the dawn of the loyalist era in 1862, Iwakura had antagonized the *shishi* by hewing to the moderate line represented by Shimazu Hisamitsu of Satsuma. When the Chōshū-backed loyalists temporarily won out in Kyoto, Iwakura was dismissed, and during his retirement of a half-decade the *shishi* did their best to terrorize him.[23]

By 1865 Iwakura was beginning to get in touch quietly with men from Satsuma, and to them and to his friends at court he began sending analyses of what was to be done. He was now very critical of the bakufu for failing to seize its opportunities to bring about kōbu-gattai, and suggested that it was time for the court to rescind the powers it had delegated to the shogun and call an assembly of daimyō. The Tokugawa, he thought, might be limited to their lands on the Edo plain. Iwakura still warned of the dangers of civil war, however, and felt that the victors, whether bakufu or tozama, would continue to dominate the court. Therefore he insisted over and over again on the need for national unity under the Imperial Throne. He also emphasized the need of controlling and utilizing the rōnin and *shishi*, and suggested that they might be assigned to selected fiefs for employment and later utilization.

In 1866 efforts were begun at the court to secure Iwakura's pardon. Since there was a majority of low-ranking nobles who stood to gain by a change in court offices, Iwakura had strong political as well as ideological support. It was not good enough as yet to effect his pardon, but it did suffice to show his standing as a new leader of court loyalism. The number and intensity of his memorials grew; and his political and strategic planning became more detailed and bold. Throughout all this Iwakura's relations with the Satsuma leaders, particularly Ōkubo Toshimichi, grew more confidential and trusting. He had accepted the necessity of working through elements of the military class, and he had chosen Satsuma han.

The death of Iemochi in 1866 seemed to Iwakura, as it did to Ōkubo, a splendid opportunity for loyalist advance. A new peti-

---

[23] The development of Iwakura's thinking can be followed through his writings, reprinted in Tada Kobun, *Iwakura Kō Jikki* (Tokyo, 1927), Vols. I and II, and the Shiseki Kyōkai edition, *Iwakura Tomomi kankei monjo* (Tokyo, 1927), I. Tokutomi, in his convenient *Iwakura Tomomi Kō*, summarizes and characterizes each of the major documents, while extended discussions of Iwakura's political development can also be found in Osatake, III, 736f., and *Ishin shi*, IV, 569-584ff.

tion by loyalist nobles asked for an amnesty for all kuge (including Iwakura), the resignation of pro-Tokugawa nobles in official posts, and an Imperial summons to the daimyō for a conference. This, too, failed, but Iwakura did not give up. He began to agitate for the development of a modern navy, the development of Hokkaido, and the establishment of a national government which would include a new Bureau of Shrines in order to guarantee the Imperial primacy. To further buttress that role, he suggested grants of land to nobles in order to increase their economic and political security and status.

Up to this point Iwakura's petitions, memoranda, and memorials had had little effect in changing court policy. They did, however, cement his relations with the Satsuma leaders and they established him as the leading loyalist among the nobles in or near Kyoto. In this manner the way was prepared for his return to favor with the loyalist *shishi* and rōnin like Sakamoto and Nakaoka Shintarō later in 1867. After the Emperor Kōmei died on February 3, 1867, Iwakura's supporters had new opportunities. The accession of a new Emperor (the later Meiji) brought a general amnesty which included Iwakura, and the substitution of a boy of fifteen for the much-respected Kōmei simplified problems of tactics and strategy.[24]

But when Tokugawa Yoshinobu, the former Hitotsubashi Keiki, became shogun in spite of their best efforts, the plotters were discouraged and not a little disturbed. In Keiki the bakufu had for the first time a shogun who combined youth (Keiki was 30) with experience and ability. Quick steps were taken to discourage further intrigues in Kyoto, and the war against Chōshū was declared ended out of respect to the court upon Kōmei's death.

The judgments of the foreigners who met Keiki confirm the excellent impression he made on most of his contemporaries. He was, wrote Mitford, "a great noble if ever there was one . . . I think he was the handsomest man, according to our ideas, that I

[24] Sasaki, *Sekijitsu dan*, p. 366, tells of rumors current at the time of the Emperor's death to the effect that he had been poisoned by order of the bakufu. It was assumed that Kōmei was opposed to Tokugawa policies, and that his death had helped the shogunal cause. But subsequent study has proved that Kōmei's death was clearly disadvantageous to the shogunate, and it is interesting to note that the post-surrender mood of disillusion in Japan extended to the "official" history of the past; some popular articles "exposed" Iwakura's part in the poisoning of the Emperor Kōmei. See Ninagawa Arata, "Ishin shi no kore dake uso ga aru: Rekishi wa motto hontō no koto o kakanuba," *Bungei Shunjū* (August 1952), pp. 158-166.

saw during all the years that I was in Japan. His features were regular, his eyes brilliantly lighted and keen, his complexion a clear, healthy olive colour. . . ." Satow found him "one of the most aristocratic-looking Japanese I have ever seen, of fair complexion, with a high forehead and well-cut nose—such a gentleman."[25]

Keiki began his administration with a set of reforms designed to modernize the shogunal institutions and make them capable of dealing with the crises that Japan faced. He first expressed these in a very general program of eight points, presented to the rōjū, which announced his intention of working for conventional virtues like fairness, the selection of men of ability, as well as new efforts for economy, trade, and stronger military forces.[26] Some of these were framed as the result of consultations with the French Minister Leon Roches, and all of them were meant to bolster the support and the performance of the bakufu. Three months after taking office, on March 11 and 12, Keiki received Roches in the Osaka castle in order to hear his views. Thereafter he repeatedly sent Itakura to consult him, and Roches' share in administrative planning became a significant element in bakufu policy. Some of Keiki's officials, and especially Oguri Tadamasa, were prepared to follow most of Roches' suggestions.

As a result of these consultations, new bureaus were set up for the navy, army, foreign affairs, finance, and home affairs, each headed by a Councillor (rōjū). Furthermore, the old system of hereditary ranks was revised to make high offices available to talent. A notable example of this was Nagai Naomune, a favorite of Keiki's, who was appointed to the Junior Council (*wakadoshiyori*) although he was not of daimyō rank.[27] Several other appoint-

[25] *Memories by Lord Redesdale*, I, 394, and Satow, *Diplomat in Japan*, p. 200.
[26] *Keiki Kō den*, III, 436.
[27] Otsuka, "Fukkoku kōshi," etc., and Honjo Eijirō, "Leon Roches to bakumatsu no shōsei kaikaku," in *Bakumatsu no shin seisaku* (Tokyo, 1935), pp. 178-214. This can be found translated as "Leon Roches and Administrative Reform in the Closing Years of the Tokugawa Regime" in *Kyoto University Economic Review* (July 1935), pp. 35-53, but the translator failed to convert the dates to the Western calendar, with the result that all dates are in error. Good accounts can also be found in *Keiki Kō den*, III, 436-464, and Ishii, *Meiji Ishin*, etc., pp. 576f. Nagai Naomune (1816-1891) was in the main stream of Western influence and training, like Katsu, and like him he continued to serve the new Meiji government. The son of an Owari daimyō and adopted into a hatamoto family, he studied in Nagasaki under the first Dutch naval detachment, then became naval commissioner, Great Inspector (*Ōmetsuke*), and finally a Kyoto official assigned to the court. Hence his importance in the closing days of Tokugawa rule. Of traditional sources

ments of this sort symbolized Keiki's willingness to break with tradition. Regular taxes were announced to tap the profits of the great rice merchants. Western clothes were substituted for traditional dress at the shogun's court. In the summer of 1867 measures were set in motion to make possible the incorporation of commercial companies as in the West. Foreign affairs, too, received different treatment, as the foreign ministers were received in audience by a shogun who sat on a chair and entertained them. Parkes, for example, received a French-cooked dinner. Keiki's brother, Tokugawa Akitake, was sent to Europe to represent him at the Paris International Exhibition, and measures were undertaken to make explicit the wider opportunities for foreign trade.[28]

In addition to these aspects of institutional and material Westernization, the return of the first group of Tokugawa scholars who had studied in The Netherlands made possible popularization of Western legal and political institutions. Tsuda Mamichi and Nishi Amane were particularly important figures in this work, and Nishi's translations of works on international law were highly prized by Keiki. In early fall of 1867, the two drew up a proposed constitution for Keiki which was designed to modernize the entire administrative structure of the bakufu.[29]

In order to rally support for this modernized bakufu, Keiki planned a council of lords that would consider and support Tokugawa measures. The Nishi-Tsuda constitution included a bicameral council of this sort. By late 1866, fifty-six han were represented in Kyoto. Keiki hoped to use these men, but he was particularly anxious to use the wisdom and services of the four or

---

for these renovation plans, the most important is that of Satō Shinen (1769-1850) who worked out a plan for centralized totalitarian government. For a discussion, with translations, R. Tsunoda, Wm. Theodore de Bary, D. Keene, eds., *Sources of the Japanese Tradition* (New York, 1958), pp. 564-578. For influence in the late Tokugawa days, Ishii Takashi, "Satō Shinen gakusetsu jissen no kito," *Rekishigaku Kenkyū* No. 222 (August 1958), pp. 1-10.

[28] Honjo. Even before this, according to Roches, the rōjū had distributed to all ministers the copy of a circular sent to the feudal lords declaring formally that "la plus entière liberté est garantie a tout sujet japonais que désirera commercer avec les étrangers dan les trois ports ouverts." And Roches could report enthusiastically, "Monsieur le Ministre, chaque jour apporte une nouvelle preuve des bonnes dispositions du Gouvernement Japonais à notre égard." *Affaires Etrangères: Documents Diplomatiques.* (Paris: Imprimérie Imperiale, 1867), pp. 357, 358.

[29] Osatake, III, 955-958. For Nishi's later career, Roger F. Hackett, "Nishi Amane —A Tokugawa-Meiji Bureaucrat," *Journal of Asian Studies*, XVIII, 2 (February, 1959), pp. 213-225.

five great lords from whose deliberations he had profited previously.

In view of the ascendancy of this vigorous shogun so willing to listen to ideas for sweeping change propounded by Roches, and with the emergence of intelligent and able men like Hara, Oguri, and Nagai into top posts, it was unlikely that the shōgun would again run the risk of alienating the powerful foreign nations. The loyalists were temporarily at a disadvantage. Indeed, some of the Mito loyalists even turned to support the bakufu cause now that it was headed by the son of their original leader, Tokugawa Nariaki. Parkes' interpreter, Satow, in a talk with Saigō Takamori, asked, "Then everything is over for the present?" "Well," he quotes Saigō as replying, "we shall be able to find him out in the next three years, I suppose."[30] A few months later, after Keiki had received the foreign ministers and made an excellent impression on them, Satow noted that "on the whole everything seemed to point to the triumph of the Shōgun over his opponents."[31]

Saigō, in a letter he wrote to Ōkubo, expressed some of the same fears. Keiki was dealing from strength and with skill, he was in control at court, the French were helping and advising him, and the outlook for a Tokugawa collapse was not promising.[32] From Iwakura, from Kido, and from Sakamoto himself, came grudging praise for Keiki and admiration for what he was doing.[33]

In fact, however, the situation was not as black as the *shishi* thought. Although Keiki was a man of great ability and experience, he had also shown in earlier meetings with the daimyō a reluctance to bend to suggestions that were not welcome to him. In the talks with the great lords that lay ahead he was to show the capacity of uniting them in irritation against his insistence on having his own way. Furthermore, the distrust that many of the Edo officials still held for him meant that he was never fully a free agent. Meanwhile at court the boy emperor, Mutsuhito, was gradually coming under the influence of Nakayama Tadayasu, an anti-foreign loyalist who had close ties, through the Konoe family, with Iwakura Tomomi and Satsuma. And just ahead lay the last great crisis in foreign affairs of Tokugawa years, the issue

---

[30] *Diplomat in Japan*, p. 182.   [31] *ibid.*, p. 198.
[32] *Dai Saigō Zenshū*, I, 813-815.
[33] *Keiki Kō den*, III, 465-466. For more estimates by the *shishi*, Osatake, III, 761-763.

of the opening of Hyōgo. "I see now," Satow remarked to Saigō, "why you attach so much importance to Hiōgo. It is your last card."[34]

3. The Kyoto Conference

In the summer of 1867 the new shogun met with the lords of Satsuma, Tosa, Uwajima, and Echizen to discuss the measures that should be taken with respect to Hyōgo and Chōshū. The conference was designed as a means of gathering support for the problems that faced Keiki's new administration. Instead of succeeding in these aims, however, it illustrated, through the manner of its convocation and the tenor of its discussions, that henceforth gatherings of this sort would serve chiefly to dramatize the disagreements current about the nature of sovereignty and leadership in Japan. The lords who assembled with Keiki had been the first to espouse conciliar organization under the slogan kōbu-gattai a half decade earlier, when they would have been its chief beneficiaries. But in 1867 Shimazu Hisamitsu, Yamauchi Yōdō, Matsudaira Shungaku, and Date Munenari were no longer as concerned with the idea of reforming the shogunate and helping it to govern more effectively; their concern was now with authority and not with assistance, and they were suspicious of any conference that might be dominated by the able shogun and used to bolster the power of his house instead of contributing to a truly national unity under the throne.

It had long been a feature of reformist thought that there should be a council of the principal lords to assist the shogun in making major decisions. Iwakura Tomomi had revived the sixteenth century precedent of Hideyoshi with a suggestion that five of the great barons might be constituted a group of Great Elders, or *Tairō*, and Saigō Takamori and others had suggested similar solutions.[35] It was assumed that such a council, headed by the shogun, would be best fitted to assure the Emperor that proposals he received represented a collective will and judgment. Keiki himself was fully conscious of the benefits he could derive from such a gathering. His original appointment to shogunal office in 1862 had come as a result of the urgings of the great barons, particularly Shimazu Hisamitsu, and Keiki had set as one of the conditions for his acceptance of the shogunal office that he should have the sup-

[34] *Diplomat in Japan*, p. 184.   [35] *Keiki Kō den*, ɪɪɪ, 387-388.

port of a council. As soon as he tried to arrange such a meeting, however, he found that it was as likely to limit as it was to strengthen his authority.

Late in 1866, after Keiki had become head of the Tokugawa house but before he was named shogun, he asked for a conference of barons to decide what was to be done about Chōshū. The court agreed to the idea, but the nobles in sympathy with Iwakura and his group felt that the conference should be called by the court rather than by the bakufu. Keiki and his councillors, on the other hand, wanted to summon the lords themselves, lest the Tokugawa power seem to be at an end. After some dispute a compromise was reached whereby the court issued a summons, worded in such a way as to make it clear that it came in response to a bakufu request, to twenty-four of the leading barons. But the lords invited to attend were of no mind to be committed to decisions that might prove unpopular or impolitic. Of the twenty-four, only five, not one of them a major figure, came to Kyoto, where they were convened, praised, and dismissed by the Emperor Kōmei. Some of those who had been invited were already in Kyoto at the time of the summons, only to become unaccountably ill and retire in haste to their fiefs for medical counsel. Thus it was clear that no conference arranged in response to bakufu requests was going to be successful.[36]

The Chōshū settlement could wait, but the opening of Hyōgo could not. When Keiki received the foreign ministers in audience in Osaka in March and April of 1867, they had made this very clear to him. Leon Roches, whom he received first, warned him of the need to open the port of Hyōgo and the city of Osaka by January 1 as stipulated in the treaties. Unless this was done, he pointed out, the foreign powers, particularly the English, would take steps to encourage the formation of a government more responsible to their desires. But if, Roches went on, Keiki guarded himself against foreign opposition in this manner, he would be able to go on with French assistance to deal with his troublesome vassals of the southwest. He should separate the court from politics and restrain the tozama lords, and he should do away with many of the petty fudai fiefs, trim the military rolls of useless samurai and substitute modern-trained and armed effectives, and speed the true unification of his country under a resurgent ba-

---

[36] *Ishin shi*, IV, 530-536; *Keiki Kō den*, III, 404f.

kufu.[37] Harry Parkes, in his interview, also supported Roches' warning by stressing the importance of Hyōgo for the British.

Keiki was responsive to these warnings. In his talks with the ministers he bore himself well, and he impressed them so favorably that the alarmed Satsuma leaders were afraid their British friends might desert them for the new shogun. Saigō made a hurried visit to Ernest Satow to make sure that no commitments of support had been exchanged. Satow reassured him, and his memoirs make clear the kind of understanding he had with the Satsuma man. "I remember receiving a visit from Saigō and others of that party," he writes, "who were not at all pleased at the rapprochement between us and the Shōgun. I hinted to Saigō that the chance of a revolution was not to be lost. If Hiōgo was once opened, then good-bye to chances of the daimiōs."[38]

Keiki decided that Hyōgo would have to come first, and on March 24 he asked for the opinions of nine of the chief han on the subject, asking that they send in their ideas within the month and meet in Kyoto with him at the end of that period.[39] But when Parkes pressed him again on the matter Keiki decided that he could not even afford to wait that long. On April 9 he submitted a request for Imperial approval of the opening of Hyōgo.[40] But the Imperial court was not prepared to give in so quickly. On April 23 it replied that it was unable to reconcile Keiki's desires with the wishes of the deceased Emperor Kōmei, and urged the shogun to seek the wishes of the feudal lords. When Keiki submitted a second request on April 26 he met with no better response.[41]

The court's refusal to cooperate with Keiki on the opening of Hyōgo had been arranged by Iwakura Tomomi and the Satsuma leaders, especially Ōkubo Toshimichi. Together they advised their friends in Kyoto that the shogun ought to be permitted to do noth-

---

[37] *Keiki Kō den*, III, 486, 436; *Ishin shi*, IV, 627; Ishii, *Meiji Ishin*, etc., pp. 576f.

[38] *Diplomat in Japan*, p. 200.

[39] *Ishin shi*, IV, 629.

[40] Keiki's request was noteworthy for the way it stressed the importance of bringing Japanese practices into line with those accepted in the West. He spoke of such changes as coming within "the natural order of things," and stressed the necessity of wiping out "the evil practices of the past." "Before many years are out," he wrote, "our military prestige will have expanded and increased. . . ." Thus the shogun, in his general orientation was expressing many of the values, and some of the language, of the later Meiji government. Translated in Beasley, *Select Documents on Japanese Foreign Policy*, pp. 308-309.

[41] Beasley, pp. 310-312, translates the texts.

ing until he had had the advantage of the advice of the great barons. By this means the plotters forced the shogun to wait for such a conference. Meanwhile they had long been at work to make such a conference a certainty by urging the reluctant participants to come. Once they had convened, the same men masterminded their moves.

Ōkubo Toshimichi and Saigō Takamori of Satsuma saw in a meeting of the leaders of the old kōbu-gattai group a means of obstructing Keiki's program. They were optimistic that their lord, Shimazu Hisamitsu, would be able to dominate such a gathering, and they were prepared with advice and counsel for him once the meetings began.

All the participants in the meeting had to be talked into coming to Kyoto, for none would come unless he had some assurance that he would find his peers there. As a result the Satsuma leaders had to divide their efforts between Shimazu Hisamitsu, Yamauchi Yōdō of Tosa, Date Munenari of Uwajima, and Matsudaira Shungaku of Echizen. Of these Yōdō, who was still not decided as to his future course and much troubled by his sense of obligation to the Tokugawa house, was expected to be the most difficult to persuade.

The Tosa rōnin helped to plan this strategy, and they benefited from it personally. Nakaoka Shintarō went to Kagoshima early in 1867 to persuade Saigō that he ought to travel to Kōchi to see Yōdō, and he undoubtedly added the suggestion that Saigō put in a good word for Nakaoka and Sakamoto. Saigō arrived in Tosa on March 23 as an emissary from Shimazu Hisamitsu, and during his visit he helped influence Yōdō to agree to a han pardon for the two men as well as official support for the Kaientai and Rikuentai. Sakamoto's letters from Nagasaki show that he was fully aware of the contribution Saigō had made to his cause.[42]

Saigō's principal purpose in coming to Tosa was to capitalize on the political opportunities the Hyōgo issue presented. In talking with Yamauchi Yōdō he stressed the need for a general revision of the government in order to ease the mind of the new and youthful Emperor Mutsuhito, and he persuaded Yōdō that Hyōgo provided the best opportunity to bring this about. Yōdō agreed

---

[42] *Sakamoto monjo*, I, 251, 270. It was immediately after this trip of Saigō's that Fukuoka Kōtei was sent to Nagasaki with the official pardon and commission as head of the Kaientai for Sakamoto.

to come to Kyoto, but he reminded Saigō that the Yamauchi bore the Tokugawa a special obligation because of past favors. In times of national emergency, however, the national interest would have to outweigh personal considerations, and therefore he agreed to come. Besides his conferences with Yōdō, Saigō also talked to a number of Tosa officials. Sasaki Takayuki was ill and unable to meet the Satsuma emissary, but he heard about the tenor of the talks from his colleagues. He recorded in his memoirs his sense of shock on hearing that Saigō was frankly reconciled to the inevitability of opening the port of Hyōgo and that he was using it chiefly as a device to embarrass the bakufu. Sasaki was unable to reconcile such devious tactics with his sense of honor, and he composed a lengthy memorial arguing against the opening of Hyōgo at all. Although the day of simple solutions and straightforward tactics was past, Sasaki's misgivings helped to account for some of the hesitation and distrust of Satsuma which the Tosa leaders showed in the months that followed.[43]

From Kōchi, Saigō went to Uwajima, where he talked to Date Munenari. Here, once again, he had to overcome his host's reluctance to mingle in national politics. Upon his return to Kagoshima, Saigō told Nakaoka how he had fared, and Nakaoka's diary provides a fascinating record of the way this low-ranking Satsuma emissary dealt with the Lord of Uwajima. Saigō took a considerably stronger line than he had with Yōdō, and in the end Date too yielded to his urgings to come to Kyoto.[44] After he returned to Kagoshima, Saigō had Nakaoka Shintarō visit Ōmura and Hirado han in Kyoto to try to build up more support there. But this came to nothing. When the conference convened, its participants were Hisamitsu, Yōdō, and Munenari, all recruited by Saigō, and Matsudaira Shungaku, who had been persuaded to come by the Satsuma leader Komatsu Tatewaki. The order of their arrival in Kyoto may serve to illustrate the degree of eagerness they had for their task. Hisamitsu of Satsuma came first on May 15, with a force of

---

[43] Sasaki, p. 383. The Chōshū loyalist Shinagawa Yajirō, who was also still not reconciled to the opening of the country, was similarly offended by Saigō's willingness to consider the opening of Hyōgo.

[44] Date tried to deflect Saigō from his purpose, but found him equal to the test. As Nakaoka recorded it, "The former lord [Date] said, 'Kichinosuke, is there a woman you love in Kyoto?' Saigō: 'There is.' The Lord: 'What's her name?' Saigō: 'Even if I told your lordship, it wouldn't do you a bit of good. So let's talk about something that will do you good.'" Ozaki, *Nakaoka*, p. 356; also in *Dai Saigō Zenshū*, I, 819.

seven hundred soldiers; Date Munenari came three days later, Matsudaira Shungaku came on the nineteenth, while Yōdō was last to arrive (June 13) and also the first to leave.

As Saigō and Ōkubo had planned, Shimazu Hisamitsu dominated the conference. Ōkubo wrote him a number of summaries of the situation in which he stressed the importance of getting a full pardon for the Chōshū daimyō together with a cancellation of all the penalties planned. His principal point, however, was that Keiki was ignoring the wishes of the late Emperor in regard to the opening of Hyōgo. As punishment, therefore, his territories should be reduced, and Keiki himself "should be summoned to join the ranks of the feudal lords as one of themselves." Thus Ōkubo now envisaged a council in which Keiki would sit with his equals. This was far from what Keiki had in mind for such a council. And although it would prove acceptable to Keiki a few months later, by then Ōkubo would no longer rest content with even this considerable achievement.[45] Saigō also prepared a number of papers for Hisamitsu. In these he emphasized the importance of combining full pardons for the exiled nobles in Dazaifu with the problems of Chōshū and Hyōgo. Saigō thought it particularly desirable to employ Sanjō Sanetomi in the court again. It was true, he granted, that the Emperor Kōmei had not approved of him. But there were extenuating circumstances, and his loyalty was undoubted.[46] Thus the loyalists, although quite willing to charge Keiki with betraying the trust of the departed Kōmei, were not afraid to go against his wishes themselves.

The lords began their visit to Kyoto by calling on the kampaku Nijō. With Hisamitsu as spokesman, they suggested that the court posts for liaison with the bakufu be opened to "men of talent." By this Hisamitsu meant to urge the employment of Ōhara Shigetomi, whom he had accompanied to Edo in 1862. He failed in this, for the court officials were hampered by the wishes of the deceased Emperor Kōmei. Instead, the lords were praised for their interest and urged to turn their efforts to external crises and political problems.

Keiki was anxious to have their support on the matter of Hyōgo,

---

[45] Text in Beasley, *Documents*, p. 313. This seems to offset a second memorial by Ōkubo and Saigō to Hisamitsu pointing out that certain steps must be taken "for the sake of the bakufu," which Osatake, III, 834, quotes to show how gradually and slowly the thoroughgoing anti-bakufu position developed.

[46] *Saigō Zenshū*, I, 220-240.

and he now invited them to his castle for a conference. But he soon discovered that they had not gathered to do him honor, as they declined to attend. A few days later, after Shungaku and Munenari had gone to Keiki's Nijō castle on their own initiative, all four of the lords deigned to make their appearance there.

The discussions centered around the order in which problems should be dealt with. Keiki wanted an immediate decision on the opening of Hyōgo, while Hisamitsu, anxious to reveal Keiki's internal weaknesses before the Hyōgo settlement could strengthen him with the foreigners, pressed for a prior settlement of the Chōshū matter. After sharp disagreements a compromise was suggested by Shungaku whereby the two matters should be settled simultaneously. Hisamitsu accepted this for a time, and the solution was also approved by Keiki. Afterwards, however, Ōkubo Toshimichi persuaded his lord to return to his original position, and Ōkubo and Komatsu went to remonstrate with Shungaku and Munenari as well. Yōdō, who was absent from all but the early meetings because of a severe mouth infection, favored Shungaku's moderate course of compromise. At this juncture Keiki held that the compromise once acceptable to all was still binding, and he reported to the court that agreement had been reached, only to be contradicted by Matsudaira Shungaku. This presented the court with precisely what it had sought to avoid, the necessity to decide between sharply antagonistic protagonists. After some vacillation, the kampaku Nijō acceded to Keiki's desires; the Imperial edict calling for the opening of Hyōgo was issued on June 26.

For Keiki it was an expensive victory. Two days later the four lords submitted a memorial to the court that made it clear that their views had been misrepresented by Keiki, and that they felt a settlement about Chōshū was prerequisite for national stability. The ill feeling generated during the acrimonious debates, and the renewed evidence of the shogunate's ability and readiness to force its will on a reluctant court, provided new fuel for the loyalist conspirators. By the end of June, Keiki's position was no longer favorable as it had at first seemed. Instead, the Kyoto talks had solidified the anti-Tokugawa front and given it new arguments, while the opening of Hyōgo produced more anti-foreign outrages. On September 11, Keiki's most trusted councillor and emissary, Hara Ichinoshin, was cut down by anti-foreign fanatics, fellow

Mito retainers, who regarded the Hyōgo opening as primarily his work.[47]

Yamauchi Yōdō was the first of the lords to return to his fief. He departed for Tosa on June 29 and the other three left early in September. Yōdō had taken a relatively minor part in the talks, partly because he was severely ill and in constant pain. He was also not in sympathy with the domineering tactics of the Satsuma men. During conferences among the lords at the Tosa residence, Satsuma troops had surrounded the estate and guarded all the exits. Hisamitsu's change of heart on the compromise solution also seemed to Yōdō evidence of bad faith, and Yōdō went so far as to order Ōkubo Toshimichi followed for a time in order to find out what was going on. Yōdō also insulted Shimazu Hisamitsu. At one gathering in the shogun's Nijō castle, he affronted Hisamitsu by playfully pulling his hair, and he quietly suggested to Matsudaira Shungaku that he communicate secretly with Keiki by sending his emissary Nakane to the bakufu councillor Itakura. There was thus a heavy burden of suspicion and resentment which combined with Yōdō's poor health to keep him away from Kyoto throughout the rest of the summer and early fall.

Since Yōdō was suspicious of Satsuma motives and unenthusiastic about the plans to embarrass Keiki, he was more than ready to consider alternative proposals that might be proposed to end the political impasse. He wanted to do nothing that might encourage the counsels for war he thought he saw developing among the loyalist leaders. He kept a wary eye on his loyalist retainers. One, Ogasawara Tadahachi, who had been won over by Nakaoka's counsel of attack against the Tokugawa, he dismissed from his post.[48] Itagaki Taisuke too was anxious to join in plans for war against the Tokugawa, and so Yōdō kept him under the special control which he reserved for retainers whose spirit he admired and whose judgment he doubted. He wanted no part of a war from which Satsuma and Chōshū would be the chief gainers, and he was still troubled by a sense of feudal obligation to the bakufu. Therefore he was sure to pay careful attention to the plans for a middle path which were worked out by Sakamoto Ryōma and brought to his attention by Gotō Shōjiro.

[47] *Ishin shi*, IV, 658.

[48] Ogasawara, as has been noted, later fought in the anti-Tokugawa army under Itagaki's command and met his death at the siege of Wakamatsu castle, the Aizu stronghold.

4. Program for a New Government

During these negotiations in Kyoto Sakamoto Ryōma was busy with his own problems in Nagasaki. Gotō Shōjirō had come to help him in the closing stages of the argument with the representatives from Kii, and the settlement for damages for the *Iroha Maru* was reached on July 1. By then Yōdō had just left Kyoto for Tosa again. Nakaoka Shintarō, who was in Kyoto during the conferences, remained there. Two weeks later, on July 14, Sakamoto and Gotō came into Kyoto with a new plan for reorganizing Japan's political system.

Sakamoto's ideas had formed during his years of service with Katsu Rintarō. He knew that a number of bakufu officials had suggested that the shogun should resign his office and his title. He had also heard suggestions about a conciliar form of government in which the shogun would remain one of the principal figures by virtue of the enormous territories which he controlled. The bakufu official Ōkubo Ichiō had thought that a council of lords might meet every five years, while lesser nobles and local councils could meet in the provinces. Similar ideas were current in many parts of Japan. Matsudaira Shungaku was familiar with them, probably through his adviser Yokoi Shōnan. In 1866 Sakamoto had talked to an Echizen man to see whether Matsudaira Shungaku could be persuaded to take the initiative in a movement for changes of this sort; a Tokugawa collateral, he thought, could put forth such ideas with the best chance of success. Shungaku had not chosen to follow this course, but Sakamoto's suggestion indicates that his scheme of the following year did not by any means represent a radical change in his thinking.[49]

Sakamoto's subsequent residence in Nagasaki exposed him to many more ideas of this sort. Students from all parts of western Japan were there to familiarize themselves with Western learning, and no feature of Western politics made a deeper impression on Japanese (and Chinese) than did constitutions. A council of lords, sharing power with the faltering bakufu, seemed a logical version of such institutions for Japan. Among Sakamoto's collaborators in Nagasaki was a man trained in Western medicine named Nagaoka Kenkichi. According to Sasaki Takayuki, it was this Nagaoka (to

---

[49] A statement by the Echizen man Sakamoto approached is given in *Sakamoto monjo*, I, 223-224.

whom he refers as Imai, another of his names) who first penned the plan for a new government which came to be known as Sakamoto's. Nagaoka was serving as Sakamoto's Kaientai secretary in 1867, and the relationship between them was undoubtedly very close. Regardless of who it was that worded the Eight-Point Plan, however, there can be no doubt that it represented ideas toward which Sakamoto had been reaching for several years.[50]

Sakamoto's scheme was based upon the assumption that a peaceful transition to group leadership was possible. It was his thought that the shogun might be persuaded to resign his powers if it was clear that by so doing he would clear the way for a new government which would be more than the exclusive preserve of a few han hiding behind the court. Sakamoto's draft used all the notes of modernity that were so common in the next two decades. Absurd and decrepit institutions would disappear, the government and commercial systems would be rationalized, and a national defence force would be established. This was an integrated program that might be expected to appeal to all, shogun or daimyō, who were afraid they might be left out in a new order.

After the solution of the *Iroha* damage suit, Sakamoto and Gotō sailed to Kyoto together. Nagaoka, the secretary, was a member of the party. The travellers knew that weighty movements were on foot in the capital, and they were anxious to be part of them. It was in this setting, on shipboard, that Sakamoto showed Gotō his Eight-Point Plan for a new government. It was a plan that might avert the necessity for force in overthrowing the shogunate.

1. Political power of the entire country should be returned to the Imperial Court, and all decrees should come from the Court.

2. Two legislative bodies, an Upper and a Lower house, should be established, and all government measures should be decided on the basis of general opinion.

3. Men of ability among the lords, nobles, and people at large should be employed as councillors, and traditional offices of the past which have lost their purpose should be abolished.

[50] Sasaki, p. 419. For Imai [Nagaoka], Teraishi, *Tosa ijin den*, ɪ (Osaka, 1914), 222-223.

4. Foreign affairs should be carried on according to appropriate regulations worked out on the basis of general opinion.

5. The legislation and regulations of earlier times should be set aside and a new and adequate code should be selected.

6. The navy should be enlarged.

7. An Imperial Guard should be set up to defend the capital.

8. The value of goods and silver should be brought into line with that of foreign lands.

> In view of the state of the nation in these days, it is vitally important to announce these eight points to the countries of the world. If these policies are carried out the fortunes of the Imperial Country will change for the better, national strength will increase, and it will not be difficult to achieve equality with other countries. It is our prayer that we may base ourselves on the path of enlightenment and virtue and that the land may be renewed with great resolution.[51]

Almost the entire Restoration program is contained within this program of Sakamoto's. Its language would be echoed in the Charter Oath of 1868, and its promise would be the basis for the complaints of Itagaki and Gotō that inaugurated the movement for representative institutions in 1874. These ideas were everywhere in the closing days of Tokugawa Japan, but it was on shipboard with Sakamoto and Gotō that they received the formulation they were to keep. For Gotō was delighted with this program. He thought that it might be the solution to his problems of reconciling Yōdō to the overthrow of the Tokugawa, and he liked its safeguards against a new Satsuma-Chōshū shogunate.

Sakamoto and Gotō entered Kyoto on July 14.[52] Yamauchi Yōdō had already returned to Tosa, and the talks with the daimyō were at an end. But the other lords were still in Kyoto, and it was particularly with the retainers of Shimazu Hisamitsu that Gotō and

---

[51] *Sakamoto monjo*, I, 297-298. The concluding summary statement is varied somewhat in some versions to read that "x, head of the daimyō conference, should submit this to the throne and then announce it to the whole nation. Whoever challenges the decision after it has been approved by the majority should be punished regardless of rank or position." Some have it that Sakamoto meant Yōdō by "x." See, for this version, Chikami, *Sakamoto*, p. 165.

[52] As dated by Nakaoka's diary. Secondary sources provide a generous selection of dates.

Sakamoto wanted to talk. They knew that plans for a violent over-throw of the bakufu were beginning to form. The shogunate's efforts to find a face-saving formula for the settlement of the Chō-shū affair were revealing its weakness;[53] although the bakufu had ignored the advice of the great lords, it was able to implement no alternative plan of its own.

At the time Sakamoto and Gotō reached Kyoto, plans for a mil-itary effort against the Tokugawa were beginning to take shape. The chief contributors and gainers from such a move would have been Chōshū and Satsuma, the two largest military powers. The morning of July 14 Shimazu Hisamitsu received the Chōshū men Yamagata Aritomo and Shinagawa Yajirō in his Kyoto headquar-ters. Hisamitsu told them that he had concluded that it would require force to overthrow the bakufu, and said that he was send-ing Saigō Takamori to Chōshū soon in an effort to tighten the al-liance between the two han. As a sign of special favor, he pre-sented Yamagata with a six-shooter pistol—more symbolic than he knew of the passing of military strength from the feudal barons to the builder of the modern Japanese army. Yamagata and Shina-gawa hurried back to Chōshū to bring their news, and the way was prepared for much closer relationships between Satsuma and Chōshū.[54]

Enthusiasm for an anti-Tokugawa war was by no means lim-ited to men of Satsuma and Chōshū. Sakamoto found his friend Nakaoka Shintarō, who was now in the service of Sanjō Sanetomi, in Kyoto. From him he heard how Nakaoka had refreshed his ties with Itagaki Taisuke during Yōdō's presence for the conferences with the Shogun Keiki. Shortly before Itagaki had returned to Kōchi with his lord, Nakaoka had arranged a meeting between him and Saigō Takamori. Saigō and Itagaki had hit it off immedi-ately. When Saigō asked Itagaki about opinion in Tosa, Itagaki had answered that he was prepared to lead his troops against the Tokugawa within the month, whether the Tosa official position changed or not. Nakaoka, afraid this might have been too direct

---

[53] The bakufu asked Hiroshima han to hint to Chōshū that a request for a pardon would be granted graciously, but Hiroshima refused even to relay the suggestion.

[54] *Dai Saigō Zenshū*, i, 860. An account in English, although not free of errors in dating, can be found in Saneatsu Mushakoji, *Great Saigō*, adapted by Moriaki Sakamoto (Tokyo, 1942), pp. 242-245. See also Tokutomi, *Kōshaku Yamagata Aritomo den* (Tokyo, 1933), i, 774f.

for a first statement, had apologized to Saigō for his friend's rashness, but Saigō had slapped his knee and exulted in the presence of a man who knew his mind. Itagaki and Nakaoka, it was clear, were in full agreement with their Satsuma friends on the necessity to use force against the Tokugawa.[55] Nakaoka also had with him in Kyoto a number of enthusiasts of Takechi's old Loyalist Party who were prepared to follow his lead.[56]

Still, when Nakaoka heard about Sakamoto's plan, he saw some merit in it. There could be no objection to a shogunal resignation. And while Nakaoka was personally of the opinion that, as he put it, the Tokugawa, who had won the country on horseback, would have to be defeated on horseback,[57] he saw the possibility that a reasonable solution like Sakamoto's, if it should be rejected by the bakufu, might provide the bridge over which a reluctant Tosa administration would agree to cross to join the ranks of fiefs prepared to use military force. The plan could serve a useful purpose so long as it was clearly understood that a refusal to surrender Tokugawa powers would lead to the use of force.

Sakamoto and Gotō were able to convince the Tosa representatives in Kyoto that it was necessary for their fief to reenter national politics. Dramatic events were in the offing, and Tosa could not afford to be out of them. In particular, as Sakamoto warned, it was essential to convince the Satsuma leaders that Tosa's long period of vacillation and hesitation was at an end. It had to be made clear that once the curtain went up, as he put it, the play would follow.[58] With arguments of this sort the two were able to persuade the Tosa Kyoto representatives that their han should take the lead in trying to persuade the shogun to surrender his powers. In no other way could Tosa protect its interest and reassure its powerful neighbors. With the arrival in Kyoto of Sasaki Takayuki, who came as Great Inspector (*Ōmetsuke*), Sakamoto and Gotō received important help for their campaign of persuasion.

---

[55] Hirao, *Rikuentai*, p. 222.

[56] *Ishin Tosa kinnō shi*, p. 1083.

[57] Iwakura put it equally colorfully by suggesting that they force Keiki to be the Ishida Mitsunari of the piece. Tokugawa Ieyasu had maneuvered Ishida into being the pawn for his power plans in 1600.

[58] From this point on the *shishi* usually refer to the political scene in terms of the theater, and it is the management of the piece (*shibai*) of which they write. Sasaki, *Sekijitsu dan*, p. 420, and Kido to Sakamoto, *Sakamoto monjo*, I, 362-364, are two examples.

Once the Tosa leaders were won over, an attempt was made to get Satsuma backing for the plan as well. Sakamoto and Nakaoka helped make the arrangements with their powerful friends, and on July 22 a Satsuma-Tosa meeting took place in a Kyoto restaurant. Satsuma was represented by Komatsu Tatewaki, Ōkubo Toshimichi, and Saigō Takamori, and Tosa by Gotō Shōjirō, Fukuoka Kōtei, Teramura Sazen, and Manabe Eisaburō.[59] Sakamoto Ryōma and Nakaoka Shintarō were also present.

Out of this meeting came an agreement for cooperation between Satsuma and Tosa which was based principally on Sakamoto's Eight-Point Plan. The draft upon which agreement was reached was provided by Gotō Shōjirō. The preamble set forth general principles:

1. It is essential first of all that we combine to establish the national polity, so that it may be made clear to all generations and all nations without shame.

2. Imperial rule must be reestablished without question, and we must join together in setting up a new political order after considering the state of affairs throughout the world.

3. There cannot be two rulers in a land or two heads in one family, and the government and regulations must return to the single control of the ruler.

4. It is a violation of the natural order that political matters should be entrusted to the office of shogun. Instead they should be returned to the various lords, who would then assist the ruler.

"The above are pressing duties that face us today, and they are the reasonable patterns for heaven and earth. Let us combine our hearts and arms and consider success, failure, or death of no consequence."

The main body of the document spelled this out in greater detail:

"Our first great duty is to seek out the national polity and struc-

[59] Hirao, *Kaientai*, p. 211. *Ishin Tosa kinnō tō*, p. 1090, however, has Sasaki among those present. Sasaki's memoirs are unclear, and he writes only of the follow-up gathering, at which he was clearly present.

ture of the Imperial Country of old so that we may face all nations without shame. For that purpose we must restore Imperial rule and study to establish an order of government within the land of such a nature that future generations will not regret our actions. There can not be two rulers in a land, or two heads in a house, and it is most reasonable to return administration and justice to one ruler. Although our Imperial family descends without a break from remote antiquity, the prefecture and district system of former days was changed to the feudal order of today and all rule ended in the hands of the bakufu, with the result that some do not even realize that there is an Emperor. When one thinks about this with the world in mind, is there anywhere else that there is a national polity like this? It is evident that we must reform our regulations and return political power to the court, form a council of feudal lords, and conduct affairs in line with the desires of the people as expressed in this manner; only then can we face all nations without shame and establish our national polity. But if in the settlement of two or three matters a noisy dispute develops and there is great confusion as to ends and means between the court, the bakufu, and the feudal lords, we will be far from a reasonable solution. On the contrary, the Imperial Country will lose its proper basis, and our intentions will be frustrated. Henceforth let us bend every effort to acquaint all nations with our fairness and impartiality, and with this principle let us establish our true basis. This is not a time to think only about the ambitions of the great lords; rather, let us strive together, so long as life is left to us. Let us at this time plan the rise of our Imperial Country, and abandoning all crafty selfishness, let us elevate the wisdom of the ruler and loyalty of subjects, seeking out the great peace and carrying out for all the people of the realm a governance of generosity, humaneness, wisdom, and compassion."

"This," the agreement continued, "we will establish along these principles:

1. Full authority for determining the government of the country is vested in the Court. All regulations and organizations of our Imperial Country will be determined by a Council to be established in Kyoto.

2. The costs of this Council will be borne by the various han.

3. The Council will have an upper and a lower house. For the upper house, nobles, and for the lower, retainers and even commoners will be selected from among those who are just and pure-hearted. Furthermore, the feudal lords will serve in the upper house by virtue of their positions.

4. There is no reason to have the office of shogun grasp the management of all national affairs. It is only natural to abolish that office at this time and have the holder return to the ranks of the feudal lords; political power must be returned to the Imperial Court.

5. All the foreign treaties covering the ports that have been opened should be taken up at Hyōgo with the ministers and stewards of the Imperial Court. New treaties should be drawn up on the basis of reason and manifest justice, and then trade should be carried on in good faith.

6. The precedents and regulations of the Imperial Court have been ordained since ancient times, but in the circumstances of the present some are no longer appropriate. Those that are corrupted should be reformed. We should establish national principles for which we will not need to feel shame in the light of customs elsewhere in the world.

7. The samurai and Lord Stewards who will be concerned with the renaissance of our Imperial Country should conduct their deliberations in such a way that they put aside personal desire and base their actions on fairness and impartiality; they should not devise clever schemes but esteem sincerity; they should have no thought for what was wrong or right in the past, but put their major emphasis on setting men's hearts at rest.

"This agreement covers the most urgent affairs which confront us today, and nothing compares with them in importance. Now that this compact has been arranged let us have no regard for success or failure, but press forward with one mind to the fulfillment of our goal."[60]

In this skillfully arranged document it is apparent that the Tosa

---

[60] *Sakamoto monjo*, I, 310-311, and also reprinted in the biographies of the leading figures.

interest was well served. The shogun would not be destroyed, but he would become "one of the feudal lords." There would not be a new shogunate or a despotic court, but a general council was to be convened to protect the general interest. Equally conspicuous was the insistence on winning and deserving foreign approval, on adapting domestic institutions, where defective, in such a pattern that they would stand the test of time and of foreign scrutiny. Indeed, in the anxiety to avoid "shame" before the "ten thousand countries" of the world, an authentic note of the Meiji period was struck.

Sakamoto had reason, therefore, to congratulate himself upon the part he had played in persuading the leaders of his han of the wisdom of a course with such goals. It had brought them into line with the leaders of the other great southwestern han, and it promised to guarantee them an equal voice in the decisions of the future. At such a time he was not inclined to be very patient with his sister's reproaches for his alliance with Gotō Shōjirō. "I don't suppose it ever occurred to you," as he put it, "that if instead of leading five or seven hundred men I were able to lead our whole realm, with its 240,000 koku, into the service of the nation, that that might be a better thing?"[61] He himself clearly thought so.

One part of the Satsuma-Tosa agreement that was not recorded in the compact was an agreement on the part of Satsuma to wait with its plans for war until Gotō had had his chance to persuade Yōdō to request Keiki's resignation as shogun. In turn, Gotō promised to return with two battalions of troops so that, if Keiki should refuse to resign, the alliance against him could move with speed and strength. Saigō, who was more interested in the second eventuality than in the first, and who shared Nakaoka's belief that Keiki would not give up without a fight, invited Gotō to a banquet before his departure. After some awkwardness at the outset, the party, at which the top Tosa and Satsuma officials in the capital were present, was successful in cementing the new personal and political relations that had been established.[62]

[61] *Sakamoto monjo*, I, 304.

[62] Saigō did not attend the party because he was ill. Sasaki did, and he provides a good account of the evening. It began badly, with the Tosa men in high spirits and their Satsuma hosts rather grim. Nakaoka whispered to Fukuoka that the geisha he was enjoying so much was also a favorite of one of the Satsuma karō. Thereafter the meeting was more successful, although less boisterous. Sasaki, *sekijitsu dan*, pp. 421-423.

Agreement between Tosa and Satsuma, which had been an aim of loyalist activists since the days of Takechi Zuizan, had finally been brought about. It would serve as prelude to a Tosa-Satsuma-Chōshū alliance. Saigō wrote his Chōshū allies to explain what had been done. The resignation of the shogun might not come off, he felt, but the Tosa cooperation with troops that was to follow made such an agreement well worth while.[63] But Gotō still needed his lord's approval, and with that in mind he journeyed next to Kōchi.

Yamauchi Yōdō immediately saw great merit in the proposal to petition Keiki to surrender on the promise of convening a council of lords. It was, as he put it, the way to save the Tokugawa house, and it offered him a perfect way of reconciling his obligations to that house with his personal interest in averting a war in which Tosa would be torn between obligation and advantage, with little enough of the latter. Therefore he approved of the idea of a memorial.

He was less willing to entrust more troops to Kyoto to be used in case the shogun refused. He did not want to seem to be coercing Keiki to resign, and he was unwilling to entrust his best troops to subordinates whose judgment might differ from his own. Once away from his control, the troops might easily be utilized by headstrong men like Itagaki to support the Satsuma and Chōshū forces that were preparing to attack the Tokugawa.

Yōdō hesitated and delayed, and as he did so the Satsuma leaders became suspicious of him again. There was even talk among the Kyoto loyalists that Tosa would have to be punished before the Tokugawa. Sakamoto and Nakaoka, who were in the city awaiting Gotō's return, were hard put to keep their friends from moves that would imperil the newly made agreement.

One step was provided by Nakaoka Shintarō, who began to work on the establishment of the auxiliary units he had been authorized to set up by Tosa. His Rikuentai, a land force which paralleled Sakamoto's Kaientai in organization, was designed to utilize some of the loyalist *shishi* and to protect them from the attacks being made against them by rōnin corps which the bakufu had organized. In case of emergency, it would provide a small, mobile force in the Kyoto area. Old friends and fellow rōnin, as

---

[63] Saigō to Yamagata, *Dai Saigō Zenshū*, I, 860f.

well as newcomers recruited from the swelling numbers of two-sworded men, were trained, armed, and housed. Nakaoka's roll of his charter members lists fifty-nine; they included men from all parts of the country, including even the Tokugawa ancestral home of Mikawa. Regulations similar to those Sakamoto had set up for his embryo navy were established to give Nakaoka absolute command of the unit. Second in command was Tanaka Kōken. The Tosa han provided the money, and Sasaki Takayuki, now stationed in Kyoto, contributed his Shirakawa residence as a center.[64]

During the same days Itagaki Taisuke, who was in charge of troops within Tosa, was working steadily to build up strength in the regular units. With Western arms and Western-style drill, he was trying to make efficient units out of status-conscious groups of swordsmen. The Tosa troops that fought so well in the Restoration battles were in large part his work.

Thus Tosa opinion was still far from united during July of 1867. Itagaki Taisuke and Nakaoka Shintarō, military specialists and advocates of forceful action, were preparing to join in the violence they expected Satsuma and Chōshū to precipitate, while Sakamoto and Gotō, who preferred compromise and peaceful means, had succeeded in staying plans for war with a proposal to Keiki to resign his powers. Yamauchi Yōdō, who would have to make that proposal, was still not sure of his course in the event the shogun refused. In view of the impatience of the Satsuma and Chōshū leaders, it was fortunate for Tosa that a new international incident diverted everyone's attention temporarily. This, too, was an incidental benefit of Sakamoto's Kaientai.

5. The Icarus Affair

On August 5, 1867, Robert Ford and John Hutchings of the British warship *Icarus* were slain in Maruyama, Nagasaki's licensed quarter. According to the hasty preliminary investigation made by the British Consul Marcus Flowers, a Kaientai ship, the *Yokobue Maru*, left the harbor the following morning only to return again later in the day. Since a Tosa han ship had left Nagasaki the same day, Flowers assumed that the guilty parties had been transferred to the Tosa ship outside the harbor for transportation back

---

[64] Ozaki, *Nakaoka*, p. 260; Hirao, *Rikuentai*, p. 250.

to Kōchi. The Kaientai stalwarts were known for their vigorous pursuit of pleasure in wine and women, and several had visited the licensed quarter the evening of the murders. It is not surprising that Flowers came to the conclusion that the murderers had been Tosa men. The bakufu, nervous because there had been several anti-foreign outbursts in the weeks immediately before, was not disposed to dispute the evidence offered by the British, the more so since it so conveniently disrupted the work of one of the great southwestern han whose loyalty was no longer certain. It was agreed that a bakufu Commissioner for Foreign Affairs would proceed to Kōchi together with Sir Harry Parkes to have the matter out with Yamauchi Yōdō himself. There seemed every chance of adding a Kōchi chapter to the story of direct punishment of anti-foreign activities which had already led to the shelling of Kagoshima and Shimonoseki.[65]

The Kōchi administration hurriedly recalled Sasaki Takayuki and a fellow Great Inspector (Ōmetsuke) from Kyoto. In talks with bakufu officials in Kyoto, Sasaki had been astonished to find the bakufu disposed to accept the flimsy circumstantial evidence that the British put forward. Indignant at the assumption that his fief was at fault, he tried to explain that all Tosa samurai were under orders not to slay foreigners, but to no avail. He was determined not to accept bakufu or British transportation to Kōchi, and since there was no Tosa vessel available he approached Saigō Takamori with a request for help in getting to Kōchi. Saigō quickly arranged passage on a Satsuma ship for Sasaki. He reminded him that Satsuma had experienced similar difficulties in the past, and suggested that the bakufu was probably seizing this opportunity of striking its vassal with a foreign fist.[66] But Sasaki and his fellows, unlike the Kagoshima men who dealt with the British in 1862, were in no mood to court a foreign war. Defeat was certain. They could not even afford bad feeling; most of the Kaiseikan debts contracted in Nagasaki through Gotō had been with the British firm of Alt and Company, and it would have been extremely awkward to incur British hostility.

As the Satsuma ship bearing Sasaki prepared to leave for Tosa, another passenger boarded in the night. Sakamoto Ryōma, whose

[65] For a representative account, Hirao, Kaientai, pp. 216f.
[66] Saigō to Sasaki, Saigō zenshū, i, 893. Sasaki, p. 434.

men were being accused of the murder, was making his first trip back to his fief since he had fled in 1862. His status was still unclear; although he had been pardoned, he did not have permission to return. He could not, as Sasaki explains, land publicly and receive the welcome and adulation of his old loyalist friends. He was permitted to come, however, for two excellent reasons. One was that his word and investigation would be essential in matters affecting the Kaientai. The second was that he bore a personal letter from Matsudaira Shungaku for Yamauchi Yōdō. Shungaku expressed sympathy for Yōdō's plight, but urged him to avoid unnecessary foreign difficulties and to reach a settlement with the British as soon as possible, even if the guilt for the murders was not fully clear. Yōdō rejected the proposition indignantly.[67]

The ships put in to Suzaki, a port west of Kōchi, whose harbor was deeper than that of Kōchi. Sasaki was worried about Sakamoto's safety: "At this time," he writes, "the pro-bakufu elements in the han government were very hostile to people who had fled, and we didn't know how it would come out." Fortunately he was able to transfer Sakamoto to a friendly captain of a Tosa naval ship while he himself went on to Kōchi to report to Yōdō. This was somewhat different from the triumphant trip home Sakamoto had assured his sister lay ahead. Sakamoto was not even able to visit his family. "I was very busy in secret negotiations," he wrote, "and couldn't get in touch with you."[68]

While the talks with the English were in progress Itagaki Taisuke and his modern troops provided an additional cause for concern. Itagaki so maneuvered his forces as to suggest plans for an attack against the foreigners, and for a time there were rumors that he planned to take such a course. When cautioned by Gotō and others, however, he countered with the assurance that he was practicing to use them against the Tokugawa and not against the British.[69]

---

[67] *Memories of Lord Redesdale*, I, 411. Satow writes, "Old Yōdō said that he had received a letter from a friend advising him to try and compromise the matter, as the English were greatly incensed at the murder of their men, but he would do nothing of the kind. If his people were guilty he would punish them; he could do no more; but if they were innocent he would declare their innocence through thick and thin." p. 269.

[68] Sasaki, p. 441. *Sakamoto monjo*, I, 336.

[69] *Ishin Tōso kinnō shi*, p. 1123. Sasaki reports that some proposed assassinating the bakufu representatives if they came dressed in Western clothes, but that he dissuaded them. p. 445.

The British failed to prove their point in the negotiations that followed. Harry Parkes presented Gotō Shōjirō, who was one of the chief Tosa negotiators, with one of the outbursts of temper for which he was famous. Satow explained in apology that his chief had formed this unfortunate habit in the course of his work in China, and Gotō later called Parkes to account for it.[70] But it was soon clear that the British had no real evidence to support their charge that the murderers had been Tosa men.

It was finally decided to adjourn the talks and the investigations to Nagasaki, where more witnesses would be available, and the official party left Suzaki on the Tosa ship *Yugao*, the former *Shooeyleen*. Sasaki went to represent Tosa, while Satow was named to represent the British interest. Sakamoto was also aboard the small steamer that left on September 9. The trip to Nagasaki took three days. Satow, who had a thoroughly unpleasant trip, unfortunately fails to note the presence of his fellow passenger Sakamoto. He sums up his impressions of the trip in these words: "Bad food, a dirty cabin, excessive heat, sullen fellow-voyagers were all accepted with the calmness of exhausted misery. The 'Shooeyleen's' boilers were old, and we steamed along at the rate of two knots an hour. Luckily the weather was calm, otherwise there was every reason to think we must have gone to the bottom."[71] Sasaki's account is scarcely more helpful. He notes that at Sakamoto's suggestion he went ashore with him at Shimonoseki to see Sakamoto's wife Oryō, but for the rest he gives no details of discussions on shipboard.[72]

As the group neared Nagasaki, Sakamoto suggested to Sasaki that he offer a reward for information that would lead to the apprehension of the criminals. This was done, but without immediate results. It could not be proved that the crime had been committed by Tosa men, and the British and the bakufu took back their charges against Tosa on October 4. The affair was not solved until

---

[70] Satow, who often bridled under Parkes' lash, encouraged Gotō to protest: "I was myself rather sick of being made the intermediary of the overbearing language to which the chief habitually resorted, and told Gotō to remonstrate with him, if he really thought this; as for myself, I did not dare to hint anything of the kind to my chief." *Diplomat*, p. 266.

[71] *ibid.*, p. 271.

[72] Sasaki, p. 453. Satow too notes "The Tosa officers also landed, one and all, on some pretext or other. . . . I went on shore to ask after old friends, and found Inoue Bunda [Kaoru], who was a perfect sink of taciturnity." p. 271.

a year later, when it was discovered that a Fukuoka samurai had killed the two English sailors and then committed suicide.[73]

One of the by-products of the investigation was that Sasaki and Sakamoto became good friends while it was in progress. Sasaki's memoirs give some indication of Sakamoto's lively interest in new ideas and tactics. The two talked together about ideas for conciliar government after the shogun should have resigned his post, and they agreed that some effort should be made to recruit Yuri Kimimasa of Echizen for the new government. Here again, a contact that Sakamoto had made in the service of Katsu was to be utilized. Sasaki was astonished by Sakamoto's readiness to consider any means, however unorthodox, to outwit the Tokugawa. In 1865 Nagasaki had been the scene of the Catholic mass attended by the Christians of Urakami, who had survived as a group despite centuries of Tokugawa scrutiny and persecution. Sakamoto speculated on the possibility of utilizing Christianity against the bakufu. "If the plans we're developing with Satsuma and Chōshū should fail," Sasaki quotes him, "what we ought to do is to use Christianity to agitate the people's minds. The confusion that results will unhorse the bakufu." It will be noted that Sakamoto accepted the Tokugawa estimate of Christianity as an unsettling, dangerous teaching. Sasaki, however, was shocked. It was all very well to use weapons against the Tokugawa, he replied, but in the case of Christianity that would not be the end of the matter. The harm would be permanent, and in the long run Christianity would be worse than the shogunate. He insisted that the basis for the national pattern had to be found in Shintō with Confucianism in an auxiliary role. He was unable to persuade Sakamoto, who argued that one ought to be able to distinguish between ends and means.[74]

From this time on Sasaki headed the Tosa administration in Nagasaki, and it was he with whom Sakamoto and Iwasaki had to deal for the Kaientai and the official han enterprises. Sasaki's memoirs made it clear that although Sakamoto and his men caused him more trouble, he thought a good deal more of them than he did of Iwasaki. Sasaki had opposed Gotō's Kaiseikan from the first as wasteful and demeaning. Gotō had ignored financial con-

[73] Parkes later apologized with a letter to Yōdō for his error. Hirao, *Kaientai*, p. 233.

[74] *Sakamoto monjo*, I, 471-472.

siderations in favor of political goals, but Iwasaki's bent was in the other direction; he felt it his exclusive task to get the han books in order. He was less generous with help for Sakamoto than the latter would have wished, and he was personally antipathetic to the boisterous men who made up the Kaientai. Sasaki had earlier objected to Gotō's profligacy, but he now thought that Iwasaki was behaving like a merchant and not like a samurai. The rational businessman and future titan of the Meiji business world found himself constantly at odds with the straightforward, uncomplicated loyalist under whose direction he was expected to work.[75]

The Kaientai, on the other hand, posed many problems for Sasaki. Nominally a Tosa organization, its rolls included rōnin from all parts of Japan. Its members had a good deal of notoriety in Nagasaki. It was perennially in debt, it enjoyed little financial success, and it was a constant drain on the han treasury.[76] Sakamoto's correspondence illustrates the problems the organization encountered. At one point he wrote to friends in Chōshū to ask whether they might not have use for some of his unemployed men. At another time he had to write in support of his friend and backer, the Nagasaki merchant Kosone, who had been arrested in Shimonoseki as a spy because he was found to be carrying a message from Tokugawa officials in Osaka for those in Nagasaki. Sakamoto assured his Chōshū contacts that Kosone's sympathies were firmly with the cause of the Kaientai, and that he had been a tower of strength to him.[77]

Although Sakamoto's main interests were political, he found time to supervise a number of business matters through the Kaientai in the fall of 1867. A contract he arranged with the Tanabe han provided that the Kaientai would transport and sell Tanabe local products in Nagasaki and buy for Tanabe there. The Kaientai was prepared, the agreement stated, to consider loans to help Tanabe han purchase its local goods, and it also offered to import Western goods as desired with the proceeds. Shortly afterward the Tanabe representative was given five hundred ryō in order to purchase local products.[78]

Sakamoto's next major venture was with a Netherlands trader,

[75] Hirao, *Ishin keizai shi*, pp. 28-29.
[76] Sasaki, p. 524.
[77] *Sakamoto monjo*, I, 324, 344.
[78] Text of agreements, *ibid*., pp. 372-376.

Hartman. The Kaientai agreed to purchase 1,300 rifles, making an initial payment of four thousand ryō with twelve thousand to follow. It is interesting to note that the down payment for this transaction was raised not in Tosa, but from Satsuma, and that a Nagasaki merchant was sent to Satsuma to have that domain arrange for a loan in the Osaka exchange. Sasaki Takayuki, who stood as informal guarantor for Tosa, also put his seal on the document. The same Satsuma loan served to cover the five hundred ryō with which the Tanabe han contract was launched. Quite evidently, Sakamoto was able to talk a very limited capital into a variety of schemes that promised considerable profit.[79]

In the case of rifles, Sakamoto's aim was to present them to the Tosa administration as thanks for his pardon. Since Sasaki guaranteed payment for Tosa, this too might be considered a sign of some commercial acumen. Satsuma, for its part, was willing to grant the initial loan since the small arms were expected to strengthen the Tosa forces that would gather in Kyoto to join the Satsuma groups there.

Activities of this sort led to new speculation about the way commerce should be organized. A document which was written in the summer of 1867 by Sakamoto's follower Mutsu Munemitsu (who would become Foreign Minister in 1894) illustrates this perfectly. Mutsu contrasted the advantages of the Western shipper, who simply charged freight for the tonnage he carried and insured its safety, with the Japanese system wherein the shipowner paid to the shipper part of the value of the goods loaded, on the premise that he would more than recover his expenditure on delivery. Mutsu felt that the Kaientai should use the Western system. He also thought that Japan ought to have commercial companies with limited liability like those in the West. In this way, he thought, it would be possible to extend Kaientai operations to all the ports of Japan. He went on to say that ship captains should be given greater responsibility, since by being able to make spot decisions they could bring back greater profits. Finally, Mutsu thought that the Kaientai should be separated into sections specializing in military and in commercial matters, with no overlap between the two. If, he seemed to say, the Kaientai would concentrate on business it would be a great deal more successful.[80]

Thus in commerce, as in politics, Sakamoto and his friends were

---

[79] Text of contracts, *ibid.*, pp. 376-379. [80] *ibid.*, pp. 317-324.

prepared to appropriate Western examples wherever they seemed applicable. The enterprises that had been begun showed the possibilities that a more rational social order would contain for profit and growth. It must be repeated, however, that Sakamoto and Mutsu did not by any means stand alone in this position. In the summer of 1867 the shogunate came to the decision that it should permit the organization of limited liability companies, and it gave up its abortive plans to limit foreign trade to the members of official guilds.[81] Political and diplomatic crises prevented immediate implementation of these plans and decisions, but it is clear that everywhere the examples of the West were finding a ready response among the curious and the impressionable, both within the shogunate and among its enemies.

The summer months of 1867 had seen a sharp change in Tokugawa fortunes. The Kyoto conference of great lords had proved that hopes of utilizing a gathering of this sort to win support for shogunal decisions could no longer succeed. The fears that the loyalists had had of success for Keiki had been replaced by hopes that he could be overthrown. Sakamoto Ryōma and Gotō Shōjirō had worked out a program for a peaceful settlement that promised, temporarily at least, to stay the plans for use of force, and while Yōdō hesitated to accept its implications a new foreign crisis had served to remind all groups that Japan could not afford the luxury of disunity indefinitely.

During all of this the nature of the role that men like Sakamoto could play thenceforth had been changing significantly. The day for intrigue and secrecy was giving way to one of formal alliances and high-level discussions. The free-wheeling rōnin were no longer as necessary to the alliances formed, for self-interest among the domains provided all the spur that was needed. Sakamoto had sensed this in seeking to renew his standing with his native domain, and he had succeeded in winning strong support from Gotō Shōjirō. But now that Tosa itself was in danger of eclipse behind the Satsuma-Chōshū councils for war, it was inevitable that Sakamoto would have to retreat from the center of the stage for the final scenes of Restoration politics.

[81] These attempts to limit and channel trade had been ably exploited by Satow and his friends among the *shishi* of the southwest to prove the need for a basic change in the handling of foreign trade and relations.

VIII. RESTORATION

*B*Y THE TIME the *Icarus* issue had been resolved and Gotō Shōjirō was able to return to Kyoto with his lord's approval of the plan to petition Keiki to resign as shogun, the time limit set by the Satsuma men for their delay in beginning a war against the Tokugawa had run out. They were ready with a new military agreement with their allies in Chōshū, while at the Imperial court Iwakura Tomomi was able to cover them with evidence of official authorization. Gotō did not give up his plans, however; the two schedules and plans proceeded simultaneously. As a result the shogun, after having resigned his powers in response to the proposal presented to him by Yamauchi Yōdō, fell victim to the plots that had been prepared for him by Iwakura and the Satsuma representatives.

The fall months of 1867 were a period of great confusion. Everyone sensed great changes in the making, and no one wanted to be caught firmly committed to the wrong side. Therefore sharp struggles about the wisdom of what was being done slowed decisions even in so committed a domain as Satsuma. Similar debates caused dissension in Tosa, and in Hiroshima they produced crazy gyrations of policy. Sakamoto Ryōma's part in the decisions of those months was a modest one, for when negotiations were taking place at a very high level the role of rōnin intermediaries and agitators became less important. Nevertheless, Sakamoto's ideas about the government that was to follow the shogun's resignation deserve careful study, for they provide the link between the vague doubts about feudalism of his early years and the dramatic reforms of the early Meiji Period in which he did not live to take part.

1. Yōdō's Petition to Keiki

Gotō Shōjirō returned to Tosa in the last week of July, 1867 to report to Yamauchi Yōdō 'that he had reached agreement with the Satsuma leaders on the lines of the program he had worked out with Sakamoto Ryōma on the way to Kyoto. Once the shogun had resigned his special administrative powers a new government, for which no one need feel shame, was to be developed in the name of the throne. Political initiative would lie with a bicameral legislature in which an upper house would represent the major feudal barons and nobles while the lower house would be based upon a broader representation, including "even commoners." In this new structure, Gotō explained to Yōdō, Keiki, still lord of the largest domains and commanding the largest income of any baron, could be expected to wield great influence. The alternative was a destructive war after which Satsuma and Chōshū, the fiefs with the largest military forces, could be expected to monopolize power fully as much as the Tokugawa had, and they might very well show less concern for Tosa sensibilities than the bakufu had. Gotō was able to report to his lord that the leaders of the Hiroshima han had agreed to his plan, and that, if Yōdō agreed, the request for Keiki's resignation would be submitted by Tosa, Hiroshima, and Satsuma jointly. Furthermore, he could report that one of Keiki's most trusted councillors, Nagai Naomune, a member of the Junior Council (*Wakadoshiyori*) had indicated to him that such a request would in all probability receive a cordial reception from the shogun. In his talks with Yōdō, Gotō stressed the imminent collapse of the Tokugawa power. He assured him that Keiki was likely to accept a request to resign, especially if it should come from someone he trusted. The plan would provide for the Yamauchi an opportunity to combine their obligations to the Tokugawa with a larger duty to the throne. Gotō had with him letters from Shimazu Hisamitsu and Matsudaira Shungaku urging Yōdō to yield to Gotō's pleas and to return to Kyoto in order to submit his memorial in person.

After some hesitation, Yōdō accepted Gotō's suggestions on August 12. He agreed that they seemed to combine honor with prudence, and he was more than willing to take the lead in a movement that would head off a destructive civil war.

On the other hand, as has been noted, he refused to give his assent to Gotō's parallel request that he bring with him several contingents of Tosa troops. Gotō argued that he had won Satsuma agreement to peaceful measures only by a promise to strengthen the anti-bakufu camp militarily in the event persuasion failed to move Keiki. But Yōdō did not want to seem to be using pressure on Keiki, and he was not certain of the judgment of his military leaders. Therefore Gotō had to return empty-handed to Kyoto, without the concession for which Satsuma had agreed to enter the plan.

The *Icarus* crisis had come before action could be taken on any of the agreements reached. Tosa was cleared of suspicion only on October 4, and until then Yōdō and Gotō were kept in Tosa for the negotiations with Harry Parkes while Sasaki Takayuki and Sakamoto Ryōma went to Nagasaki to carry on the investigation there. During this time, there was plenty of opportunity for argument about the wisdom of the course that had been agreed upon. Yōdō had made his decision, but his advisers and retainers were far from united as to its merits.

A number of men who styled themselves loyalists objected to any measures that would fall short of war. The loyalist movement had lost the overtones of gōshi and shōya interests that had hurt it a half decade earlier, and its supporters were now in high office. Of these, none objected more strongly to the proposal to ask Keiki to resign his powers than Itagaki Taisuke. Itagaki had returned from Yōdō's summer meetings in Kyoto enthusiastic about the possibilities of a war in which Tosa would support Satsuma and Chōshū. He had acquired several hundred rifles of American make, and he had trained his troops throughout the summer. He felt so strongly about his position that he talked of having his followers flee the han and join his command in Kyoto if he should be unable to convince his lord. Yōdō was aware of Itagaki's displeasure, and he tried to allay it by promoting him to Great Inspector (Ōmetsuke) and placing him in charge of all military reform in Tosa. This diverted and channeled Itagaki's energies for a time and until the end of the *Icarus* negotiations he was busy with his program of modernization for the Tosa armed forces.[1]

By the time the *Icarus* crisis was past, his forces were ready for action, and Itagaki's opposition to the petition to Keiki strength-

---

[1] Nakaoka, who was in Kyoto, contributed a comparison of military reforms in Satsuma and Chōshū for Itagaki's use. He wrote that the Satsuma changes were on the English model, and not, in his opinion, well suited to Tosa. Samurai there received niggardly stipends, so that many Tosa ashigaru were better off than Satsuma samurai. The entire military class had joined in the reforms, and officials and privates trained together. Nakaoka also noted that Satsuma subsistence allowances for troops in the Kyoto area were extremely low; despite this, morale was high. In Chōshū, on the other hand, he thought he saw a better model for Tosa. There he had seen many men with large stipends who were thoroughly spoiled and worthless for a modern military system. To overcome this the Chōshū, leaders had built up militia units made up chiefly of those of low ranks and in which even commoners were included. The final principle, adopted after a period of trial and error, was the enlistment of one man for each fifty koku of income. Nakaoka recommended this for Tosa, instead of trying to build on upper- and middle-rank samurai. Here one finds still an echo of the gōshi-shōya contempt of their betters. "Heidan," in *Shunketsu Sakamoto Ryōma*, pp. 362-364, 534-535.

ened. A Tokugawa resignation without prior defeat and loss of territory, he thought, would mean little change in the situation. He had heard (as had Sasaki Takayuki in Nagasaki) that Gotō and Sakamoto had assured Yōdō that Keiki would undoubtedly be appointed kampaku in the new Imperial government that would follow his resignation, and he was bitterly opposed to this. Yōdō finally decided he would have to relieve Itagaki of his command, and before he himself left Tosa for Kyoto again he went so far as to issue orders for Itagaki to study in America.[2] The orders were never carried out, and Itagaki, who regained command of the troops at the last, gained fame by leading one of the best balanced land forces of those that fought against the Tokugawa in 1868. Had Yōdō persevered in his intention to send Itagaki to America, the career of the future democratic leader might well have been very different.[3]

Yōdō was also under pressure from many of his conservative retainers who thought it rash to urge the shogun to resign. Unable to adjust to the facts of Tokugawa weakness, they feared that punishment would follow such presumption. On September 17, Yōdō assembled his retainers and informed them that he had definitely decided to present a memorial to the shogun. He explained that in view of the great urgency of conforming with Western examples Japan had to change its course; and that the abandonment of the old shogunal institutions was one requirement of the times. He went on to state that his course was in harmony with the real interests of the shogun, and he assured them that he would in no wise countenance the use of force against the bakufu. Thus Yōdō was restraining his military enthusiasts and reassuring his conservatives.[4]

Once his decision was made to petition the shogun, Yōdō ordered one of his court Confucianists, Matsuoka Kiken, to prepare the text of the memorial that he and Gotō had planned.[5] In content and phraseology, the memorial could be traced to the eight-point program that Sakamoto and Gotō had discussed on ship-

---

[2] *Ishin shi*, IV, 714; Hirao, *Rikuentai*, pp. 224-225, *Yōdō Kō*, pp. 233-234.

[3] Itagaki visited the West in the 1880's, after he was already established as a popular hero. He returned convinced of the need for national unity in the face of Western condescension, and he was more inclined to cooperate with the Meiji government for a time. Cody, *ibid.*

[4] Hirao, *Yōdō Kō*, p. 234.

[5] For Matsuoka's biography, Teraishi, *Tosa Ijin den*, p. 147. See also *Ishin shi*, IV, 728f.

board. It was in two parts. A personal statement by Yōdō was followed by a more specific plan signed by his retainers.

Yōdō began by pointing out that the present state of national disunity was "a great disaster to us and of great happiness to the foreigners. This is exactly what they have been hoping for." He saw little point, he wrote, in discussing the origins and causes of the situation, but he stressed the need to reconstruct the political order with the cooperation of all groups so that a government "for which no shame need be felt before future generations or foreign countries" might be set up. Yōdō wrote that he himself was temporarily unable to come to Kyoto because of a severe illness; but that he was sending several of his retainers with detailed recommendations he hoped the shogun would consider.

The supplementary statement repeated Yōdō's conviction of the need for establishing a state structure that would endure throughout all time. Yōdō's retainers explained that their chief had been turning over these ideas ever since the Kyoto meetings earlier in the summer. His suggestions were, as usual, eight in number:

1. Authority to govern the whole country is vested in the Imperial court. Therefore all legislation of the Imperial country should originate with a Kyoto Deliberative Council (*Gisei-jo*).

2. This Council should be divided into two sections, with legislators of the upper to be lords and nobles, and those of the lower to include rear vassals and even commoners, all to be selected from upstanding and sincere men.

3. Schools appropriate for those of various ages should be established everywhere to give instruction in learning and technology.

4. Foreign relations should be carried out at Hyōgo. New treaties based on enlightened reason should be negotiated with the foreigners by Imperial ministers after consultation with the han. Commercial transactions must be carried out in all sincerity lest the foreigners lose faith in us.

5. The establishment of land and naval forces is of first importance. A military center should be set up between Kyoto and Settsu (Naniwa-Hyōgo), and an Imperial guard should

be established to guard the court. What we must have is a force which will have no equal in the world.

6. Since medieval times administrative orders have been issued by the military. Since the entry of Western ships into the ports, the country has been in disorder and the nation has been distressed; in view of this it is inevitable that administrative authority should be changed. We must reform the errors of the past, and, not contenting ourselves with the leaves and branches or stopping at minor regulations, we must make a fundamental revision.

7. The procedures and regulations of the Imperial court are of great antiquity, but in view of the situation we face today it is not surprising that they do not meet our needs. We must abolish wrong customs and establish a national basis that will make a complete change, in order to stand as unique in the world.

8. The members and ministers charged with deliberation must carry out their plans, put aside all self-interest, and base themselves on impartiality. In making a new beginning they must avoid the controversies of the past and concentrate on the problems that lie ahead. They must carry out the general will and avoid abuses.[6]

This document bore the signatures of Teramura Sazen, Yōdō's Chamberlain (*Sobayōnin*), Gotō Shōjirō, Fukuoka Kōtei, and Kō-yama Kunikiyo. Once the memorial was ready, Gotō left for Kyoto on September 22. Because of stormy weather he did not reach there until October 1.

2. Preparations for War

Gotō found the political scene in Kyoto drastically changed. When he left in July Satsuma had been ready to hold back until the request to secure Keiki's resignation had been tried, but subsequently his allies had concluded that there was little likelihood of his securing Tosa participation in their plans. They were aware of the complications which the *Icarus* affair had caused for Tosa,

---

[6] The text of the memorial from *Ishin shi*, iv, 728, 732-736. Another translation can be found in Ishii Ryosuke, ed., *Japanese Legislation in the Meiji Era* (W. J. Chambliss, tr., Tokyo, 1958), pp. 708-711.

but in view of the failure to send Tosa army units to Kyoto they no longer felt themselves bound by the agreements which had been made during the summer. They were afraid that by further delay they might lose the trust of their friends in Chōshū, and they were also urged to stronger measures by their friends at the Imperial court. And in talks with British diplomats the dangers of further assistance from France for the bakufu were held up to heighten the sense of urgency and crisis.

The French danger was magnified in debate while it dwindled in fact. The influence of Leon Roches with the bakufu administration remained great, and in response to the plans Roches had worked out with Tokugawa officials France's share of Japan's foreign trade had grown markedly. Technology, weapons, and even the language taught in the shogunate's institute for foreign learning, renamed the *Kaiseijo*, gave evidence of the effective work of Napoleon III's representative. Bakufu leaders like Oguri Tadamasa remained adamant in their insistence on the need for further French help, and the trip to France by Tokugawa Akitake in the summer of 1867, followed by the mission of Kurimoto Joun, who arrived in Paris September 14, left little doubt of the reliance the shogunate placed on its French connection.

Roches, however, had lost the backing he required in Paris. With the replacement of E. Drouyn de Lhuys by the Marquis de Moustiers as Foreign Minister in the fall of 1866 a much more cautious policy was inaugurated. Diplomatic disasters in Mexico and the lengthening shadow of Prussia in Europe had made the Empire less intent on Asian exploits, and new instructions to Roches urged him to maintain good relations with the shogunate without alienating the daimyō, who, it seemed to Paris, might succeed the bakufu as national leaders. Questions about French policy that had been raised in the House of Commons were also cited as additional reasons for caution. Roches disputed the wisdom of these instructions, and he insisted vigorously on the certainty of a Tokugawa victory. He praised Keiki's abilities in the most enthusiastic terms, and argued that the true French interest lay in giving the bakufu full help to overcome its enemies. But he failed to convince his superiors, although they did not remove him from his post. When Tokugawa Akitake came to France the money available for his support (paid out by Fleury Herard as agent for the bakufu commercial interests negotiated earlier) proved disappointingly meager, and when Kurimoto Joun came to Paris later he made it his first business to confirm and deplore this apparently lukewarm attitude in dispatches to Edo. Full French support, it was apparent, would fall far short of the enthusiastic promises of M. Roches.[7]

Both the British and the Satsuma representatives had some knowledge of this change of heart in Paris. Harry Parkes had sent to Paris his adviser von Siebold, who reported fully on the penurious reception that the bakufu representative received in Paris. Also in France was a Satsuma representative, Iwashita Masahira, who wrote home about the difference between attitudes in France and those of France's representatives in Japan. Indeed, the very presence of a Satsuma mission, allowed to exhibit at the Paris International Exposition of 1867 as representatives of an independent state, argued that the French position was far from supporting Roches' extravagant promises and hopes.[8] To be sure, there was no certainty that official coolness in France would be accompanied by a cancellation of earlier promises in Japan. Distance also blurred reports by the time they arrived in the Far East, and in most cases they had furthermore to be evaluated against other, more alarming, reports that came in.[9]

However accurate the knowledge of French intentions which the Satsuma leaders and British diplomats may have possessed, they spared no effort in attempting to spur each other on with grim pictures of what the other could expect from a future changed through French assistance. On August 26 Saigō Takamori had a long and instructive talk with Ernest Satow in Osaka. One of his Satsuma colleagues had warned that the English were about to betray their Satsuma friends in return for an agreement

[7] Ishii, *Meiji Ishin*, pp. 590ff.

[8] Roches did his best to minimize the effects of this by transporting the goods to France and seeing to it that they would be displayed in a single Japanese pavilion; the French consul in Nagasaki explained this to the Governor there, assuring him of Roches' "sincère Dévouement au Gouvernement de TaiKoon . . . qui est là seule pour le bonheur du Japon. . . ." Nagasaki Prefectural Library, document dated 28 October 1866, s/W. Drury.

[9] Including an earlier report to Satsuma from Iwashita which had it that "One finds many strong supporters of the bakufu among the French; rumors have it that in about three years there won't be any daimyō any more, and that they will be defeated and converted into men of wealth and standing, but without any political power, as was the case in France and other countries." Ishii, *Meiji Ishin*, p. 591.

with the bakufu, and Saigō wanted to satisfy himself that this was not so. Nothing could have been farther from the mark. Satow later summarized British policy in these terms: "The British legation . . . were determined that so far as their influence went, the Mikado should be restored to the headship of the nation, so that our treaties might receive a sanction that no one would venture to dispute, and for this purpose it was necessary that the constitution of the Tycoon's government should be modified in such a manner as to admit the principal daimiōs (or clans rather) to a share in the distribution of power."[10] The Satow-Saigō conversation can be followed from Satow's memoirs and from two long letters Saigō wrote to Kagoshima, and it is interesting to see the way in which each tried to drive the other into a stronger stand by calling in the French bogey.

Saigō began by telling Satow that the French were making capital out of the diplomatic gains won by the British. While Britain struggled to open more ports, the French had arranged with the bakufu to secure monopoly trading rights with a guild of merchants especially authorized by the shogunate to deal with the foreigners. Satow, Saigō noted with satisfaction, became very angry.[11] Satow, who fails to record his own reaction, notes that he did report this to Harry Parkes, whose reaction, as always, was violent. "This piece of news," he writes, "inflamed the chief's wrath, who immediately got hold of the prime minister and insisted upon the scheme being abandoned. A new proclamation . . . was extorted by dint of great diplomatic pressure. . . ."[12]

Satow then seized the French issue to threaten Saigō with it. He told Saigō what he already knew, that the bakufu was conspiring with French advisers to speed the unification of Japan under the shogunate by dint of aid from technicians, military advisers, and, if necessary, troops. Satsuma and Chōshū, as the two greatest fiefs, were to be brought to their knees first of all, and whatever resistance followed would also be dealt with by force. Satow had a solution to suggest: Britain would be willing to lend its backing to Satsuma and Chōshū in their struggle to restore Imperial government. If it were known that French intervention would be followed by British intervention, Napoleon III would

---

[10] *A Diplomat in Japan*, p. 244.
[11] Saigō to Katsura Uemon, *Saigō Zenshū*, I, 900.
[12] *Diplomat*, p. 256.

not be likely to take the risks involved. The British goals were simply stated. There should be a single sovereign, with the feudal lords under him so that Japan's national polity would be similar to that of Britain.[13]

Saigō was impressed by the tenor of Satow's talk, and he closed his report to Ōkubo with the significant observation, "Satow's tone toward the bakufu is very disparaging."[14] But Saigō wanted no part of a British-French intervention in Japanese politics. "I told him," he wrote Ōkubo, "that whatever came of it, we Japanese would do our utmost in the cause of reforming Japan's political structure and that we had no cause to trouble foreigners with it."[15] Saigō's report of the same conversation to his superior, the Satsuma karō Katsura Uemon, stated his feelings more explicitly: "[British help] . . . would be different from the other matters in which we have consistently tried to make the Englishmen get their backs up and be angry; although we have tried to separate them from the French and make them oppose the help the French are giving, to go along with this proposal of his for this kind of assistance would be unpardonable. So I declined and chose the proper path, . . . we can be at ease about the matter."[16]

But the principal factor which impelled the Satsuma leaders to take a stronger stand on the issue of an anti-Tokugawa war was the necessity of maintaining friendly relations with their allies in Chōshū. The original alliance between the two domains had been largely defensive in nature. Until its status was settled Chōshū was still technically an enemy of the court, and its leaders were still unable to participate openly in the planning and conspiring that took place in Kyoto. Dependent upon Satsuma protection and concealment, they were quick to harbor suspicion and to take offense against their erstwhile allies, who seemed to be temporizing at the capital. And their suspicions were sharper because of the vacillation Satsuma seemed to show between the Tosa com-

---

[13] From Saigō's report to Ōkubo Toshimichi of August 26, in *Saigō Zenshū*, I, 880-892. Satow, *Diplomat*, pp. 254-255, gives the same letter in translation, and explains that it was given to him in 1906 by "my old friend Matsugata Massayoshi." His translation differs in that Japan's national policy is to be "similar to the system of all other countries," while Saigō's ori .nal has "similar to that of England."

[14] *Saigō Zenshū*, I, 892.

[15] *ibid.*, p. 887. Again, Satow's version differs: "I replied that we would exert ourselves for the transformation of the Japanese government and we had no justification (?) vis-à-vis foreigners." *Diplomat*, p. 255.

[16] *Saigō Zenshū*, I, 904.

promise program and a joint military effort with Chōshū.

As has been described, Shimazu Hisamitsu received two Chōshū emissaries in audience after the failure of the Kyoto conferences on July 17, 1867. He had stated to them his conviction that the bakufu would have to be struck down by force, and said he was ready to make final arrangements for military cooperation. Saigō Takamori was to come to Chōshū soon to coordinate the planning, and Kuroda Kiyotaka, another Satsuma loyalist, accompanied the Chōshū men as far as Osaka. The Chōshū men, Yamagata and Shinagawa, returned to their fief full of elation. As sign of Hisamitsu's favor Yamagata had the six-shooter he had been given, and as promise of the future they had received statements of the Satsuma intention to petition the court for authority to punish the bakufu for its arrogance against the Emperor. Yamagata had succeeded to Takasugi's command of the militia units after Takasugi's death in May, and he now drew up tactical plans to discuss with Saigō Takamori when he should arrive. Yamagata planned assaults on the centers of the shogunal power near Kyoto and a quick strike to eliminate Keiki himself, followed by summons to the barons of the Kyoto area to assemble and cooperate with the Satsuma-Chōshū ("Imperial") forces. The Kansai plain was to become the base from which direct assaults on Kyoto could be launched.[17]

Just when these military plans were taking shape in Chōshū, the Satsuma emissary arrived on August 15. It turned out to be Murata Shimpachi and not Saigō Takamori, and with him he brought the details of the Satsuma agreement with Tosa to work for a peaceful settlement instead of tactical plans for battle. The Chōshū administration was quick to scent the danger of a Satsuma defection. Remembering the disasters that had followed its last attempt at independent action, it decided to send several men back to Kyoto together with Murata to find out exactly what the Satsuma men had in mind. Shinagawa Yajirō, one of those who returned with Murata, talked with Komatsu Tatewaki, Saigō Takamori and Ōkubo Toshimichi. The reports he brought back to Chōshū contained reassuring evidence of Satsuma's intention to fight. The Satsuma leaders had convinced him that they had little confidence in the agreement they had worked out with Tosa for peaceful persuasion. They already had one thousand troops ready

[17] Mushakoji, in *Great Saigō*, pp. 244-245, gives the fullest treatment of this to be found in a western language.

in Kyoto. When the day for action came, one third of these were to guard the Imperial palace, which would be the center for those nobles who would side with the insurrection. Another contingent would attack the Aizu headquarters in Kyoto. It was felt that, as in 1864, this was virtually the only han that would provide real support for the Tokugawa cause. The rest of the Satsuma troops would put the bakufu's Horikawa military headquarters to the torch. Furthermore, the Chōshū men were told three thousand more men would be sent from Satsuma with the mission of assaulting the bakufu's Osaka castle and seizing the Tokugawa gunboats, while still another thousand men, presently in Edo, would combine with anti-Tokugawa forces there, march on Kōfu, and block whatever Tokugawa troops might be sent to relieve Kyoto.[18]

At this late date the Satsuma schedule for war was delayed by sharp arguments about the wisdom of the course the youthful leaders had persuaded Hisamitsu to follow. It was all very well for Saigō and Ōkubo to assure their colleagues that even if they failed some other han would finish their work, but the Kagoshima councillors were less prepared to risk their inheritance. During the late summer of 1867 a vigorous struggle was waged for direction of Satsuma policy. The higher-ranking groups, who preferred a more cautious line, denounced the young leaders as the Party of Extremism (*Kyūgeki tō*), while the latter charged their elders with a "pedestrian" view (zokuron). Thus the same struggle that had been carried on in other fiefs came to Satsuma. Ōkubo Toshimichi and Saigō Takamori had Hisamitsu's ear, however; perhaps more important, they also had the enthusiastic support of the great majority of their fellows. They managed to commit their han, step by step, to their counsels. On October 3 a force of three thousand troops entered the port of Osaka from Kagoshima. Once there it was under Saigō's command, and thereafter the balance shifted. Saigō thought it dangerous to leave so large a body of troops exposed to attack from the Tokugawa garrisons in Osaka, and he arranged with friends at court for Imperial permission to bring them to Kyoto. This changed the military picture within the capital completely; Satsuma strength in Kyoto was soon reputed to be as high as ten thousand men.[19]

[18] *Ishin shi*, IV, 676-677, gives the diary of a member of the Chōshū party, Kashimura Kazuma; this plan is also given as a speech by Saigō in Mushakoji, *Great Saigō*, pp. 252-253.
[19] *Ishin shi*, IV, 679.

Gotō Shōjirō returned to Kyoto two days before the new Satsuma units arrived from Kagoshima. He was dismayed to discover that plans for military action were so far advanced. Saigō and Ōkubo told him that they had concluded from his long absence in Tosa that they would have to take matters into their own hands. Saigō reminded Gotō of his promise to bring troops with him from Tosa to aid in plans for war, and he was little pleased by Gotō's explanation that Yōdō was opposed to the use of force.

Gotō did his best to dissuade the Satsuma leaders. His efforts can be traced through the diary of Teramura Sazen, Yōdō's Chamberlain, who came with him to Kyoto.[20] After his first attempt to get Satsuma to return to its agreements of July had failed, Gotō tried for a delay in the execution of the plans for war. He found Saigō inflexible. If Tosa wanted to try to get Keiki to resign, he assured him, it was acceptable to Satsuma, but the Satsuma schedule could not be changed. To make things worse, Gotō discovered that the Hiroshima domain, whose councillor Tsuji Shōsō had supported his earlier efforts, was showing signs of casting its lot with the Satsuma and Chōshū effort.[21] Thus there seemed every likelihood of a military campaign in which Tosa would have to choose between two sides, neither of them to its liking.

Gotō was unable to keep the Satsuma leaders from going ahead with their plans for war. On October 12 Ōkubo Toshimichi and Ōyama Kakunosuke went to Chōshū to draw up the final plans for action, and they completed them there on October 16. In talks with Kido Kōin, Itō Hirobumi, Shinagawa Yajirō, and other Chōshū men, they agreed that October 23 would be the date for action. Satsuma troopships would arrive in Chōshū before then, and Chōshū forces would be mobilized and waiting. Ōkubo suggested that the allies use as pretext for war a bakufu request that Chōshū send two representatives to Osaka, in order to have it appear that Chōshū had come to petition for the pardon that could no longer be denied. Ōkubo thought this could be made to seem a violation of the Imperial court's expressed wishes for a compromise settlement. Satsuma, which had troops in the capital, was to open the fighting with a determined drive to secure the person of

---

[20] *Teramura Sazen shuki*, in Iwasaki Hideshige, ed., *Ishin nichijō sanshū* (Tokyo, 1926), III.

[21] *Ishin shi*, IV, 727.

the Emperor, while Chōshū units would play a major role in the land fighting that followed.[22]

To complete the discomfiture of the Tosa representatives in Kyoto, the Hiroshima han, which bordered on Chōshū and therefore lay along the route of advance of the Chōshū armies, now agreed to join in the new military plans. Hiroshima signed an agreement with Chōshū on October 20. The Hiroshima administration, like all the secondary actors in the drama, acted more from prudence than from conviction. For when word came from Kyoto that Gotō was making some headway with his proposals for a petition to Keiki, Hiroshima tried to withdraw from the alliance again, and to the last it tried for full membership in both camps.[23] There were few reckless or adventurous statesmen in a period when all sensed that great changes, whose exact nature was still unclear, were imminent.

Just as war seemed certain, controversies erupted within the Satsuma leadership group again. Teramura, whose diary records the anxious work of the Tosa men in Kyoto, noted that there were still two parties in Kagoshima, and even two within the Satsuma group in Kyoto. Saigō and Ōkubo, he recorded, were determined to use force whatever the obstacle, but their position had been weakened by the failure of the troops that had been promised the Chōshū leaders to arrive by the October 23 deadline. Once again suspicion of Satsuma intentions arose in Chōshū. Ōkubo and Saigō were on the point of returning to Satsuma from Osaka to see what was wrong.

Then, October 28, the Satsuma karō Komatsu Tatewaki, whose position had been consistently more moderate than that of Saigō and Ōkubo, informed Gotō Shōjirō that the idea of petitioning the shogun was gaining some ground in Kagoshima. He recommended that Tosa should forward its memorial to the bakufu immediately, on its own.

The two plans were now set in motion simultaneously, each in a race against time. On October 28 Gotō presented the Tosa memorial to Itakura Katsukiyo of the bakufu's Council of Elders. He warned him that plans for war against the Tokugawa were still in progress, and that there was very little time to be lost. At the

[22] *ibid.*, pp. 680-681.
[23] *ibid.*, p. 740.

same time copies of the memorial were sent to the court Chancellor (kampaku), Nijō Nariaki, and the residence of the strongest Tokugawa supporter, the lord of Aizu, as well as to the Satsuma Kyoto headquarters.[24] Three days later the Hiroshima daimyō, not to be outdone, added his own urgent request to Keiki to resign. On November 1 the troops Satsuma had promised to send to Chōshū finally arrived at Mitajiri. Ōkubo and Saigō cancelled their plans for a trip to Kagoshima, and their planning for war resumed. On November 3 Hiroshima agreed to resume its place in the alliance preparing for military action. Thus the petition to Keiki had been submitted, and the preparations for war were speeding up.

3. The End of the Bakufu

Sakamoto arrived in Kyoto on November 4. He had been detained in Nagasaki by the *Icarus* investigation, and thereafter he had finally made the return to Tosa he had planned so long. His Kaientai had been cleared of complicity in the Nagasaki murders and he himself was in excellent standing with Sasaki Takayuki and other han officials.[25] With him Sakamoto brought the rifles he had recently imported through the Netherlands trader Hartman.[26] His reception was all that he had desired; old enmities had been so far forgotten that it was safe for remaining members of Takechi's Loyalist Party to gather to greet their old friend. Sakamoto was full of information about national politics for his friends. "I have just arrived at Urado on a Hiroshima steamer, and I've brought a thousand rifles with me," he wrote a friend. "On the way I stopped at Shimonoseki and heard the latest news from Kyoto. Things are coming to a head there. I hear it will come at the end of this month or early next month. Satsuma is moving two big companies of troops to Kyoto two days from now, and I hear Chōshū has promised to send troops, I think three battalions, to Osaka. While I was at Shimonoseki Ōkubo Toshimichi came there as a Satsuma messenger. . . . What's happening in our prov-

[24] *ibid.*, pp. 737, 741.

[25] Sakamoto had helped avoid a second incident with foreigners by making prompt report of an attack by Tosa men on foreign sailors in Nagasaki. Sasaki, *Sekijitsu dan*, p. 482.

[26] The extent of Sakamoto's generosity is not clear since, as will be remembered, Sasaki had signed as guarantor for the shipment and Satsuma money had paid for the shipment.

ince? How about Gotō Shōjirō? What's Itagaki doing? I must meet you soon, for I have a lot to tell."[27]

Sakamoto's visit included a visit to the home he had fled in 1862. Unfortunately few documents survive to record the conversations in which he brought his friends and relatives up to date.[28] The accounts that have come down suggest that he was insistent that Tosa should move quickly, and that he wanted his han to play a leading role in the days ahead—if by petition, then through Gotō; if it came to war, then through Itagaki. Indeed, he went so far as to write Kido "I am considering shifting my contact to Itagaki Taisuke."[29] He could not stay away from the political center very long, however; he left Tosa again on October 27, and arrived in Kyoto on November 4.

Sakamoto found the city electric with expectation. Rumors were everywhere, and some of these attached to him. By now his reputation as a mysterious manipulator had outrun the facts of his influence, and some of the popular sheets that circulated throughout the city reported that he had come prepared to lead 300 Kaientai followers in Kyoto. In reality he had five or six men available to him at that time.[30] Nor did he take much part in the high-level discussions and negotiations that were in progress.

Sakamoto did, however, utilize his old contacts to learn about all the plans that were afoot. The same day he entered the city he met Nagai Naomune, Keiki's trusted Junior Councillor. In several talks with Nagai Sakamoto asked whether the bakufu thought it possible to withstand the attack of the Satsuma, Chōshū, and Hiroshima armies. When Nagai replied that victory under such circumstances would be doubtful, Sakamoto observed that in that case Tokugawa Keiki had no real choice in considering the Tosa suggestion that he resign.[31] At the same time, Sakamoto tried to allay the impatience of Nakaoka Shintarō and the Satsuma military leaders by assuring them that military action would win much wider support if they waited a little longer for the shogun's decision.

Sakamoto also had discussions with Gotō about the degree to which Keiki should be made to lay down his powers. The Tosa

---

[27] *Sakamoto monjo,* I, 385. The letter is dated two days before the original Satsuma-Chōshū deadline for action.

[28] *ibid.,* pp. 408ff., does give, however, an account by a man named Motoyama which tells of Sakamoto's impressive news and documents.

[29] *ibid.,* p. 382.   [30] *ibid.,* p. 412.   [31] Hirao, *Kaientai,* pp. 254-255.

memorial had asked him to resign his special political authority, but it did not specify his resignation of the title of shogun. At one point Sakamoto thought he had found a middle path, and wrote Gotō to offer a solution that might not be too difficult for bakufu men to accept. "If," he suggested, "we move the Edo mint to Kyoto and control the currency, then even though the office of shogun remains the same in name it will actually be nothing we need to fear."[32] This should not be taken to mean that Sakamoto's real aims were so modest, but it may serve to indicate how difficult it was for even committed loyalists to imagine a system in which the regime that had ruled the land for two and a half centuries would be done away with completely. And it certainly shows Sakamoto poles removed from the Satsuma insistence on total humiliation for the Tokugawa.

Meanwhile the war party continued its preparations. With military plans complete, and with the new strength which the Satsuma troop movements had created, all that was lacking was a proper authorization for the declaration of war.

This was provided by a handful of nobles under the leadership of Iwakura Tomomi at the court. With his release from confinement in the spring of 1867 Iwakura had begun regular visits to Kyoto. In these he cultivated the Satsuma leaders, and he formed a close working relationship with Ōkubo Toshimichi. He also did all he could to redeem himself in the eyes of the exiled nobles at Dazaifu; Sanjō Sanetomi and the others had long considered Iwakura an unprincipled turncoat who secretly favored the bakufu cause, and their loyalist rōnin followers had threatened his life constantly. Iwakura repaired his fences with Dazaifu through the mediation of Nakaoka Shintarō and Sakamoto Ryōma.[33] When these men became convinced of his ability and sincerity, they brought the word to Sanjō at Dazaifu.[34]

After his standing in the loyalist camp improved, Iwakura did his best to win influence at Kyoto. His two most important contacts were Nakayama Tadayasu, maternal grandfather of the young Emperor Mutsuhito, and Nakamikado Keishi. Since his

---

[32] *Sakamoto monjo*, I, 418.

[33] It is worth noting that Nakaoka, on a visit to Iwakura in the summer of 1867, brought as gift a copy of Fukuzawa's *Conditions in the West*, a book he had first read himself.

[34] For these negotiations, *Hirao, Rikuentai shimatsu ki*, pp. 245-250. Also *Ishin shi*, IV, 687.

advice had to be extended largely through letters, Iwakura employed as assistant a Shintō scholar, Tamamatsu Misao, to write his papers for him.[35] He then began sending vigorously argued analyses of the political situation to his friends at court. In these he did his best to build up court support for Satsuma and Chōshū as the best instruments of punishment of the bakufu. Although his progress was slow, since the top court officials were securely on Keiki's side, Iwakura gradually gained in influence and boldness. His papers presented ideas for a new government with considerable detail, and Tamamatsu worked out for him a model that was based as much as possible on the days of the legendary Jimmu. After Iwakura showed this to his Chōshū and Satsuma contacts, they took steps to see that the standards and flags described were ready for use by the eventual "Imperial" army.

On November 4, the day Sakamoto reached Kyoto, and while the Shogun was still considering the Tosa request, the Satsuma leaders sent word to Iwakura asking that he and his supporters at court draw up an Imperial decree ordering "loyal" daimyō to attack the bakufu. Iwakura commissioned Tamamatsu to draft this. The document contrasted Japan's awkward governing system with the progressive systems in effect elsewhere in the world, and stressed the need of a basic revision of Japan's government. It went on to point out that the bakufu institutions were out of harmony with Japan's true national traditions, and ended by authorizing the punitive campaign. Iwakura, Nakayama, and Nakamikado proceeded to secure approval of this from the boy Emperor. Nakayama, who had easy access to young Mutsuhito, secured his seal on the document, and it was carefully smuggled out of the court under the nose of the watchful bakufu.[36] Together with a decree restoring the Chōshū lord to favor, these documents were delivered to Ōkubo (for Satsuma) and Hirozawa (for Chōshū) on the ninth of November.[37]

These preparations were not quite as secret as the conspirators wished, for word of them reached the bakufu and helped to speed

---

[35] Tamamatsu (1810-1872) was a member of a Kyoto family and had studied under a national scholar (*Kokugakusha*) named Okuni Furumasa. He was a fervent loyalist, and his personal bent may have been reflected in a number of the papers he wrote for Iwakura.

[36] An equally good case can be made out for the proposition that the Emperor never saw the decree, and that the entire maneuver was a fabrication disguised as loyalty by later official historians. See Tōyama Shigeki, *Meiji Ishin*, p. 206.

[37] *Ishin shi*, IV, 692, 706ff.

Keiki's decision. Keiki's councillors were far from enthusiastic about the Tosa program. Some, like Oguri Tadamasa, still favored complete reliance upon French aid they thought was available. Even those who opposed war were uncertain about the details of the Tosa proposition. Matsudaira Shungaku, for instance, despite his part in the development of just such a solution, now wondered whether the conciliar government the Tosa memorial proposed would not be too different and too Western to fit Japanese needs. Would it not, he asked in a letter to Itakura, produce parties and confusion, rather than unity and direction? On the other hand, men like Katsu Rintarō and Nagai Naomune endorsed the proposal heartily, confident that cooperation now would reap rich dividends in power and influence later.[38]

Keiki, under the pressure of assurances relayed from Gotō by Nagai that war could not long be delayed, finally summoned all daimyō and important han officials in Kyoto to his Nijō castle on November 8, the day before Iwakura's edict reached Satsuma. Gotō was among those who were summoned, and he went conscious that the die was cast. Sakamoto wrote him when he heard that a meeting was scheduled, assuring him excitedly that he and his handful of Kaientai stalwarts stood prepared to defend him with their lives and to die in an assault upon the bakufu if the shogun should fail to resign his powers.[39]

Later that same day Gotō sent a hasty note to Sakamoto. "I have just returned from the palace . . . ," he said. "The shogun indicated to us his intention of handing over his administrative powers to the throne, and tomorrow he will petition the Court to this effect. Henceforth there will be a council chamber with an upper and a lower house. . . . Truly this is the event of a millennium; I could not delay in telling you of it, for nothing could cause more rejoicing in the country. . . ."[40]

The meeting had been a quiet one. Keiki had indicated his plans to those assembled, and they had filed out without comment or expression. The only men who had stayed behind to thank Keiki for his sacrifice and laud him for his courage were Komatsu of Satsuma, Gotō and Fukuoka from Tosa, Tsuji from

---

[38] For Keiki's deliberations, *Keiki Kō den*, IV, 79ff.
[39] *Sakamoto monjo*, I, 419.
[40] *ibid.*, p. 420.

Hiroshima, and the representatives of Uwajima and Bizen. Enthusiasm for Keiki's nobility and bearing ran high even among the *shishi* in that time, and Sakamoto wrote of his readiness to die for so great a man.[41]

The Imperial court received Keiki's petition on November 9. Although he had accepted the office of shogun, Keiki wrote, his "government and his administration of justice have not a little been at fault. The situation of the present day is ultimately due to his deficiency in virtue, for which he is filled with humiliation." Intercourse with the outside world made it essential to have a unified government, and therefore he deemed it his duty to return his political powers, to seek the opinion of the country, "and to protect the land in common accord with all."[42] It will be seen that Keiki was resigning his powers but not renouncing his influence.

On the same day the "Imperial" rescript that had been prepared at Iwakura's behest authorizing force against the bakufu was transmitted to Satsuma and Chōshū. Saigō, Ōkubo, and Komatsu sped to Kagoshima. On the way the Satsuma leaders conferred in Yamaguchi in order to coordinate with their Chōshū counterparts plans for the military action that was to follow. Once in Kagoshima, they persuaded their lord to return to the capital. The nominal daimyō, Tadayoshi, left Kagoshima on December 8 with three thousand troops. After a stop in Chōshū, he reached Kyoto on December 18. By then formidable bodies of Chōshū troops had also disembarked at Nishinomiya, within striking distance of Kyoto.

Like his Satsuma counterparts, Gotō rushed to Tosa to urge Yōdō to return to Kyoto. In view of the uncertainty that continued at the capital, however, Yōdō's retainers were divided as to the course he should follow. In particular, his conservative vassals opposed his departure from Kōchi strenuously. In a long memorial that may stand as the final expression of the conservative vested interest in Tosa, they criticized the entire drama that was taking place in Kyoto as one staged by extremists and upstarts, men who dealt with fugitives and rōnin. But Yōdō, after some

[41] Hirao, *Kaientai*, pp. 259-260.
[42] Translated in Asakawa, *The Documents of Iriki*, p. 377.

hesitation, decided he should go. He reached Kyoto on January 2, 1868.[43]

Gotō returned earlier, as did Saigō and Ōkubo. The Satsuma leaders were dismayed to find that the political confusion in Kyoto was so great that their allies at court had decided to ask them to return the rescript they had prepared calling for punishment of the Tokugawa. Keiki's decision to resign his special powers had created more confusion than it had solved. He had been told by the court to continue to defend and protect the realm, and to defer all decisions until a conference of daimyō could be convened. The document was sufficiently obscure and ambiguous to require a request for clarification from Keiki. When he became suspicious that he was being given responsibility without authority, he sent in his resignation as shogun also. By that time about fifty daimyō were in Kyoto, and it seemed possible to hold a conference. But the court, which was still dominated by officials accustomed to looking to the bakufu for direction, was full of uncertainty. It seemed likely that Keiki would indeed dominate the conference that had to be called, and this was exactly what the Satsuma leaders did not want.

It was against this background that Ōkubo, Saigō, and Iwakura laid their final plans. They agreed they would have to act soon if they were to stage a successful coup at Kyoto. Not until December 27 did they reveal to Gotō and Teramura their plans for the future; Teramura's diary records the shock of the Tosa leaders at their discovery of the way in which it was planned to humble the former shogun. The court offices which had been the channels for communication between the bakufu and Kyoto for two centuries, and which were staffed with bakufu supporters, were to be abolished and their incumbents dismissed. Other channels for shogunal control and information in Kyoto were also to disappear. A coup was to replace the Tokugawa guards on the Imperial palace gates with troops of Tosa, Satsuma, Hiroshima, Echizen, and Owari. Most important of all, the Tokugawa would have to surrender their lands to the throne and receive a new allotment, vastly smaller, from the new regime. Prince Arisugawa would be made head of a temporary government.[44]

Keiki's surrender was thus going to be much greater than any

[43] Hirao, *Yōdō Kō ki*, p. 266.
[44] Teramura Sazen, p. 501.

Gotō, Yōdō, or Sakamoto had intended. His authority was to be peeled off in the order in which it had developed. The outer layer, administrative authority, he had already given up, confident of a role in any new organization that might be worked out. Then, aware that he might be placed in a false position, he had added his resignation as shogun, a title his ancestors had won with the sword. This too was dispensable, for the ties that bound his vassals to him could survive the loss of his title. The one thing essential to him was continued presence in the ranks of the powerful barons. If this were ruled out, his fate would be sealed. And that was precisely what Iwakura, Saigō, and Ōkubo had in mind.

Gotō searched vainly for some way of combatting this plan. Execution was originally set for January 2, and he persuaded the plotters to delay a day until the arrival of Yamauchi Yōdō. But that was his only success.

On the eve of the coup d'état a small meeting was held at the residence of Iwakura Tomomi. Representatives of Satsuma, Tosa, Hiroshima, Echizen, and Owari heard the final plans, and agreed to provide the troop units needed for the military phase. After preparations were complete, Iwakura went to the palace in the pre-dawn hours of January 3 to secure the young Emperor's approval. Simultaneously troops of the han represented in the meeting moved in to seize the gates of the Imperial palace. Then, after a few carefully selected nobles, daimyō, and councillors had been admitted, the young Emperor appeared before them to read a proclamation that the old order had been restored. The Tokugawa regime was officially at an end.

Yamauchi Yōdō was dismayed by the course events had taken. He feared that a general war might be ignited, and he felt an injustice was being done to Keiki. In the conferences that followed Yōdō protested vigorously against the severity of the plans for Tokugawa Keiki, and for a time he won Echizen and Owari to his side. He was checked only after Saigō and Iwakura let it be known that Yōdō was not likely to survive further obstruction to their will. When this news reached Gotō Shōjirō and Fukuoka Kōtei, they dissuaded their lord from further protest. In swift succession the program that had shocked Gotō and Teramura so recently was then enacted. A new government, under the leadership of an Imperial prince and staffed by members of the groups represented in Iwakura's house that night, and supported by the armed might of Satsuma, Chōshū, and Tosa, began to take shape.

Keiki was fearful that his angry vassals would precipitate a ruinous civil war, and therefore he retired to Osaka to remonstrate with the court from a distance. The loyalists were now able to denounce him for disobedience.

In Osaka Keiki received Leon Roches in an audience interrupted by Sir Harry Parkes, who claimed priority on the ground of superior diplomatic rank. Keiki explained to the two envoys that he had been the victim of a stratagem. Satow, who was present as interpreter, noted Keiki's feeling that the proposal of a congress had been intended only to throw dust in his eyes. The proclamations of the new government, Keiki said, had been "a pre-concocted matter; they had it all ready on paper, and took these measures without consulting anyone." "One could not, but pity him," Satow writes, "so changed as he was from the proud, handsome man of last May. Now he looked thin and worn, and his voice had a sad tone."[45]

On January 27 Keiki yielded to the insistence of his vassals and tried to reenter Kyoto with a strong force. In the fighting that followed the Tokugawa troops were defeated, and with this battle of Fushimi the war against the Tokugawa began. On the whole, however, the war was not waged with the vigor the Tokugawa forces could have mustered, for Keiki had little enthusiasm for war. Edo was surrendered without a battle after conferences between Katsu Rintarō, for the Tokugawa, and Saigō, for the Imperialist forces—the same two who had worked out the compromise settlement for the first Chōshū expedition. At the Aizu keep of Wakamatsu, bitter last-ditch resistance by Tokugawa partisans made Itagaki Taisuke, who led the loyalist forces, a popular hero. The fighting on Honshu was over early in the fall of 1868, and the last resistance on Hokkaido, where the Tokugawa navy held out, ended in June of 1869.

Before the war was more than launched, however, and while the support of all factions was most desperately needed by the new regime, the court issued the famous "Charter Oath" in April 1868. This incorporated once again the principal features of the Tosa program of the previous year. Its drafts were the product of collaboration between Yuri Kimimasa of Echizen, Fukuoka Kōtei of Tosa, and Kido Kōin of Chōshū. All three had been influenced by and had influenced Sakamoto, and the language they used

---

[45] *Diplomat*, p. 302.

continued the terminology already familiar in the earlier programs.

1. Assemblies shall be widely convoked and all measures shall be decided by open discussion.

2. The government and the governed shall be of one mind, and the national economy and finances shall be greatly strengthened.

3. Civil and military officials as well as the common people shall achieve their aims, and thus the people's minds shall not grow weary.

4. All absurd customs of olden times shall be abandoned, and all actions shall be based on international usage.

5. Knowledge shall be sought for all over the world, and thereby the foundations of Imperial rule shall be strengthened.[46]

These promises of "assemblies" and government decisions by "open discussion," a state in which all classes would be united and free to "achieve their aims," were evocative of the language of the proposals of Sakamoto and Gotō, while the concluding intentions of doing away with "absurd customs of olden times" in favor of procedures "based upon international usage," and of seeking knowledge throughout the world in order to strengthen the "foundation of Imperial rule," were in harmony with almost every draft plan of the last months of Tokugawa days. Thus the new regime, during the uncertainty and distrust attendant upon a military campaign that many feared would lead to a new military despotism, found it prudent to revert to some of the promises of government by agreement that had been used by Gotō and Sakamoto to win over the bakufu itself.[47] In so doing it also provided an authorization for more responsible government that would be invoked by the makers of Japan's modern constitutions.

4. Sakamoto and the New Government

Sakamoto and Nakaoka did not live to see the Meiji government come into existence. During the uncertainty that followed

[46] Of many versions I have used that of Nobutaka Ike, *The Beginnings of Political Democracy in Japan* (Baltimore, 1950), p. 36.

[47] This purpose of the Charter Oath is emphasized by Tōyama Shigeki, *Meiji Ishin*, p. 228.

the shogun's resignation, suspicion and hate flared in Kyoto. Disorder accompanied the uncertainty as men tried to settle old scores, and the two Tosa men were among its victims. They had little part in the political maneuvering that followed Keiki's resignation, and they did not long outlive it. There is little record of Nakaoka's work in those weeks; he was still head of his Rikuentai, and still preparing for war against the Tokugawa. There is better material for Sakamoto, and it is useful to piece this together with a view to understanding the way he saw the future of Japanese politics. In doing so one is struck again by the rapidity with which radical solutions became first acceptable and then taken for granted. For while there is evidence that Sakamoto thought of Keiki as holding a high position in a new administrative structure based upon the feudal society of his day, there is also evidence that his thinking was moving in the direction of a post-feudal and more modern society by the time of his death.

After it was certain that Keiki was surrendering his powers, a group of Sakamoto's cronies gathered at his Kyoto inn to discuss the form of the new government. Sakamoto seems to have held for a regime headed by a kampaku (the ancient court office once utilized by the Fujiwara and subsequently controlled by the shogunate). Under him would be *gisō*, selected from among princes, nobles, and barons of vision and integrity. These men, he thought, would head the ministries of the regime. Sakamoto seems to have assumed that the lords of the great southwestern fiefs (Shimazu, Mōri, Yamauchi, Date, Nabeshima) and leading nobles (Iwakura, Higashikuze, Saga, Nakayama) would fill these posts. In other words, the principal actors of the decade would continue to dominate the scene. And if, as rumor had it, Sakamoto thought of Keiki as kampaku, then his initial plans were modest indeed. Sakamoto and his friends added to these names a group of councillors, or *sangi*. These men would head government departments at the assistant minister level. Ozaki, one of the participants in the conference, reports general agreement on names like Komatsu Tatewaki, Saigō, and Ōkubo of Satsuma, Kido of Chōshū, Gotō and Sakamoto of Tosa, and Yuri Kimimasa and Yokoi Shōnan of Echizen. Thus Sakamoto would himself have emerged as a member of this strategic group. The Tosa enthusiasts for military action

against the bakufu (Itagaki and Nakaoka) as well as Sanjō Sanetomi were not mentioned.[48]

The new regime as announced in January went much farther
than these plans. The ancient titles of kampaku and gisō, long
limited to certain families and associated with subservience to the
Tokugawa, were abolished. The title sangi was utilized, however,
and for a time the Restoration leaders used it to guide their superiors who held the higher posts.[49]

During the next few weeks, while the main actors in the drama
travelled to Satsuma, Chōshū, and Tosa to bring their lords up to
date, Sakamoto had time to do some planning of his own. In a
letter to his brother he explained his silence by saying that he was
"working day and night for our country."[50]

On November 26, 1867, Sakamoto left Kyoto to visit the Echizen
castle town of Fukui. His purpose was to visit one of the most
able young samurai of Matsudaira Shungaku's fief, Yuri Kimimasa.
Yuri had been in detention since the fall of 1863, allegedly for
overstepping his authority during a mission to Satsuma, but actually because of the dislike the conservative han leaders had for
him. Sakamoto came accompanied by a Tosa metsuke, and the
Echizen officials considered his visit sufficiently important to justify a relaxation in Yuri's restrictions. He was allowed to go to Sakamoto's inn in the company of police officials, and the two men
talked with the Tosa and Echizen metsuke sitting with them.
Sakamoto considered Yuri a finance expert, and he had come to
discuss economic problems of the new regime. The conversation
opened with Sakamoto's explanation that the form of the new government was not yet certain, and that a war might still break out.
If the former bakufu refused to cooperate, he said, the Restoration
leaders were prepared to fight. Unfortunately, the Imperial government had neither money nor military strength, and it could
expect to attract confidence and support only by developing these.
He wanted Yuri's advice. Yuri argued that if the Son of Heaven
ruled, then he had a right to the riches of his subjects, especially
in the cause of their safety and security; wealth, in this sense, was
an instrument to be used for the general security. The best way to

[48] From notes by Ozaki Saburō. *Sakamoto monjo,* I, 414-415.
[49] For the titles used by the early Meiji government, Robert Wilson, *Genesis of
the Meiji Government in Japan, 1868-1871.* Univ. of Calif. Press, Berkeley, 1957.
[50] *Sakamoto monjo,* I, 425.

raise money quickly, he thought, was to issue gold certificates, and he recommended this course of action. Yuri later wrote that Sakamoto was grateful for such useful advice.[51] Sakamoto's high appraisal of Yuri's talents may have played a part in Yuri's appointment to a finance ministry appointment in the new Meiji government soon afterward.

On his way back to Kyoto Sakamoto worked out a new eight-point program for the new government. This was to be his last piece of political programming. Its points were as follows:

1. The most able men in the country should be invited to become councillors.

2. The most able lords should be selected and given court positions, and the meaningless titles of the present should be set aside.

3. Relations with foreign countries should be carried out after proper deliberation.

4. Laws and regulations should be drawn up. When a new code, free of weaknesses, has been agreed upon, the lords should abide by it and have their subordinates implement it.

5. There should be an upper and a lower deliberative assembly.

6. There should be an army and a navy ministry.

7. There should be an Imperial guard.

8. The Imperial country should bring its valuation of gold and silver into line with international usage.

These points should be taken up with two or three of the most able and far-seeing samurai; then, when the time for the conference of lords comes, (x) should become head of the conference and respectfully suggest to the court that these steps be proclaimed to the people; whoever then protests disrespectfully against such decisions should be resolutely punished, and no deals should be made with the powerful or the nobles.[52]

It is usually thought that Sakamoto intended for Yōdō to play

[51] Mioka Takeo, *Yuri Kimimasa den* (Tokyo, 1916), pp. 125-128, gives Yuri's account of the talks. Some interesting sidelights on Yuri's difficulties in these years can be seen in the account of an American who went to Fukui to teach. W. Griffis, *The Mikado's Empire* (New York, 1871), Book II, "Personal Experiences."
[52] *Sakamoto monjo*, I, 427-428.

the role he marked out for "x." The strong insistence in these eight points for a public statement laying down the general principles of equity and common sense that were to prevail in the reorganization of Japan is clearly related to the purpose and content of the Charter Oath which was issued during the spring of 1868. And, it will be recalled, it was Yuri Kimimasa who drew up the first version of that oath. Since this program, in Sakamoto's own hand, has survived into recent times, there is little question of the general trend of his thought. He envisaged a system in which particularly able lords, beginning with his own, would replace the powerless functionaries of the old court system. But the power of the lords would be transitional, and moderated immediately by the selection of "men of talent," among whom Sakamoto and his comrades must inevitably have included themselves. It would also have been limited permanently by the workings of a deliberative assembly which would operate under a system of law selected more for applicability than for tradition. Finally, an Imperial guard and Imperial military and naval strength would work to limit, and, if necessary, punish, any efforts that might be made to frustrate these plans in the name of local autonomy. The national armed forces would be used to chastise any who were so blind or so discourteous as to obstruct the new regime.

There is one other index to Sakamoto's thinking in the days after Keiki's resignation. An unfinished pamphlet entitled *Hanron*, "Discussion of the fiefs," is usually considered a product of Sakamoto's mind, if not his brush. The attribution to Sakamoto is not certain, but there seems little doubt that the work can serve as an indication of the sort of thinking that Sakamoto and his friends were doing,[53] and it most probably represents Mutsu Munemitsu's recollection of Sakamoto's conversation.

[53] For years *Hanron* was known only through the translation which the Yokohama British Consul General, J. Carey Hall, made for Harry Parkes. This was reprinted in the *Japan Chronicle* for June 21, 1911, and again by Chikami, *Sakamoto Ryōma* (1914), who noted that no original survived. Since attribution was so uncertain, the editors of Sakamoto's papers decided against including it in their volumes. In the 1930's Osatake discovered an original of the document (struck from a wood block and marked "Two hundred copies"), which he republished in *Tosa shidan*, 46 (1934). This was dated 1868 and bore the initials Y. M. In his section on Sakamoto in *Bakumatsu Ishin no jimbutsu* (1935) Osatake states his reasons for accepting this as a work by Sakamoto. Its preface begins with the statement that "an old friend of mine in a certain han discussed the problems of the fiefs with me, and what I have written is his opinion." The friend in question,

Hanron begins with a general discussion of problems arising from the Restoration. There is, it notes, a general agreement that changes should be made, but no agreement as to what is needed or how it should be introduced. There are those who are swept by every current tide and who "glance hurriedly into Japanese translations of European works, or question those who have crossed the seas as to social institutions of the West," contrasted to others who are bound by what they have read in historical writings and who try to turn the clock back to antiquity. Unfortunately, few are aware of the meaning of history and of the times in which they live. What is needed is the ability to sense the spirit of the age and to foresee whether movements will succeed or fail. Indeed, the pamphlet notes, there have been only two great examples in Japanese history of men with this ability. In the fourteenth century Kusunoki Masashige, the loyalist hero, realized the futility of his cause and died by his own hand. More recently, the shogun realized the impossibility of his position and voluntarily resigned his powers.

It is time, the pamphlet continues, that national affairs are decided on the basis of a broad consensus. The same ought to be true of affairs within the fiefs. "The rule which applies to the government of the Empire is fully as applicable to the government of the feudal domains." Bad government is inexcusable, however lofty its source; good government is that which is subject to the approval of public opinion.

The pamphlet has much to say about the injustice of hereditary rank. By what right, it asks, does a lazy, thoughtless man come into power and authority? Most of the feudal lords have been born to sloth and luxury, and even when they reach maturity they still show childish traits of irresponsibility and selfishness. In their magnificent garments they do not feel the winter wind, and they neither know nor care if people are dying of starvation and cold. Far from recognizing the significance of their times, they are intent upon self-gratification. And this is true not only of the barons, but also of their chief retainers.

---

it goes on, circulated his views among his comrades in "his company." Hirao Michio, who reprints Osatake's copy in his *Kaientai* (1941), suggests the Y. M. be taken as Mutsu Munemitsu (then Yonosuke), who was from Kii and a member of the Kaientai. But it remains possible that Sakamoto's secretary, Nagaoka Kenkichi, a man with a good deal of Western learning, was the "friend" in question.

"Offices are constantly filled by unqualified men, and corruption is so rife as to defy all attempts to suppress it."

But the author of *Hanron* is no populist. He agrees that the lower ranks are for the most part stupid, shortsighted, and easily discouraged. They prefer the easy way out, and under direct representation they would vote for friends instead of sages. The way to deal with this is through a system of indirect representation, a "system which is followed in other countries." In every fief, the lord should first inform his retainers that "old customs are going to be abolished and an entirely new system is going to be inaugurated." Old ties of obligations will then be broken, and a new compact can be entered into by all the vassals who meet on an equal footing. This done, the lords can end the whole system of inherited rank and income, and "dismiss at one stroke the entire body of officers, regardless of seniority."

The newly homogeneous community of retainers should then select its own leaders according to a ratio of offices to numbers which is first worked out. From those selected in the first ballot will come the constituency for the second and more important vote, as elected electors select the most able and worthy leaders. Thereby the dangers of popular dolts achieving leadership will be kept to a minimum. And, the author goes on, after this is done the commoners themselves ought to select their leaders similarly for the more humble tasks of everyday life. Here the pamphlet breaks off, with the promise to take up further points in future sections.

Hanron is a document of extraordinary interest. Many things suggest that the attribution to Sakamoto is sound. The high praise for Keiki is easily reconcilable with the reverence with which Sakamoto regarded him at the time of his resignation. Stories of faithful retainers who have suffered punishment for reform attempts put one in mind of Yuri Kimimasa and other of Sakamoto's friends. The contempt for the privileged orders at the top of the feudal hierarchy recalls the line of protest that distinguished the Tosa Loyalist Party of Takechi Zuizan, and the irreverent attitude which Sakamoto had long shown as a rōnin, free of normal obligations and respect for authority. The seizure of the device for indirect representation as a solution to the problem of feudal office shows again the quick receptivity which

Sakamoto and his friends showed for foreign ideas and institutions that offered solutions for immediate problems.

But the things that *Hanron* does not say are equally interesting. There is no explicit mention of an end to the feudal order, although the revisions in rank and office that are discussed would certainly have sounded its death knell before very long. Nor does the pamphlet say very much about the Imperial system; indeed, it says, bad government is inexcusable, even if it comes from the Mikado. Emperor worship was slow to grow in the first months of the Meiji period, and Gotō even reported to Satow that some "were afraid that the extremists might go further and abolish the Mikado."[54]

Even without radicalism of this order, however, the type of thinking represented in *Hanron* would have made difficult the type of Satsuma-Chōshū oligarchic control that proved so objectionable to Tosa leaders in the years that followed. It may be suggested that the pamphlet represents a late statement of the position of the low-ranking warriors for whom entrenched privilege was still the principal problem. After the feudal hierarchy had crumbled, this sort of enthusiasm for Western representative institutions temporarily lessened, only to revive as Iwakura and his friends invoked the increasingly sacred name of the Meiji Emperor to fasten their own rule upon the country. When the form of the new political monopoly became evident, the language used here by Sakamoto Ryōma and his friends to protest against entrenched privilege would be utilized by his feudal superiors, Itagaki and Gotō, in renewed demands for a legislative chamber.

5. *The Warriors Become* KAMI

In the midst of this programming, almost a month before the coup that replaced the shogun's guards at the Imperial palace and before the Satsuma leaders had returned to Kyōto, Sakamoto and Nakaoka were slain in their inn. An attack similar to the one he survived at Fushimi found Sakamoto unprepared to meet his assailants; this time no friendly hotel maid gave the warning that might have saved his life.

[54] Diplomat in Japan, p. 297. Satow says of the new offices as Gotō described them: "This looked rather what we had suggested to Gotō as the framework of the future executive."

Sakamoto returned to Kyoto from Fukui on November 30, 1867. He then began the meetings with his friends in which he worked out the eight-point plan for the new government, and he discussed, or wrote, the ideas contained in *Hanron*. Kyoto was still in a state of tremendous confusion. Rumors swept the city. Bakufu supporters were greatly, and, as it proved, justly concerned lest backstage plotting should cost pro-Tokugawa lords whatever influence remained to them. They were suspicious and resentful of all who had conspired against them, and few of those conspirators were better known or more reputed for their ability than Sakamoto. The units that had been organized to help police the capital were the most likely to seek to deal with upstarts and revolutionaries. One of these, the *Shinsengumi*, had been recruited from rōnin in Kyoto, while another, the *Mimawarigumi*, was made up of younger sons of Tokugawa retainers. The two organizations numbered several hundred by 1867. Organized to deal with rōnin plots, they were ruthless and efficient. It was from units of this sort that Sakamoto and his friends had experienced the greatest hostility and danger. Sakamoto's escape of a few years earlier from the Teradaya was by now a famous one, and many of his friends, among them Kido Kōin, warned him that bakufu agents were likely to make another attempt to kill or capture him. In recent scuffles in Kyoto the Shinsengumi had been hurt; its members, their pride aroused, were particularly aggressive and dangerous.

Sakamoto was aware of this, but his natural buoyancy and optimism made it difficult for him to keep his guard up very long. For a time his Kyoto headquarters had been at the shop of a soy sauce merchant on Kawaramachi, the Ōmiya. The proprietor provided Sakamoto with a rear room, above the storehouse, which had exits that permitted rapid flight to a nearby temple. After his return from Fukui, however, Sakamoto became ill with a cold and moved to a more accessible forward room to avoid the inconvenience of the other.

Here, on the evening of December 10, he was joined by Nakaoka Shintarō. The night was very cold. The two talked in Sakamoto's bedroom, seated on opposite sides of a hibachi, their faces bright with the light thrown on them by a small lamp next to the brazier. Sakamoto, who had recently been ill, was somewhat pale, Nakaoka vigorous and in the best of health. Two other men were present in the room, a follower of Nakaoka's and a hotel employee; Sakamoto's servant Tōkichi sat in the outer room. After a while Sakamoto asked one of the men to go out to get him something to eat. The other decided to accompany him, leaving Sakamoto and Nakaoka to continue their conversation.

Then came a knock below. Tōkichi answered the door. It was a stranger who identified himself as coming from Totsukawa, an area which produced revenue allocated to the Imperial court. Tōkichi, who knew that Sakamoto had contacts there, turned to take the visitor's card upstairs. By the time he came back to the stairway prepared to admit the visitor, three men had come upstairs without his leave. One of them cut Tōkichi down, while the other two rushed past him to attack Sakamoto and Nakaoka. Neither of them had a chance to unsheath his sword. Sakamoto was cut down first, with numerous and savage cuts in his head and face, body, and limbs. Nakaoka fared little better. He was less spectacularly wounded, but nevertheless mortally cut. He was still alive to explain what had happened when Tanaka Kōken, his second in command in the Rikuentai, arrived to find his friends lying in a pool of blood. Nakaoka's spirits and courage were still strong, but his strength ebbed rapidly. Tanaka tried to encourage him by reminding him of the miraculous recovery Inoue Kaoru had made after an assault in Chōshū, and he reminded him how necessary his role would be in the war that lay ahead, but it was to no avail. Nakaoka lingered on for two more days and breathed his last on the twelfth. He was twenty-nine, Sakamoto thirty-two.[55]

The *shishi* who gathered to mourn had quick thoughts of vengeance. In the Restoration wars the Shinsengumi and Mimawarigumi received short shrift when captured, but the details of Sakamoto's death were never fully learned. One of the men who had stood guard downstairs during the attack confessed his part in 1870 and was placed under domiciliary confinement in Shizuoka. Years later he wrote a long confession, but Tanaka and other *shishi* disputed its details because they seemed to conflict with the story they remembered. At any rate the full details of the decision and responsibility for the murders were never learned.[56]

[55] *Sakamoto monjo*, II, 357ff., for the details as recorded by those who were there and who investigated the murders.
[56] Hirao, *Kaientai*, pp. 274-275.

The Restoration leaders lamented the loss of both *shishi*. Iwakura particularly regretted the death of Nakaoka, but on the whole Sakamoto's warm and engaging personality won him more eulogies, as they had won him more friends. "Nakaoka was a sage," Tanaka Kōken wrote, "Sakamoto a real hero."[57] Kido Kōin wrote the epitaph for the two tombs in a temple graveyard in Kyoto's Higashiyama. From Dazaifu Sanjō Sanetomi sent the poetic tribute,

> The warriors are surrounded by their valor,
> And, as gods, they still protect the country.[58]

Sakamoto's evolution as a national hero furnishes an illuminating example of the development of modern Japanese nationalism. It did not come about overnight, for it required time and success at the difficult tasks of nation-building before those who had led the way could be appreciated for what they had helped bring about. When the time of appraisal arrived, Sakamoto was ideally equipped to share in the laurels. His romantic career and his buoyant, self-confident bearing and correspondence lent themselves extraordinarily well to the image the nation wished to hold of its Restoration *shishi*. A cluster of stories illustrating his quick intelligence, his practical bent, his indifference to position and power, his nonchalance in money matters, and his calm and casual bearing in time of danger, fitted him equally well for the roles of sage and warrior. Overgenerous attribution of a booklet entitled "Secret Writing of the Great General" is further indication of the popular image of Sakamoto, in that the confident and violently anti-Tokugawa sentiments expressed therein, and the insistence upon the importance of seizing opportunities as they arise, all seemed fully consistent with the career of the man.[59] At the same

[57] *Seizan Yoei*, p. 235.

[58] Hirao, *Kaientai*, p. 273.

[59] For a discussion of this work and its problems, see K. Shiomi, "Sakamoto Ryōma goroku to tsutaerareta *Ei Shō Hiki* ni tsuite," *Rekishi gaku kenkyū* (1957, 6), No. 208, pp. 39-41. The book was first reputed to be Sakamoto's in Chikami, *Sakamoto*, and Hirao Michio accepted it as such in an early work on the Kaientai. Later he rejected it, although, like most writers, he accepts Sasaki's judgment that it was the sort of thing Sakamoto might have done in the late years of Tokugawa rule and that some member of the Tosa circle probably penned it. Shiomi puts forward as proof of this the diary of an Aizu man who was assigned to mix with and spy on the rōnin, and who reports seeing a very secret and violently anti-Tokugawa pamphlet by this name.

time, Sakamoto's lack of involvement with the Meiji government or its opposition made him a hero in whose praise all could agree and unite.

The first biography of Sakamoto appeared in 1883, entitled *Biography of Sakamoto Ryōma, Our Country's Matchless Hero.* Half history and half fiction, it left everything for later scholarship, but it marked the first step in the creation of the popular image of Sakamoto. As Japanese national feeling and pride grew toward the end of the 1880's, Sakamoto's reputation was among those to benefit. In 1891 he was posthumously honored, as was Nakaoka, by an award of the Fourth Imperial Rank. From then on he figured prominently in fictionalized accounts of the Restoration. The memoirs of surviving Restoration leaders also gave him generous praise. He has been above all a Tosa hero, and his statue on Katsura bench, overlooking Urado Bay, symbolizes his role as maritime pioneer and national leader.

It remained for the Meiji Emperor's consort to give meaning to Sanjō's assertion that Sakamoto, as a kami, would continue to protect the country. Twice before the Japanese defeat of the Russian fleet in Tsushima Straits, the Empress dreamed that she saw Sakamoto. The second time he introduced himself in these words: "Your Majesty, this humble servant was born in Tosa and is named Sakamoto Ryōma. I pray Your Majesty may rest in peace, for I will take care, as far as my limited abilities allow, of the fate of the Imperial Navy."[60] Sakamoto's fame needed no new laurels, but with this assistance from the Imperial palace his place in legend was secure. The popular image of the courageous hero grew until it overshadowed the less spectacular deeds of the rōnin adventurer, but both are of compelling interest for the light they throw on the development of modern Japan.

[60] I have adapted the English wording given by Chikami, *Sakamoto*, introduction, iv-v. Chikami's biographer notes that the author knew English so well that he wrote both of his biographies (the other being of Napoleon) in English before reworking them in Japanese. *Zoku Tosa ijin den* (Kōchi, 1923), pp. 297-299.

IX. THE RESTORATION IN TOSA

*M*OST of the generalizations that have been applied to the Restoration period illustrate the difficulty and danger of generalizing from the pattern of one fief or one area. It would be even more unwise to base interpretations upon the experience of one man or one group of men. If such attempts were to be made, they should be based on trends in Satsuma or Chōshū, the fiefs which furnished the major drive for the Tokugawa defeat. The situation in Tosa was, in any event, extremely unusual. The ruling house was bound by feelings of great obligation to the Tokugawa; it was led by an able daimyō who knew his mind, and he, in turn, was served by a hierarchy of vassals and retainers many of whom, still rooted in the countryside, traced their lineage back to the pre-Tokugawa days of Chōsogabe. This was a situation not to be duplicated elsewhere in Japan. But even after these disclaimers for Tosa have been made, it will remain useful to relate the intellectual and social trends experienced by Sakamoto and Nakaoka to those that followed their death in order to see the degree to which their development may have been representative and prophetic of the broader national scene in which the restoration of Imperial rule was only the beginning, and not the culmination, of revolutionary changes.

1. The Stages of Response to the West

At the outset it will be well to restate the assertion made earlier, that the outstanding intellectual and political experience in the formative years of the Restoration activists was the discovery that their society was incapable of successful resistance to the Western threat. This should not be taken to mean that the Western threat was the only, or even the chief, factor in the changes which followed the coming of Perry. Intellectual trends had prepared the way for discrediting the political and social order of Tokugawa days. The emphasis on Confucian teachings of loyalty that the *gōshi* and *shōya* sons received in the private academies tended to combine with their resentment of inferiority to provide much of the raw material for men prepared to strike out for a new political order and opportunity. But the fact remains that these conditions had long been present, and that it was the Western threat that precipitated them into action by posing danger to the sacred country and to the Imperial tranquility. Preconditions for resentment and reaction had long been present, but legitimate justification for action lay in the assumed priority of larger and higher goals. The activity of Restoration days was never justified in terms of a particular social resentment, but was at all times professedly "selfless" and idealistic. These energies developed according to the schedule determined by the interaction of foreign and domestic strains. What began as anti-foreignism continued as anti-Tokugawa agitation, and ended, in *Hanron*, as anti-feudal sentiment. The justification of most of this, in terms of Imperial well-being, was reasonably constant, and the language and terminology were astonishingly consistent. Nevertheless there were substantial changes of content that lay beneath the phrases, changes that derived from a new awareness of what was at stake in the world and what was wrong in Japan.

In the case of Sakamoto, there were four stages whereby he became aware of the significance of the Western problem. The first of these began with the arrival of Perry's flotilla, and it continued through the approval of Harris' commercial treaty by Ii Naosuke. These days when no young man of spirit and ambition could have failed to be conscious of the crisis that faced the country. Urgent defense measures called the samurai back to their profession of arms. In Tosa there was the development of the People's Corps, emergency levies which included commoners and which were commanded by *gōshi*. Everywhere in the han an emphasis on fencing helped to channel the indignation and the ambition of youths into the pursuit of excellence in traditional arms. Sakamoto, who had been sent to Edo for special work in swordsmanship and who met there the most vigorous and active members of his class and generation, was naturally swept up into the enthusiasm and resentment of the decade; it was as natural for him to promise his family that he would not return home without having struck off a foreign head as it was to join with his counterparts from other areas of Tosa and from other fiefs in discussing measures that should be taken to drive out the foreigners.

Within Tosa, during the same years, Yamauchi Yōdō sought, by backing the proposals and protégés of Yoshida Tōyō, to build political, military, and economic strength so that his realm could improve its standing relative to its neighbors in the years that lay ahead. It was thus a period that restored the han, and many of its retainers, to life. The bakufu's consciousness of weakness, expressed in requests for advice, activated the daimyō. The long-standing prohibitions on contacts between fiefs, which had been built up to guard against combinations inimical to the Tokugawa, seemed to bear little relevance to the need for united effort and planning against the outside world. Bakufu moderates like Abe Masahiro encouraged such trends at the outset. As a result the great tozama daimyō, Yōdō among them, dared to put forth proposals affecting even the shogunal succession by the end of the decade. But it was also a time in which information was still hard to come by; wisdom was concentrated in few hands. The old guard of han office-holders, wedded to their privileges, had little interest or, if one believes their critics, ability to adjust to the problem; and the low-ranking members of the samurai class, cut off from realistic estimates of barbarian strength and capabilities and subject only to calls for vigilance and militancy, had no consciousness of the complexity of the problems that their betters faced. Reforming bureaucrats like Yoshida Tōyō were therefore vulnerable to criticism and attack unless they had the strong backing of an able and an active lord. At the end of the period Ii Naosuke removed this protection and restraint by punishing Yōdō for his part in efforts to swing the shogunal succession to Hitotsubashi Keiki.

The second period of Sakamoto's response began with the murder of Ii Naosuke in 1860. In the rising tide of fury against the bakufu and its policies for admitting the foreigners and punishing Yōdō, the young swordsmen, Sakamoto among them, developed hopes for a cooperative program with their counterparts in Satsuma and Chōshū which might force the bakufu to pay more honor to the court and to act on the Emperor's presumedly anti-foreign desires. This was the period in which Takechi Zuizan and his Loyalist Party emerged. Their extremism fed on the vacillation which the bakufu showed before the growing ambition of its future adversaries. The young loyalists were stimulated by the competition between Satsuma and Chōshū for sponsorship of the Imperial cause against the Tokugawa, and their excitement was spurred on by Chōshū favor and kuge irresponsibility. The violence that Takechi and his men unleashed so casually would have been impossible without the ability of Chōshū and Tosa power to set at nothing (temporarily, at least) Tokugawa police forces, and without the enthusiasm and optimism of young court nobles like Sanjō Sanetomi and Anenokōji Kintomo, the extremists would have had a much more difficult time cloaking their assassinations with the authority of the Imperial will. But since they did have such support, they could claim to be absolutely pure in their motives; party names full of Righteousness and Enlightenment entitled them to unleash the Punishment of Heaven upon their political enemies. Theirs was a day of extremism and emotionalism, of heroism, ruthlessness, and cruelty. The lowly struck down their superiors or absconded from their control. Anti-foreignism was raised to the level of a cult and an ideology, and it sought its justification in the essence of the non-foreign, the sacred Emperor and land. Anti-foreignism still meant striking at the foreigners and at all who might be considered pro-foreign. It was a cause and not a tactic, espoused, in Tosa at least, by enthusiasts whose intellectual innocence permitted them the luxury of consistency and purity of ideology. It was in this mood that Sakamoto fled his home to join a rōnin rising and that Nakaoka deserted his family and responsibilities to rush to Edo to preserve Yōdō from whatever dangers he might face there. The crisis seemed to justify abandonment of normal goals and repudiation of nominal superiors, and it offered the opportunity to do great things for the country as well as for one's own fame and name. It made *shishi* of swordsmen; self-motivated and self-confident activists of what had been other-directed, respectful noncommissioned officers in the feudal hierarchy.

The third stage in this response to the West came with the discovery that the foreigners could not be driven from Japan by force; it led to the substitution of reason for emotion. While the activists had previously seen their problems with simple-minded directness, they now learned to develop a measure of sophistication and moderation. For many of them this transition had the aspects of a religious experience, one in which they were converted to a new way of thinking because of overpowering evidence of the inadequacy of their earlier ideas. The change did not come in the same way or at the same time for any two men. For some, a ride on a steamship brought enlightenment; for Inoue Kaoru it came when he saw the forest of masts of Western ships in the Shanghai harbor. For Sakamoto it came the night of his visit to Katsu Rintarō. Excited and tensed for the supreme effort he thought he would have to make, he was suddenly ready to accept the guidance and leadership of the man whose calm replies broke his will to fight. Not all the activists, of course, were so converted. Some went on to kill and be killed. But Sakamoto went on to serve his Tokugawa sponsor in hopes of strengthening the national defense. In the course of his duties he made the contacts and gained the experience that made him such an important figure in late-Tokugawa days. Nakaoka, for his part, shared the dangers and discoveries of the Chōshū loyalists, and gradually came to the conclusion that the foreigners were to be dealt with only after a period of borrowing and learning. Jōi, he now realized, had been practiced elsewhere by men of patience and will; if Washington had waited until he had the armed strength to drive out the English barbarians, the Japanese too should be able to wait until the moment appropriate to their cause arrived. This sudden ability to see the events of the day in broader, world-wide range and in historical depth made statesmen of the Tosa *shishi*.

While they were learning these lessons, their erstwhile associates in Tosa were falling victim to the counter-purge of Yamauchi Yōdō, with the result that those who failed to learn and grow diminished in number and in influence. Thereafter the Tosa administration, if it wished to tap loyalist energies and contacts for future participation in national politics, had to use Sakamoto and Nakaoka, for they alone of the original group had retained their freedom of maneuver and maintained their contacts outside the han. Meanwhile the reforms of the new leaders whom Yōdō had placed in power, reforms built upon a program of self-strengthening similar to the one worked out earlier by Yoshida Tōyō, meant that Tosa would have new strength and influence to offer future allies when once it returned to compete for national leadership.

Up to this point the phases of individual and group response in Tosa had been to a considerable degree the result of the appearance of the West. The fourth stage in the career of Sakamoto and Nakaoka, however, was largely a response to the bakufu. Tokugawa vacillation between moderation and force, opening and delay, had been of course a variable that affected earlier moods as well. But in 1864 the bakufu's pleasure with its apparent victories encouraged rash attempts to restore the powers that had been slipping away. Chōshū units had been driven from Kyoto the previous September, and subsequent effort to regain national leadership had brought that fief failure and new opprobrium as an "enemy of the court." The foreigners had helped by forcing Chōshū to capitulate. In possession of an Imperial mandate and enjoying the support of all its major vassals, the bakufu called for a military expedition against Chōshū. In the presence of a force greater than any they could muster, the Chōshū loyalist leaders who had been responsible for fief policy since 1862 capitulated, and they were replaced by conservatives who were willing to meet the bakufu terms. The Edo conservatives now thought they saw the way clear for a total recovery. They began to agitate for a new expedition and total humiliation for Chōshū. French help for a sweeping program of modernization seemed to offer hope of a new bakufu-dominated central government which could crush opposition in other areas as it would first have done in Chōshū. They also decided to revive the system of alternate attendance, the cornerstone of earlier Tokugawa control of the daimyō. And they decided that the councillors and officials who, during the period since 1862, had dealt with the lords of Satsuma, Uwajima, and Tosa as though they were equals instead of subordinates, could now be sacrificed. Matsudaira Shungaku and Hitotsubashi Keiki found that their influence was at an end unless they shifted their position to conform with the new "hard" line. The naval commissioner Katsu Rintarō, who had sheltered so many rōnin in his Hyōgo school, was dismissed. It was symbolic of the times that this dismissal shifted Sakamoto Ryōma from Tokugawa to Satsuma protection.

The last stage thus became one of economic and political planning to upset the bakufu. The men of the southwestern fiefs now began to think that if they did not act in time the bakufu would. They believed every story they heard about French assistance for the Tokugawa, and they realized the dangers that a second Chōshū expedition held for them. In this setting Sakamoto and Nakaoka helped to bring about the alliance between Satsuma and Chōshū, and Sakamoto's early Kaientai helped to cement the alliance by carrying grains and guns between Kagoshima, Shimonoseki, and Nagasaki. And then, as anti-Tokugawa feeling grew among the Satsuma and Chōshū leaders he knew, Sakamoto became a middleman for ideas as well as trade. Drawing on the things he had heard from Katsu Rintarō and Ōkubo Ichiō, ideas probably reinforced through his contacts with Yokoi Shōnan and men in Nagasaki, conversant with the West, he now drew up his eight-point program for a political system in which power would pass from the bakufu to a council of great lords; the shogun, as first among equals, would still wield great influence. These were ideas Sakamoto's Chōshū and Satsuma friends were not likely to sponsor, for they could aspire to inherit the Tokugawa role. Tosa could not. Since the Tosa leaders were now ready to reenter national politics, Sakamoto's program fitted their needs perfectly, and it became, with minor changes, the Tosa program.

Sakamoto and Nakaoka undoubtedly moved farther and faster than the majority of their contemporaries. But it is safe to say that the stages through which they passed were those through which their generation had to move. In other men and other areas the vacillation between submission and revolt was determined by the manner in which rank and power affected the risks which alternative courses seemed to hold, but the successive stages of indignation and of action were in large measure universal throughout Japan. And everywhere the increasing tempo of change in national politics had a way of rendering programs of reform obsolete almost before they could be implemented.

The Sakamoto who had passed through these stages had combined patriotism with ambition. Initiator of the proposal the last shogun had accepted, commander of the Kaientai, and widely praised and blamed as a mysterious contact man who counted for a great deal, he was as different from the young *gōshi* loyalist who fled Tosa in 1862 as *Hanron*, with its proposals for equality and elected officials, was from his early letters home to Tosa. Like so many of his generation, Sakamoto had exploited the opportunities to learn of and from the West with good effect.

It is impossible to read the literature of the period without being impressed by the influence exerted by the power and example of the West. Fukuzawa's famous little book *Seiyō Jijō* circulated in thousands of copies, and it was very close to being the textbook for an age. Its influence is visible in Sasaki and Nakaoka, and it was given as a present to nobles (Anenokōji and Iwakura) who were in need of enlightenment. An earlier interest in Western studies was by no means prerequisite to this readiness to learn from the West, although it naturally enabled men like Katsu to speak with particular authority.

The conviction of the need to reorganize Japan in such a way as to make possible effective utilization of Western technology was, indeed, so general among a small number of leaders that it seemed for a time a race between Satsuma-Chōshū and the bakufu, each determined to build national unity at the expense of the other. Bakufu leaders who, like Oguri Tadamasa, relied upon France, and Chōshū figures like Kido Kōin were in basic agreement as to what their society needed. The power and attraction of the West had created an astonishing degree of agreement on what was to be done.

It can not, of course, be maintained that men like Oguri could have succeeded in carving out their program. The bakufu reformers would have had much more to combat in the sense of vested interests, and their program would have run counter to, instead of benefiting from, the rising popularity of the Imperial cause that followed foreign penetration of the sacred land. Sakamoto's program, which became Tosa's, sought to bridge these two by giving the principal Tokugawa houses and the great domains equal representation in a new conciliar system. One suspects that this would have produced equity at the cost of the strong leadership that the times required. The experiments with representative institutions in early Meiji years suffered from the fact that the oligarchy was seldom disposed to share its real power with a council, but their failure was also owing to the fact that the consciousness of what needed to be done was still concentrated in too few hands, so that measures for reform continually ran afoul of local and personal interests. One suspects that Sakamoto's council, had it gone into effect, would soon have required steps by the leaders of the southwestern han to strengthen their authority. It may well be that the Tosa program gained, in retrospect, attraction from the fact that it was never really tried.

The war campaign against the Tokugawa solved the problem of Tokugawa conservative backers by defeating them, and it helped solve the leadership problem by revealing the degree to which the southwestern fiefs were controlled by the young reformers. It was fortunate for the Meiji reformers that so many of the men who had to be shoved aside like Yamauchi Yōdō and the shogun Keiki were in basic accord with their plans, and that they possessed a sense of history that enabled them to accept their own removal with calmness and dignity. The daimyō, Yōdō is quoted as saying,

were only in the way when it came to building a new Japan; he himself, after a short period of service in the new government, retired to a life of pleasure and died in 1874 at the age of 46.[1]

2. The Leaders and Their Aims

It is sometimes suggested that a sharp break should be made between the Restoration, with its goals of Return to Antiquity (*Fukkō*), and the Meiji Restoration which followed with its slogans of Enlightened Rule (*Meiji*) and Civilization and Enlightenment (*Bummei kaika*). From the fact that only a small number of leaders were fully aware of what was needed at the time of the Restoration, many of them soon to fall prey to assassins (Sakamoto, Nakaoka, Yokoi Shōnan, Ōmura Masujirō; Yokoi's assassins had hopes for Gotō Shōjirō as well), some writers suggest that a new group of bureaucratic leaders with, on the whole, new and more modern goals, replaced the earlier group. With a few exceptions, it is suggested, most of the Restoration men were concerned with a return to the past, while the next group were intent upon advancing into the future.[2] We may leave for others the application of this generalization to the national scene; was it true of Tosa?

In Tosa the distinction to be drawn is not between Restoration and Meiji leadership, but between obscurantist Loyalist and enlightened Restoration leaders. The former, as exemplified by Takechi Zuizan, seem to have held very little promise for the creation of a strong and modern nation-state. But they were dealt with by Yamauchi Yōdō long before the Restoration. A few, like Sakamoto and Nakaoka, managed to survive the shift and serve the han interest in the Restoration drama. But this Loyalist-Restoration change, it must be repeated, was quite another thing than the just-mentioned Restoration-Meiji shift. In Tosa there was a remarkable continuity in leadership and aims in the days after Sakamoto's death, and what change there was (as in Itagaki, who was still firmly anti-foreign in 1867) came about through education and not through assassination or replacement.

Tosa continued to be led by disciples of Yoshida Tōyō, men who had returned to activity after Yamauchi Yōdō resumed con-

[1] For Yōdō's opinions as reported by Gotō, *Hakushaku Gotō Shōjirō*, pp. 415-422.
[2] For a concise statement of this, Sakata Yoshio, "An Interpretation of the Meiji Reformation," Silver Jubilee Volume, Zinbun Kagaku Kenkyusyo, Kyoto, 1954.

trol of han affairs in 1863. They enjoyed the support and trust of Yōdō, who was able to control the conservatives, and they encountered little opposition from the old Loyalist groups, who had nowhere else to turn. Of this group Gotō Shōjirō, the best politician and the best manipulator, served for a time with distinction in the "national" government, as did Fukuoka Kōtei and several others. Yōdō himself, after his reluctant agreement to join the anti-Tokugawa war, was given a number of honorific positions and titles during the months when national unity was desperately needed for the war. He was successively Minister (*Gijō*), then head of the Ministry of Internal Affairs (together with Matsudaira Shungaku), and finally president of the upper house set up under the governmental reorganization of June 1868 (a plan close to the "Tosa program"), a function in which he supervised the drafting of some of Japan's first parliamentary codes. After the war was won and the need for support was less pressing, however, Ōkubo, Iwakura, and the other leaders of the faction that had forced the issue ended their experiments with the councils championed by the Tosa leaders, and they had less need for figureheads like Yōdō.

Gotō Shōjirō initially served in the new Department of Foreign Affairs with the title of Councillor (*Sanyo*), and he played an important part in the negotiations with the foreign powers in the months after the political turnover. He served also as governor of Osaka. It was largely at his urging that Edo was selected as the new capital (renamed Tōkyō September 3, 1868); thereafter he followed the new government to Tokyo. Fukuoka Kōtei, also named Sanyo, served in bureaus charged with the preparation of codes of law and institutional reorganization, and, together with Yuri Kimimasa of Echizen, helped draw up the Charter Oath of April 1868. Fukuoka also helped plan the reorganization of June 1868 (the *Seitaisho*, under which Yōdō served as head of the upper house), a task in which the planners used Fukuzawa's *Seiyō Jijō* as one of their sources for information about procedures in the West. But, as has been mentioned, these experiments with the Tosa program came to an end when the Tokugawa defeat made it possible to develop an all-powerful executive without fear of having dissidents rally to the bakufu cause.

It was Itagaki Taisuke who achieved the greatest fame in early Restoration days. After Yōdō agreed to commit Tosa troops to the war, Itagaki led the forces he had equipped and modernized north to the neighboring han of Takamatsu and Matsuyama, which capitulated, and then on to the island of Honshu for the major battles. Itagaki and his troops distinguished themselves particularly in the long and successful siege of the Aizu castle of Wakamatsu. He emerged from this campaign something of a national hero. Moreover, his experience in this last of Japan's feudal wars convinced him of the need for activating the commoners and developing in them a sense of participation in national affairs. The local farmers, he noted, took no part in the fighting, and observed the proceedings with perfect calm, intent only on selling as much food to either side as safety permitted. It was not very long after this that word from Europe acquainted Itagaki with the resistance the commoners in France had put up against the armies of Prussia, and the Tosa documents during the sweeping reforms of the next few years made much of the need to develop a spirit of patriotism like that of the French.

Itagaki's forces also provided opportunities for glory for other Tosa leaders; Tani Kanjō and Kataoka Kenkichi distinguished themselves in the army. At Kyoto Nakaoka Shintarō's lieutenant Tanaka Kōken led the Rikuentai detachment against the Tokugawa units. In Nagasaki Sasaki Takayaki organized Sakamoto's Kaientai men to seize the headquarters of the Tokugawa administrators there, and until the arrival of Matsukata Masayoshi of Satsuma, Sasaki held that important port city. Itagaki was by no means the only Tosa leader to take part in the wars, but he was certainly the most prominent of those who did so.

Upon conclusion of the fighting in northern Honshu, the Tosa han rewarded both Itagaki and Gotō with promotions from mounted guard (umamawari) to elder (karō), the highest of the retainer ranks. Fukuoka and others received less spectacular advancement. The central government also rewarded them with gifts of money (still calculated in rice). For a time Gotō's prominence in the central councils was greater than that of Itagaki, who, according to Gotō's biographer, professed to Gotō that he was better suited for military than for political tasks, and urged Gotō to represent their common interest in the government.[3] Itagaki nevertheless remained in Tokyo, as did most of the other prominent leaders. Yōdō himself was there, and as a result the city was the center for both Tosa and national concerns. In Tosa an

[3] *Hakushaku Gotō Shōjirō,* p. 386.

administration under Yamauchi Toyonori was responsive to directives from Tokyo, with the result that many of the officials were, as Tani Kanjō (one of their number) put it, resentful that the large number of han leaders were wasting Tosa money at the capital; "They thought it like falling from Heaven to Hell to return to Tosa, and it was considered much too cruel to ask any of them to go back home." Tani's summary of the han budget for 1870 shows over one-third devoted to Tokyo costs, exclusive of military expenditure there; less than one-sixth went for administration within Tosa.[4]

In 1869 political conditions were still extremely unsettled, and as a result the Tosa leaders continued to spend most of their effort and money on measures to strengthen Tosa defenses. It was considered a matter of months before warfare between Satsuma and Chōshū would break out, and many conferences were devoted to the problem of the Tosa role in such a war. It was agreed that the han had lost ground because of its reluctant and partial participation in the war against the Tokugawa, and that plans should be readied for immediate entry into the next conflict. It was not easy to decide which side to join. The Tosa ruling family had connections with both the Mōri of Chōshū and the Shimazu of Satsuma, but because the ties with the Satsuma house had been closer, and because political relations with Satsuma since Sakamoto's work with Saigō had been amicable, the han leaders agreed that they would cast their lot with the Shimazu cause. In the spring of 1870 Yamauchi Toyonori visited Kagoshima for formal talks with his Satsuma counterpart. The Tosa military leaders had decided that with the outbreak of war they would rush their full military strength to Kyoto, thereby establishing a clear basis for claims of service to the Imperial (and the Satsuma) cause.

These plans required diplomatic preparations within Shikoku to make certain that neighboring han would not attack once the Tosa forces were away. Conversations were initiated with each of Tosa's twelve neighbors, and after agreement was reached a council of delegates was convened at Kompira in Sanuki. It will be noted that the Tosa delegates again thought in terms of conciliar organization. The assembly was designed as a way of pooling information and promoting mutual trust among the realms represented. But its achievements were not impressive. In the first year

[4] *Tani Kanjō ikō* (Tokyo, 1912), I, 318f.

of its life Tani Kanjō found the delegates poorly selected and indifferent to their responsibilities; they failed to observe national affairs or even those of their own han, he noted, and "did nothing but get together and spend money in drinking and amusement." The experiment ended in failure.[5]

In the meantime vigorous steps were taken to strengthen the Tosa armed forces. In Tokyo a French army officer was hired to give instruction in European drill and tactics, and a number of officers of the (now-disbanded) bakufu armed forces were retained as teachers. The Tokyo measures were under Itagaki's general direction. He placed his main emphasis on the building of a balanced force that would include cavalry and engineers as well as artillery and infantry. Similar reforms were carried out in Tosa under the direction of Tani Kanjō and Kataoka Kenkichi. As a result Tosa was able to contribute a small but well-trained and well-equipped force to the national government when the final measures of centralization were taken in 1871.[6]

Since the military reforms were paralleled by efforts to bring Tosa up-to-date in terms of Western technological education, it was inevitable that the han debt should rise. Despite nominal direction from Tokyo after the lords of Tosa, Satsuma, Chōshū, and Hizen petitioned the court to accept the return of their registers in March, 1869, local autonomy continued to be the rule. In July 1869 the young daimyō Yamauchi Toyonori was named Governor of Tosa. The autonomy of centuries was not to be reversed by a change in titles of this sort, and as a result the Tosa budget continued to be the product of local needs and intentions. Thus despite nominal disapproval of official trade on the part of the former domains (a trade which was, by definition, non-modern, and, furthermore, dangerous to the degree that it made possible local strength) Tosa han trade continued as important as before. Iwasaki Yatarō had resigned his position as Tosa agent in Nagasaki after disagreements with Sasaki Takayuki in 1868, but he soon reemerged as director of the office of the Tosa firm in Osaka which was opened in 1868. This office now outdistanced the older Nagasaki station in the volume of foreign and domestic trade. The firm, although outwardly a private (Iwasaki) firm, was actually as

---

[5] *ibid.*, and Numata Yorisuke, "Toshū han no taisei hōkan undō to sonogo no kōdō" in Shigakkai, ed., *Meiji Ishin shi kenkyū*, pp. 705-706, for text of the treaty negotiated with neighboring fiefs.

[6] Numata, *loc.cit.*

much a han enterprise as ever. After central government control improved in intensity and competence, however, there was no alternative to making reality conform to name, with the result that trade that had been private only in name became so in fact. With Iwasaki's purchase of the assets of the Tosa han the basis was laid for the Mitsubishi firm and one of the great financial and industrial empires of modern Japan.[7]

Trade with the Nagasaki and Osaka stations was only one of the devices which the han used to meet its expenditures in the years immediately following the Restoration. Samurai incomes were heavily taxed with emergency "loans" and military taxes, and a new tax system brought house lots, businesses, and even religious institutions into the tax structure for the first time. In addition the han borrowed money vigorously from Tosa, Osaka, and foreign merchants. At the abolition of the han in 1871 the total debt was 922,389 ryō, slightly more than one year's tax income. The Nagasaki officials were the recipients of vigorous protests from foreign firms that wanted payment from Tosa,[8] and ultimately many of the obligations to the foreigners (which totalled 180,000 ryō) were settled by turning ships still unpaid for over to the government and to Iwasaki. Besides these measures, the fief also issued a great deal of paper money.[9]

[7] Hirao, *Ishin Keizai shi no kenkyū* pp. 29-46. As Gotō's biographer describes it, "Beginning with the Osaka station, all the assets and the debits of the han official trade ended up in Iwasaki's hands. The han steamers passed to the Ministry of Finance for a time, and then they were sold very cheaply to the Mitsubishi Company, with the result that it became a private shipping concern. Count Gotō's assistance and Iwasaki's ability were well matched, and *Daisanji* Hayashi Yūzō exerted himself not a little to help." *Hakushaku Gotō Shōjirō*, p. 415.

[8] The Nagasaki library files contain a number of complaints forwarded by British consul Flowers, who reported (as on February 13, 1868) that "Messrs. Alt & Co. inform me that the Prince of Tosa is indebted to them in the sum of twenty-seven thousand, four hundred and seventy-nine dollars and that they are unable to obtain payment from his Representative here, Mr. Iwasaki. I have the honor to request you will be pleased to recover this amount, and in the event of payment being refused, I beg you will detain the steamers in harbour belonging to said Prince of Tosa, until a satisfactory arrangement be come to with Messrs. Alt & Co." Two days later another communication concerned a "separate claim of $77,500 against said Prince, being for the final installment of the purchase money of the 'Shoeyleen'" (the ship that had taken Sakamoto, Sasaki, and Satow to Nagasaki some months earlier). The same archives contain material bearing on a prior Tosa attempt, in April 1867, to borrow $100,000 Mexican from the Netherlands (at 1% interest) on a Tokugawa guarantee of payment. The documents concerned are Dutch efforts to make sure of the Tokugawa guarantee, but there is no evidence that the guarantee or the loan were forthcoming.

[9] The paper money issues are discussed in Hirao, *Ishin keizai shi no kenkyū*, pp. 88-160, while the broader problems of han finance of the period are treated in his *Kōchi han zaiseishi*, pp. 51-55.

There can be no doubt that all of this bore heavily on the people of Tosa. Tani noted later that "the value of money fell rapidly while prices rose higher and higher. Much of our rice and other products were illegally carried out to foreign markets, the supply of goods grew short everywhere, and the government and the people suffered from poverty and distress. The government . . . tried to overcome the difficulties by purchasing various kinds of local products and exporting them to Osaka, but it was always forestalled by the merchants with whom it competed. Most of its undertakings ended in failure, with the result that people lost confidence in the government. . . ." To meet this problem he submitted plans for recalling most of the people unnecessarily consuming Tosa income in Edo, for checking corruption, and for restoring some of the sumptuary measures of earlier days.[10]

This crisis of finance, coupled with the dangerous trend of national politics, must have been an important element in the vigor with which Itagaki and his colleagues attacked social reforms in the same period. The samurai, rapidly losing their military utility and weighing down the public payrolls, were inviting targets for reform-minded modernizers. Military rank determined income, and stipends were the major burden on the government. At the same time the modern troops that Itagaki had trained and equipped included non-samurai, men who were often better qualified to accept discipline and to function as part of a larger unit.

The central government in Tokyo provided the authorization for much of this, but the Tosa men, after a slow start, went well beyond the government's proposals. When the fief registers were first "returned" to the court and the lords declared governors in 1869, the government leaders abolished the rank of daimyō and grouped the former lords together with the court nobles (kuge) as a new class to be known as kazoku (aristocracy). Then, at the end of the year, new orders came out cancelling the numerous gradations of the samurai class in favor of two categories, *shizoku* (warrior, or knights) and, for the former "lower samurai," *sotsuzoku* (soldiers). Below these last, the old groupings of peasant, artisan, merchant, and the mean classes (*Eta* pariahs and "unclean" or "nonhuman," *hinin*), were to be levelled out as "commoners" (*heimin*). These orders to the former fiefs became law in Tosa in regulations that were issued on December 26, 1869. As in

[10] *Tani Kanjō ikō*, I, 315-324, for Tani's "My 18 point plan for economic reforms for Tosa."

other fiefs they were interpreted with some freedom, however, and as a result relative standings in the social hierarchy did not change very much. It is extremely interesting to note the compromises that were made, for these suddenly establish with clarity what the value of rank actually was in late Tokugawa Tosa.

The warrior or knightly class was subdivided into five main groups, three of which had two levels, making a total of eight ranks.[11] They were as follows:

Shizoku	First Class:	Yamauchi branch families; *karō*; quasi-*karō*.
Shizoku	Second Class:	*Chūrō, umamawari*; new *umamawari*
Shizoku	Third Class,	
	Upper:	*Koshōgumi*; new *koshōgumi*.
	Lower:	*Rusuigumi*; new *rusuigumi*.
Shizoku	Fourth Class,	
	Upper:	Five grades of Shintō shrine officials; *gōshi*; *kachi*; quasi-*kachi*.
	Lower:	*Kumigai*; personnel of the nine Shintō shrines.
Shizoku	Fifth Class,	
	Upper:	*Jinshoku* (shrine officials); original *ashigaru; ashigaru*.
	Lower:	Other grades of ashigaru; village shrine keepers (*jajin*); *ōjōya-bangashira*

The sotsu were similarly arranged with a total of six ranks in three classes. It will be noted that these classifications were extremely generous. Shizoku numbered some 7,250 (30,500 including dependents), and sotsu 3,700 (17,681 including dependents).[12] The numerous compliments paid the confusing ranks of Shintō shrine personnel may be taken as a reflection of the ideological purity of the day, with its emperor-emphasis and anti-Buddhist propaganda. But perhaps the most striking feature of this arrangement is the fact that *gōshi* and even ashigaru (foot soldiers) made the coveted shizoku rank. Among "commoners," *shōya* group leaders (like Nakaoka Shintarō) were created shizoku. Other *shōya* were listed among the sotsu, those with sur-

---

[11] Hirao, *Ishin keizai*, etc., pp. 162-167.

[12] *Hansei ichiran*, I, 152; Kikkawa Hidezō, *Shizoku jusan no kenkyū* (Tokyo, 1942), p. 59.

names being given precedence in rank over those without. But virtually all the Restoration leaders in Tosa would have been shizoku. The final group of Itagaki, Gotō, and Fukuoka, of course, were of the very highest strata.

The Tosa reforms thus began slowly, and there was reason to conclude that they lagged behind the wishes of the central government for a time. One reason these measures were so mild is that every effort was made to take stock of opinions of the men who staffed the han administration.

This changed in January 1870 when Itagaki returned to Kōchi together with Gotō and Fukuoka Kōtei. Gotō remained relatively inactive for a time, but Itagaki and Fukuoka immediately took over the policy-making posts in Kōchi. There were several reasons for their return. In Tokyo extremely conservative aristocrats were temporarily in the ascendancy, with the result that Shintō was receiving more attention than was reform. Within the group of samurai leaders unity was also weakening. The end of the anti-Tokugawa war made it less necessary to conciliate minority groups, with the result that the Satsuma and Chōshū men seem to have been less interested in Tosa opinions than they were earlier. But more important than personal differences was the fact that the central government was still too weak and disunited to carry out reforms of any great significance. As a result the leaders of the southwestern fiefs decided to return to their domains and to reestablish political control there, strengthening their military forces in case fighting should break out again, and set a pattern of social and institutional reform that might provide a pattern for national changes later. Kido Kōin and Ōkubo Toshimichi also returned to Chōshū and to Satsuma at this time; Saigō Takamori had been home for some time.[13] Itagaki later explained that it was his purpose to reform and bypass the oligarchic control which prevailed in Tokyo by reforming Tosa first—somewhat the way in which adventurers in later decades talked about reforming Korea (through Kim Ok-kiun), China (through Sun Yat-sen), and Manchuria (through the Kwantung Army) as a model for the home country.

Itagaki's proposals had to be cleared with Yōdō and with members of the central government in Tokyo. Immediately after being appointed as *Daisanji* (the highest post under an administrative

[13] *Gotō Shōjirō*, pp. 399-403; Hirao, *Ishin keizai*, pp. 171-172.

reform that had been instituted in the summer of 1869) Itagaki and Fukuoka returned to Tokyo to present their proposals to the government in the name of Governor Yamauchi Toyonori. Their memorandum began with the statement that all men were by rights equal. Hereditary occupations should be abolished, "whether those of samurai, civil, or military posts, so that all people may become the same subjects of the nation." Officials ought to be selected from commoners and sotsu as well as samurai, and a new standing army should be set up to replace the samurai forces. Finances should be arranged by converting samurai stipends to bonds. "The only difference between farmers, artisans, and merchants," their document went on, "is that of occupation; it should have nothing to do with social status." They concluded by proposing a census registration law that would affect all classes impartially. An accompanying statement explained that the system of social stratification derived from Tokugawa feudalism, and ought to be abolished together with the governmental system that had been overthrown. "Customs like these do not exist in any civilized country; such ranks are artifically assigned, and deprive people of the rights which heaven has given them." The samurai ought to be deprived of their security, in which they consumed their food in idleness. Far better that "each man be engaged in the pursuit of knowledge and try to serve his country with his learning; this is as heaven wills it."[14] The proposal did not, of course, advocate an end to class distinctions and titles, but it did suggest ways of making them meaningless.

The Tokyo response was favorable, though not entirely enthusiastic. There were those who pointed out that there was inequality among all classes, and that it would be unjust to level only samurai incomes and status. The giving of bonds in lieu of lands or stipends, however, seemed a reasonable compromise between the obligations to the past and the needs of the present, and so the proposals were approved. Itagaki and his fellows were eager that Tosa should be made a testing ground for principles they thought would soon be needed everywhere in Japan; they talked about abolishing the sotsu rank, and also wanted to end the permission for samurai to carry swords. The government in Tokyo went along with the former, with Kōchi as experiment, but

[14] Hirao, *Ishin keizai*, pp. 178-180, and a document marked "Proposal presented on the twenty-fifth day of the tenth moon of 1870," in the Kensei shiryō shitsu, National Diet Library, Tokyo.

delayed its approval for banning the wearing of swords. The Tosa proposals were well ahead of the timetable being followed elsewhere in Japan. The Kōchi men found interest in their ideas on the part of men from Chōshū, Uwajima, and other fiefs, but those areas were content to delay comparable measures until they had the chance to see how they worked out in Tosa.

Itagaki and Fukuoka returned to take up their tasks with enthusiasm. A major part of the problem lay in explaining to the samurai what was being done. Early in 1870 the han government issued a proclamation on "The Principle of Equality of the Four Classes." "Man is the most precious of the creatures on earth," it began, "and possesses a wonderful and mysterious nature; he has intelligence and ability, so that he is said to be the most wonderful of creatures. This cannot be reconciled with the separation into samurai, farmer, artisan, and merchant, or with the division into superior and inferior in terms of worth." It was an evil of medieval feudalism that the right of service in arms and government had been restricted to the samurai, with the result that commoners felt themselves unconcerned by the outcome of war. Henceforth office should be open to ability, in order to cultivate a society in which all could achieve their aspirations. The country would benefit as all classes competed in service. In the recent war in Europe the French had been defeated, but the common people had given their all during the long siege. Japanese should develop the same spirit. True national unity and real national wealth depended upon the enlightenment and activation of the commoners; the riches of the people were those of the government and the poverty of the people was that of the government, and no distinction could be made between the two.

In the weeks that followed, the Tosa administration announced that all incumbents in official and military positions were discharged and new men (no doubt often the same ones) were appointed. Commoners were recruited for the army. Hereditary stipends of samurai were changed to pensions in the form of bonds. Three years' bonds were given in a lump sum in order to encourage samurai to invest them in new enterprises. The abolition of feudalism and full central control which came in August of 1871 interrupted this program before it was complete, but by then the Tosa measures had anticipated many of the steps that would later be carried out elsewhere in Japan.

Other measures, less spectacular, continued the pattern of removing samurai privileges. Punishments for acts of discourtesy to samurai were repealed, and the samurai right of private punishment and vendetta was withdrawn. Check stations at the borders of the realm were removed, and commoners were permitted free entry and exit from Tosa. Samurai were permitted, and encouraged, to enter trade. There were also a number of experiments with council chambers. On April 22, 1870 the first of these, restricted to the family heads of the three highest categories of shizoku, opened for two meetings each month. It met in the residence of the council head, and a petition box was placed outside the gate in order to solicit the voice of the people as in earlier times. The composition of this chamber marked it as a feudal relic, however, and it was disbanded two months later. The next attempt went to the other extreme. The *Shūgisho* which convened on August 2, 1870 was made up of village heads, elders, group leaders, and town ward leaders. It had little rapport with the upper ranks which still controlled the fief administration. It was the project of Fukuoka Kōtei, and came to an end when he withdrew to return to the central government shortly after the council was set up. A final and more promising effort for a two chamber system was designed to combine the representation of both groups. Before it was implemented, however, the abolition of fiefs of 1871 put an end to such local experiments.[15] These reforms could not fail to alarm the upper classes. But although there was much grumbling and evasion, no violence broke out, perhaps because the commoners did not seize their new privileges right away.

Itagaki's plans for reform did not end with these measures. During 1870 he impetuously set out to modernize Tosa with all the speed he could manage. New privileges granted included permits for restaurants and theatres, and a new era for private enterprise included regulations for brothels in Kōchi. Foreigners were brought in to teach and to advise on reform of the codes of law. Special announcements were issued to samurai explaining why the foreigners had been invited, in the hope that they would meet courtesy instead of assassins.[16] Old handbooks of feudal days designed for ruling and controlling the commoners were ordered

[15] *Kōchi Shi shi*, pp. 639-644. Hirao, *Kōchi Ken no rekishi*, pp. 145-146.
[16] *Kōchi Shi shi*, pp. 646, 651ff.

burned, and even the portraits of the Yamauchi daimyō of the past were destroyed. Similarly the effort to establish Shintō, with its concomitant campaign against Buddhism, received warm support from Itagaki's administration. The best of Kōchi's temples were pulled down and innumerable pieces of sculpture and art were destroyed. The political overturn was becoming a cultural revolution.[17]

Radical as these measures were, their roots lay in the kind of thinking that produced *Hanron*, and they were carried out by the same men who led Tosa in late Tokugawa days. Itagaki, Gotō, and Fukuoka, all three disciples of Yoshida Tōyō and favorites of Yamauchi Yōdō, dominated the administration. Junior men like Sasaki Takayuki and Tani Kanjō gained in experience and prominence, but they were not in charge. Both of them were inclined to think Itagaki rash and impractical and Gotō somewhat wily and self-centered, but their written verdicts to this effect were penned after Itagaki and Gotō had parted company with the central government while they themselves stayed on.

It can not, then, be said that the make-up of Tosa's leadership changed in the years after the Restoration, but the content of their programs did change as new concerns made necessary new measures. At first political and diplomatic thinking continued to be set in the framework of feudal competition with Satsuma and Chōshū of earlier days. The Tosa men anticipated a break between the two, and were prepared to take full advantage of it. Military reforms and alliance with neighboring fiefs on Shikoku were undertaken to make this possible. Efforts were made to continue official trade in order to supplement normal revenue. Then, in order to provide the regional unity which was required, the leaders also set in force sweeping political, social, and cultural reforms. Gradually the new political situation made it possible and necessary to anticipate the construction of a different sort of society. One senses in the documents of the period the conviction that true national unity can be gained neither under Satsuma-Chōshū auspices nor under the institutions of decaying feudalism. Hence the efforts to use Tosa as a testing ground for reforms that might be applied in the nation at large in future years. Thought was now given to the problem of producing in the commoners a

---

[17] Numata, "Toshū han no taisei hōkan undō to sono go no kōdō," p. 709.

sense of participation in the national purpose and destiny, and out of this came radical measures of social reform.

As in late Tokugawa days, it was the West that provided the model for the kind of society that was needed. True unification and true patriotism required a levelling process which would bring Japan's practices into line with those of the rest of the world. The French had shown the benefits of patriotism, as opposed to the nonchalant farmers whose indifference had astonished Itagaki outside the besieged castle of Wakamatsu. "If the principle of humanity [i.e., equality] replaces that of samurai, and if each man is encouraged to work for others and their welfare, every single person in the country will readily provide military service and sacrifice his life for the country when war breaks out," was the way the Kōchi proposal to the central government put it. Only a prosperous people could support real national strength. The "national debt of England," the same proposal added, was enormous, "larger than that of any other country in the world. Yet Englishmen are all rich and prosperous. A government can not do anything when its people are badly off, even if it has a rich treasury."[18] These ideas, only slightly refined and sophisticated, would reappear in the proposal calling for a National Council chamber which Itagaki, Gotō, and their fellows issued after they withdrew from the government in 1873. This belief in the necessity to unify and utilize popular interest and enthusiasm motivated much of Itagaki's subsequent career in the democratic movement, and it helps to account for the consistently nationalistic tone of the propaganda for democratic institutions in the Meiji period.

3. The Problem of Class Interest

Ever since E. H. Norman's classic synthesis of Japanese studies on the Restoration,[19] the interpretation of the Restoration as the outcome of a coalition between merchants and lower samurai has been almost taken for granted. Norman used Chōshū for his study in depth, and then and later he concluded that the combination of able and discontented merchants and samurai had utilized peasant and lower class pressures only to frustrate them in

---

[18] "Proposal," etc. National Diet Library.
[19] *Japan's Emergence as a Modern State* (N.Y., 1940).

the land tax, conscription, and police measures that followed in the 1870's.[20] Although Tosa, as has been noted, was far from typical, it will be useful to look again at the Tosa scene to evaluate these propositions. For Tosa was an important area, and if, instead of such a nation-wide coalition of interest groups, local characteristics can be shown to have determined the course of events there, it will show the need of caution in working out any pattern of social analysis viable for Japan as a whole in a day when administrative and social measures encouraged and perpetuated localisms everywhere.

At the outset it must be emphasized that in a society in which political initiative and action were limited to so small a number it sufficed for a very small minority to adopt a program for it to be realized. It needed no larger stirrings of class interest. Only some elements within the group with influence and authority needed to become aware of the necessity for changes in the face of the Western threat. Were those few representative of a special class interest?

In Tosa one must first repeat the distinction, made earlier, between the Loyalist and the Restoration movements. In many instances and individuals the two overlapped, but the differences between them were important. Of these the former, the Loyalist movement of Takechi's day, was to a large degree dominated by *gōshi* and *shōya*. There were feelings of intense hostility between these groups and their superiors; the antagonism had been shown in numerous complaints before the coming of Perry, and it contributed to the rapidity with which the Loyalist movement caught hold in the early 1860's. The split between *gōshi* and *shōya* and their superiors was not merely one of rank or political frustration, although these entered in, but probably more basically one of country against town. The village leaders were bitterly resentful of efforts to limit their wealth and authority in the interests of the new han monopolies and projects, and the old order which they sought to resurrect was one in which no feudal middlemen would interpose between the honorific court and the all-powerful rural leaders. But in view of the need for greater, rather than less, cen-

<hr>

[20] *Soldier and Peasant in Japan: The Origins of Conscription* (N.Y., 1943), and *Feudal Background of Modern Japanese Politics* (N.Y., mimeographed, 1945). Albert Craig's forthcoming *Chōshū in the Meiji Restoration*, however, serves as an essential corrective for Norman's treatment of Chōshū.

tralization after the coming of the West, their hopes of carrying out such a utopian program would in any case have been doomed; as it happened, however, they had no real chance. After a promising beginning they lost all influence in late Tokugawa Tosa. Their adjustment to the early Meiji situation is one we shall note below.

But these sectional interests were not translated directly into the political programs of the loyalist years. To begin with, many of the most important *gōshi* figures sprang from urbanized families which had purchased the rank. When close to power they prepared programs for economic measures comparable to those their fellows had earlier found so objectionable. And their activities and writings were usually national, and never narrowly local or sectional, in emphasis and appeal.

The Tosa Restoration movement, on the other hand, was necessarily led by bureaucrats of rank and status who had the capability of affecting official decisions and policies. They were "lower samurai" only in relation to the handful of privileged incompetents who held power at the time of Perry's arrival. These few seem to have been incompetent and uneducable; their inability to read the translation of Perry's letter in 1853, and Gotō's decision to by-pass them by addressing Yōdō in *kambun*, reveal how little they could contribute in terms of alternatives to the programs worked out by their inferiors. The men who led Tosa in Restoration days—Gotō, Itagaki, Fukuoka—were disciples of Yoshida Tōyō and favorites of their daimyō. Their programs for reform depended upon keeping the *gōshi* and *shōya* in their place, but once this was done they had no hesitation in utilizing parts of the loyalist political propaganda when it became necessary for continued Tosa influence on the national scene. These "upper samurai," as they must be called, kept a secure grip on power in Tosa during the Restoration years.

It is a good deal more difficult to discern any measure of merchant influence and direction in the events that have been described. To a degree the *gōshi* and *shōya* represented merchant interests as well as agricultural, since they played a dual role in the countryside. But their ideology and values were distinctly non- (and really pre-) commercial, and they would have been irate indeed had they been told they were a nascent *bourgeoisie*. Town (Kōchi) merchants, on the other hand, were in league with, and utilized by, the han monopolies. Of course not all of them could be employed in this way, and many clearly resented the Kaiseikan and its new monopolistic powers; but the latter, and not the merchants, helped make possible Tosa Restoration role. It is worth noting, however, that in the days after the Restoration han efforts to continue and strengthen monopolies fell victim to merchant sabotage; in Tani's words, "the government . . . was always forestalled by the merchants, with whom it competed."[21] The tension and resentment brought out under the political uncertainty of the time must have been present for many years, but it cannot be proved that they caused the political uncertainty.

On the national scene, Sakamoto's activities profited from numerous merchant contacts. This was inevitable, for his trading activities and his need for protection and capital brought him into paths previously trod only by merchants. His friendships with Shiraishi and Itō, Chōshū merchants with an interest in trade between fiefs, and with the Nagasaki merchant Kosone, were profitable and enjoyable for all concerned. But it would be overstepping the evidence at hand to suggest that these men represented autonomous merchant interests or that they influenced Sakamoto and his friends in that behalf. The equality of classes, the permits for new enterprises previously restricted in Tosa, and the withdrawal of the han from trading channels it had previously monopolized obviously created new possibilities for merchants. But the pressure for this came only partly from merchants. One should not lose sight of the fact that old-fashioned men like Sasaki Takayuki felt that official trade tended toward inefficiency and corruption, and that it made for burdens upon the commoners, and therefore urged its discontinuance. Equally important pressure came from the modernizers, who pointed to the doctrines of free trade which prevailed in the 19th century West. However tempting it is to postulate, it is at present impossible to establish merchant interest at work in the implementation of these reforms.

In early Meiji times the *shōya-gōshi* interest, on the other hand, continued to be a recognizable and highly vocal one, and it is instructive to observe the way in which it was exercised in the great crises that agitated Tosa in the middle of the 1870's. Although the evidence at hand is too sectional to permit sweeping verdicts, it does provide material for questioning the adequacy of the thesis

[21] See n. 10, above.

which holds that the early Meiji "democratic" movement was responsive to the wishes of rural leaders who resented the utilization of an onerous land tax for urban industrialization.[22]

Shōya and gōshi were to be found in generous proportion in the Restoration armies of Tosa, and after the war against the Tokugawa came to an end and they made vigorous efforts to improve the titles and status they were accorded. They alone, they complained, were expected to give up the status and rank they had achieved during the fighting. These complaints were unavailing.[23] But there were other compensations. Both groups fared rather well in the new ranks of shizoku and sotsu that were announced. Much more important was the fact that, while remaining patterns of subinfeudation were ended and samurai stipends sharply reduced, the gōshi were recognized as owners of their lands, to which they ultimately received "modern" titles. Shōya, although often displaced in authority as rural organization and administration were rationalized, were usually large owners as well, with the result that their prestige and influence remained more or less constant while that of their samurai betters dwindled rapidly.[24]

These shifting standards of prosperity played a role in the democratic movement of the next decade. Itagaki and Gotō returned to Tokyo to serve in the central government in 1871, but it was not long before the argument over war with Korea (a course which Gotō had advised as early as 1869) found them unable to have their way. Disgruntled with the way in which their colleagues had choked off a move that would clearly have had the support of the samurai class, they resigned their posts and, together with their colleagues from Hizen, issued the famous call for a constitution that inaugurated the Movement for People's Rights (Jiyū Minken undō). Other Tosa men loyal to Itagaki left the Konoe Guards and followed their leaders to Tosa. When they arrived there many of them were shocked by the changes in their old homes. The samurai who had invested their bonds in new enterprises had shown such lack of business acumen that the phrase "warrior business methods" (shizoku shōhō) had been

[22] The fact that the Jiyūtō of the 1880's was supported, inter alia, by rural sake brewers and land lords has been pointed out by most writers, many of whom go on to draw a causal connection on this point.

[23] For petitions, Hirao, Nagaoka son shi, pp. 101-110.

[24] Kōchi ken nōchi kaikaku shi, pp. 110-114; Matsuyoshi, Shinden no kenkyū, p. 308.

added to the language. Match factories, restaurants, and a wide variety of other enterprises had been begun enthusiastically only to fail miserably.[25] A galloping inflation of paper money rendered the bonds worth only part of their declared value. The residences of the feudal great, now taxed, had changed hands, and restaurants and public houses of all sorts had been established in them. Household goods and possessions of even the karō were being hawked in the streets. "Our situation is so hard," a petition for government help read, "that many families are unable to live together; mothers, fathers, and children have to make separate arrangements; some of us work as rickshaw men, and many take work by the day."[26]

The return of the military men from Tokyo added fuel to this discontent, and in a short time a number of factions had formed. One, which ultimately took the name *Reinansha*, represented a coalition of those holding conservative social and philosophical positions. Its ideology was that of Imperial loyalty, and to bolster this in the domain it imported a loyalist scholar from Kyoto to teach young men. The Reinansha represented a combination of pre-Restoration loyalism with other elements of conservatism; it was to be found in all parts of Tosa, and its roots lay in the rural interests that had found earlier expression in the *gōshi* and *shōya* movements.[27] A second organization, the *Chūritsusha*, was set up by Sasaki Takuyuki with government funds as a counterweight to other groups and a source of intelligence about other movements. The *Risshisha* (Achieving one's aim society) which Itagaki set up in 1874 was centered in Kōchi, and made up of his samurai followers.[28] It combined plans for samurai assistance with education in the problems and values of the modern world. Schools were set up for the study of Western learning and law, and cooperative ventures were organized to provide livelihood for the impoverished retainers who needed help. At the same time the Risshisha served to keep alive and to further the agitation for a constitution and popular rights.

---

[25] Tosa *shizoku shōhō* is treated in Hirao, *Ishin keizai shi*, pp. 188-217.
[26] *Nagaoka son shi*, p. 123.   [27] *ibid.*, pp. 113ff.
[28] The best study of the *Risshisha* is by Hirao Michio, *Risshisha to minken undō* (Kōchi, 1955). The name, as Sir George Sansom has pointed out, was taken from the title of the famous Japanese translation of Samuel Smiles' *Self Help*, so that it might perhaps best be rendered as "Self Help Society." For a local study of membership and appeal of these organizations, see *Nagaoka son shi*, p. 114.

Such local studies as are available indicate that Itagaki's movement was bitterly resisted by the *gōshi* and *shōya*, most of whom preferred the Reinansha conservatism. As landlords they were now comfortable and wealthy social leaders, and they looked upon the agitation for political rights as dangerous radicalism that failed to take proper account of Imperial sovereignty. And since the Risshisha men were also the object of surveillance by government officials and supporters in Kōchi, their path in Kōchi was not an easy one. Had it been otherwise, the movement would have been a good deal more difficult to control. At the present state of our knowledge, then, it would seem clearly incorrect to say that the lower samurai used peasant energies to achieve a turnover after which they choked off the ambitions which flared up again in the democratic movement. In Kōchi, at least, it might be more accurate (though also exaggerated) to suggest that the *gōshi-shōya* had utilized samurai ambitions to establish their own social and economic primacy, after which they deserted their erstwhile benefactors and allies. Certainly no greater contrast could be found than that offered by the smug, contented *gōshi* squirearchy and their impoverished former superiors after the mid-1870's.

Until 1877 many of the Risshisha men and their enemies thought that the Restoration scenes might be reenacted, and that a few bold strikes could still bring about the destruction of Satsuma and Chōshū domination and replace it by a new coalition in which Tosa interests would fare better. But in that year Saigō Takamori's attempt to use force by marching his Satsuma samurai up to Tokyo proved a failure, and it ended with his death. Tosa men loyal to the government helped to crush Saigō; Tani Kanjō was the Kumamoto commander whose stand doomed the insurgents' plans. Until word of Saigō's death reached Tosa, however, the central government was afraid that Itagaki would lead his men into action in Saigō's support.[29] That he did not do so was owing largely to his conviction that the time for old-fashioned measures of this sort was past. Itagaki deprecated plans that some of his friends worked out for a quick strike against government headquarters at Osaka and for assassination of prominent government officials. When these men proved unable to get weapons,

[29] Sasaki Takayuki, now a staunch government supporter, utilized all his contacts in Tosa to keep the government posted on Itagaki's activities. Local administration and police of course added to the pressure.

and when it became clear that Saigō was losing, talk of open rebellion came to an end. Thereafter the only way to oppose the
government was by "modern" political movements, and this was
the path that Itagaki followed.[30]

It will be seen from this brief summary that it is difficult, on the
basis of present research, to assign a class interest to the actions
of men like Itagaki and his followers in pre- and post-Restoration
days. Cliques and factions within the upper samurai were, to be
sure, much in evidence, and so were the antagonisms based on
rank and privilege throughout the ruling class. The more rural interests of the *gōshi* and *shōya* made themselves felt during the
brief periods when the Loyalist movement in Tosa was responsive
to a widespread and vocal opinion, but this unity and enthusiasm
does not seem to have been recovered in the years after 1864. Nor
can these sectional and local concerns be shown to have exercised
very great influence on the actions and ideas of Sakamoto Ryōma
or Nakaoka Shintarō. Once they entered politics, their concerns
were usually with national dangers and needs.

It is also necessary to speak with caution about the ideological
position of the Tosa figures. The modern reader is to some degree,
one suspects, the victim of several decades of "official" Restoration history in which Shintō purity and Imperial reverence were
emphasized to the exclusion of broader national and narrower personal goals. In the case of men like Sakamoto and Nakaoka, the
schooling they received did, it is true, plant very strong ideas
about the importance of the Emperor in their minds. This is particularly true of Nakaoka, who, perhaps because he had more
formal schooling than Sakamoto, frequently concluded a document with exhortations in the Shintō language of the unity of worship and government. Still, it would be a mistake to conclude that
many of those who supported Yōdō or the bakufu, or both, would
not have been willing to agree with all or most of such language.
The disagreement was more likely to be found in the area of
means and possibilities, and it was usually based on practical considerations and judgments. Total loyalism and complete ideological purity were luxuries that those with experience and responsi-

[30] Government investigations of several of the Tosa plots resulted in sentences
for Kataoka Kenkichi, Hayashi Yūzō, and Takeuchi Tsuna (whose son, Yoshida
Shigeru, is perhaps the last notable representative of the Tosa political tradition associated with Itagaki.)

bility could seldom maintain. The low-ranking *gōshi* tended to see things in sharp distinctions of black and white, and they failed to understand how their superiors could hesitate when faced with the truth. Those in the upper brackets, on the other hand, even Itagaki himself, were too much aware of the immaturity of the court nobles, and too conscious of the complexities of the situation, to take so rigorous a stand. They tended to talk less about the sacred cause, and they were more prepared to develop plans for constitutions that would lessen any future Imperial absolutism that could serve to cloak Satsuma or Chōshū interests. Even in the case of Sakamoto Ryōma, it is striking to note how seldom he articulated sentiments of belief in Shintō. For him the restoration of Imperial rule was indeed a precondition of effective national unity, but the expressions that came most naturally for him were voiced in terms of achievement and ambition.

It is perhaps this sense of individual purpose and daring, expressed in a period of national crisis, that most distinguished the Restoration heroes from so much of earlier Japanese and Chinese history. The self-confidence, conviction, and arrogance that made the *shishi* such formidable antagonists were something new. Since they professed obedience to an (unknowable) Imperial will, they could not be controlled or guided by their fellows. Self-motivated, they established a tradition of dissent and personal intervention that survived to become one of the most dynamic aspects in modern Japanese politics. It was a tradition to which future revolutionaries would lay claim. In the 1880's the Tosa writer Ueki Emori, who became Itagaki's assistant, was one of the first to seize upon this. He quoted with approval Kusaka Genzui's praise of the man who despised those who concerned themselves with trifles and praised those who were "magnanimous, lofty, and different"; he published a "record of patriotism" about the Tokugawa *shishi*, and strove for their contempt for gain, their self-confidence, and their courage.[31] Nor was the *shishi* heritage restricted to radicals. The Meiji educational system, designed in an age when Samuel Smiles was a best seller, did its best to implant goals of achieve-

[31] Ueki, *Mutenzatsuroku* (ed. Morishita, Kōchi, 1957), pp. 256ff. Ienaga Saburō, *Kakumei shisō no senkakusha* (Tokyo, 1955), p. 50; for detailed treatment, Eiji Yutani, "Ueki Emori: Tradition and Change in Meiji Japan" (unpublished M.A. thesis, University of Washington, 1960).

ment and self-realization in every school boy breast.[32] Thus one might consider this spirit of Sakamoto's a political harbinger of the social dynamism of Meiji Japan. It was also a spirit that attracted the idealistic and ambitious from other Asian countries. At the end of the Meiji period, the adventurers who worked with revolutionaries elsewhere in Asia told their friends and protégés about their own heroes, and together the conspirators laid claim to this heritage. As Sun Yat-sen put it, "We are the *shishi* of the Meiji Restoration."[33]

The *shishi* tradition has also been full of temptation for zealots inclined to flout authority and decency in carrying out their concept of "the highest duty of all," and the words, names, and examples of the Restoration activists have been invoked as justification for shocking deeds of violence long after other forms of protest have become available. The ambivalent reaction of a public struck by feats of daring and encouraged to focus on problems of provocation or instigation instead of on individual responsibility for taking life has helped to confirm young fanatics in a favorable view of their own reckless fury. Nevertheless they are wrong in considering themselves the heirs of the Restoration *shishi*. Far from giving reality to the values of their society, they are instead showing, in a shocking flash-back, how much the world Japanese live in has changed in less than a century. The phrases of a century before are today archaic and obscurantist. No one can mistake the difference between the best of the Restoration figures, who forsook the path of violence when presented with a rational plan for progress, and the self-proclaimed successors who turn their backs on reason and resort to violence in a vain attempt to return their land to the irrationality of an outworn and discredited myth.

The individual purpose and daring of the late Tokugawa *shishi* tended, in the overwhelming majority of cases, to be set in an atmosphere of broad agreement on goals, though not on methods. The things that divided progressives and conservatives, when analyzed, were frequently matters of execution and timing; who should lead, and when, but not where. As a result the consensus

---

[32] R. P. Dore, *City Life in Japan* (London, 1958), pp. 191ff., describes this emphasis on "getting on" in the Meiji educational system.

[33] I have studied the work of the late Meiji *shishi* and "China rōnin," as they called themselves, in *The Japanese and Sun Yat-sen* (Cambridge, 1954).

among the minority who were politically articulate was striking. Was this partly because the problem could be explained as a "foreign" one, so that broad agreement on defence of the national political and cultural integrity could be maintained? Undoubtedly this helped. But in the final evaluation the answer must be sought in the strength and vitality of the values which underlay Tokugawa society, values that could survive the collapse of the political order because it was revealed to represent the negation, and not the expression, of the political ideal. The channels of authority survived the fall of those who held authority, and they remained available for the use of those who followed. Divisions were limited to the elite, and even there they were usually overshadowed by agreement. So it is that Keiki, who was pushed aside, like Sakamoto, who in all probability would have been pushed aside, could become a Restoration hero for historians and those who read them.

This consensus of Restoration times also serves to illumine the contrast with the Japan of a century later. The once sacred national essence, revealed hollow by defeat, has been rejected; no political ideal exists, while outside influence, in a world no longer as agreed as the nineteenth century West on the nature of the good society, has become divisive. Postwar Japan has shown a surface agreement expressed in terms like democracy, prosperity, and internationalism which often seems to obscure a deeper division on the ends and goals of the society that is to be built. Ironically, however, this may also have its compensations, as Japan's achievements of modernization, separated from the nationalist mystique that once accompanied them and set now within the framework of a more democratic and attractive society, can better hope to appeal to other lands. In this sense it may yet prove that the goals of Restoration leaders, who sought to bring their country's state structure up to those of other lands so that their descendants would not "feel shame" before the countries of the world, have been as well served by the displacement of the Imperial ideal as they were by its formulation a century ago.

CHRONOLOGICAL TABLES

Year & Era	National Developments	Tosa	Sakamoto (and Confederates)
Ka'ei 1853	Arrival of Perry	Yōdō dismisses top officials	to Edo for study of fencing; joins special defence corps
Ansei 1854	Netherlands detachment gives instruction at Nagasaki to Katsu and others	Yoshida Tōyō administration and reforms in economic, defence; People's Corps	
1856	Arrival of Townsend Harris, preparation of commercial treaty	1856 Takechi Zuizan sent to Edo	1856 in Edo again, comes under Takechi's influence
1857	Bansho Shirabesho opened	1857 Takechi returns to Tosa	1857 to Tosa
1858	Ii Naosuke appointed Tairō; succession to Iemochi, not Keiki; punishment for *shishi*, daimyō, nobles who opposed	1858 Mito messengers try to contact Tosa loyalists	1858 sent to contact Mito men at border
		1859 Yōdō put under house arrest by Bakufu	
Man'ei 1860	Mission to United States; Oguri, Katsu, Fukuzawa members; first trade treaty now in effect	Tosa man attached to U.S. mission	
	March: assassination of Ii Naosuke by Mito, Satsuma shishi opens loyalist years	Yoshida Tōyō continues internal reforms; codification; *Kainan Seiten*	
	Aug.: death of Tokugawa Nariaki plunges Mito into factional disputes	Aug.: partial relaxation of restrictions on Yōdō	
Bunkyū 1861	Chōshū puts forward Nagai Uta's plan for mediation between Court and Bakufu (*kōbu-gattai*)	Growing repute of Takechi in national fencing, loyalist circles	emissary, lieutenant of Takechi
	Princess Kazu wed to shogun	*Oct.: Takechi forms Tosa Loyalist Party* (Kinnōto)	Sakamoto, Nakaoka, members of Loyalist Party
1862	Feb.: attack on Andō fails	Takechi unable to persuade Yoshida Tōyō	
	April: Hisamitsu arrives Kyoto, outbids Chōshū for court support		April: Sakamoto flees Tosa
	May: Hisamitsu crushes *rōnin* in Teradaya	May: Yoshida Tōyō killed full freedom for Yōdō	
	July: Ōhara mission, acc. Hisamitsu, to Edo; on return, Richardson incident	July: loyalists accompany Toyonori to Kyoto (arr. Sept.)	
	New administration (Shungaku, Keiki) relaxes *sankin-kotai* regulations	Nov.: Sanjō-Anenokōji mission (acc. Toyonori) app't.; leaves for Edo Dec.	Dec.: Sakamoto tries to kill Katsu, instead is converted to his position and service Nakaoka and party to Edo

Year & Era	National Developments	Tosa	Sakamoto (and Confederates)
Bunkyū 1863	Shogun's first visit to Kyoto June: Chōshū shells ships at Shimonoseki July: Chōshū in full ascendancy in Kyoto; Anenokōji murdered Aug.: British shell Kagoshima Sept.: Satsuma-Aizu coup drives Chōshū out of Kyoto: Sanjō, other nobles flee to Chōshū Desperate risings in Yamato, Ikuno	Feb.: Yōdō to Kyoto from Edo May: *Yōdō returns to Tosa, begins suppression of loyalists* July: Mazaki, Hirai, Hirose, *hara-kiri* *Nakaoka flees Tosa* Tosa *rōnin* prominent in Chōshū, other fighting	Katsu secures han pardon for Sakamoto Hyōgo academy for naval training Dec.: Sakamoto put in charge of Hyōgo training
Ganji 1864	Shogun's second visit to Kyoto Aug.: abortive Chōshū invasion of Kyoto Sept.: Western ships shell Shimonoseki Nov.: Katsu dismissed as Commissioner of Navy Dec.: shogunate launches expedition against Chōshū as "enemy of court" compromise settlement worked out with help of Saigō; Sufu suicide	Aug.: Gotō becomes Yōdō's first minister; new series of reforms begun; abortive rising at Noneyama by loyalists	Sakamoto hears of plans for resignation of shogun from Katsu, Ōkubo Ichiō. Nov.: Katsu dismissed from post; Sakamoto gets Satsuma protection
Keiō 1865	refugee court nobles moved to Dazaifu Chōshū loyalists revolt, capture control of han June: Tokugawa conservatives secure decision for Second Chōshū exped. Programs for French assistance worked out with Leon Roches Harry Parkes arrives as British Minister	*Kaiseikan* announced; plans for export to Nagasaki Takechi suicide	future *Kaientai* begun at Nagasaki as way of importing Western arms and ships for Satsuma and Chōshū; trips to Shimonoseki Dec.: purchase of *Union*, arms for Chōshū
1866	Feb.: commercial arrangements with French completed Mar. 7: Satsuma-Chōshū alliance worked out in secret Satow pamphlet on British policy July: shogunate meets disaster in attack on Chōshū Aug.: Shogun Iemochi dies	Tosa administration turns to reconsider loyalist chances; Sasaki to Dazaifu Sept.: Gotō to Nagasaki; to Shanghai Nakaoka document to Tosa loyalists rules out immediate exclusion	Mar. 7: *Sakamoto helps bring about Satsuma-Chōshū alliance* Survives attack in Teradaya; trip to Kagoshima; returns to take part in fighting at Shimonoseki

Year & Era	National Developments	Tosa	Sakamoto (and Confederates)
Keiō 1867	Keiki (Yoshinobu) new shogun; vigorous program of reforms; French, through Roches, as advisers June: Conference of lords of Satsuma, Tosa, Uwajima, Fukui, with shogun on opening of Hyōgo, punishment of Chōshū Satsuma-Chōshū plans for war Nov. 9: *Keiki petitions court to accept return of political powers*	Tosa support for Sakamoto, Nakaoka *Iroha* negotiations Iwasaki replaces Gotō as chief of Tosa interests in Nagasaki Tosa-Satsuma agreement *Icarus* crisis delays action Sept.: Yōdō decides to petition Keiki to resign powers Oct. 28: petition submitted to Keiki	Sakamoto app't. head of *Kaientai* July: *Eight-Point Program* Aug.: *Icarus* crisis Nov.: Sakamoto arrives Kyoto Dec. 10: killed together with Nakaoka in Kyoto
Meiji 1868	Jan.: coup relaces Tokugawa with allied troops in Kyoto; "Restoration" announced Jan. 27: Keiki tries to reenter Kyoto; "Fushimi-Toba" incident begins war April: "Charter Oath" restates principal features of Sakamoto-Tosa program Sept.: Edo, renamed Tokyo, new capital.	Tosa units take Takamatsu, Matsuyama, take part in campaigns to north, esp. Wakamatsu; cause foreign crisis by attack on French at Sakai; ceremonies of remembrance for loyalists killed at Noneyama	
1869	fiefs returned to court, lords declared governors Tokugawa resistance ends on Hokkaido	samurai ranks changed	
1870	cautious measures of liberalization; "National Teaching" experiments	Itagaki, Fukuoka, and program of "equal rights"	
1871	abolition of fiefs, establishment of prefectures.	experiments with council chambers	

LIST OF WORKS CITED

I. Books in Western Languages

Affairs Etrangères: Documents Diplomatiques. Paris, 1867.

Alcock, Sir Rutherford. *The Capital of the Tycoon: A Narrative of a Three Years' Residence in Japan,* 2 vols., New York, 1863.

Asakawa, K. *The Documents of Iriki,* 2nd ed., Tokyo, 1955.

Beasley, W. G. *Great Britain and the Opening of Japan,* London, 1951.
———. *Select Documents on Japanese Foreign Policy, 1853-1868,* London, 1955.

Bellah, Robert N. *Tokugawa Religion: The Values of Pre-industrial Japan,* Glencoe, Ill., 1957.

Courant, Maurice. *Ōkoubo,* Paris, 1904.

de Bary, W. Theodore, and Tsunoda, R., eds. *Sources of the Japanese Tradition,* New York, 1958.

Doeff, H. *Herinneringen uit Japan,* Haarlem, 1833.

Dore, R. P. *City Life in Japan,* London, 1958.

Fukuzawa Yukichi. *The Autobiography of Fukuzawa Yukichi* (tr. Eiichi Kyooka), Tokyo, 1948.

Griffis, W. *The Mikado's Empire,* New York, 1871.

Hall, John W. *Tanuma Okitsugu (1719-1788): Forerunner of Modern Japan,* Harvard, 1955.

Harrison, John. *Japan's Northern Frontier,* Gainesville, 1955.

Ike, Nobutaka. *The Beginnings of Political Democracy in Japan,* Baltimore, 1950.

Ishii Ryosuke. *Japanese Legislation in the Meiji Era* (tr. W. J. Chambliss), Tokyo, 1958.

Jansen, Marius B. *The Japanese and Sun Yat-sen,* Cambridge, 1954.

Meijlan, G. F. *Japan: Voorgesteld in schetsen over de zeden en gebruiken van dat ryk, byzonder over den Ingezetenen der stad Nagasaky,* Amsterdam, 1830.

Mushakoji Saneatsu. *Great Saigō* (tr. Sakamoto Moriaki), Tokyo, 1942.

Norman, E. H. *Japan's Emergence as a Modern State,* New York, 1940.
———. *Soldier and Peasant in Japan: The Origins of Conscription,* New York, 1943.
———. *Feudal Background of Modern Japanese Politics* (mimeographed), New York, 1945.

Redesdale, Lord (Hugh Mitford). *Memories by Lord Redesdale,* 2 vols., New York (n.d.).

Sansom, George B. *The Western World and Japan,* New York, 1950.

Satow, Sir Ernest. *A Diplomat in Japan,* Philadelphia, 1921.

Smith, Thomas C. *The Agrarian Origins of Modern Japan*, Stanford, 1959.

Takekoshi, Yosaburo. *The Economic Aspects of the History of the Civilization of Japan*, 3 vols., London, 1930.

Teng, Ssu-yü, and Fairbank, John K. *China's Response to the West*, Harvard, 1954.

Tsudzuki, K. *An Episode from the Life of Count Inouye*, Tokyo, 1912.

van der Chijs, J. A. *Neerlands Streven tot Openstelling van Japan voor den Wereldhandel*, Amsterdam, 1867.

van Meerdervoort, J. L. C. Pompe. *Vijf Jaren in Japan (1857-1863)*, 2 vols., Leiden, 1868.

von Siebold, P. F. *Open Brieven uit Japan*, Deshima, 1861.

Warriner, Emily V. *Voyager to Destiny: the Amazing Adventures of Manjiro, the Man Who Changed Worlds Twice*, Indianapolis, 1956.

Wilson, Robert. *Genesis of the Meiji Government in Japan, 1868-1871*, Berkeley, 1957.

II. Books in Japanese

Abe Dōzan. *Kaigun no senkusha: Oguri Kōzuke no Suke seiden*, Tokyo, 1941.

Bakumatsu keizai shi kenkyū. ed. Honjō Eijirō, Tokyo, 1935.

Chikami Kiyoomi. *Sakamoto Ryōma*, Tokyo, 1914.

Dai Nihon Ishin shiryō. part 3, Vols. 4, 7, Tokyo, 1940, 1944.

Dai Nihon Komonjo: Bakumatsu gaikoku kankei monjo. ed. Tokyo Teikoku Daigaku, Vol. 18, 1925.

Dai Saigō Zenshū. ed. Okawa Shigeyoshi, 3 vols., Tokyo, 1926.

Fukushima Nariyuki. *Yoshida Tōyō*, Tokyo, 1927.

Godai Ryūsaku. *Godai Tomoatsu den*, Tokyo, 1936.

Godai Tomoatsu kankō kai. ed. *Godai Tomoatsu hishi*, Osaka, 1960.

Haruyama Ikujirō. *Hirano Kuniomi den*, Tokyo, 1933.

Hansei ichiran. Tokyo, 1928-1929, 2 vols.

Hijikata Hisamoto. *Kaiten jikki*, Tokyo, 1900.

Hirao Michio. *Yōdō Kō ki*, Tokyo, 1941.

———. *Yoshimura Toratarō*, Tokyo, 1941.

———. *Kaientai shimatsu ki*, Tokyo, 1941.

———. *Rikuentai shimatsu ki*, Tokyo, 1942.

———. *Ishin Kinnō ibun sensho: Sakamoto Ryōma, Nakaoka Shintarō*, Tokyo, 1943.

———. *Takechi Zuizan to Tosa Kinnō Tō*, Tokyo, 1943.

———. *Kōchi han zaisei shi*, Kōchi, 1953.

———. *Tosa nōmin ikki shikō*, Kōchi, 1953.

———. *Tosa han gyogyō keizai shi*, Kōchi, 1955.

———. *Nagaoka son shi*, Kōchi, 1955.

LIST OF WORKS CITED

Hirao Michio. *Risshisha to minken undō*, Kōchi, 1955.

——. *Tosa han ringyō keizai shi*, Kōchi, 1956.

——. *Tosa han kōgyō keizai shi*, Kōchi, 1957.

——. *Ishin keizai shi no kenkyū*, Kōchi, 1959.

Honjo Eijirō. *Bakumatsu no shin seisaku*, Tokyo, 1935.

Ienaga Saburō. *Kakumei shisō no senkakusha*, Tokyo, 1955.

Iohara, Ryūjirō. *Hijikata Hakushaku*, Tokyo, 1914.

Irimajiri Yoshinaga. *Tokugawa baku-han sei kaitai katei no kenkyū*, Tokyo, 1957.

Ishii Takashi. *Meiji Ishin no kokusaiteki kankyō*, Tokyo, 1957.

Ishin nichijō sanshū. ed. Iwasaki Hideshige, 5 vols., Tokyo, 1925.

Ishin shi. ed. Ishin shiryō hensan jimukyoku, 6 vols., Tokyo, 1939-1941.

Ishin Tosa kinnō shi. ed. Zuizan kai, Tokyo, 1911.

Iwai Ryūtarō. *Mitsubishi Konzern tokuhon*, Tokyo, 1937.

Iwakura Tomomi kankei monjo. ed. Ōtsuka Takamatsu, 8 vols., Tokyo, 1925-1933.

Jinketsu Sakamoto Ryōma den. Osaka, 1926.

Kagoshima ken shi. 5 vols., Kagoshima, 1939-1943.

Katsu Rintarō (Kaishū). *Kaishū Zenshū*, 10 vols., Tokyo, 1929.

Katsuta Magoya. *Ōkubo Toshimichi den*, 3 vols., Tokyo, 1911.

Kikkawa Hidezō. *Shizoku jusan no kenkyū*, Tokyo, 1942.

Kinsei sonraku kenkyū kai. *Kinsei sonraku jichi shiryōshū: Tosa no kuni jikata shiryō*, Tokyo, 1956.

Kōchi chihōshi kenkyūkai. *Kōchi Ken rekishi nempyō*, Kōchi, 1958.

Kōchi Ken, ed. *Kōchi Ken nōchi kaikaku shi*, Kōchi, 1952.

Kōchi Ken shiyō. Osaka, 1924.

Kōchi Shi shi hensan iinkai. *Kōchi Shi shi*, Kōchi, 1958.

Koda Shigetomo. *Ōshio Heihachirō*, Tokyo, 1910.

Kodama Kōda. *Kinsei nōmin seikatsu shi*, Tokyo, 1957.

Kumazawa Kazue. *Seizan Yoei: Tanaka Kōken Haku shoden*, Tokyo, 1924.

Kure Shūzō. *Shiiboruto Sensei, sono shōgai oyobi kōgyō*, Tokyo, 1926.

Kurihara Ryōichi and Ueda Tomoi. *Itagaki Taisuke Kun den*, Tokyo, 1893.

Kuzuu Yoshihisa. *Tōa senkaku shishi kiden*, 3 vols. Tokyo, 1933-1936.

Matsuyoshi Sadao. *Shinden no kenkyū*, Tokyo, 1936.

——. *Tosa han keizaishi kenkyū*, Tokyo, 1930.

Matsuzawa Takurō. *Man'yō to Kamochi Masazumi no shōgai*, Tokyo, 1943.

Mikami Sanji. *Edo jidai shi*, 2 vols., Tokyo, 1943-1944.

Mioka Takeo. *Yuri Kimimasa den*, Tokyo, 1916.

Nakahama Tōichirō. *Nakahama Manjirō den*, Tokyo, 1936.

Nakamura chō yakuba. *Nakamura Chō shi*, Kōchi, 1950.

Naramoto Tatsuya. *Kinsei hōken shakai shiron,* Tokyo, 1948.

Numata Jirō. *Bakumatsu yōgaku shi,* Tokyo, 1950.

Ogata Hiroyasu. *Kamochi Masazumi,* Tokyo, 1944.

Ōmachi Keigetsu. *Hakushaku Gotō Shōjirō,* Tokyo, 1914.

Osatake Takeshi. *Meiji Ishin,* 4 vols., Tokyo, 1942-1948.

Ozaki Takuji. *Nakaoka Shintarō,* Tokyo, 1926.

Sakamoto Ryōma kankei monjo. ed. Iwasaki Hideshige, 2 vols., Tokyo, 1925.

Sakazaki Bū. *Gekai Suikō,* Tokyo, 1902.

Sanjō Sanetsumu shuroku. ed. Iwasaki Hideshige, Tokyo, 1925.

Sasaki Takayuki. *Kinnō hishi: Sasaki Rō Kō sekijitsu dan,* Tokyo, 1915.

Seki Junya. *Hansei kaikaku to Meiji Ishin,* Tokyo, 1956.

Shibusawa Eiichi. *Tokugawa Keiki Kō den,* 8 vols., Tokyo, 1916.

Shigakkai, ed. *Meiji Ishin shi kenkyū,* Tokyo, 1930.

Shisho Kai, ed. *Katō Shisho den,* Fukuoka, 1933.

Tada Kobun. *Iwakura Kō jikki,* 3 vols., Tokyo, 1927.

Takechi Zuizan kankei monjo. ed. Hayakawa Junzaburō, 2 vols., Tokyo, 1916.

Tanaka Sōgorō. *Iwasaki Yatarō den,* Tokyo, 1940.

Tani Kanjō ikō. 2 vols., Tokyo, 1912.

Teraishi Masaji. *Tosa ijin den,* Kōchi, 1914.

———. *Zoku Tosa ijin den,* Kōchi, 1923.

Tokutomi Iichirō (Sohō). *Iwakura Tomomi Kō,* Tokyo, 1932.

———. *Kōshaku Yamagata Aritomo den,* 3 vols., Tokyo, 1933.

———. *Tosa no kinnō,* Tokyo, 1929.

Tomoatsu kai, ed. *Kindai no ijin: ko Godai Tomoatsu den,* Tokyo, 1921.

Tosa han gōshi chōsa sho (Tosa shiryō sōsho). Kōchi, 1958.

Tōyama Shigeki. *Meiji Ishin,* Tokyo, 1951.

Ueki Emori. *Muten zatsuroku,* ed. Morishita, Kōchi, 1957.

Yamazaki Masatada. *Yokoi Shōnan den,* Tokyo, 1942.

Yoshida Tōyō ikō. ed. Ōtsuka Takematsu, Tokyo, 1929.

III. Articles in Western Languages

Beasley, W. G. "Councillors of Samurai Origin in the Meiji Government 1868-9," *Bulletin of the School of Oriental and African Studies,* xxx (London, 1957).

Brown, Sidney. "Kido Takayoshi and the Meiji Restoration: A Political Biography, 1835-1877," unpublished doctoral dissertation, University of Wisconsin, 1952.

———. "Kido Takayoshi, Japan's Cautious Revolutionary," *Pacific Historical Review,* xxv, 2 (1956).

Cody, Cecil E. "A Study of the Career of Itagaki Taisuke (1837-1919),

A Leader of the Democratic Movement in Meiji Japan," unpublished doctoral dissertation, University of Washington, 1955.

Craig, Albert. "Chōshū in the Meiji Restoration," unpublished doctoral dissertation, Harvard University, 1959.

———. "The Restoration Movement in Chōshū," *Journal of Asian Studies*, xviii, 2 (1959).

Fukuzawa Yukichi. "Kyūhanjō" (tr. Carmen Blacker), *Monumenta Nipponica* (Tokyo, 1953).

Grinnan, R. B. "Feudal Land Tenure in Tosa," *Transactions of the Asiatic Society of Japan*, xx, 2 (1893).

Goodman, Grant K. "The Dutch Impact on Japan (1640-1853)," unpublished doctoral dissertation, University of Michigan, 1955.

Hackett, Roger F. "Yamagata Aritomo: A Political Biography," unpublished doctoral dissertation, Harvard University, 1955.

———. "Nishi Amane—a Tokugawa-Meiji Bureaucrat," *Journal of Asian Studies*, xviii, 2 (1959).

Hall, John W. "Bakufu and Chōnin," *Occasional Papers*, Michigan Center for Japanese Studies, 1 (1951).

Henderson, Dan F. "Patterns and Persistence of Traditional Procedure in Japanese Law," unpublished doctoral dissertation, University of California, 1955.

Hiraga Noburu. "Tosa in the Meiji Restoration," unpublished M.A. thesis, University of Washington, 1955.

Honjo, Eijiro. "Leon Roches and Administrative Reform in the Closing Years of the Tokugawa Regime," *Kyoto University Economic Review* (Kyoto, 1935).

———. "The Views of Various Hans on the Opening of the Country," *Kyoto University Economic Review*, xi, 2 (1936).

Jansen, Marius B. "New Materials for the Intellectual History of 19th Century Japan," *Harvard Journal of Asiatic Studies* (1957).

———. "Takechi Zuizan and the Tosa Loyalist Party," *Journal of Asian Studies*, xviii, 2 (1959).

Naff, William E. "The Origins of the Satsuma Rebellion," unpublished M.A. thesis, University of Washington, 1959.

Sakai, Robert K. "Feudal Society and Modern Leadership in Satsuma han," *The Journal of Asian Studies*, xvi, 3 (1957).

Sakata Yoshio. "An Interpretation of the Meiji Reformation," Silver Jubilee Volume, Zinbun Kagaku Kenkyusyo, Kyoto, 1954.

Smith, Thomas C. "The Japanese Village in the 17th Century," *Journal of Economic History*, xii, 1 (1952).

———. "Landlords and Rural Capitalists in the Modernization of Japan," *Journal of Economic History*, xvi, 2 (1956).

————. "The Land Tax in the Tokugawa Period," *Journal of Asian Studies*, xviii, 1 (1958).

Tsukahira, Toshio. "The Sankin-Kōtai System of Tokugawa Japan," unpublished doctoral dissertation, Harvard University, 1951.

Webb, Hershel F. "The Mito Theory of the State," *Researches in the Social Sciences on Japan*, Columbia University East Asian Institute Studies, no. 4, ed. John E. Lane, New York, 1957.

Yutani, Eiji. "Ueki Emori: Tradition and Change in Meiji Japan," unpublished M.A. thesis, University of Washington, 1960.

IV. Articles in Japanese

Egashira Tsuneji. "Kōchi han ni okeru Bakumatsu no shinseisaku," *Bakumatsu keizaishi kenkyū*, Tokyo, 1925.

Hara Heizō. "Tenchū-gumi kyohei shimatsu kō," *Tosa shidan*, 62 (1938), 63 (1938).

Hirao Michio. "Bakumatsu rōnin to sono hogo oyobi tōsei," *Meiji Ishin shi kenkyū*, Shigakkai, ed., Tokyo, 1930.

————. "Gotō Shōjirō no Nagasaki Shanghai shuchō to sono shimei," *Tosa shidan*, 52 (1935).

————. "Kōchi han no mimpei seido," *Tosa shidan*, 35 (1931).

————. "Kōchi shi no konjaku," *Kōchi ken kenchiku shikai hakkō* (n.d.).

————. "Mizonobuchi Hironojo," *Tosa shidan*, 29 (1929).

————. "Tempō 'Okoze gumi' shimatsu," *Tosa shidan*, 36 (1931).

Honjo Eijirō. "Leon Roches to bakumatsu no shōsei kaikaku," *Bakumatsu no shin seisaku*, Tokyo, 1935.

Ikeda Yoshimasa. "Tempō kaikaku ron no saikentō: Tosa han o chūshin ni shite," *Nihon shi kenkyū*, no. 31 (1957).

————. "Hansei kaikaku to Meiji Ishin: Kōchi han," *Shakai Keizai shigaku*, 212, 5 (1957).

————. "Tosa han ni okeru Ansei kaikaku to sono hantai ha," *Rekishigaku kenkyū*, 205 (1957).

Irimajiri Yoshinaga. "Tosa han 'chōnin gōshi' no kaisei ni kansuru ichi shiryō," *Shakai kagaku tōkyū*, 1 (1956).

Ishii Takashi. "Satō Shinen gakusetsu jissen no kito," *Rekishigaku kenkyū*, no. 222 (1958).

Nagami Tokutarō. "Nagasaki jidai no Sakamoto Ryōma," *Tosa shidan*, 29 (1929).

Numata Raisuke. "Toshū han no taisei hōkan undō to sono go no kōdō," *Meiji Ishinshi kenkyū*, Shigakkai, ed., Tokyo, 1930.

————. "Tosa koku taka kō," *Rekishi Chiri*, 28, 1 (1916).

Otsuka Takematsu. "Fukkoku kōshi Leon Roches no seisaku kōdō ni tsuite," *Shigaku zasshi*, xLVI (1935).

Ozeki Toyokichi. "Kambun no kaitai ni tsuite," *Tosa shidan*, 24 (1928).

Sakata Yoshio. "Meiji Ishin to Tempō kaikaku," *Jimbun Gakuhō*, 2 (1952).

Shimmura Izuru. "Ransho yakukyoku no sōsetsu," *Shirin*, I, 3 (1916).

Shiomi Kaoru. "Sakamoto Ryōma no Ganji gannen," *Nihon Rekishi*, 108 (1957).

———. "Sakamoto Ryōma goroku to tsutaerareta Ei Shō Hiki ni tsuite," *Rekishigaku kenkyū*, 208 (1957).

———. "Saitaniya no koto nado," (n.p., n.d.).

Takezaki Gorō. "Sakamoto Ryōma Sensei keizu: Ōhama ke yori izuru," *Tosa shidan*, 76 (1941).

Tōyama Shigeki. Hara Heizō, "Edo jidai goki ikki kakusho," *Rekishigaku kenkyū*, 127 (1947).

A NOTE ON SOURCES

The books and articles used in this study may be found, with relevant bibliographical data, in the List of Works Cited as well as in the footnotes, where the frequency of citation will also suggest my evaluation of their relative importance and reliability. The discussion of sources which follows makes no attempt at complete coverage, but hopes, through a description of materials available for earlier Tosa, the Restoration *shishi*, and Kōchi local history, to give some idea of the significance of these matters for Japanese historiography as well as a view of the possibilities for further work on local history as it relates to the Meiji Restoration.

1. Documentary Sources for the History of Tosa

The main collection of documents for Tosa during the Tokugawa period became, in modern times, the private property of the Yamauchi daimyō family. As with the records for other han in Tokugawa times, this great mass of documents with its details of finance, administration, cadastral registers, ceremonial, retainer families, and chronicles of court and realm bore convincing evidence through its sheer bulk of the bureaucratic maturity of Tokugawa institutional life. (For a detailed description of a representative han documentary depository, that of Okayama, see John W. Hall, "Materials for the Study of Local History in Japan: Pre-Meiji *Daimyō* Records," *Harvard Journal of Asiatic Studies* 20, pp. 1-2 (1957). After World War I the Yamauchi documents were moved to Tokyo, where the family established a Center for the Compilation of House History (*Kashi Hensanjo*). Three historians—Numata Raisuke, Fukushima Nariyuki, and Hirao Michio—served as archivists and editors, dividing the Yamauchi history into periods for their own responsibility and following in general the pattern of the *Dai Nihon Shiryō* for a projected compilation. By 1945 their labors had produced several hundred volumes in manuscript when the great fire raids on Tokyo reduced their work to ashes. Some Yamauchi documents which had been left in Kōchi in the family residence survived, but others, which had been put for safe keeping in the Kōchi Prefectural Library, were lost when that city, in its turn, was destroyed in a fire raid on July 4th, 1945. The war thus removed the possibility of a documentary survey as complete as those that can be made for Kanazawa (Kaga) and Yamaguchi (Chōshū) and as is being made for Okayama.

Nevertheless the sources for Tosa history are impressive in scope and quality. Among the Yamauchi documents that have survived are records for the early nineteenth century and a *Yamauchi Toyonori Ki*, covering 1865 to 1871, that parallels the well-known *Shimazu Hisa-mitsu Kō Jikki* in structure. Also extant are records of the han trade through Nagasaki which include contracts and details of transactions. Among the treasures that remain, for the earlier period, is the cadastral survey of 1590 (*Tensho chikensho*), which has miraculously survived in 368 fascicules. This extraordinary document details and assigns every plot of land in late 16th century Tosa, and it is one of the two or three of that period in all Japan that have survived the ravages of storm, fire, and neglect. It is now being transcribed with commentary by Hirao Michio for publication by the Kōchi Prefectural Library. By 1960 5 volumes, for Tosa, Nagaoka, and Aki districts, had appeared.

There are several major compilations of Tokugawa times that, although little exploited by historians as yet, are certain to yield rich dividends for future study. Some mention of them and of the manner of their compilation will add further insight into the development of literacy and scholarship in Tokugawa days.

The first of these is the *Nanroshi* (南 路 志), or History of the Southern Circuit, compiled by a wealthy merchant Mutō Munekazu (1741-1813) with the assistance of his sons. The Mutō house had interests in lumber, lime, dry goods, drugs, and paper, and it owned reclaimed lands as well. The family heads were appointed to posts as *shōya*. They were well educated, and disciples of the Shintō scholars of the school of Motoori Norinaga and his disciples. With a well-developed interest in letters and antiquity and the means to indulge it, the head of the house set about compiling a history of Tosa. In 120 Japanese-style volumes he divided his work into qualitative and chronological divisions, including a final section of documents. Two complete copies of this work survive, one in the Tokyo University Historiographical Institute and one in the Ueno Branch of the National Diet Library. Volumes 9 to 33 of the original, covering the history and geography of all Tosa villages, are now being published in Kōchi; the first appeared in 1960. There are also four shorter, less important supplements to this basic set.

A second set of tremendous variety and interest is *Tosa no Kuni gunsho ruiju* (土 佐 国 群 書 類 从), or Classified Collection of Materials on the Province of Tosa, put together by Yoshimura Shumpo (1836-1881). Yoshimura, who was born a farmer's son, studied Japan's classics under Kamochi Masazumi, who was, as has been noted, Takechi's uncle. Again, the nationalistic and antiquarian bent of the National Learning produced a scholarly compilation. Yoshimura became a *shōya* in his twenties and held this office until the abolition of feudalism in the Meiji Period. In organization and approach he modelled his life work on the famous Tokugawa *Gunsho ruiju* of Hanawa

Hokiichi (1746-1822), but he restricted himself to the Tosa of Chōso-gabe and Yamauchi times. As with *Nanroshi*, the set survives in its full 307 volumes in two copies, one in the Tokyo University Historio-graphical Institute and the other in the Ueno branch of the National Diet Library. Some of the set's most notable excerpts, such as the Chōsogabe Code, have been reprinted in *Nihon keizai taiten* (54 vols., 1928-1930), *Kinsei shakai keizai sōsho* (36 vols., 1914-1917), and in the recent *Kinsei sonraku jichi shiryō-shū: Tosa no kuni jikata shiryō* (Tokyo, 1956, 588 pp.), but the bulk of the material in this series has yet to be made widely available or to be utilized. In the set can be found, for example, complete records of peasant revolts, with docu-mentation; detailed records of the rise and fall of hundreds of re-tainer families, discussions of education, registers of Buddhist temples, local gazeteers, and verbatim accounts of the questioning of Nakahama Manjirō upon his return to Japan.

A third set of great importance, *Tosa shiryō*, or Tosa Historical Sources, was lost in the bombing raid that destroyed Kōchi on the fourth of July, but since some of its items have been reassembled it deserves mention here. Its compilation was authorized by the prefec-tural government in 1912, and it was carried out by scholars who went to great efforts to locate materials that had not been included in the above-mentioned sets. When completed in 1923, the collection in-cluded 617 items. It existed in one copy. After the library burned it seemed that only the numerous review articles published by the li-brary in its Monthly Report from 1925 to 1940 would remain to indi-cate its strength, but more recently the library staff has been able to reassemble important parts of the collection from the sources on which it originally drew. The set was particularly strong in documents per-taining to late Tokugawa times. It included much of an official nature (e.g., documents relative to the government of Kōchi City, regulations for elders and village heads, etc.) and therefore, even in its partial reconstruction it provides material of very great importance.

The fourth and last of these great sets to be mentioned here is the *Kenshōbo* (熏章薄), or Charter Register, a compilation of laws, edicts, regulations, and notices issued in Tosa during the Tokugawa period. Its 68 volumes were compiled sometime during the last years of Tokugawa rule by Kanematsu, a *shōya* in Hata District who began with the intention of compiling rules and regulations essential for *shōya* in their work. The only complete set of the work is in the Economics library of Kyoto University; Kōchi University has a par-tial set consisting of perhaps one third of the whole. Despite its tre-mendous importance, this set too has received little attention so far from scholars.

It was suggested earlier that a survey of these materials and the manner in which they were compiled could yield useful insights into Tokugawa Tosa. Take a large, literate, underemployed warrior class become bureaucrats. What more logical than to expect to find them improving their leisure and consuming their substance on prestigious projects of literary and historical merit in the manner endorsed by their Confucian tutors? Yet of these sets we owe the three done in Tokugawa times to a merchant, a farmer become *shōya*, and a *shōya*. It is clear that the appeal to tradition voiced in the petitions of the *Shōya* League and the love of learning that characterized the leisure habits of Nakaoka Shintarō were by no means isolated instances of scholarship among the well-to-do commoners. Where were the samurai? No doubt a good many of them were editing and copying the formal records and chronicles that were destroyed in the fiery holocaust brought on by their successors a century after Tempō. But many more were spending their time in the search for and enjoyment of office, contemptuous of the diligent scribblers who concerned themselves with the records of the past. The samurai and their activities were more glamorous in the short run, but less enduring in the long pull, and one reason nineteenth century Japan was able to slough them off so successfully was that they had been pensioned off for years without being any the wiser.

2. The Restoration Period

The documentary and secondary material available to a historian of the Restoration is so vast that it would require an essay many times longer than this to do it justice. The volume is so great partly because of the central place the Restoration holds in Japanese historiography. After decades during which the Restoration was the special preserve of official historians who sought to document the patriotism of the Meiji leaders, it suddenly became a battle ground for new contestants concerned with the ideology and politics of resistance who wanted most to determine the point at which "progressive" developments had been thwarted by the leaders of the counter-revolution who established modern Japan's "absolutism."

For years historians considered it beneath their dignity to deal with anything more recent than "Recent Times," as the Tokugawa Period is termed in Japanese. During that period only official bureaus and family-sponsored committees busied themselves with the restoration of Imperial rule. The interpretation followed was necessarily one which stressed the virtue of those who sought to right the Tokugawa wrongs, and the sets subsidized by the families of Meiji statesmen or by the government itself were not likely to introduce the possibility of self or class interest in detailing the activities of their principal subjects. The six-volume set produced under the sponsorship of the Ministry of Education, in fact (*Ishin shi*, Tokyo, 1939-1941), had representatives of Satsuma, Chōshū, Tosa, and Hizen on the council which directed the work to make sure that all would receive their due of praise and credit. Nevertheless this work, conveniently indexed and carefully done, remains an essential source for the chronology and narrative of those turbulent years. The monumental work of Osatake Takeshi, *Meiji Ishin* (Tokyo, 4 vols., 1942-1949) adds further detail. The last work of this pioneer historian of the Meiji period, this work profits from a lifetime of reading in the sources, published and unpublished, and with *Ishin shi* it sets a framework of narrative detail that will not have to be redone.

Documentary compilations undertaken, but still incomplete, for the Restoration Period include the Historical Materials for the Restoration (*Ishin shiryō*, Tokyo, 19 vols., 1938-1942), Documents Relating to Foreign Affairs at the end of the Shogunate (*Bakumatsu gaikō kankei shiryō*, 33 vols., Tokyo, 1910-1959) and, for the early days of the Meiji government and the war against the Tokugawa holdouts, Records of the Revival of Antiquity (*Fukkō ki*, Tokyo, 15 vols., 1930-1931).

No single compilation can challenge the excellence of the work done by the Society for Publishing Historical Sources, the Nihon Shiseki Kyōkai. Its series on the Restoration contains 186 printed volumes, issued between 1915 and 1931, providing the papers of most of the principal participants in those events, letters, diaries, records, and statistical material. The contents range from impressions noted by the first Japanese visitors to the Western world (collected in "Records of the Period when the Barbarians Entered the Ports," *Ihi nyūkō roku*, 2 vols., 1930-1931) to the sources for the Chōshū Kiheitai militia (*Kiheitai nikki*, 4 vols., 1918, and include a statistical analysis of the various fiefs in late Tokugawa days (*Hansei ichiran*, 2 vols., 1928-1929), drawn on by W. G. Beasley in "Feudal Revenue in Japan at the Time of the Meiji Restoration," *Journal of Asian Studies*, XIX, 3 (1960). The papers of nobles, statesmen, and activists of all camps are represented. For this study the volumes devoted to Sakamoto Ryōma (*Sakamoto Ryōma kankei monjo*, 2 vols., 1926), Takechi (*Takechi Zuizan kankei monjo*, 2 vols., 1916) and Yoshida (*Yoshida Tōyō ikō*, 1929) were of particular importance. Mention should also be made of the diary of Date Munenari (*Zaikyō nikki*, 1916) and Matsudaira Shungaku's *Saimu kiji* (12 vols., 1920-1922).

In addition to these volumes the principal activists naturally came in for a good deal of attention from biographers, particularly in prewar days. Sakamoto received full-scale treatment in a work by Chikami

Kiyoomi, *Sakamoto Ryōma* (Tokyo, 1914), a less reliable work compiled on the occasion of a projected monument and entitled *Jinketsu Sakamoto Ryōma den* (Osaka, 1926) and the very careful work of Hirao Michio, "A Complete Account of the *Kaientai*" (*Kaientai shimatsu ki,* 1941). More recently Professor Shiomi Kaoru of Nara has been studying the life of Sakamoto, and I have profited from several of his articles which are cited in the text.

Nakaoka Shintarō, whose fragmentary diary and correspondence failed of inclusion in the Nihon Shiseki Kyōkai series, can be traced through the biography of Hirao Michio, *Rikuentai shimatsu ki* (Tokyo, 1942), the less reliable *Nakaoka Shintarō* of Ozaki Takuji (Tokyo, 1926) which, however, reprints the diary, and Hirao's collection of his letters and analyses of the political situation, *Ishin Kinnō ibun sensho: Sakamoto Ryōma-Nakaoka Shintarō sensho* (Tokyo, 1943).

For the wealth of biographical material available on other Restoration participants it is sufficient to list as guide the bibliography compiled by Takanashi Kōji, *Ishin shiseki kaidai: denki hen* (Tokyo, 1935). Critical notes accompany each of the thousands of items listed there, and it provides comprehensive coverage for all works published before 1934. It remains an essential point of beginning for anyone planning serious work on a Restoration figure, for few important works of biography have appeared since 1935. One, which is of particular interest, was compiled by a society formed to commemorate the seventy-fifth anniversary of Godai Tomoatsu's death, *Godai Tomoatsu hishi* (Osaka, 1960, 395 pp.). Practically each major Restoration figure has been the subject of at least one excellent biographical set, whose natural partiality toward its subject can usually be balanced and checked by reference to the biographies of the man's principal contemporaries. When we read of each of the major figures that he became convinced of the necessity to end feudal divisions in 1870, for instance, it is indicative not so much of a solitary, individual stroke of genius (as the authors would usually have it) as of a widespread consensus that emerged in the face of Japan's administrative handicaps in the presence of the strength and efficiency of the West. Thanks to the convenience of these materials the Restoration statesmen have in recent years begun to provide agreeable topics for doctoral dissertations in American universities, and, as the volume of these increases, the possibility nears of a useful work of reference for Western scholars. Already slated for publication in the Harvard Historical Monographs is Roger F. Hackett's *Yamagata Aritomo*. Mention should also be made of Cecil E. Cody's "Itagaki Taisuke (1837-1919), a Leader of the Democratic Movement in Meiji Japan" (University of Washington, 1955), Sidney D. Brown's "Kido Takayoshi and the Meiji Restoration: A Political Biography 1835-1877" (University of Wisconsin, 1952), and Joyce Lebra's "Japan's First Modern Popular Statesman: A Study of the Political Career of Ōkuma Shigenobu (1838-1922)," (Radcliffe, 1958).

The Restoration materials described thus far are largely documentary compilations, chronological narratives, and biographical studies. On the whole little work of this sort has appeared in Japan since World War II, as the main stream of analysis has turned on concerns that arose in the early 1930's in connection with Japan's militarism and aggression. This literature is set in formulations that derived from the new framework of Marxist analysis first given full expression in the theses of the Japan Communist Party. Current political decisions could be made only after "scientific" judgments of Japan's progress on the historical escalator that was to lead to "socialism," and in such determination the place and meaning of the Restoration assumed critical importance. For intellectuals anxious to relate their studies to the world in which they lived and unenthusiastic about adding to the praise of statesmen already well-heralded, this analysis had great attractions, and before very long the younger scholars were dismissing the careful work of those who had hitherto dominated the field as "one thing after another" (raretsu) history. For them the problem became one of whether the Restoration represented a victory of, or simply an advance toward, bourgeois society and capitalism; if the former, socialism could be seen to lie ahead, while if not, the struggle would be longer and the tactics different. The reactionary Japanese government lent this scholarship dignity by its disapproval of those who produced it, and the flow of ink in Japan as historians debated the nature of Japanese capitalism very nearly kept pace with the flow of blood in China as that capitalism pursued, in the language of the polemicists, its inevitably imperialist course. Histories of the controversy about the nature of Japanese capitalism run to several volumes. For many participants the problem was limited to the working out of definitions to fit Japan's experience into preconceived categories, but for others the challenge was more serious, and they produced a literature of considerable importance despite its limited scope.

This tide continued after World War II, for a time in greater volume than ever, as historians continued to wonder where and why their society had missed the path of progress. Few societies, it is safe to say, are as displeased by their recent past as are the Japanese, and one will look in vain for the kind of praise that earlier writers showered on the Meiji leaders. The public school textbooks, which reflect the productions of the scholarly pamphleteers, have in the 1950's become one of the principal battlegrounds between those who write them and the conservatives who find them unpatriotic and propagandistic.

Probably the outstanding product of the newer trends, and by all odds the most important and thought-provoking short work on the Restoration, is Tōyama Shigeki's *Meiji Ishin* (Tokyo, 1951), a work which, while Marxist in conception and analysis, is soundly based on the sources. It provides a convenient and moderate statement of Restoration analysis against the background of two decades of Marxist-oriented research.

Of late there are signs that the Marxist polemic has begun to wane. Again, the situation is related to current politics. The reverses suffered by the "progressive" forces in elections have begun to give some reason for thinking that they have separated themselves from the aspirations and interests of the people by an excess of doctrinal and theoretical speculation. The corollary of this for the historians has been a call to return to the stuff, and particularly the figures, of history in order to communicate with the readers once more. Hence new attempts which, by inference, compare the struggle against the unequal treaties in the nineteenth century with the struggle against American bases, thereby renewing contact with some Meiji leaders. Out of the same movement has come an ambitious series of short biographies of late Tokugawa and Meiji leaders published by the Yoshikawa Kobunkan. Inoue Kiyoshi's biography of Sakamoto Ryōma is yet to appear.

The problems of foreign policy which had so great an impact on Restoration politics were much emphasized by prewar Japanese historians, but they received a good deal less attention during the Marxist search for and identification of internal contradictions. W. G. Beasley's authoritative introduction to his *Select Documents on Japanese Foreign Policy, 1853-1868* (London, 1955) provides the best statement of the interaction between domestic and foreign policy in the Restoration period, and his bibliographical pages characterize the large body of Japanese works. The most significant items to be added to his list are the very substantial works of Ishii Kaoru, *Bakumatsu bōeki shi no kenkyū*, Tokyo, 1944, and *Meiji Ishin no kokusai teki kankyō* (Tokyo, 1957). This last, of which I have made extensive use, rephrases the material in a Marxist vocabulary in which international imperialist capitalism sought to ally with a native Japanese "absolutism" to choke off a true bourgeois development which would have threatened European manufacturers with competition. This much is not very impressive, but the book is extensively documented in its treatment of the late Tokugawa scene, particularly for French policy, and it includes Satow's statement of policy which was not previously available. I have also profited from the use of Netherlands sources, particularly the account of the opening of Japan by van der Chijs, *Neerlands Streven tot Open-stelling van Japan voor den Wereldhandel* (Amsterdam, 1867); I have also used these materials in an earlier study of the *Bansho Shirabesho*, the Tokugawa response to the need for more information about the West, in "New Materials for the Intellectual History of Nineteenth Century Japan," *Harvard Journal of Asiatic Studies* (20, pp. 3-4, 1957).

3. Regional and Local History: Tosa

I have drawn heavily on recent works about Tosa history in the preparation of this volume, and since future Western scholarship is, I think, going to have to take increasing note of the kind of detail that local historians provide in Japan, it will be worthwhile to summarize some of the trends in work on Tosa.

Local history in Tosa is not a recent development. *Tosa shidan* is probably one of the best periodicals in the local history of any area in Japan. It first appeared in 1917; in all, 99 issues have appeared, and their contents range from substantial articles of analysis and description to the bits of local piety and antiquarianism that fill so many journals of local history. Among the most frequent contributors on matters of solid historical merit have been Ozeki Toyokichi (1877-1940) and Hirao Michio (b. 1900), who has also republished the essence of some earlier articles in several of his postwar books.

Local historians naturally left few stones of Tosa's Restoration road unturned. A basic work, and one much cited above, is the History of Tosa Loyalism in the Restoration (*Ishin Tosa Kinnō shi*), published in 1911 by "The Society to Honor Takechi Zuizan." Its bias is apparent; "lower samurai," *gōshi* and *shōya*, are its heroes, but it is a useful narrative for the period and fuller on many matters than any other work. Reference has also been made to the biography of Tanaka Kōken (Mitsuaki) (*Seizan yoei*, 1924) whose collection of Restoration materials in Sakawa, Kōchi Prefecture, contains a rich variety of pictures, scrolls, letters, and other mementos of the *shishi*. Extremely useful and interesting are the memoirs of Sasaki Takayuki as he tells the "Secret History" of the Loyalist movement, *Kinnō hisshi: Sasaki Rō Kō sekijitsu dan* (Tokyo, 1915). Sasaki's diary survives in a copy in the Tokyo University Historiographical Bureau.

Prefectural governmental and private agencies have also provided important syntheses of provincial history. The most important of these is still the "Materials for the History of Kōchi Prefecture," *Kōchi ken shi'yō* (Osaka, 1924). This extremely useful work contains a rich variety of materials, and has an appendix the Genroku code of Tokugawa times, one of the best sources for the administrative and bureaucratic structure of Tosa under Yamauchi rule. Equally valuable is the recent publication of the Kōchi city government, *Kōchi Shi shi* (1958), much of the text of which is by Hirao Michio. This is far more than a history of Kōchi City alone; Vol. ɪ, the only one to appear thus far, tells a good deal of Tosa history, adds much new data (such as *gōshi* resident in Kōchi City), and carries the story into early Meiji days. Less valuable, but also of use, is the two volume *Kōchi Ken shi* issued in 1949. Also worthy of mention is the brief and readable *Kōchi Ken no rekishi* by Hirao Michio, Kawamura Genshichi, Sekita Hidesato, and Yokogawa Suekichi, published in Kōchi in 1956 and designed in part for students in secondary schools.

Social and economic history have profited from attempts to reinterpret materials previously available in the light of current historical approaches and from enthusiastic efforts to preserve and make available what survived the flames of World War II. Professor Irimajiri Yoshinaga of Waseda University has recently collected and in part, rewritten many studies he published over the years in Waseda University periodicals under the title *Tokugawa baku-han sei kaitai katei no kenkyū* (Tokyo 1957). His accounts of the *gōshi* system and the interrelationships with merchants proved especially useful for the preparation of this work. A young scholar who is steeping himself in the documentary sources on Tosa history, particularly the *Kenshōbo*, Ikeda Yoshimasa, has already published several articles which have been cited above, and he will undoubtedly be heard from a good deal in the future.

Documentary collections have been provided in the series *Kinsei sonraku jichi shiryō shū* (materials bearing on self-government of villages in recent times), the second volume of which, *Tosa no kuni jikata shiryō* (Tokyo, 1956) makes available a large number of legal codes, *gōshi* regulations, and petitions and memorials, some of which have been cited in the chapters above. The series of volumes devoted to reprinting the late sixteenth century cadastral survey, *Chōsogabe chikensho*, of which 5 volumes have appeared to date, have already been mentioned. The hundred-article Code of Chōsogabe Motochika (1597) has also come in for study and interest. (Judge) Inoue Kazuo's commentary, *Chōsogabe okitegaki no kenkyū* (Kōchi, 1955) provides an authoritative point of departure for serious study of the document and period, for which it is the best single source for political and social analysis. Judge Inoue's very important earlier work, *Han hō, Bakufu hō to Ishin hō* (Han law, Bakufu law, and Restoration law; three volumes, 1940), although unfortunately very rare (almost the entire printing was destroyed by fire), is a basic work for anyone interested in the problems it treats; most of his firsthand material is drawn from Tosa.

In recent years the Kōchi City Public Library has been publishing a large number of small volumes about the prefecture. Some resemble modest gazetteers of villages or districts, while others are devoted to historical topics. The majority of the latter have been by Hirao Michio, who has done his best to make available the excerpts from documents now lost that he collected during his years of service in the Yamauchi archives. Most of these extended essays include discussions of and commentary on documentary material which is supplied in very generous amounts, and they add up to a comprehensive coverage of what is known of the economic life of the Tosa domain in Tokugawa days. There are volumes on finance (*Kōchi han zaisei shi* 1953, 122 pp.), peasant revolts (*Tosa han nōmin ikki shi'ko*, 1953, 151 pp.), fisheries (*Tosa han gyogyō keizai shi*, 1955, 227 pp.), lumber (*Tosa han ringyō keizai shi*, 1956, 230 pp.), industrial enterprises (*Tosa han kōgyō keizai shi*, 1957, 255 pp.), agriculture (*Tosa han nōgyō keizai shi*, 1958, 261 pp.), economic ventures in Restoration times (*Ishin keizai shi no kenkyū*, 1959, 218 pp.), and the final one in the series, *Tosa han shōgyō keizei shi* (Kōchi, 1960) treats commerce. To these can be added the earlier essays by Matsuyoshi Sadao, *Tosa han keizai shi kenkyū* (Tokyo, 1930) and *Shinden no kenkyū* (Tokyo, 1936). It would seem that the historians of Tosa, despite the loss of the repositories of official documents, are making such determined efforts to collect and collate documents which survived the fires that the loss of the official han documents may actually prove to have been something of a blessing in disguise.

It remains to be said that several works in progress or in press seek to draw on the kind of interest in local history that has been evident in Tosa. Albert Craig's forthcoming *Chōshū in the Meiji Restoration* (Harvard University Press) draws on secondary sources of recent years as well as on the basic *Bōchō kaiten shi* to treat the Restoration scene in Chōshū. At the University of Michigan John W. Hall has been engaged for many years on an institutional survey of the Okayama han in close collaboration with Taniguchi Sumio and other local historians, and their use of one of the great surviving documentary collections will provide an authoritative picture of the structure of a regional bureaucracy of Tokugawa times. And for Tosa I have in progress a collection of documents, chosen from the works above, with commentary, which will attempt to illustrate something about the way the system worked, and in particular the points at which strains developed in the stratified, stagnant society of the textbook legends. "Conditions tended," according to Lafcadio Hearn, "to the general happiness . . . there was no need for supreme effort of any sort—no need for the straining of any faculty. Moreover, there was little or nothing to strive after; for the vast majority of the people, there were no prizes to win." Hearn's Tokugawa idyl would have seemed a concentration camp to Sakamoto Ryōma, and I suspect that his forbears would not have thought very much more highly of it during their progress from sake brewers to gōshi.

BIOGRAPHICAL NOTES

Abe Masahiro 阿部正弘 (1819-1857), fudai daimyō of Fukuyama (100,000 koku) from 1837 to 1857, member of Senior Council (rōjū) 1843-1857, circularized daimyō for advice at time of Perry mission, consulted principal daimyō personally.

Andō Nobumasa 安藤信正 (1820-1871), fudai daimyō of Iwakitaira (50,000 koku) from 1847 to 1862, member of Senior Council 1860-1862, object of an abortive assassination plot in 1862.

Anenokōji Kintomo 姉小路公知 (1839-1863), member of a court family which traced its importance to the Restoration of Emperor Godaigo in 1334; sided with loyalist nobles, headed, with Sanjō, the mission to Edo escorted by Tosa daimyō in 1862, assassinated in Kyoto upon return.

Chōsogabe (Chōsokabe) Motochika 長宗我部元親 (1539-1599), warrior chief who emerged as daimyō of Tosa during sixteenth century; Morichika 盛親 (1575-1615), last of the line, was deprived of fief by Tokugawa Ieyasu after battle of Sekigahara in 1600, reemerged in the fighting for Osaka in 1615 as supporter of Hideyori, and was executed. Many Tosa gōshi and shōya traced ancestry to Chōsogabe retainers, thereby finding legitimization for disloyalty to Tokugawa and Yamauchi.

Date Munenari (Muneki) 伊達宗城 (1818-1892), tozama daimyō of Uwajima (100,000 koku) from 1844-1858, thereafter, from retirement, an important figure among the feudal lords in Kyoto; served the Restoration government in a number of important diplomatic and governmental posts.

Fukuoka Kōtei (Takachika) 福岡孝弟 (1835-1919), Tosa samurai who entered government service as disciple of Yoshida Tōyō and rose rapidly in the han bureaucracy; he was sent, with Gotō Shōjirō, to Kyoto with the suggestion the shogun resign in 1867; thereafter he served the new government in a variety of posts. He drafted the "Charter Oath" of 1868, supervised legal and educational changes, was a member of the Privy Council, and created Viscount in the new peerage of 1884.

Fukuzawa Yukichi 福澤諭吉 (1834-1901), Kyushu samurai who became the outstanding popularizer of Western knowledge in nineteenth century Japan; a student of Ogata Koan in Osaka, he founded the present Keiō University in Edo, accompanied several Tokugawa missions to the West, and wrote, in *Seiyō jijō*, an account of the West extremely influential among the Restoration figures.

Glover, Thomas (1841-1911), principal partner in the Nagasaki firm of Glover and Co., who rendered much assistance to agents of the southwestern daimyō intent upon acquiring experience, information, and armament from the West. Itō, Inoue, Godai, and many others managed to go abroad through his assistance, and Itō was later able to show his appreciation by having the Third Order of the Sacred Treasure bestowed upon Glover by the Meiji Emperor.

Godai Tomoatsu 五代友厚 (1834-1885), Satsuma samurai who was assigned to study in Nagasaki, travelled to Shanghai to purchase Western ships, travelled and studied in England, and played an important role in Satsuma's imports of Western technology and armament. After the Restoration he served in several governmental posts before entering private life as industrialist; by the time of his death he had launched a wide variety of enterprises in mining, textiles, and transportation.

Gotō Shōjirō 後藤象二郎 (1838-1897), Tosa samurai and disciple of Yoshida Tōyō who came to head the Tosa bureaucracy at the end of the shogunate. With experience in Shanghai and Nagasaki, where he helped Sakamoto Ryōma, he saw the benefit for Tosa of a voluntary shogunal resignation and helped persuade Yamauchi Yōdō to put the proposal forward. After serving in the Meiji government for a time he resigned together with Itagaki in 1873 over the issue of war with Korea, and thereafter took a prominent part in the liberal party movement. In 1882 he travelled in Europe with Itagaki; subsequently he several times held cabinet posts. At the same time he took part in numerous commercial and industrial ventures.

Hara Ichinoshin (Tadanari) 原市之進 (忠成) (1830-1867), Mito samurai and retainer of the last shogun, regarded as the most able of his assistants. Assassinated in 1867 by anti-foreign fanatics.

Hijikata Hisamoto 土方久元 (1833-1918), son of a Tosa *gōshi*, after several years of study in Edo with Satō Issai and others he became committed to a firm loyalist position. He entered the service of the noble Sanjō, accompanied him to Mitajiri and to Dazaifu, and did all he could to raise support for the loyalist cause through friends in Satsuma, Chōshū, and Tosa. After the Restoration he served the new government in a number of posts, and for a time was Minister of Agriculture and Commerce. Most of his service was directly for the Imperial house, culminating in his appointment as Imperial Household Minister in 1887. He was created Count in the new peerage.

Hirai Shūjirō (Waizan) 平井収二郎 (隈山) (1833-1863), Kōchi loyalist who took a prominent part in organization and plans of Takechi's Loyalist Party. While Takechi accompanied the Anegakoji-Sanjō mission to Edo in late 1862 Hirai was left behind in Kyoto to maintain contacts with other fiefs and nobles there; after return of the mission he was one of the party which secured authorization for political reforms from a Kyoto noble before returning to Kōchi. For this act, deemed disrespectful toward his feudal superiors, he was ordered to commit suicide upon the return of Yōdō to Kōchi.

Hirai Zennojō 平井善之丞 (1803-1865), Tosa samurai (umamawari) who joined Takechi's loyalist movement and who gained bureaucratic importance during the shifts in han administration that followed the murder of Yoshida Tōyō. Although not brought to trial or punished in the changes that followed the return of Yōdō he lost power and influence, and died before Tosa rejoined the loyalist front.

Hirano Kokuo (Kuniomi) 平野国臣 (1828-1864), Fukuoka samurai who took a vigorous part in the loyalist plotting, gaining particular fame for the rising at Ikuno after which he was executed together with thirty-seven followers.

Hirose Kenta 弘瀬健太 (1836-1863), Tosa loyalist who was an early follower of Takechi's, helped arrange the entry of the young daimyō Toyonori into Kyoto in 1862, accompanied, with Takechi, the Anegakoji-Sanjō mission to Edo, and thereafter returned to Tosa expecting responsibility for reorganizing the administrative system, only to fall victim to Yōdō's purge of loyalists.

Hitotsubaṣhi Keiki (Tokugawa Yoshinobu) 一橋慶喜 (徳川慶喜) (1837-1913), the last shogun; a son of Tokugawa Nariaki, he was adopted into and inherited the Hitotsubashi family (100,000 koku), 1847-1859, and 1862-1867, when he became shogun; after his resignation he was named Prince in the new peerage.

Ii Naosuke 井伊直弼 (1815-1860), fudai daimyō of Hikone (350,000 koku) from 1850 to 1860, Regent (Tairō) from June 1858 until his assassination in March 1860. His "Ansei Purge," which struck at major daimyō, activated their retainers in opposition to the shogunate.

Ike Kurata (Sadakatsu) 池内蔵太 (定勝)(1841-1866), Tosa samurai son who entered the loyalist movement during a period of study in Edo. He fled Tosa for Chōshū in 1863, and was enrolled in units that fought in Kyoto, in Yamato (with Yoshimura Toratarō), and in Chōshū during the unsuccessful attempts to resist the foreign ships. He then entered Sakamoto's Kaientai and was lost when a ship sank.

Inoue Kaoru (Bunta) 井上馨 (聞多) (1835-1915), Chōshū loyalist and Meiji statesman, student of Yoshida Shōin, studied in England through help of Glover, helped arrange alliance with Satsuma, held wide variety of offices in Meiji government, was created Marquis, and associated particularly with efforts to speed capitalist developments (as Mitsui adviser) and achieve diplomatic equality.

Itagaki (Inui) Taisuke 板垣 (乾) 退助 (1837-1919), Tosa samurai (umamawari) who first entered official life as disciple of Yoshida Tōyō. He reorganized the Tosa military shortly before the Restoration, and led them in the wars against the Tokugawa. Subsequently he led in the movement to reform ranks in Tosa, entered the Meiji government only to withdraw in protest against the decision not to go to war with Korea, and led the movement for representative government. He held cabinet posts several times, but retired from active politics after 1900.

Itō Hirobumi (Shunsuke) 伊藤博文 (俊輔) (1841-1909), Chōshū loyalist and Meiji statesman, closely associated, in policy and person, with Inoue Kaoru; chief of the Meiji statesmen and architect of the Meiji Constitution. Created Prince.

Itō Sukedayu 伊藤助大夫 (n.d.), Shimonoseki merchant with whom Sakamoto corresponded several times and who apparently aided loyalist emissaries.

Iwakura Tomomi 岩倉具視 (1825-1883) Kyoto noble who backed marriage of Princess Kazu to Tokugawa Iemochi, was banished for his own safety during loyalist years, and reemerged as principal court contact of Satsuma leaders during last year of shogunate. After Restoration played an important role in Meiji regime; best known for his leadership of mission to the Western world in 1872-1873; created Prince.

Iwasaki Yatarō 岩崎彌太郎 (1834-1885), low-ranking Tosa disciple of Yoshida Tōyō who rose through a succession of fiscal posts; responsible for Tosa trading stations in Nagasaki and Osaka in late Tokugawa days, he succeeded in gaining control over the han capital investments and used them to form the basis for one of Japan's great fortunes in Meiji times, the Mitsubishi firm.

Iwashita Masahira 岩下方平 (1827-1900), Satsuma samurai who was sent to France in 1866, reporting thence on Bakufu-French relations to Kagoshima; served the Meiji government in a number of administrative assignments such as governor of Kyoto; created Viscount, served in House of Peers.

Kamochi Masazumi 鹿持雅澄 (1791-1858), Tosa teacher of the national classics and of poetry, who gained a wide following. An uncle of Takechi Zuizan, he numbered among his students many of higher rank like Sasaki Takayuki.

Kataoka Kenkichi 片岡健吉 (1843-1903), Tosa samurai (umamawari) who rose through the military bureaucracy as a lieutenant of Itagaki in late Tokugawa days; served under Itagaki during the wars against the Tokugawa, and, after a tour of Europe, retired from government service together with Itagaki in 1873. Thereafter he took a prominent part in the movement for representative government, in the Christian church, which he joined, and in the YMCA movement.

Katsu Rintarō (Kaishū, Awa, Yasuyoshi) 勝麟太郎 (安房)(海舟) (1823-1899), son of a Tokugawa hatamoto who received training in Western studies, was assigned to instruction under the Netherlands naval detachment at Nagasaki, and became Tokugawa Naval Commissioner, a post in which he sheltered Sakamoto. One of Keiki's councillors, he opposed an all-out stand against the anti-Tokugawa armies, arranged the surrender of Edo to Saigō, and served the new government with distinction in a number of naval posts and as adviser.

Kido Kōin (Katsura Kogorō) 木戸孝允 (桂小五郎)(1833-1877), Chōshū loyalist leader who negotiated the Satsuma-Chōshū alliance with Saigō and Ōkubo. Thereafter he played a leading role in the new government's Charter Oath, abolition of feudalism, and other reforms; he accompanied Iwakura to the West in 1872-1873, resigned his posts in protest against the Formosan expedition of 1874, and died during the Satsuma rebellion.

Komatsu Tatewaki 小松帯刀(1835-1870), Satsuma karō who worked closely with Ōkubo and Saigō in planning the alliance with Chōshū and the overthrow of the Tokugawa. One of the highest-ranking men to be numbered among the *shishi*, he was in the front rank of Meiji leaders when illness brought his career to an end.

Kōmei, Emperor 孝明天皇 (1831-1867), succeeded to throne in 1846.

Kominami Goroemon 小南五郎右衛門(1812-1882), Tosa official who came into prominence during Tempō reforms of Mabuchi Kahei and again with Yoshida Tōyō. Together with Hirai Zennojō, he was one of the few samurai of rank who sided with Takechi's loyalist movement in 1862-1863, with the result that he was stripped of rank and family name during Yōdō's counter purge. He was restored to office and honor in Meiji times, and served both the Kōchi and the national administration in a variety of administrative posts until his retirement in 1877.

Kondō Chōjirō (Akira) 近藤長次郎 (昶)(1838-1866), Tosa merchant's son who showed such aptitude for study, particularly of Western learning, during a period of residence in Edo that the han granted him privileges of swords and family name, plus rations, in order to claim his services. He preferred, however, to enter Katsu's Hyōgo academy, and thereafter he was one of Sakamoto's group. His services in securing the *Union* for Chōshū at Nagasaki were so valued that Itō Hirobumi recommended to his lord that study abroad be arranged as a reward for Uesugi Sōjirō (as he then called himself); when his Kaientai comrades heard of his talks with Itō and Glover, however, they abused him for seeking self-advantage and drove him into suicide.

Kurimoto Joun 栗本鋤雲 (1822-1897), Tokugawa foreign affairs specialist who was born into a line of doctors, trained in medicine and Western learning, raised in rank and given diplomatic assignments, the most important of which was a mission to France. While he was there the shogunate was overthrown, and upon his return to Japan he entered newspaper work, taking a prominent part in the formation and direction of several prominent Meiji papers.

Kuroda Kiyotaka 黒田清隆 (1840-1900), Satsuma specialist in Western gunnery who played a prominent part in the military and diplomatic arrangements with Chōshū at the end of the shogunate. He served the new government in numerous and important posts, among them that of Prime Minister in 1888.

Kusaka Genzui 久坂玄瑞 (1840-1864), Chōshū loyalist, student of Yoshida Shōin, who had close relations with Takechi Zuizan's loyalist movement in the early 1860's. He took a leading part in urging a thoroughly anti-foreign program upon his lord, organized the assault on the British legation, championed the shelling of foreign ships in the Shimonoseki Straits and the invasion of Kyoto in 1864, and committed suicide when it failed.

Mabuchi Kahei 馬淵嘉平 (1793-1839), student of swordsmanship and of *Shingaku*, the merchant creed, who was named to high office during Tosa's Tempō reforms only to be denounced and dismissed shortly after on ideological grounds. During his ascendancy Yoshida Tōyō first gained prominence.

Matsudaira Katamori 松平容保 (1836-1893), Tokugawa collateral, daimyō of Aizu (230,000 koku) 1852-1869, named Protector of Kyoto 1862-1864 and 1864-1868, organized special units to combat rōnin; his Wakamatsu castle, which was taken by Tosa troops in war against Tokugawa, offered stout resistance. Although Katamori's top retainers were punished by the new government, he himself was treated with relative leniency, though not permitted to regain importance.

Matsudaira Shungaku (Keiei, Yoshinaga) 松平春嶽 (慶永) (1828-1890), Tokugawa collateral, daimyō of Fukui (320,000 koku) from 1838 to 1858; took leading part in campaign to secure shogunal succession for Keiki in 1857-1858, appointed to special offices in shogunate from 1862-1864, one of outstanding lords of kōbu-gattai faction. Held a number of posts in Meiji government during its early years, and was praised and rewarded by throne.

Matsuki Kōan 松木弘庵 (1832-1893), Satsuma student of Western learning who accompanied first mission to Europe in 1861 and 1862; captured by British forces which shelled Kagoshima (with Godai), he arranged settlement; later studied in England, served shogunate as instructor in Western learning, and, after Restoration, as Terajima Munenori, became important official of new regime, serving in diplomatic, educational, legal, and Imperial household posts.

Matsuoka Kiken 松岡毅軒 (1814-1877), Tosa court Confucianist who gained prominence under Yoshida Tōyō, whose codification of administrative procedure, the *Kainan seiten*, he rendered in Sinico-Japanese (*kambun*). He drew up the memorial urging the shogun to resign, and went on to serve the new government in a number of posts having to do with education and the study of constitutional systems.

Mazaki Sōrō (Tetsuma) 間崎滄浪 (哲馬) (1834-1863), Tosa loyalist ideologue, descendant of a family in remote Hata District. Through study in Edo he became well versed in classical studies, and upon his return to Tosa his fame as scholar and teacher brought him a large following. One of the most important figures in Takechi's loyalist movement, he arranged, together with Hirose and Hirai, the "court" authorization for administrative reforms in Tosa, for which impertinence he was ordered to commit suicide by Yōdō upon his return to his fief.

Miyoshi Shinzō 三吉愼蔵 (n.d.), Chōshū samurai attacked with Sakamoto in Teradaya in 1866 and a friend and frequent correspondent thereafter.

Montblanc, Comte Descantons de, title granted Baron of Ingelmunster by Belgian monarch in 1841; known to many late Tokugawa travellers in Europe, entered into commercial agreements with Satsuma representatives, visited Japan at time of Restoration and drew up initial statement for foreign representatives at request of Terajima (see under Matsuki) in 1868.

Mutsu Munemitsu (Yōnosuke, Date Shōjirō) 陸奥宗光 (陽之助, 伊達小二郎) (1844-1897), Kii samurai; left his (Tokugawa) fief to join *shishi* in Kyoto; entered Katsu's naval training academy, Sakamoto's Kaientai. Served new government in wide variety of posts, best known for diplomatic service which culminated in period as Foreign Minister during which unequal treaties were revised and war with China was waged.

Nagai Naomune 永井尚志 (1816-1891), younger son of a Tokugawa collateral daimyō (of Okudono, Mikawa) adopted into a hatamoto family; became a specialist in naval training, studied under Netherlands contingent in Nagasaki, advanced through many shogunal posts, member of *Wakadoshiyori* under Keiki, took part in last stand of Tokugawa units in Hokkaido, pardoned by new government and served in legislative and *Genrōin* posts.

Nagai Uta 長井雅楽 (1819-1863), Chōshū official responsible for a plan whereby his lord took the leadership in a movement for kōbu-gattai in 1862; a Satsuma version which was more favorable to the court, weakened his support in Kyoto and consequently in Chōshū; when the fief adopted a loyalist and exclusionist position to regain leadership over Satsuma in court backing, Nagai was forced to accept responsibility for his failure by suicide.

Nakae Chōmin 中江兆民 (1847-1901), son of a Tosa low-ranking samurai, was sent by the han to study Western learning in Nagasaki, where he concentrated on French. Later he studied in Edo, served briefly as interpreter for Leon Roches, and, after the Restoration, taught French in Tokyo. After a period of government service and study in France he entered the democratic movement, becoming known for his advocacy of French political philosophy, atheism, and materialism.

Nakahama Manjirō 中濱萬次郎 (1827-1898), Tosa fisherman rescued at sea by American ship in 1841, taken to Massachusetts and educated there (as John Mung); sailed on whalers, took part in Gold Rush, and with earnings persuaded whaler to put him ashore on Ryukyus in 1851. Thereafter served Satsuma, Tosa, shogunate, and early Meiji government as source of information about West, as interpreter, instructor in whaling, teacher.

Nagaoka Kenkichi (Makoto) 長岡謙吉 (恂) (1834-1872), Tosa student of medicine with periods of study in Edo and Nagasaki, where he came under Sakamoto's influence and served as Kaientai secretary. Besides his share in the eight-point program, known for an anti-Christian tract (written after the Urakami Christians were discovered); took part in Restoration wars.

Nakaoka Shintarō 中岡愼太郎 (1838-1867), Tosa *shōya* loyalist leader; fled han during Yōdō's counter purge, worked with Sakamoto for Satsuma-Chōshū alliance, formed Rikuentai, assassinated with Sakamoto.

Nakayama Tadayasu 中山忠能 (1809-1888), court noble who took prominent part in Kyoto resistance to shogunate's handling of early treaties with the West; uncle of Meiji Emperor, he became, with Iwakura, essential channel for access to court for Satsuma leaders planning overthrow of Tokugawa.

Nasu Shingo 那須信吾 (1829-1863), adopted son of a Tosa *gōshi* and charter member of Takechi's Loyalist Party; one of the three who murdered Yoshida Tōyō in 1862; thereafter fled Tosa and received shelter from Kusaka Genzui and from Satsuma friends; took part in Yamato rising of Yoshimura Toratarō in 1863; killed in fighting while accompanying Kyoto noble Nakayama Tadamitsu.

Nonaka Kenzan 野中謙山 (1615-1663), Tosa administrator who devised intellectual, economic, and political policies which established Tosa as one of great fiefs. Began *gōshi* recruitment, increased income through official monopolies, and sponsored Confucian studies of Yamazaki Anzai and Tani line of teachers.

Ogasawara Nagamichi 小笠原長行 (1822-1891); Tokugawa official (son of daimyō of Karatsu), member of Senior Council (1865-1868), commander in second expedition to chastise Chōshū, after which he was briefly relieved of his office; after Restoration sided with last stand of Tokugawa followers on Hokkaido, thereafter lived in retirement.

Ogasawara Tadahachi (Makino Shigeyuki) 小笠原唯八 (牧野茂敬)(1829-1868), Tosa official who was one of Yōdō's most trusted retainers in early years of loyalist movement, serving as emissary, helping to restrain violence of low-ranking *shishi*, supervising suppression of Noneyama demonstrators. Subsequently he became convinced of need for overthrow of Tokugawa and was deprived of his rank and office for time. Took part in Restoration wars (as Makino Shigeyuki), and was killed at Wakamatsu siege.

Oguri Tadamasa 小栗忠順 (1827-1868), son of a Tokugawa bugyō, advanced rapidly in late Tokugawa times; accompanied first embassy to United States; City, Finance, Naval Commissioner; most outspoken advocate of all-out aid from France; captured and executed by Imperial troops in Restoration war.

Ōkubo Ichiō 大久保一翁 (1817-1888), one of most important and farsighted Tokugawa officials in closing decade; associated with Institute for Investigation of Barbarian Books, Commission of Army, Kyoto, Foreign Affairs, urged Keiki to resign powers; after Restoration served Tokugawa interests in Shizuoka, was appointed Governor by new regime, also served in Genrōin; Viscount.

Ōkubo Toshimichi (Ichizō) 大久保利通 (一蔵) (1830-1878), Satsuma Restoration leader and principal member of Meiji government until his death; principal adviser of Shimazu Hisamitsu and close collaborator with Iwakura Tomomi; provided strong central control during first decade of Meiji in suppression of rebellions of Etō (Saga) and Saigō (Satsuma), assassinated 1878.

Parkes, Sir Harry (1828-1885), veteran Foreign Office official whose career in China began at the age of fifteen; served as interpreter and consul at all major treaty ports in China, ap-

411

pointed Minister to Japan in 1865, a post he held until 1833, when he was transferred to China.

Roches, Leon (1809-1901), French Minister to Japan who arrived in 1864; carried on vigorous campaign to effect French commercial and political primacy by policy of loans, technical and military aid to Tokugawa; under his influence military and naval training, as well as teaching in shogunate's foreign learning institute, became French-oriented, and Bakufu statesmanlike Oguri depended upon full French assistance. He was unprepared for the Tokugawa fall, and his mission ended in failure for Napoleon III.

Saigō Takamori 西鄉隆盛 (1828-1877), Satsuma leader in the anti-Tokugawa movement, military specialist; left Meiji government in 1873, led unsuccessful revolt against it in 1877.

Sakamoto Ryōma 坂本龍馬 (1835-1867), Tosa loyalist, follower of Takechi Zuizan, then of Katsu Rintarō; organized Kaientai; helped bring about Satsuma-Chōshū alliance; eight-point program the basis for proposed compromise.

Sakuma Shōzan 佐久間象山 (1811-1864), Matsushiro samurai who became noted advocate of opening the country in order to strengthen it with Western technology. Teacher to Yoshida Shōin and many others, his services sought by many fiefs, Sakuma was killed in Kyoto by anti-foreign zealot.

Sanjō Sanetomi 三條實美 (1837-1891), son of Sanetsumu (1802-1859); Court noble related to Tosa daimyō whose strongly anti-foreign stand endeared him to the Tosa *shishi*; journeyed to Edo with Anegakoji in 1862 to demand expulsion of foreigners, raised in office at court in 1863, forced to flee Kyoto after expulsion of Chōshū, after which, with other refugee nobles, he lived at Mitajiri and Dazaifu, served by Tosa and other rōnin. After Restoration served in many important posts, including, for short period, Prime Minister; created Prince.

Sasaki Takayuki (Sanshirō) 佐々木高行 (三四郎) (1830-1910), Tosa samurai (umamawari) who held loyalist views but did not join Takechi's movement; he rose in importance in late Tokugawa days, headed Tosa Nagasaki station, served Meiji government in several posts and accompanied Iwakura on mission abroad in 1872. Although dissatisfied with many decisions of Meiji government he differed sharply with Itagaki's democratic movement, and, with Hijikata, supervised detection and suppression work in Tosa for time. Later served in Privy Council, created Marquis.

Satow, Sir Ernest Mason (1843–1929), interpreter for Harry Parkes, known to many of Restoration *shishi*; later Minister to Japan.

SHIMAZU 島津 BARONS OF SATSUMA (KAGOSHIMA) AND TOZAMA DAIMYŌ UNDER TOKUGAWA RULE:

Hisamitsu (Saburo) 久光 (三郎) (1817-1887); as regent for son Tadayoshi, who succeeded to rule after Nariakira, was effective ruler of Satsuma 1859-1868.

Nariakira 斎彬 (1809-1858), daimyō 1851-1858 (770,000 koku); widely respected as one of ablest feudal lords, promoter of Keiki's succession at time of death.

Tadayoshi (Mochihisa) 忠義 (茂久) (1840-1897), son of Hisamitsu, adopted by Nariakira as successor; nominal daimyō, 1859-1868; named governor of Kagoshima by new government for time; created Prince.

Shiraishi Seishirō 白石正一郎 (1811-1880), Shimonoseki merchant who specialized in water-borne trade, dealt with Satsuma, enthusiastically supported *shishi* with food, money, lodging, and became known as "chivalrous merchant"; the Chōshū lord recognized his merit by raising him to samurai rank.

Sufu Masanosuke 周布政之助 (1823-1864), Chōshū official principally responsible for bringing about his fief's shift from the kōbu-gattai program to the anti-foreign program in 1862; the principal voice in fief councils thereafter, he committed suicide when, at the time of the first campaign against his domain, his policies seemed to have brought failure.

Takasugi Shinsaku 高杉晋作 (1839-1867), Chōshū loyalist, student of Yoshida Shōin, organizer of militia units (Kiheitai and others); travelled to Shanghai, organized military victory over Chōshū conservatives in 1865 and over Tokugawa in 1866, died of illness before Restoration.

Takechi Zuizan (Hanpeita) 武市瑞山 (半平太) (1829-1865), Tosa *gōshi* who recruited and led the Tosa Loyalist Party, gained influence as a master of swordsmanship, intrigued with confederates in Satsuma and Chōshū to bring about a three-fief unity of program, and to achieve this engineered the murder of Yoshida Tōyō in 1862. After a brief period of ascendancy he was checked by the return of Yōdō to power, and ordered to commit suicide for actions unbecoming his station.

Tanaka Kōken (Mitsuaki) 田中光顯 (1843-1939), Tosa rōnin who fled to Chōshū, assisted Nakaoka Shintarō in Rikuentai, then went on to serve new regime in military posts (General), travelled abroad on inspection missions, served in Genrōin, eleven years as Imperial Household Minister. Created Count. Library of Restoration materials, Seizan Bunko, in Sakawa, Tosa.

Tani Kanjō 谷干城 (1837-1911), Tosa samurai who, although sympathetic with Takechi's teachings, did not openly join his movement. Several periods of study in Edo made him well versed in classical and military teachings, and he took an important part in military training and campaigns in late Tokugawa years. In Meiji times he continued his military service, especially during Satsuma rebellion, promoted "Japanism" and reverence for the Emperor, opposed both the oligarchy and the Itagaki followers. Created Viscount.

TOKUGAWA SHOGUNS AND FAMILY MEMBERS:

Akitake 昭武 (1853-1910), eighteenth son of Nariaki and daimyō of Mito, sent to Paris to represent shogun for International Exposition in 1867; returned to Japan after Restoration; to France for study, 1877.

Iemochi 家茂 (1846-1866), fourteenth shogun (1858-1866) whose accession was preceded by campaign for Keiki.

Ienari 家斉 (1773-1841), eleventh shogun (1787-1837) whose long reign was followed by Tempō reforms.

Iesada 家定 (1824-1858), thirteenth shogun (1853-1858), incompetent, who demonstrated the desirability of a mature, able shogun, thereby lending weight to supporters of Keiki.

Nariaki 齊昭 (1800-1860), lord of Mito (1829-1844), strong

exponent of policy of strength with foreigners, began trend of seeking support in Kyoto.

Yoshinobu: see under Hitotsubashi Keiki.

Uesugi Sōjirō: 上杉宗次郎 see under Kondō Chōjirō.

Yamagata Aritomo 山縣有朋 (1838-1922), Chōshū loyalist military leader who succeeded to Takasugi Shinsaku's command and planned the final campaigns against the Tokugawa. With Itō, one of the two most important statesmen of the Meiji government; builder of modern army, bureaucracy; Prime Minister; created Prince.

YAMAUCHI (YAMANOUCHI) 山内, BARONS OF TOSA (KŌCHI), TOZAMA DAIMYŌ, 202,600 KOKU:

Kazutoyo 一豊 (daimyō 1600-1605), founder of the line, received fief from Tokugawa Ieyasu.

Toyonori 豊範 (daimyō 1859-1871), d. 1886; nominal ruler after Yōdō's forced retirement, controlled either by him or other relatives.

Toyoshige (Yōdō) 豊信 (容堂) (daimyō 1848-1859), d. 1872, one of most important lords of late Tokugawa days.

Toyosuke 豊資 (daimyō 1809-1843), d. 1872; consistent force for conservatism and vested interests throughout reform plans and proposals.

Yokoi Shōnan 横井小楠 (1809-1869), Kumamoto samurai who entered employ of Matsudaira Shungaku of Fukui; advocate of opening the country, of conciliar organization to secure unity; murdered by reactionary while undertaking political task of planning council for new government.

Yoshimura Toratarō 吉村寅太郎 (1837-1863), Tosa *shōya* who fled fief to enter main stream of loyalist movement, led abortive rising in Yamato in 1863, took own life.

Yoshida Tōyō (Genkichi) 吉田東洋 (元吉) (1816-1862), most trusted minister of Yamauchi Yōdō and sponsor of Itagaki, Gotō, Fukuoka, Iwasaki, and others; modernized by strengthening han controls over Tosa products, hesitated to endanger lord's life during Ii purge, and, having alienated loyalists of Takechi, was assassinated by them in 1862.

Yuri Kimimasa 由利公正 (1829-1909), Fukui samurai (originally Mioka Hachirō), vigorous advocate of modernization after coming of Perry; as adviser to Matsudaira Shungaku known to many of *shishi*, and highly esteemed by Sakamoto. Took part in drafting Charter Oath in 1868, currency reforms, Iwakura mission, governor of Tokyo, Genrōin, created Viscount.

INDEX

Abe Masahiro, 47, 56, 57, 58, 60, 67, 349; biographical note, 401
Abe Masatō, 193, 212
Abe Sadato, 208
Aizawa Seishisai, 54
Aizu han, 141, 142, 180, 185, 199, 232, 280, 323, 326, 334, 357; cooperation with Satsuma, 181
Alcock, Rutherford, 11
Alt & Co., 248, 276, 305, 360n
Andō Nobumasa, 113, 125; attacked, 126, 127; biographical note, 401
Anenokōji Kintomo, 130, 132, 138, 143, 144, 162, 350, 353; mission to Edo, 133; assassinated, 139; contacted by Katsu, Sakamoto, 168, 169; biographical note, 401
Ansei Reforms, 72, 73, 74
Arai Hakuseki, 18
Arisugawa, Prince, 126, 332
Asano, Hiroshima daimyō, 213
ashigaru, Tosa, 26

bakufu (shogunate), 99, 106, 201, 202; organization, 3-8; reforms after 1860, 126-29; and Sanjō-Anenokōji mission, 134; authorization to govern, 139; first expedition against Chōshū, 193, 194; second expedition, 211, 232, 235, 236; relations with France, 214, 320 (and see Roches, France); further reforms, 280, 283, 284, 311; and Icarus affair, 305; responsibility for final stage of response, 351; see also Tokugawa Keiki
Bansho Shirabesho, 65, 155
Bumbu Kan, 76
bummei kaika, 355

Charter Oath of 1868, 244, 296, 334, 335, 339, 356
Chiba Sadakichi, 82, 162
China, Western advances in, 16, 19, 20, 53, 62, 159, 199, 208
Chōshū, 8, 40, 49, 54, 55, 87, 99, 107, 113-20, 125, 129-32, 134, 137, 138, 140, 141, 143, 146, 148-50, 177, 185, 186, 191, 206-10, 214-22, 248-55, 258, 260-63, 274, 278-82, 286; Tempō Reforms, 42; reply to Perry letter, 57; kōbu-gattai plan, 127, 128; shells foreign ships, 139, 175; invades Kyoto, 142, 182; Shimonoseki bom-

barded, 176; first expedition against, 193, 194, 199-202; revolt of Takasugi, 202, 203, 204; second expedition against, 211-13, 215, 219, 232-40; peace formula, 287, 291; Satsuma alliance and provisions, 220, 221; preparation for war with Satsuma against bakufu, 297, 311
Chōsogabe, 22, 27, 28, 48, 347; farmer-soldiers, 30; biographical note, 401
Chōsokabe, see Chōsogabe
Chu Hsi, 16, 35, 95
Chūritsusha, 373
chūrō, 25
Chūyūtai, 199-202, 205
Clarendon, Lord, 257
Confucian learning and schools, 7, 16, 18, 19, 95
Council Chamber, plans for, 168; in eight point program, 295-99; in Satsuma-Tosa agreement, 301; in Yōdō's petition, 316; in Sakamoto's final plan, 338; in Charter Oath, 335

Daigoku Maru, 264
daimyō, 6; fudai daimyō and attitude on Perry, 55, 61; and Keiki, 279; see also bakufu, Tokugawa Keiki
Date Munenari, 60, 194, 279, 286, 289, 290, 291, 292, 336; biographical note, 401
Dazaifu, 194, 204, 211, 218, 219, 221, 223, 248, 249, 262, 291, 328, 345
de Lhuys, E. Drouyn, 318
de Moustiers, Marquis, 318
Doeff, Hendrik, 187
Drake, U.S. merchant, 254
Dutch studies and scholars, 18, 43, 54

Fabius, Lt. G., 62, 63
Fillmore, President, 56, 72
Flowers, English Consul, 304
Ford, Robert, see Icarus
France, 185, 213, 221, 222, 250, 255, 258, 272, 285, 287, 318-21, 330, 354, 357, 365, 363; total aid for bakufu, 259
Fujita Tōko, 54, 73, 104
fukuoku-kyōhei, as han policy, 247
Fukuoka han, 205, 236, 370; politics, 202

417